MEETING THE CHALLENGE OF HUMAN RESOURCE MANAGEMENT

While communicating is a vital skill for managers at all organizational levels and in all functional areas, human resource managers are expected to be especially adept communicators, given the important interpersonal component of their roles. Practitioners and scholars alike stand to benefit from incorporating an updated and more nuanced view of communication theory and practice into standard human resource management practices.

This book compiles readings by thought leaders in human resource management and communication, exploring the intersection of interests, theories, and perspectives from the two fields to highlight new opportunities for research and practice. In addition to covering the foundations of strategic human resource management, the book:

- offers a critical review of the research literature on topics including recruitment, selection, performance management, compensation, and development
- uses a communication perspective to analyze the impact of corporate strategy on human resource systems
- investigates the key human resource management topic of the relationship between a company's human capital and its effectiveness
- directly discusses the implications of communication literature for human resource management practice

Written at the cross-section of two established and critically linked fields, this book is a must-have for graduate human resource management and organizational communication students, as well as for high-level human resource management practitioners.

Vernon D. Miller is an Associate Professor in the Department of Communication and Department of Management at Michigan State University, USA.

Michael E. Gordon is a Professor at the Rutgers Business School—New Brunswick, USA.

MEETING THE CHALLENGE OF HUMAN RESOURCE MANAGEMENT

A Communication Perspective

Edited by
Vernon D. Miller and
Michael E. Gordon

Routledge
Taylor & Francis Group

NEW YORK AND LONDON

First published 2014
by Routledge
711 Third Avenue, New York, NY 10017

and by Routledge
2 Park Square, Milton Park, Abingdon, Oxon OX14 4RN

Routledge is an imprint of the Taylor & Francis Group, an informa business

© 2014 Taylor & Francis

The right of Vernon D. Miller & Michael E. Gordon to be identified as editors of this part of the work has been asserted by them in accordance with sections 77 and 78 of the Copyright, Designs and Patents Act 1988.

Library of Congress Cataloging-in-Publication Data

   Meeting the challenge of human resource management : a communication perspective / edited by Vernon D. Miller & Michael E. Gordon.
      pages cm
   Includes bibliographical references and index.
   1. Communication in personnel management.   I. Miller, Vernon D. (Vernon Dubose), 1955–   II. Gordon, Michael E.
      HF5549.5.C6M34   2014
      658.3—dc23   2013046595

ISBN: 978-0-415-63020-7 (hbk)
ISBN: 978-0-415-63021-4 (pbk)
ISBN: 978-0-203-09798-4 (ebk)

Typeset in Bembo
by Apex CoVantage, LLC

Printed and bound in the United States of America by Publishers Graphics, LLC on sustainably sourced paper.

CONTENTS

PREFACE

Although organizational communication is a vibrant academic discipline, it only occasionally addresses issues of how effective human resource management (HRM) is created and maintained as a consequence of human interaction. Though not indifferent to communication, HRM researchers seldom explore the potential for expanding an understanding of the field's practices by considering its foundation in human communication. In our judgment, these are both unexpected and serious oversights.

Neglect of communication issues in HRM is unexpected given the apparently widespread belief that there is an intimate connection between the two fields in the minds of many students and practitioners of HRM. Specifically, many report that choosing to pursue a career in HRM was based on the conviction that they were "people persons" who loved working with and providing assistance to others. It seems to be almost an article of faith that individuals with a penchant for interacting with other people are well suited to the HRM profession. Clearly, empathy for people and a willingness to undertake the challenges of working with others are important personality facets of HRM practitioners (indeed, for all managers), and these characteristics may, in fact, account for the difference between failure and success in performing HRM roles.

Neglect of communication issues in HRM also represents a serious oversight in the development of HRM practitioners and programs. Despite the assumption that communication is a vital component of the field, communication courses rarely are incorporated in degree and certificate programs that prepare individuals for careers in HRM. Instead, training, especially at the graduate level, typically focuses on the analytic side of the profession, which is generally viewed as more relevant to the strategic interests of the organization. Hence, courses on employment law, human resource information systems, compensation, selection, and training dominate the curricula of these programs. Such emphasis, unfortunately, appears to reflect acceptance of a limited role for communication that simply entails the *delivery* of informative messages about various HRM policies, activities, and services. For example, the rare communication course in an HRM curriculum is most likely to address various skills such as writing that are obviously important means for disseminating messages. This analytic focus is a serious oversight because it implicitly undervalues the role played by communication in organizations, in general, and HRM, in particular, and thereby circumscribes the instrumentality of communication as a means for attaining more significant organizational objectives.

Communication and HRM scholars have, from time to time, exhibited interest in the overlap between their disciplines and have produced a patchwork of literature in this hybrid area of scholarship. For example, though there are numerous communication studies pertaining to the giving and receiving of feedback, we, ourselves, are among a very few who have written about the potential of a communication perspective for improving specific HRM programs designed for performance appraisal and organizational disengagement. Further, a number of communication scholars have investigated how the career development of new employees begins by learning the organizational ropes (i.e., employee socialization), but few (aside from Kramer) have pursued a communication perspective on formal career development by means of promotion from one rung on the organizational ladder to the next. Rather than just providing advice on the delivery of messages (for example, recommending clever but untested scripts for use by managers to handle an employee's objections during an appraisal interview), these writings recognize the importance of communication in making sense of social situations for ourselves and others. For example, we address the effects of the social context and audience analysis on communication effectiveness. More importantly, our work draws attention to the structure of interactions by examining the communication roles of both managers and employees in attaining the didactic objectives of HRM programs that jointly create a social reality better suited to the interests of the organization and its members.

It is fair to say that the literature that has considered the relationship between communication and HRM is scattered across the leading journals and books in different academic disciplines, and it has yet to develop an accepted focus. It is our hope that this book will help communication and HRM scholars recognize the viability of the intersection of their interests, theories, and perspectives and that it will lead to the development of useful new, concerted streams of research that explore the communicative foundations of, and opportunities within, HRM. By considering the communication dynamics associated with training, work/family life issues, and employee compensation (to name just a few HRM areas), we believe it will be possible to improve these standard practices with consequent benefits for organizations and their members. In particular, we hope that HRM scholars and practitioners will profit from exposure to an updated and more nuanced view of communication theory and practice.

Additionally, formal consideration of the contributions that communication researchers have made to traditional HRM practices may invigorate the former to expand their efforts to contribute further to the HRM discipline.

ACKNOWLEDGMENTS

Preparation of an edited book obviously requires the collaboration of many individuals. Normally, these are individuals renowned for their scholarship in specific fields of study related to the primary subject of the book. In our case, this meant joining forces with scholars who are recognizable for their expertise in the theory and research pertaining to the major activities comprising the practice of human resource management. We are most gratified that a group of highly regarded scholars contributed original chapters that address the viability of an intersection of disciplinary interests, theories, and perspectives in the fields of communication and HRM.

Consequently it is only fitting that we thank the contributors who have produced cutting-edge work in a narrow time frame. Although many academic departments no longer reward the writing of book chapters, each scholar quickly embraced the main ideas guiding our effort and then produced high-quality works. More than anything, they were very patient with us as editors, responding to our queries—and, in some cases, challenges—with calm and diligence. Our endeavor would have had limited chances of success without them, and we are grateful for their insight, work, and enthusiasm.

We would also like to thank the three distinguished scholars who, rather than preparing remarks about a single HRM practice, offered their reactions to particular sets of the contributed chapters. Instead of simply summarizing the contents of the chapters, they were asked to play the familiar communication role of discussant at a professional meeting—in other words, proposing evaluative and integrative remarks regarding the papers that were presented. Specifically, the three were asked to comment on whether the contributors actually identified viable and interesting intersections of HRM and communication research with the potential for advancing HRM research and practice.

We appreciate the perspective provided by these discussants. The inclusion of their comments represents our commitment to a broader view of communication, from message sending and receiving to daily formal and informal interactions to symbolic meanings derived from leaders, policies, and structures. This broader view embraces the challenges of daily coordination within and across units, how individuals derive meaning, and how individuals succeed or fail in their jobs as communicators. This view also embraces the awareness, as championed by Karl Weick, Scott Poole, Francois Cooren, and others, that enterprises emerge from and are maintained by communication processes. That is, entities are socially constructed from micro-interactions that ultimately define the social reality of what takes place at the macro-organizational level. This academic endeavor is devoted to expanding the understanding of HRM and is more likely to succeed as a result of the dialogue among the contributors and discussants begun in this book that hopefully discloses the communicative essence of its traditional practices.

Michael E. Gordon, Rutgers University
Vernon D. Miller, Michigan State University

PART I

INTRODUCTION

1

COMMUNICATION AND HUMAN RESOURCE MANAGEMENT

Historic Ties and New Relationships

Michael E. Gordon and Vernon D. Miller

It is a truism that communication is the bedrock of organizations. Consequently, communicating is a vital skill for managers serving at all organizational levels and in all functional areas. Managers must possess the communication skills that make it possible for them to successfully listen, receive and give instructions, fashion introductions, and ask questions. Because the interpersonal component of their jobs is important, human resource management (HRM) professionals are expected to be especially adept communicators. For example, presenting, interviewing, mediating, teaching, and serving as a liaison are only a few of the necessary communication tasks that human resource managers must display to succeed in their positions.

Above and beyond the communication skills required of individual human resource managers, the HRM function plays a vital communication-centric role in organizations. The performance of the HRM function is highly dependent upon its ability to communicate with its internal (e.g., line managers) and external (e.g., business partners) clients. Although this perspective is seldom emphasized when discussing the field, HRM professionals are expected to support, supervise, or, in some cases, perform significant communication functions in organizations. For example, relaying vital information to employees regarding their benefits and organizational offerings represents one obvious and important communication responsibility of human resource managers. Further, implicitly and, from time to time, explicitly, HRM professionals serve as partners in employee development, organizational change efforts, and the management of information systems. Therefore, HRM professionals not only help to fulfill the informational needs of employees, but their actions influence and assist the functioning of organizations as coordinated, meaning-centered systems. Recent research supports this view that "high quality communication may help to effectively bring across the desired employee behaviors that are motivated and rewarded through HR practices, which then feeds into unit performance" (Den Hartog, Boon, Verburg, & Croon, 2013, p. 1657).

It follows from the innate relationship between the two fields that formal and specific consideration of communication in the development and delivery of HRM practices should result in benefits for organizations and their members. To this end, communication and HRM scholars have, from time to time, exhibited interest in the overlap between their disciplines. For instance, researchers using an assimilation framework have examined the communication processes surrounding individuals' transition through recruitment and selection, socialization, role development, job transfer, and exit (Jablin, 2001). Other researchers have examined how particular interviewing tasks associated with HRM might be improved by considering principles of communication (e.g., Gordon, 2011; Gordon & Miller, 2012; Gordon & Stewart, 2009). This literature is scattered across the leading journals in different academic disciplines and, unfortunately, has yet to develop a clear scholarly identity. Further, it is fair to say that considerable communication research focuses on issues that are not presently recognized to be of substantial importance by HRM professionals. Deadrick and Gibson (2007) spoke of the divergence of interests that characterizes the "research-practice gap in HR" (p. 131).

It is our thesis and that of our fellow contributors that the effectiveness of HRM is dependent on recognizing and incorporating appropriate communication practices. We hope that our work will help communication and HRM scholars recognize the viability of this hybrid intersection of interests, theories, and perspectives and that it will lead to the development of useful new, concerted streams of research. This book is intended to encourage the development of a potentially symbiotic relationship that can nourish both fields. HRM scholars and practitioners could profit from consideration of an updated and nuanced view of communication theory and practice. In turn, formal consideration of the interactive requirements of HRM professionals and the organizational practices for which they are responsible could invigorate communication scholars to contribute further to the HRM discipline.

History of Human Resource Management

Discussions of the evolution of HRM from its roots in personnel management have quietly acknowledged the importance of communication. From its beginning, implicit in the tasks to which personnel managers were assigned is an important responsibility for wide-ranging communication activities. For example, personnel managers came into being as "welfare secretaries" who were responsible for dealing with worker complaints stemming from the harsh working conditions brought on by the factory system around the turn of the 20th century. Scott and Clothier (1925), authors of what is generally regarded to be the first comprehensive textbook dealing with personnel management, defined the goal of the emerging field as "establishing wholesome relationships between management and men" (p. iv). This remains the primary responsibility of HRM as noted by Croucher and Rizov (2012), who state that "forms of HRM all emphasize alignment of employer and employee interests" (p. 633). Throughout the ages, therefore, HRM has viewed itself as an engine for promoting the establishment of sound interpersonal relationships. "As employers began to understand the need for professionals who could play a middle role between employees and employers, the personnel manager's role emerged" (Losey, 1998, p. 42).

The nature and scope of HRM has been enlarged since its inception to reflect the ideas about work and workers espoused by a succession of schools of management thought, employment laws, and people's prevailing attitudes about work. Personnel managers originally performed transactional services in establishing and maintaining records on a firm's employees and administering pay and benefit programs. The field expanded when companies began to implement the ideas of Frederick W. Taylor (1911) and his disciples in the school of scientific management. In the decade after 1910, there was widespread acceptance of their principles, which required identifying workers with appropriate skills to perform each job, teaching them to perform their jobs in the "one best practice" (p. 8), and directly linking workers' pay to their output. The success of these practices depended on the clear transmission of information about how jobs should be performed. "Taylor even recommended that managers prepare job cards that gave workers precise instructions for their tasks; in this way, there could be no misunderstandings or ambiguities about the nature of the work" (Mumby, 2013, p. 65). Personnel managers soon assumed jurisdiction over employee selection, training, and compensation along with the responsibility for communicating clearly about these matters.

The seeds of the human relations school were sown in 1924 with the onset of studies conducted at the Hawthorne Works of Western Electric Company that flowered with the publication of Roethlisberger and Dickson (1939). The studies offered evidence that workers need to be understood in order to be satisfied and productive, as well as required management to promote better employee communication, cooperation, and involvement.[1] Whereas formal, downward communication was the focus of scientific management, the importance of upward and informal communication was recognized by the human relations school. For example, during this time personnel managers acquired a valuable tool for promoting upward channels of organizational communication with the publication of the first survey of employee attitudes, which was conducted by Kornhauser and Sharp (1932) at the Badger-Globe mill of Kimberly-Clark.

> In many ways, the work initially performed by the founding researchers of this school still provides the touchstone for many of the central questions that present-day organizational communication and management scholars are asking themselves—questions having to do with the *social* dimensions of organizational life. (Mumby, 2013, p. 81, italics in the original)

World War II was the stimulus for the expansion of personnel management. With the exodus of male workers from business organizations to armed services duty, companies were compelled to meet wartime production goals by hiring a more diverse workforce that included women (e.g., Rosie the Riveter) and people of color, who formerly were denied access to many industrial jobs. The role of the personnel manager now encompassed recruiting, testing, training, mediating, and monitoring employee morale and job performance with, for that time, nontraditional workers, and these practices introduced special communication challenges.

A period of labor unrest followed the war and ushered in important federal legislation to deal with organized labor. Personnel managers were expected to apprise organizations about compliance with a maze of new regulations, executive orders, and court decisions (Losey, 1998). Unlike their responsibilities for promoting conformity with an overarching legal environment that dealt with employment rights, personnel managers also began introducing ideas about creating internal organizational environments that promoted worker satisfaction and motivation as suggested by Douglas McGregor's Theory Y (1960) and Rensis Likert's Four Systems of Management (1961). These theories drew attention to the importance of informal communication. For example, McGregor called for a transformation of supervisor control over subordinates by means of formal authority to a state of interdependence based on the development of a mutual understanding of role requirements (1960, chap. 2). Further, McGregor (1972) expressed unease about the incompatible communication roles of judge and counselor that supervisors were expected to enact in the traditional performance appraisal.

During the 1970s, traditional personnel activities were increasingly oriented toward the planning needs of top management. Recognition that successful organizational performance is dependent on the amalgamation of financial, technological, and people resources required HRM to function as an integral component of the business as opposed to an employee support system. Today, it is clear that HRM departments are judged in terms of their ability to provide human capital that enables the enterprise to operate effectively and competitively and to implement its business strategies successfully. Indeed, many now refer to the field as strategic HRM.

Obviously, ensuring that its practices support the strategic goals of the organization requires substantial attention to communication with HRM's internal and external clients. Effective HRM is consistent with General Electric's ideas about the "boundaryless" organization (Ashkenas, Ulrich, Jick, & Kerr, 1995) in which communication regularly occurs both within the confines of its own department as well as in collaboration with outsiders. Traditional HRM work is now conducted jointly with line managers (e.g., integrated or cross-functional work teams) as well as staff from other functional areas (e.g., HRM and finance department personnel may join forces to offer programs on personal investment to other business units). Further, the leverage afforded by supply chain management has instilled recognition of the benefits of involving both upstream and downstream business partners in the design and delivery of HRM practices.

Finally, today's global economy obliged HRM to deal with a host of new employment issues. A variety of different organizational forms emerged (e.g., modular organizations and virtual teams) as a result of powerful new computer and telecommunication technology. The nature of employment also has changed. Lifetime service with a single employer appears to be a thing of the past, replaced by a changing array of employment relationships (e.g., contingent, part-time, and temporary labor). Shifting work assignments (e.g., work teams of various types, projects) have rapidly replaced the concept of a "job." Clearly, the global economy has brought in its wake many challenges for HRM that require its practitioners to find the right words to establish "wholesome relationships between management and men" (Scott & Clothier, 1925, p. iv).

The Structure of HRM

The increasingly rapid pace of change in the workplace has made identifying the boundaries of HRM and defining its most distinguishing characteristics a difficult task. Over the years HRM has gradually encompassed more practices and expanded its influence on organizational decision making. This growth led scholars to propose various groupings of its practices. Beginning with the work of Mark Huselid, it was argued that coherent sets of practices were the appropriate unit of analysis when investigating the impact of HRM on firm performance (Becker & Huselid, 1998; Huselid, 1995).

Acceptance of the "coherent sets of practices" approach sparked a debate over the appropriate contents of those bundles. Pfeffer (1994) proposed a universalistic doctrine that all organizations should adopt a set of 16 high performance work practices (e.g., incentive pay, employment security, and training and development) that affect relevant outcomes (e.g., productivity and profitability). Other researchers adopted a contingency approach that recommended bundling specific HRM practices to conform to various characteristics of the organizational context (e.g., Delery & Doty, 1996). Different alignments of practices result from reliance on different contingency factors. For example, Snell (1992) organized HRM practices based on their linkage to three types of organizational control: behavior control (e.g., practices that regulate the actions of employees on the job); output control (e.g., practices that tie rewards to performance of the job); and input control (e.g., staffing, training, and development practices). Lepak and Snell (2002) focused on HRM practices suited for different employment modes (e.g., knowledge work, job-based employment, contract work, and alliance/partnerships), whereas Verburg, Den Hartog, and Koopman (2007) found support for four configurations of HRM practices (bureaucratic, professional, market, and flexibility) that were appropriate for different organizational structures. Finally,

Posthuma, Campion, Masimova, and Campion (2013) created a nine-category taxonomy of high performance work practices by analyzing two decades of peer-reviewed articles. The taxonomy, based in part on previously published systems of types, groups, or categories of these practices, contains familiar categories of HRM programs, including compensation and benefits, training and development, recruiting and selection, and performance management and appraisal.

The organizational role is the systematizing principle we have chosen to identify as "coherent sets of practices." Organizational role is a concept that is familiar to HRM practitioners, and role theory has provided a valuable and oft-used theoretical framework for research on the behavior of individuals in organizations. "In their pure or organizational form, roles are standardized patterns of behavior required of all persons playing a part in a given functional relationship" (Katz & Kahn, 1978, p. 43). With an eye toward the responsibility of HRM in helping mold a sustainable social order in the organization, roles afford a useful perspective because organizational members are linked by the functional interdependence of the roles they are expected to play.

Role expectations for any position evolve in the minds of members of its role-set (i.e., occupants of other interdependent organizational roles), who communicate their presumptions about behavior to the incumbent. Role sending occurs by means of the communicative acts of the members of the role-set that provide information that varies in terms of prescriptiveness and specificity and that embody influence attempts intended to elicit behavior that conforms to role expectations. "In most organizations, role behavior is largely dependent on role sending" (Katz & Kahn, 1978, p. 193).

Consistent with this description, we present an overview of HRM that emphasizes the part that it plays in staffing practices (i.e., those intended to manage employee role changes), developing practices (i.e., those intended to prepare employees to assume a current or future role in the organization), and conserving practices (i.e., the various steps taken to assure the availability of employees to perform their organizational roles). When viewed through the prism of organizational roles, the special communication requirements of HRM professionals and their programs become apparent.

Staffing

HRM professionals are responsible for managing the movement of individuals currently occupying roles outside of the firm (e.g., students attending college or employees of a competitor) into suitable organizational roles. These practices are more recognizable in terms of traditional HRM nomenclature—for example, recruitment and selection. Communication is obviously important in reaching individuals who possess the qualities sought by the organization for the positions that must be filled and interesting them to apply. Further, HRM has important communication tasks in connection with employee selection. Effective hiring decisions are dependent upon the collection and evaluation of information descriptive of the applicants (e.g., interviewing). Lastly, outside-inside role changes will be most successful when HRM takes the lead in the socialization activities necessary to onboard new employees. "Learning the ropes" obviously entails both formal and informal sources of information about the organization.

HRM also is responsible for assisting employees to move from one organizational role to other suitable organizational roles. HRM manages these role changes by means of promotion and transfer policies and procedures. However, before people are willing to trade the roles they play within an organization for new roles inside that organization, appropriate communication is necessary to convince them that such a role change will be beneficial.

Finally, HRM must supervise the departure of employees from their current organizational roles for new roles outside of the firm (e.g., employment by a different business, retirement, or new life directions such as going back to school). Communication plays a role in apprising employees about the administrative procedures required to terminate employment and the services available for identifying new organizational roles with other firms. Due to the frequently high costs associated with turnover, organizations often use the exit interview to deduce the reasons that employees depart.

Developing

HRM is responsible for the development of employees of all ranks and stations in order that they may perform their organizational roles at a high level. To this end HRM must train employees to assure that they possess the knowledge and skill required to assume the organizational roles to which they are currently assigned. Appraisal systems that provide meaningful feedback on performance also must be created to ensure effective execution of current organizational assignments.

HRM also must work with executives and division directors to create plans for employees' futures, including special assignments that prepare them for the assumption of more responsible roles within the organization. Communication behaviors and systems are vital for the fulfillment of these developing practices. Effective communication is necessary in order that "employees have some idea of what skills will be valued in the future and what experiences are considered important in developing these skills" (Beer, Spector, Lawrence, Mills, & Walton, 1984, pp. 88, 89).

Conserving

HRM professionals are charged with the difficult tasks of anticipating and remediating issues within the organization's control that may affect employees' availability and willingness to perform their organizational roles. These activities are referred to as conserving. For example, compensation programs are intended to attract and retain qualified employees, while safety and health programs help ensure the well-being of employees, thereby enabling them to do their jobs. Efforts to assess and promote job satisfaction also are conserving programs because employees who are dissatisfied with their jobs are more likely to contemplate finding other work (Liu, Mitchell, Lee, Holtom, & Hinkin, 2012).

HRM must find ways to communicate in a more formal manner to keep employees in whom the organization has invested staffing and developing resources. To accomplish these tasks, HRM professionals must assess work climates within each unit as well as organization-wide; facilitate information exchanges on compensation systems; facilitate monitoring, training, and remediation related to work safety issues; and address issues associated with a diverse workplace. They must also assist managers in information dissemination regarding family leave benefits and develop creative programs to meet workers' schedules where family issues threaten to interfere with employee contributions. To this end, HRM professionals now work closely with information systems personnel for the effective distribution of information and use of social media across the organization.

Our organizing system results in a categorization of HRM practices that approximates those of other scholars. For example, when describing the way that effective HRM professionals contribute to an organization, Losey, Meisinger, and Ulrich (2005) identified categories of HRM practices that correspond closely to our system. "People—finding them, motivating them, keeping them, and exiting them when necessary—are central to what we do" (p. xxii). Similarly, high performance organizations are those whose HRM practices are strong in each of our three designated areas. Based on approximately 1,400 responses to the *High Performance Organization Survey 2007*, high performance organizations were described as having the following three distinguishing characteristics:

- They are more likely to promote the best people for a job, make sure that performance expectations are clear, and convince employees that their behaviors affect the success of the organization;
- They are superior in terms of clarifying performance measures, training people to do their jobs, and enabling employees to work well together; and,
- Their employees are more likely to think the organization is a good place to work (American Management Association, 2007, p. vii).

Plan of the Book

The goal of this book is to identify linkages between the disciplines of HRM and communication in order to facilitate research on the communicative aspects of HRM. In pursuit of this goal, our contributors summarize communication research on selected HRM topics and point out where research on communication issues could benefit theory, research, and application in organizational settings. Their input is segmented into sections in keeping with the previously described staffing, developing, and conserving functions. Providing a capstone to each section, a senior distinguished scholar discusses the contributed chapters' positions and advocacy.

Chapter 2 is a prelude to the discussions of particular HRM practices. Sue Hutchinson considers the importance of communication in fulfilling HRM's strategic role. The traditional view of HRM as a specialized functional department that simply provided information about staffing, training, and pay to organizational decision makers has given way to an integrated view of HRM as a full partner with real influence in strategic management. Strategic human resources management (SHRM) must link traditional HRM policies and practices to organizational strategy. Further, linkages among traditional HRM practices must be considered in order to create synergies that produce the greatest boost toward attainment of organizational goals. HRM managers must know what information should be shared with other members of the organization, when that information must be made available, and by what means that information should be shared. The role of eHRM is discussed in this context.

Staffing

In chapter 3, James Breaugh examines recruitment research pertaining to the presentation of information about an organization that increases its attractiveness to qualified applicants. HRM professionals face choices of communication methods (e.g., Internet posting boards, college campus recruitment service) and the nature of information to convey (e.g., realistic job previews) regarding the open position and employment conditions in the organization. Breaugh identifies communication issues that require additional research in order to improve recruitment practices, including the challenges inherent in the use of social media, the importance of incorporating prospective supervisors and coworkers into the process, the need to develop methodologies for conducting studies of the comparative effectiveness of different recruitment methods, and the potential difference between encoded recruitment messages and those that are perceived when decoded by applicants.

Chapter 4 is devoted to the selection of employees. Robert Dipboye focuses on communication requirements that facilitate collecting and interpreting applicant information in order to improve subsequent employment decisions. These requirements differ depending upon whether an analytical or intuitive selection model is adopted by the organization. Despite the concurrence of research that indicates the superiority of the analytical approach, its usefulness is limited by a number of largely technical issues as well as barriers stemming from various environments, including the HRM function itself, the organizational culture, and the external environment of the organization. Dipboye encourages researchers to examine how communication processes could assist management of the boundaries between selection processes and these environments and might affect the psychometric quality of assessments.

Prospective employees acquire information and form expectations about potential job choices from many sources, a process known as anticipatory socialization. Socialization is a transitional process involving the movement from being an organizational outsider to an organizational insider, according to Talya Bauer, Berrin Erdogan, and Lauren Simon. Chapter 5 treats the socialization of new employees as a process of reciprocal influence mediated by communication between new employees and organizational insiders. New employees' proactive behaviors and information seeking influence their successful entry into new organizational roles, although individual differences affect the inclination of newcomers to engage in these communication activities. HRM professionals are among several categories of insiders who contribute to newcomers' successful onboarding by helping to convey established organizational culture. Internalization of the organizational culture is an important indicator of successful newcomer adjustment.

Once people have been hired and have assumed an entry-level position, HRM must effectively manage internal organizational mobility. In chapter 6, Michael Kramer and Carrisa Hoelscher focus on HRM's responsibilities for identifying employees who are capable of and interested in changing organizational roles and providing them with sufficient information about new positions. They examine the changes in communication activity that occur in each phase of employee promotions and transfers. Communication issues are compared in the cases of domestic and international transfers, the latter being complicated by obvious challenges to increase the communicative competence of expatriates in the new cultural environment. Unintended consequences of these role changes (e.g., acceptance problems in new work settings) are discussed in terms of their bases in communication. In this vein, organizations must be aware of the powerful intended and unintended messages it sends about what the organization values in its personnel by promoting or transferring particular individuals who possess and display certain traits and behaviors.

In chapter 7, Michael Gordon examines the exit interview, an institutionalized conversation intended to reveal departing employees' actual reasons for leaving. Researchers have found that little useful information is disclosed about organizational conditions (e.g., abrasive supervision) that "pushed" people to seek employment elsewhere, but rather that departing employees typically report less threatening, extra-organizational ("pull") factors (e.g., starting a family) as the basis for their voluntary turnover. HRM professionals and researchers have long been concerned about the reliability of the information collected during exit interviews. Gordon suggests that more accurate information about employee turnover might be collected using communication research on self-disclosure and deception detection.

Developing

A traditional role for HRM is the development of personnel so that employees of all ranks and stations can manifest a high level of performance. In chapter 9, Jeremy Fyke and Patrice Buzzanell expand the view of communication as simply a transmission tool in the context of employee training, relying, instead, on a communication-as-constitutive-of-organizing (CCO) approach focused on the ongoing social construction of meaning among organization members in all phases of training. The CCO perspective assumes that meanings are actively produced, reproduced, maintained, and resisted in and through interactions. This orientation makes it important to consider the characteristics of those organizational members negotiating these to-be-learned items: trainers who view their roles as facilitating rather than teaching or instructing by drawing out issues germane to trainees' working lives, and trainees who represent particular audiences with whom the interactions will occur. This training *as* communication model is explicated in discussions of familiar training issues, including needs assessment, training methods and practices, training evaluation, and transfer of training.

It is critical that performance management systems provide employees with meaningful feedback to promote effective performance of organizational assignments. In chapter 10, Michael Gordon and Vernon Miller discuss several communication issues that give rise to the most problematic component of performance management systems, viz., the appraisal interview. For instance, reliance on most rating scales encumbers appraisers with a vocabulary that is typically ill-suited to the discussion of performance. Further, the communication role of the appraiser is complicated by interview procedures that treat both performance and salary issues during the same conversation. In light of the paucity of research based on actual appraisal interviews, they suggest consideration of conversation analysis as a methodology for examining the interchange of information during performance reviews.

The subject of leadership always has been the focus of discussions about how to promote better performance among organizational members. Dennis Tourish addresses the role of HRM and communication related to leadership in chapter 11, a topic of considerable importance considering the widespread disappointment in leadership in organizations and the vast sums expended on its development. Leadership is recognized as a distinctive social practice in which certain individuals are accorded the right to define social reality for others, largely by means of communication. Tourish points out that most leadership theories (e.g., transformational theories) posit unbounded leader agency while ignoring the importance of upward communication from followers (including dissent) in constructing this social reality. Instead, leadership should be recognized as an organized, fluid process of co-orientation and co-construction between myriad interacting organizational members. Tourish recommends a variety of managerial practices that promote upward communication, thereby recognizing the legitimacy and importance of followership in creating leadership.

Chapter 12 examines the communicative role of HRM professionals in organizational change management efforts. Laurie Lewis reviews research on collaboration in the planning processes, the development of "buy-in" by employees, negotiating implementation, and resistance to change. The essential, yet often difficult, process of organizational change must be implemented through communication, thus highlighting the necessity of involving all those affected by the proposed change in a dialogue with change agents to define the new social reality. Three communication challenges of HRM professionals during change are addressed, viz., soliciting employee input about change, disseminating information and contending with alternate framing of change, and creating ways to surface and resolve perceived problems with change initiatives.

Conserving

A variety of HRM programs affect employees' availability and willingness to perform their organizational roles. Because job satisfaction is related to the intent to turnover, Paul Leonardi, Jeffrey Treem, William Barley, and Vernon Miller discuss HRM's use of attitude surveys in chapter 14.

They consider communication issues related to what information is sought, how information is gathered, and how feedback garnered about employee attitudes is disseminated to various audiences in the organization. Consistent with the notion that organization emerges from communication, the authors describe a multi-method approach that entails the collection of information from different sources within the organization in order to understand better how it operates and to identify potential enablers and constraints on strategic changes planned by management.

It is axiomatic in HRM that compensation policies and practices are an important influence on an organization's ability to attract and retain a qualified workforce. Less studied and developed is the important role played by communication in achieving the desired outcomes of compensation programs. In chapter 15, Ingrid Fulmer and Yan Chen address the significance of employee perceptions of compensation practices and how these are influenced by what they learn about the compensation system, how organizations communicate those details, and how they affect attitudinal and behavioral reactions to the system. Some problems attributed to pay systems do not, in fact, reside with the compensation program but rather with how it is communicated to and understood by employees during its implementation. Importantly, they note widespread managerial diffidence about their ability to communicate information regarding compensation, yet little work has been done that might assist managers to provide accurate information about these matters.

Workplace safety policies and practices seek to reduce risks of injury and illness that could interfere with the ability of employees to work. In chapter 16, Robert Sinclair, Kyle Stanyar, Anna McFadden, Alice Brawley, and Yueng-Hsiang Huang discuss the role of communication in providing employees with health and safety knowledge and in encouraging safe and healthy behavior. While the organization climate and communication climate are concepts with which communication scholars are familiar, Sinclair and co-authors describe safety and health climates as reflections of the degree of consensus among employees about these two strategic priorities. The sense-making processes from which these climates emerge are strongly influenced by the behavior of supervisors, the occupational context, and the temperaments of individual employees.

The forces of globalization and more scrupulous legal environments have made it advisable for business organizations to create opportunities and work environments that will attract and retain a diverse workforce. In chapter 17, Eddy Ng and James Barker describe several approaches that organizations can use to communicate their commitment to diversity. Importantly, these authors also describe the thin line that HRM professionals must negotiate to avoid problems stemming from efforts to promote diversity, principally those frequently associated with affirmative action programs. The organization climate is considered an important influence on the meanings derived by employees from HRM attempts to manage diversity. Ng and Barker discuss the manner in which language affects the development of organizational climates that support diversity.

Throughout the last four decades, work-life issues that complicate the continued employment of valued workers, especially women, have been prominent media copy and an increasing focus of corporate policy. Unfortunately, according to Caryn Medved, little research literature exists on work-life communication and the responsibility of HRM in communicating effective policies about this matter. Consequently, Medved devotes much of chapter 18 to pointing out fertile areas for communication research on a variety of matters that appear to affect an organization's ability to retain valued employees in the face of personal and family demands. A review of interdisciplinary work-life policy research, the small yet bourgeoning body of work-life communication research, and HRM-related work-life communication research are interwoven around three communication roles HRM professionals play in the implementation of work-life policies: resource, coach, and strategist. Coworker communication in job-sharing relationships, career counseling regarding work-life issues, and workplace interactions between part-time and full-time employees represent useful subjects of study. Successful communication about all these work-life issues is dependent on the credibility of the messages.

In chapter 19, Keri Stephens, Eric Waters, and Caroline Sinclair argue that new information and communication technologies (ICTs) have become central to understanding the organization's communication practices, notably organizational translucency and eHRM. ICTs have transformed the roles played by HRM, particularly those in the conserving category. For example, ICTs have changed meeting practices and provided new meeting formats (e.g., dispersed meetings, multicommunicating, and videoconferencing) in ways that may temper negative effects on people's sense of well-being and may increase job satisfaction. The development of eHRM has made it possible for HRM to move away from exclusively providing one-on-one assistance and to adopt a self-service type of one-to-many support (e.g., a central repository of compensation and benefit information). HRM now is challenged to assist employees to use these new technologies and overcome their consternation at having to adopt new methods for performing their jobs.

William Schneper and Mary Ann Von Glinow report that the importance of communication in all facets of HRM is magnified in globally dispersed organizations. After describing the scope and role of communications technologies in bringing about globalization in chapter 20, they argue that the nature of communication flow within a multinational corporation (MNC) reflects the mind-set of the management as they evolve from ethnocentric to geocentric organizations. The choice of individuals for foreign assignments is still an essential HRM function, and intercultural communication competence and global mind-set are important considerations. An MNC's language policy influences the type of individual attracted to the MNC while simultaneously affecting interunit communication and the power of individual employees.

Commentary Chapters

Readers are encouraged to ponder the ideas regarding communication presented in association with the HRM practices in each section of the book. To assist such reflection, the services of an important scholar have been secured to serve as discussant at the end of each section. Neal Schmitt in chapter 8 provides his thoughts about the collection of staffing chapters; Patricia Sias comments about the material pertaining to developing programs in chapter 13; and the diverse programs intended to assure conserving are reviewed in chapter 21 by Gary Latham. Finally, chapter 22 affords Vernon Miller and Michael Gordon the opportunity to highlight themes presented across the three sections of the book, identifying the breadth of communication research and the fertile directions for future communication studies that will improve HRM policies and actions.

Note

1 The findings of the Hawthorne studies have been questioned frequently based on methodological shortcomings and theoretically biased interpretations of the empirical results (e.g., Levitt & List, 2011).

Bibliography

American Management Association. (2007). *How to build a high-performance organization: A global study of current trends and future possibilities.* Retrieved from www.gsu.edu/images/HR/HRI-high-performance07.pdf.

Ashkenas, R., Ulrich, D., Jick, T., & Kerr, S. (1995). *The boundaryless organization: Breaking the chains of organizational structure.* San Francisco, CA: Jossey-Bass.

Becker, B., & Huselid, M.A. (1998). High performance work systems and firm performance: A synthesis of research and managerial implications. *Research in Personnel and Human Resource Management, 16,* 53–101.

Beer, M., Spector, B., Lawrence, P.R., Mills, D.Q., & Walton, R.E. (1984). *Managing human assets.* New York: Free Press.

Croucher, R., & Rizov, M. (2012). Union influence in post-socialist Europe. *ILRReview, 65*(3), 630–650.

Deadrick, D.L., & Gibson, P.A. (2007). An examination of the research–practice gap in HR: Comparing topics of interest to HR academics and HR professionals. *Human Resource Management Review, 17*(2), 131–139.

Delery, J.E., & Doty, D.H. (1996). Modes of theorizing in strategic human resource management: Tests of universalistic, contingency and configurational performance predictions. *Academy of Management Journal, 39*(4), 802–835.

Den Hartog, D.N., Boon, C., Verburg, R.M., & Croon, M.A. (2013). HRM, communication, satisfaction, and perceived performance: A cross-level test. *Journal of Management, 39*(6), 1637–1665.

Gordon, M.E. (2011). The dialectics of the exit interview: A fresh look at conversations about organizational disengagement. *Management Communication Quarterly, 25*(1), 59–86.

Gordon, M.E., & Miller, V.D. (2012). *Conversations about job performance: A communication perspective on the appraisal process.* New York: Business Expert Press.

Gordon, M.E., & Stewart, L.P. (2009). Conversing about performance: Discursive resources for the appraisal interview. *Management Communication Quarterly, 22*(3), 473–501.

Huselid, M.A. (1995). The impact of human resource management practices on turnover, productivity, and corporate financial performance. *Academy of Management Journal, 38*(3), 635–672.

Jablin, F.M. (2001). Entry, assimilation, disengagement/exit. In F.M. Jablin & L.L. Putnam (Eds.), *The new handbook of organizational communication: Advances in theory, research, and methods* (2nd ed., pp. 732–818). Newbury Park, CA: Sage.

Katz, D., & Kahn, R.L. (1978). *The social psychology of organizations.* New York: John Wiley & Sons.

Kornhauser, A.W., & Sharp, A.A. (1932). Employee attitudes: Suggestions from a study in a factory. *Personnel Journal, 10*(11), 393–404.

Lepak, D.P., & Snell, S.A. (2002). Examining the human resource architecture: The relationships among human capital, employment, and human resource configurations. *Journal of Management, 28*(4), 517–543.

Levitt, S.D., & List, J.A. (2011). Was there really a Hawthorne effect at the Hawthorne plant? An analysis of the original illumination experiments. *American Economic Journal: Applied Economics, 3*(1), 224–238.

Likert, R. (1961). *New patterns of management.* New York: McGraw-Hill.

Liu, D., Mitchell, T.R., Lee, T.W., Holtom, B.C., & Hinkin, T.R. (2012). When employees are out of step with coworkers: How job satisfaction trajectory and dispersion individual- and unit-level voluntary turnover. *Academy of Management Journal, 55*(6), 1360–1380.

Losey, M. (1998). HR comes of age. *HRMagazine, 43*(3), 40–53.

Losey, M., Meisinger, S., & Ulrich, D. (2005). *The future of human resource management.* Hoboken, NJ: John Wiley & Sons.

McGregor, D. (1960). *The human side of enterprise.* New York: McGraw-Hill.

McGregor, D. (1972). An uneasy look at performance appraisal. *Harvard Business Review, 50*(5), 133–138.

Mumby, D.K. (2013). *Organizational communicaion: A critical approach.* Los Angeles: Sage.

Pfeffer, J. (1994). *Comparative advantage through people: Unleashing the power of the workforce.* Boston: Harvard Business School Press.

Posthuma, R.A., Campion, M.C., Masimova, M., & Campion, M.A. (2013). A high performance work practices taxonomy: Integrating the literature and directing future research. *Journal of Management, 39*(5), 1184–1220.

Roethlisberger, F. J., & Dickson, W. J. (1939). *Management and the worker: An account of a research program conducted by the Western Electric Company.* Cambridge, MA: Harvard University Press.

Scott, W.D., & Clothier, R.C. (1925). *Personnel management: Principles, practices, and point of view.* London: A.W. Shaw.

Snell, S.A. (1992). Control theory in human resource management: The mediating effect of administrative information. *Academy of Management Journal, 35*(2), 292–329.

Taylor, F.W. (1911). *Principles of scientific management.* New York: Harper & Brothers.

Verburg, R.A., Den Hartog, D.N., & Koopman, P.L. (2007). Configurations of human resource management practices: A model and test of internal fit. *International Journal of Human Resource Management, 18*(2), 184–208.

2

THE IMPORTANCE OF COMMUNICATION IN FULFILLING THE STRATEGIC ROLE OF HRM

Sue Hutchinson

Interest in the field of strategic human resource management (SHRM) has grown rapidly since the 1980s, but it is "an area of difficult definitions and contentious theory" (Boxall, 1996, p. 59) and complex to understand. There is some debate, for example, as to whether SHRM is a new discipline that is distinct from HRM, and opposing views exist on how the management of people may be critical to the success of organizations—a central tenet of SHRM. Although SHRM has been extensively researched, one key area, communication, has been neglected. Yet communication is an integral part of the strategy-making process and is generally considered essential to the establishment of a strong HRM system that allows for the creation of an organizational climate conducive to high performance (Bowen & Ostroff, 2004).

I begin by considering the distinguishing features of SHRM and introducing some key theoretical models that seek to explain how HRM links to performance, thereby framing the discussion on the role of communication in SHRM. Then I discuss the role of some key factors in the communication process—notably line managers, the HRM function, and the role of e-HRM in facilitating a move to a more strategic role for the HRM function. I conclude by identifying avenues for further research.

I have been selective in what is covered, and, therefore, several important aspects of communication are not addressed. For example, different communication channels are not explored (other than the role of e-HRM). Further, I do not address interpersonal communication between employees, even though it is closely related to organizational culture and climate, also vital in any strategic approach to HRM.

What Is SHRM?

Although definitions vary, there appears to be a consensus that SHRM focuses on linking HRM to organizational strategy in some way. Underlying this consensus is the notion that how people are managed will influence performance, and this relation is critical to the long-term success of the organization (Lepak & Shaw, 2008; Truss, Mankin, & Kelliher, 2012). In analyzing different definitions and interpretations of SHRM, Truss et al. (2012) suggest that it is the following:

> An overarching approach to people management within the organization in a broad, strategic sense. The focus is on the longer-term strategic needs of the organization in terms of its people, rather than day to day HR policies and practices. (p. 87)

The approach thus adopts a "macro" perspective by focusing on HRM at the level of the firm in contrast to the more traditional functional view of HRM (Lepak & Shaw, 2008).

The notion of fit or alignment plays a central role within SHRM. Not only must the HRM strategy and its underpinning policies and practices align with organizational strategy, but the policies and practices themselves must be linked to ensure that they are mutually supportive and that they promote the goals of the organization (Truss & Gratton, 1994; Wright & McMahan, 1992). In other words, there are vertical and horizontal dimensions to SHRM. Another distinguishing feature of SHRM is that the day-to-day management of human resources is devolved to line managers (Truss & Gratton, 1994), thus, in theory at least, freeing up the HRM function to play a more strategic role.

The concept of alignment has its origins in research on the linkage between HRM and performance that has dominated much of the SHRM literature. Although this research has generally supported the notion that there is a positive, albeit weak, relationship between HRM and performance, consensus is lacking on how this is achieved. There were initially two main schools of thought in this area. The contingency perspective, or "best fit" approach, argues that HRM strategies should be aligned with the organization's strategy and other contextual conditions (e.g., Schuler & Jackson, 1987). The universalist perspective ("best practice") focuses on a generic set of mutually supportive high performance or high commitment work practices (e.g., Arthur, 1994; Huselid, 1995; MacDuffie, 1995). More recently, a third perspective has entered the debate stemming from the resource-based view of the firm and emphasizing HRM as an important strategic resource (Wright, Dunford, & Snell, 2001; Wright & McMahan, 1992). It suggests that competitive advantage can be achieved from a firm's internal resources and capacities under certain conditions, viz., resources must be value producing, rare, imperfectly imitable, and without strategically equivalent substitutes.

The SHRM Process

Recent research has examined the mechanisms underlying the HRM practices-performance relationship. This has come to be known as the "black box" problem (Purcell, Kinnie, Swart, Rayton, & Hutchinson, 2003; Wright & Gardner, 2003). One principal model developed by Wright and Nishii (2005) postulates five critical steps in the HRM causal chain: (1) intended HRM practices, leading to (2) actual practices, leading to (3) perceived practices, leading to (4) employee reactions, and finally resulting in (5) performance outcomes. The model posits that employees' perceptions of HRM practices and employee reactions (attitudes such as job satisfaction and commitment and performance-related behaviors) are key mediating variables through which HRM practices influence performance. Furthermore, there may be a gap between intended practices—for instance, those designed to support HRM strategy—and the actual HRM practices that are implemented. In other words, it is not just the design of HRM policies that is important but the effectiveness of these policies as they are implemented.

The linkage between actual practices and perceived practices represents the "communication challenge" (Wright & Nishii, 2005, p. 14). This model builds on the work of Bowen and Ostroff (2004), who link HRM practices to employee reactions using communication theory, arguing that HRM practices can be viewed as communications devices that aim to send messages or signals from employer to employee about what is appropriate behavior. For example, a team-based incentive pay scheme sends out important messages about the ability of work teams. However, HRM practices can be communicated in unintended ways and may be understood idiosyncratically as, for example, when two employees interpret the same practice differently (Bowen &

Ostroff, 2004; Guzzo & Noonan, 1994). Therefore, HRM practices are likely to lead to desired outcomes only if they are perceived by employees in intended ways. To achieve such agreement regarding the actual purpose of the various practices, Bowen and Ostroff (2004) advocate the creation of a "strong situation" that is high in distinctiveness, consistency, and consensus.

Other theories have also been used to explain this relationship between HRM practices and performance. Nishii, Lepak, and Schneider (2008), for example, used attribution theory to explore the way in which workers interpret HRM practices and show how these interpretations can shape employee responses. The psychological contract is another useful framework for explaining why experiences with HRM practices may vary between individuals. The SHRM process, therefore, provides considerable potential for further research and integrating HRM theories/research with communication literature.

Linking Communication With Strategic Outcomes

Various models have been proposed for how HRM strategy, policies, and practices should align with organizational strategy in order to achieve performance goals. Schuler and Jackson's (1987) framework, for example, takes a behavioral perspective arguing that employees need to be encouraged to behave in ways that support the organization's strategies and that it is the role of HRM to elicit and reinforce these behaviors. Based on the three strategic options outlined by Porter (1985) of cost leadership, quality enhancement, and innovation, they identify the different types of HRM practices that are necessary to achieve different kinds of role behaviors that are needed for different competitive strategies. For instance, a strategy of innovation will require behaviors focused on risk taking, creativity and cooperation. Appropriate HRM techniques would include selecting highly skilled staff, appraisals based on individual and team performance, a high level of discretion, and broad career paths.

There is a clear role for communication in establishing these strategic linkages between organization strategy and HR strategy, policy, and practices. First, there is a need to communicate the firm's strategic direction. Typically, this is captured in vision and/or mission statements, and these are said to be most effective when expressed clearly and simply (e.g., Truss et al., 2012). A vision statement is normally a formula of inspirational words about what the organization will look like in the future, whereas a mission statement focuses on the organization's present state, although in practice organizations often blend the two. Such statements can be underpinned by value statements that articulate overarching principles for the psychological contract and can signal which attitudes and behaviors are important for organizational effectiveness. For example, an information technology firm with a vision focusing on inventing new products might adopt a value statement such as, "We value creativity." The HRM strategy flowing from this vision is likely to suggest the promotion of a creative work environment (Posthuma, Campion, Masimova, & Campion, 2013).

Statements by themselves, however, are not enough. They have to be disseminated appropriately and acted upon by the organization. Otherwise, employees will not understand and will not be committed to attainment of the organization's objectives. This emphasizes the importance of having a strongly integrated management approach. In their research on the link between people management and organizational performance, Purcell and colleagues (Purcell et al., 2003; Purcell, Kinnie, Swart, Rayton, & Hutchinson, 2008/2009) use the concept of the "Big Idea"—a mission supported by strong values and culture—to illustrate this point (see Box 1). One way in which organizations can show some of the strategic linkages is by using the balanced scorecard approach (Kaplan & Norton, 1996). Although criticized for its rigidity, the key advantages of this approach are that it provides a direct line of sight between employee goals, business unit objectives, and the organization's objectives and that it attempts to balance long-term and short-term requirements.

The Big Idea

The Big Idea was described as "a clear mission underpinned by values and a culture expressing what the organization stands for and is trying to achieve." In Jaguar Cars (now Jaguar Land Rover), for example, the Big Idea is quality.

The Big Idea may be described by five distinct elements:

- embedded
- connected
- enduring
- collective
- measured and managed.

When translated into practice, Big Ideas espouse values that are embedded in organizational policies and practices. These values interconnect the relationships with customers (both internal and external), culture, and behavior and provide the basis upon which employees should be managed (particularly important in customer-facing organizations). The values must also endure, even during difficult times, and provide a stable basis on which policies can be built and changed. The Big Idea is also a collective endeavor that serves as a "glue" that binds people and processes together for one common goal. Finally, the Big Idea can be managed and measured, providing not just the means of measuring performance, but also a way of integrating different functional areas of the business, both horizontally and vertically.

(Source: Purcell et al., 2003, pp. ix–x)

Linking Communication With Other HRM Practices

Supporting these vertical links is a range of HRM policies that must be configured in such a way that they are mutually supportive and consistent. Research suggests that combining HRM practices into a coherent and integrated "bundle" has stronger effects on performance than individual practices (Combs, Liu, Hall, & Kitchen, 2006; MacDuffie, 1995). This is based on the assumption that, first, practices have an additive effect, and second, that synergies occur when one practice reinforces another. For example, sharing information enhances the likelihood of the success of team working and other problem-solving groups because it encourages the exchange of ideas. Communication practices that allow information to be exchanged are an important component of this "bundle" and appear to have a positive relationship with performance (Posthuma et al., 2013). Pfeffer (1998), for example, lists information sharing on financial performance as one of his seven interlinked "best practices" in HRM. Further, Guest, Michie, Conway, and Sheehan's (2003) study of HRM and performance identifies two-way communication, including informing and consulting on business plans and employee surveys, as a best practice.

The reasons why communication is a best practice are wide ranging. Formalized communication mechanisms help clarify goals, connect individual work with organizational strategy, and reduce uncertainty (Posthuma et al., 2013). They also increase employee commitment to the organization, reduce perceived breach of the psychological contract, and strengthen manager-employee relationships (e.g., Guest & Conway, 2002; Pfeffer, 1998). Marchington and Wilkinson (2012) suggest that open communication about strategy and performance measures conveys a symbolic and important message that employees are trusted with such information and thus have a role to play in building a climate of mutual trust and understanding between employees and employers. Formal information sharing practices are also a way of reducing the impact of unofficial channels, such as the "grapevine," which are typically associated with rumors and inaccurate information.

The Critical Role of Line Managers

Merely having a strategy in place is not sufficient on its own. Attention also must be paid to the strategy implementation process, as suggested by Wright and Nishii's (2005) model of the HR causal chain. A key actor in this process is the line manager who directly supervises employees. Acting at the interface between the organization and its workforce, line managers are in an apposite position to translate and communicate organizational information, such as strategic intentions and decisions, procedures, and policies, to front-line staff. As Floyd and Wooldridge (1997) observe in discussing the role of middle managers, they "perform a coordinating role where they mediate, negotiate, and interpret connections between the organization's institutional (strategic) and technical (operations) levels" (p. 466). Similarly, Townsend, Wilkinson, Allan, and Bamber (2012) note in their research on ward managers (lower level line managers), "the line manager is a critical role, which interprets and disseminates the signals from senior executives and conveys them to front-line staff" (p. 278). In sum, line managers at all levels of the organization are in a position to "strengthen, ignore, or even undermine the messages" senior managers wish to be conveyed (Marchington & Wilkinson 2012, p. 4).

In models of SHRM, line managers are expected to deliver and implement organizational HRM policies and practices. Indeed, in most organizations today it is the line manager, not HRM specialists, who routinely handles the operational aspects of recruitment and selection, performance management, training, learning and development, reward, and absenteeism (Hutchinson & Purcell, 2010; Perry & Kulik, 2008). As "HRM agents" of the organization, line managers mediate the effect of HRM practices on attitudes and behavior (Purcell et al., 2003; Purcell & Hutchinson, 2007). For example, research by Purcell and colleagues shows that the way line managers implement and enact HRM, or "bring policies to life" (Hutchinson & Purcell, 2003, p. 12) and show leadership, strongly influences employees' attitudes, as reflected in job satisfaction and employee commitment. Indeed, "poorly designed or inadequate HRM policies can be 'rescued' by good management behavior in much the same way as 'good' HRM practices can be negated by poor front-line manager behavior or weak leadership" (Purcell & Hutchinson, 2007, p. 4). Research on leader-member exchange, perceived supervisory and organizational support, and the psychological contract confirm the importance of manager-employee relationships and the role of the line managers in implementing HRM (e.g., Guest & Conway, 2002; Rhoades & Eisenberger, 2002; Uhl-Bien, Graen, & Scandura, 2000).

Studies show that there is frequently a disconnect between intended and actual HRM policies, and this can be explained by line management behavior (e.g., Hutchinson & Purcell, 2003; Khilji & Wang, 2006; McGovern, Gratton, Hope-Hailey, Stiles, & Truss, 1997). This is particularly the case for direct methods of communication, such as team briefs and cascading information, that are heavily reliant upon line manager discretion for how they are executed (Cox, Marchington, & Suter, 2009). This disconnect is problematic if, as theorized in models of the HRM causal chain, HRM policies affect performance through employee perceptions of HRM practices.

A key reason for this disconnect is that line managers face considerable difficulty in implementing their HRM roles effectively due to problems of work overload, competing work priorities, ambiguous processes and practices, lack of skills and knowledge, lack of commitment, and inadequate organizational support (Maxwell & Watson, 2006; Nehles, van Riemsdijk, Kok, & Looise, 2006; Perry & Kulik, 2008; Purcell et al., 2009). In particular, communication, a key skill for good people management, is often thought to be lacking. Although studies are sparse, there is some evidence that both the style and content of manager communication affects employee attitudes. Den Hartog, Boon, Verburg, and Croon's (2012) study suggests that clear, informative, and useful communication by managers is important in effectively implementing HRM and, indeed, may be even more crucial than the specific content of the HRM practices. The importance of the quality of managers' communication is also suggested in signaling theory, which implies that if managers' communication on organizational issues is unclear or inconsistent, then employees receive confused signals. When employees receive confusing signals, they are likely to rely on their own subjective interpretations of what is offered in terms of HRM.

The HRM Function and Communication

The HRM function becomes more strategic when it moves from a mainly administrative function to a strategic partnering role. Exactly how this is to be achieved has been the subject of considerable debate among practitioners and academics, and this question has given rise to many different proposals for classifying the roles played by HRM. One of the best known and most widely practiced models is Ulrich's (1997) business partnering model that describes three types of HRM roles: HRM shared services handle the transaction work; HRM centers of excellence offer specialist knowledge and develop HRM policy for the organization; and the HRM business partner normally embeds HRM with senior line managers to influence and support strategy development and implementation. In addition to affording the HRM function a more strategic role, the model, if implemented properly, promises considerable benefits, including improved service efficiency and consistency, reduced costs, and an increased business focus.

One of the central roles of a strategic HRM function must be to communicate the organization's vision, its culture, and its goals through the choice and design of HRM policies and practices. For example, the use of a competency framework in performance management, recruitment and selection, and training and development sends powerful messages about the types of behaviors the organization values. A strong HRM system is one in which its policies are communicated to all employees and managers to ensure that they are fully understood and to encourage consistency in application (Bowen & Ostroff, 2004). A lack of knowledge and understanding of HRM policies and procedures has been shown to constrain management effectiveness in people management (Hutchinson & Purcell, 2010; Nehles et al., 2006). Policies and procedures need to be written in accessible language that avoids jargon, is relevant, is easy to understand, is straightforward to deliver, and is not overly bureaucratic and cumbersome. Finally, HRM must assure that line managers have the appropriate communication skills and confidence to conduct effective performance appraisals, give feedback, support training and development, and have "difficult conversations" with their staff (Hutchinson & Purcell, 2010).

Arguably there is also a role for HRM professionals in channeling employees' views to senior management. Introducing and administering upward communication practices often are accomplished with mechanisms such as employee attitude surveys and suggestions schemes. HRM professionals should also seek to influence downward corporate communication policies by advising on when major policy decisions that affect employees (e.g., redundancies or mergers) should be communicated and how they should be disseminated—in other words, what channels should be used and who should be involved and at what level. Finally, lateral communication is also vital for HRM professionals in order to build effective relationships with communication colleagues across the business who may or may not reside in the HRM function. Clarity is needed about which function (e.g., HRM, internal communications, public relations, or marketing) takes overall responsibility for the design, development, and implementation of communication strategy and processes within organizations. Argenti (1998) reports survey evidence that 80 percent of top corporations in the United States placed responsibility for employee communications with the corporate communication function, arguing that companies recognize that internal messages should be aligned with messages to external constituents. But if employee communication is so critical to shaping employee attitudes and behaviors, then there is a strong case for responsibility resting with the HRM function.

e-HRM

HRM's ability to use communication mechanisms may also assist in its efforts to become a strategic business partner, and electronic human resource management (e-HRM) is a tool that has the potential to play a key role in SHRM. Its use has increased considerably over the last decade, particularly for transactional HRM, although the extent to which this improves efficiency and effectiveness is debatable. This increase has gone hand in hand with other changes in the delivery of HRM such as shared service centers, outsourcing, and the devolution of HRM to the line (Parry & Tyson, 2011). Defined as "a way of implementing HRM strategies, policies and practices in organizations through a conscious and directed support of and with the full use of web-based technology" (Ruël, Bondarouk, & Looise, 2004, p. 281), e-HRM is both an entity (the technological aspect) and a process (Marler & Fisher, 2013). It is distinct from human resource information systems (HRIS) in that e-HRM reaches all employees at all levels of the organization, whereas HRIS affects only those working in the HRM function (Marler & Fisher, 2013).

It is claimed that e-HRM has the capacity to offer substantial benefits. The literature suggests there may be three main types of impact on the HRM function: operational, relational, and transformational (Lepak & Snell, 1998; Parry & Tyson, 2011; Ruël et al., 2004; Ruël, Bondarouk, & Van der Vald, 2006). Operational consequences comprise efficiency and effectiveness gains, including a reduction in HRM staff, speedier processes, cost savings, releasing staff from administrative work, and improving the quality of HRM services for internal customers (Ruël et al., 2004; Strohmeier, 2007). Relational outcomes refer to "new and extended interactions between actors" (Strohmeier 2007, p. 28) such as providing managers and employees remote access to HRM databases and information. Transformational outcomes are associated with changes to the HRM function and, more specifically, improving the strategic orientation of the HRM function. It is argued that by releasing HRM professionals from administrative work, more time is available to spend on strategic activities, although whether this can be achieved in practice is questionable.

Strohmeier (2007) notes that "the decisive question whether e-HRM is able to transform HRM into an appreciated business partner that provides value to the organization is only parenthetically addressed," finding mixed results and only "some isolated hints" that e-HRM may contribute to a more strategic role of HRM (p. 28). Similarly, Marler and Fisher's (2013) review of the empirical research finds that the evidence that e-HRM can facilitate a move to a more strategic role is weak, although they note that none of the studies reviewed specifically examined any strategic outcomes such as fit with business strategy. However, as Parry and Tyson (2011) note, a strategic impact does not just mean increased involvement in implementing organizational strategy. Their case study research in ten UK-based firms indicates that there are other ways in which e-HRM can enable HRM to support organizational strategy, such as developing organizational capability through better resourcing and learning systems, helping to clarify strategic choices through more accurate data on cost and performance, and providing more comprehensive employee data to aid strategic planning and decision making.

Nevertheless, there can be no doubt that achieving transformational outcomes is difficult, and more research is needed in this area. As Marler (2009) notes, achieving a strategic orientation "requires quite a radical shift of focus from cost reduction to customization" (p. 521). HRM functions trying to move from a mainly administrative role to a strategic role may find this transformation difficult, particularly if senior management treats the HRM function as a cost center or does not consider it as critical to organizational strategy. Transformational outcomes may not be attained should HRM staff lack the skill and ability to rise to the challenge of a more strategic role (Parry & Tyson, 2011). HRM staff may also be redeployed to other activities such as shared service centers or other technology support roles rather than more strategic roles (Parry, 2011). Thus, the introduction of e-HRM alone is not sufficient for an HRM function to become strategic (Marler, 2009).

Future Research Recommendations

In summary, if HRM is to contribute to organizational success and become "strategic," then SHRM must link with organizational goals, and individual HRM policy areas must be interlinked and mutually supportive. Attention also needs to be paid to the process, in particular implementation and the meaning employees attach to HRM practices. The role line managers play in delivering HRM practices and their communication style is fundamental to achieving the benefits of good HRM strategies and policies. There is a clear role for communication in SHRM, although explicit references to communication as a key component of the strategy process is often lacking. HRM professionals can play vital roles at both the strategic level, by assisting in the design of HRM and communication strategy, and at the operational level, by the way they communicate HRM policies and practices to employees and employers and by the way they provide support to line managers. While e-HRM has the potential to provide a platform for transforming the HRM function to a more strategic role, the evidence that this actually happens in practice is weak.

These conclusions suggest ample avenues for further research, and the following areas are recommended. Overall, more research is required to understand the SHRM process. In particular, future research might usefully be devoted to the mechanisms through which intended practices translate into actual practices and to the influences on employees' perceptions of practices (see Fulmer and Chen's chapter 15 on the problems of deriving the intended motivational impact of compensation programs if they are not understood by employees). As Wright and Nishii (2005) note, there are exciting avenues for integrating relevant theories from SHRM, organizational behavior, psychology, and communication literature.

More specifically, research is needed to understand the roles played by line managers in HRM. Front-line managers at the lower levels of the management hierarchy, in particular, are frequently overlooked in research and in practice in the field of SHRM. These managers potentially have the greatest impact on employees because they usually have larger teams to supervise and because of their proximity to, and regular interaction with, employees (Becker, Billings, Eveleth, & Gilbert, 1996). Greater understanding is needed on the way front-line managers' roles in HRM are defined in different contexts and how they are experienced and on the factors that enable and inhibit line managers in delivering effective HRM. Communication research can provide useful insights into how to handle "difficult conversations" with staff (e.g., delivering bad news, raising issues of poor performance or misconduct) and communicating recognition.

There is little literature on the role of HRM professionals with respect to communicating HRM strategy, policy, and practices to employees and managers and on the types of communication practices that are most effective. Different communications channels achieve different objectives and need to be fit for purpose. For example, newsletters, the intranet, videos, and general forum meetings may be best for messages about strategic directions and intentions but do not necessarily drive behavioral outcomes. Closer communication between managers and employees, such as one-to-one meetings and performance reviews, may be more appropriate for addressing behavioral issues. A related matter is HRM involvement in corporate communication policies—how and when major policy issues that affect employees should be communicated and who should be responsible for the communication strategy, HRM or another specialist function.

Strohmeier (2007) notes that e-HRM is a "new and intriguing field of research at the intersection of HRM and information systems" (p. 34). Despite the rapid increase in the implementation of e-HRM, the theoretical and empirical research in this area is still at an embryonic stage, particularly when compared with the general information technology literature and the strategy literature. Marler and Fisher (2013) identify four gaps in the research: a stronger theoretical foundation for e-HRM research; a greater focus on strategic outcomes; examination of e-HRM from a resource-based view;[1] and more macro-level and longitudinal quantitative studies to explore the causal relationship between e-HRM and SHRM.

A final and perhaps more controversial area to study concerns the relationship between communication and performance. Academics, practitioners, and policy makers have mostly taken it for granted that communication is good—that communication can bring about improved organizational performance and, indeed, the more communication the better. Communication is a means of fostering employee involvement, and direct communication, as discussed earlier, is identified as a key practice in studies linking HRM to performance. However, the relationship between communication and performance is complex. Rodwell, Kienzle, and Shadur's (1998) study, for example, found communication to be negatively related to performance, yet positively related with teamwork, job satisfaction, and commitment. Zimmerman, Sypher, and Haas (1996) question the "communication metamyth," which makes the assumption that more communication is better for all organizations. They argue that this undifferentiated view of communication ignores the organizational context, the quality of communication, and the type of communication channel (e.g., informal, such as the "grapevine," versus formal, such as team briefings). Clearly, further research is needed to unravel the nature of the relationship between communication and performance.

Note

1 Although not addressed in this chapter, some commentators dismiss information technology as a resource with the characteristics necessary to create a sustained competitive advantage, arguing, for example, that it is not rare and is easily imitated.

Bibliography

Argenti, P.A. (1998). Strategic employee communications. *Human Resource Management, 37*(3–4), 199–206.

Arthur, J.B. (1994). Effects of human resource systems on manufacturing performance and turnover. *Academy of Management Journal, 37*(3), 670–687.

Becker, T.E., Billings, R., Eveleth, D., & Gilbert, N. (1996). Foci and bases of employee commitment: Implications for job performance. *Academy of Management Journal, 39*(2), 464–482.

Bowen, D., & Ostroff, C. (2004). Understanding the HRM-firm performance linkages: The role of the "strength" of the HRM system. *Academy of Management Review, 29*(2), 203–221.

Boxall, P. (1996). The strategic HRM debate and the resource-based view of the firm. *Human Resource Management Journal, 6*(3), 59–75.

Combs, C., Liu, Y., Hall, A., & Kitchen, D. (2006). How much do high-performance work systems matter? A meta-analysis of their effects on organizational performance. *Personnel Psychology, 59*(3), 501–528.

Cox, A., Marchington, M., & Suter, J. (2009). Employee involvement and participation: Developing the concept of institutional embeddedness using WERS2004. *International Journal of Human Resource Management, 20*(10), 2150–2168.

Den Hartog, D.N., Boon, C., Verburg, R.M., & Croon, M. (2012, April 3). HRM, communication, satisfaction and perceived performance: A cross level test. *Journal of Management*. doi: 10.1177/0149206312440118.

Floyd, S., & Wooldridge, B. (1997). Middle management's strategic influence and organizational performance. *Journal of Management Studies, 34*(3), 465–485.

Guest, D.E., & Conway, N. (2002). Communicating the psychological contract: An employer perspective. *Human Resource Management Journal, 12*(2), 22–38.

Guest, D.E., Michie, J., Conway, N., & Sheehan, M. (2003). Human resource management and corporate performance in the UK. *British Journal of Industrial Relations, 41*(3), 291–314.

Guzzo, H.A., & Noonan, K.A. (1994). Human resource practices as communications and the psychological contract. *Human Resource Management, 33*(3), 447–462.

Huselid, M.A. (1995). The impact of human resource management practices on turnover, productivity, and corporate financial performance. *Academy of Management Journal, 38*(3), 635–872.

Hutchinson, S., & Purcell, J. (2003). *Bringing policies to life: The vital role of line managers.* London: CIPD.

Hutchinson, S., & Purcell, J. (2010). Managing ward managers for roles in HRM in the NHS: Overworked and under resourced. *Human Resource Management Journal, 20*(4), 357–374.

Kaplan, R.S., & Norton, D.P. (1996). *The balanced scorecard: Translating strategy into action.* Boston: Harvard Business School Press.

Khilji, S.E., & Wang, X. (2006). Intended and implemented HRM: The missing linchpin in strategic international human resource management research. *International Journal of Human Resource Management, 17*(7), 1171–1189.

Lepak, D., & Shaw, J.D. (2008). Strategic HRM in North America: Looking to the future. *International Journal of Human Resource Management, 19*(8), 1486–1499.

Lepak, D., & Snell, S. (1998). Virtual HR: Strategic human resource management in the 21st century. *Human Resource Management Review, 8*(3), 215–234.

MacDuffie, J. (1995). Human resource bundles and manufacturing performance: Organizational logic and flexible production systems in the world auto industry. *Industrial and Labor Relations Review, 48*(2), 197–221.

Marchington, M., & Wilkinson, A. (2012). *Human resource management at work* (5th ed.). London: CIPD.

Marler, J.H. (2009). Making human resources strategic by going to the Net: Reality or myth? *International Journal of Human Resource Management, 20*(3), 515–527.

Marler, J.H., & Fisher, S.L. (2013). An evidence-based review of e-HRM and strategic human resource management. *Human Resource Management Review, 23*(1), 18–36.

Maxwell, G.A., & Watson, S. (2006). Perspectives on line managers in HRM: Hilton International's UK hotels. *International Journal of Human Resource Management, 17*(6), 1152–1170.

McGovern, F., Gratton, L., Hope-Hailey, V., Stiles, S., & Truss, C. (1997). Human resource management on the line? *Human Resource Management Journal, 7*(4), 12–29.

Nehles, A.C., van Riemsdijk, M., Kok, I., & Looise, J.C. (2006). Implementing human resource management successfully: A first-line management challenge. *Management Review, 17*(3), 256–273.

Nishii, L., Lepak, D., & Schneider, B. (2008). Employee attributions of the "why" of HR practices: Their effects on employee attitudes and behaviors, and customer satisfaction. *Personnel Psychology, 61*(3), 503–545.

Parry, E. (2011). An examination of e-HRM as a means to increase the value of the HR function. *International Journal of Human Resource Management, 22*(5), 1146–1162.

Parry, E., & Tyson, S. (2011). Desired goals and actual outcomes of e-HRM. *Human Resource Management Journal, 21*(3), 335–354.

Perry, E.L., & Kulik, C.T. (2008). The devolution of HR to the line: Implication of perceptions of people management effectiveness. *International Journal of Human Resource Management, 19*(2), 262–273.

Pfeffer, J. (1998). *The human equation: Building profits by putting people first.* Boston: Harvard Business School Press.

Porter, M.E. (1985). *Competitive advantage: Creating and sustaining superior performance.* New York: Free Press.

Posthuma, R.A., Campion, M.C., Masimova, M., & Campion, M.A. (2013). A high performance work practices taxonomy: Integrating the literature and directing future research. *Journal of Management, 39*(5), 1184–1220.

Purcell, J., & Hutchinson, S. (2007). Front-line managers as agents in the HRM-performance causal chain: Theory, analysis and evidence. *Human Resource Management Journal, 17*(1), 3–20.

Purcell, J., Kinnie, N., Hutchinson, S., Rayton, B., & Swart, J. (2003). *Understanding the people and performance link: Unlocking the black box.* London: CIPD.

Purcell, J., Kinnie, N., Swart, J., Rayton, B., & Hutchinson, S. (2008/2009). *People and performance.* Abingdon, VA: Routledge.

Rhoades, L., & Eisenberger, R. (2002). Perceived organizational support: A review of the literature. *Journal of Applied Psychology, 87*(4), 698–714.

Rodwell, J.J., Kienzle, R., & Shadur, M.A. (1998). The relationship among work-related perceptions, employee attitudes, and employee performance: The integral role of communications. *Human Resource Management, 37*(3–4), 277–293.

Ruël, H.J.M., Bondarouk, T.V., & Looise, J.K. (2004). e-HRM—innovation or irritation: Explorative empirical study in five large companies on Web-based HRM. *Management Revue, 15*(3), 364–380.

Ruël, H.J.M., Bondarouk, T.V., & Van der Vald, M. (2006). The contribution of e-HRM to HRM effectiveness. *Employee Relations, 29*(3), 280–291.

Schuler, R., & Jackson, S. (1987). Linking competitive strategies with human resource management practices. *Academy of Management Executive, 1*(3), 207–219.

Strohmeier, S. (2007). Research in e-HRM: Review and implications. *Human Resource Management Review, 17*(1), 19–37.

Townsend, K., Wilkinson, A., Allan, C., & Bamber, G. (2012). Mixed signals in HRM: The HRM role of hospital line managers. *Human Resource Management Journal, 22*(3), 267–282.

Truss, C., & Gratton, L. (1994). Strategic human resource management: A conceptual approach. *International Journal of Human Resource Management, 5*(3), 663–686.

Truss, C., Mankin, D., & Kelliher, C. (2012). *Strategic human resource management.* Oxford: Oxford University Press.

Uhl-Bien, M., Graen, G.B., & Scandura, T.A. (2000). Implications of leader–member exchange (LMX) for strategic human resource management systems. In G. Ferris (Ed.), *Research in Personnel and Human Resource Management* (pp. 137–185). Greenwich, CT: JAI Press.

Ulrich, D. (1997). *Human resource champions: The next agenda for adding value and delivering results.* Cambridge, MA: Harvard Business School Press.

Wright, P.M., Dunford, B., & Snell, S. (2001). Human resources and the resource-based view of the firm. *Journal of Management, 27*(6), 701–721.

Wright, P., & Gardner, T. (2003). Theoretical and empirical challenges in studying the HR practice—firm performance relationship. In D. Holman, T.D. Wall, C. Clegg, P. Sparrow, & A. Howard (Eds.), *The new workplace: A guide to the human impact of modern working practices* (pp. 331–330). New York: John Wiley & Sons.

Wright, P.M., & McMahan, G. (1992). Theoretical perspectives for strategic human resource management. *Journal of Management, 18*(2), 295–320.

Wright, P.M., & Nishii, L. (2005). Strategic HRM and organizational behavior: Integrating multiple-level analysis. *Working Paper Series*, Cornell University.

Zimmerman, S., Sypher, B.D., & Haas, J.W. (1996). A communication metamyth in the workplace: The assumption that more is better. *Journal of Business Communication, 33*(2), 185–204.

PART II
STAFFING

3

EMPLOYEE RECRUITMENT

James Breaugh

Regardless of the type of organization, an employer's success is dependent upon the quality of its workforce. Because the manner in which an employer recruits affects the type of individuals it hires, it is not surprising that the topic of employee recruitment has received substantial attention from researchers (see Dineen & Soltis, 2011, for a review of this research) and practitioners (see Breaugh, 2009, for examples of innovative recruitment practices used by employers). In this chapter, I focus on recruitment as a communication process between an organization with job openings to fill and individuals who may be interested in applying for them.[1]

At the outset, two issues should be noted. First, given the breadth of the recruitment literature, choices had to be made in terms of what topics to cover. This chapter focuses on external recruitment defined as such:

> an employer's actions that are intended to (1) bring a job opening to the attention of potential job candidates who do not currently work for the organization, (2) influence whether these individuals apply for the opening, (3) affect whether they maintain interest in the position until a job offer is extended, and (4) influence whether a job offer is accepted. (Breaugh, 2008, pp. 103–104)

Second, although emphasis is placed on an organization as the sender of a recruitment-related message, the perspective of a job applicant as the message recipient is also addressed because applicant-related variables influence the effectiveness of recruitment communications.

The Perspective of a Job Applicant

Research (e.g., Uggerslev, Fassina, & Kraichy, 2012) has established that whether a person applies for a job (and ultimately whether a job offer is accepted) is strongly related to its perceived attractiveness. Among the job and organizational attributes that determine the attractiveness of a position are the tasks involved, pay, benefits, coworkers, supervision, location, autonomy, advancement opportunity, and organizational reputation. The importance of these and other attributes suggest that they should be addressed during the recruitment process. Because some attributes (e.g., tuition reimbursement) may only be important to some recruits, an employer should allow sufficient opportunity for job applicants to ask knowledgeable sources (e.g., an HR recruiter, a prospective coworker) questions about job attributes. An individual's expectancy of receiving a job offer also has been linked to a position's attractiveness. Specifically, studies have shown that individuals often downgrade an advertised position if they perceive they are unlikely to receive a job offer (Uggerslev et al., 2012).

When making decisions about job openings, individuals often draw inferences about unknown aspects of a position from known aspects (Harold, Uggerslev, & Kraichy, 2013). For example, an organization's reputation can affect an applicant's evaluation of a job opening, not only because individuals want to impress others by being affiliated with a respected organization (Highhouse, Thornbury, & Little, 2007), but also because they infer that an employer's reputation signals other job attributes about which they lack information (Cable & Turban, 2003). Research also has shown that time delays during the recruitment process may be interpreted by applicants as an indicator that they were not the top choice of the employer for a job opening (Becker, Connolly, & Slaughter, 2010).

Two findings concerning the accuracy of recruits' perceptions should be noted before addressing specific aspects of the recruitment process. Applicants' perceptions of a job opening are not always accurate, and they may lack insight concerning their abilities, needs, and so forth (Dunning, 2007). An absence of self-insight can be problematic when an employer provides accurate information about a position so that recruits can make informed job choice decisions, but the recruits lack sufficient self-awareness for determining whether a job is a good fit.

Targeting Individuals for Recruitment Messages

In beginning the recruitment process, an employer needs to decide on the types of job applicants it wants to attract (e.g., those with prior work experience). Several factors should be considered when deciding whom to recruit, including: (a) what type of person is likely to be initially attracted to a job with the employer (i.e., will the person value what the organization offers and, therefore, be likely to submit an application?), (b) what type of individual is likely to possess the personal characteristics (e.g., education, values) needed to be hired, and (c) whether a job offer is likely to be accepted by the type of person targeted (will an employer's job offer be competitive with other offers a recruit may receive?).

Several authors have noted the significance of the decision about whom to target. However, there is little empirical research directly relevant to this topic (Dineen & Soltis, 2011). For example, although former employees who performed well are potentially valuable recruits based on the assumptions that they possess accurate job expectations and relevant skills, few studies have compared the recruitment of former employees against other potential targeted groups (e.g., new college graduates). Nonetheless, empirical studies, theoretical articles, and practitioner reports suggest that targeting certain groups would be beneficial. For example, individuals have been found to be more attracted to an employer if prospective coworkers were perceived as similar to themselves in terms of personality characteristics (Devendorf & Highhouse, 2008). This attraction could result from individuals wanting to work with similar coworkers and/or perceiving they were more likely to receive a job offer if the employer had previously hired people who were similar to them. Because a job offer is less likely to be accepted if an applicant is required to relocate, individuals who reside in the same locale as the job opening represent another potentially useful group to target (Becker et al., 2010). Theoretical treatments of the topic (e.g., Breaugh,

2008) suggest the benefits of targeting individuals who have a family member who works for the organization or have worked in jobs similar to an advertised position (in both cases, the individuals recruited should have more realistic job expectations).

Breaugh (2009) discussed how two employers targeted certain types of individuals for recruitment. Borders, the former international book and music retailer, targeted senior citizens based on data showing that, compared to younger employees, seniors did not have higher medical costs or absenteeism and, indeed, had better performance and retention. RightNow Technologies, located in Bozeman, Montana, had difficulty filling positions in marketing and engineering using job advertisements placed in newspapers in cities in the western United States. Based on the assumption that some former Montana residents might welcome the opportunity to return home, RightNow tried targeting alumni of Montana State University to fill vacant positions and found it to be quite effective.

The decision an employer makes with regard to the type of individuals to recruit should affect subsequent recruitment decisions. For example, with regard to recruitment methods, if an organization has targeted seniors for recruitment, it might be wise to work with AARP or to visit senior-oriented community centers to publicize job openings. If an employer has targeted relatives of current employees, its recruitment messages may convey less information about itself than if it were recruiting individuals who would be less familiar with the organization.

Recruitment Methods

Having selected the type of individuals to target for recruitment, an employer needs to decide how to reach these individuals with its recruitment message. In the past, organizations frequently relied on advertisements placed in newspapers, job postings at the work site, college campus recruiting, and its current employees for developing an applicant pool. However, technological advances (e.g., the Internet, social media) offer employers a greater choice of ways to reach targeted recruits today. Given the number of recruitment methods available (e.g., direct mail, job fairs), my discussion of recruitment methods is necessarily limited.[2]

Attracting the attention of the people you want to recruit is a fundamental communication issue. In some cases, this may not be difficult. For example, college students who are about to graduate may be attentive to the job postings of companies that will be interviewing on their campus. In contrast, sometimes it is not so easy to attract the attention of targeted individuals. For example, an employer might be interested in recruiting individuals who are currently employed by its competitors. Many of these individuals may not be looking for a job. Research on goal-directed attention (Breaugh, 2013) suggests that individuals who are not looking for a job will be less likely to attend to a job advertisement. If they do, they are likely to process it superficially. All else being equal, certain methods (e.g., being contacted by a current employee of a hiring organization) are more likely to attract attention than others (e.g., an organization using its Web site to passively recruit).

Research has shown the use of employee referrals to be one of the most effective recruitment methods. Compared to individuals recruited by other methods, individuals referred by current employees of an organization have been found to be superior in terms of skills, education, and work experience (Castilla, 2005; Yakubovich & Lup, 2006). Given these advantages, it is not surprising that researchers also reported that employee referrals were more likely to receive job offers and, if hired, were more likely to perform at a higher level and were less likely to quit their new jobs.

The positive outcomes linked to the use of current employees to generate recruits are due to two primary factors (Dineen & Soltis, 2011). First, when discussing a job opening with a potential recruit, a current employee is likely to communicate a detailed and realistic view of what working for the employer would involve. If the person doing the referring works in the department with a job opening, the current employee should be especially able to provide important information concerning the type of projects currently being worked on, coworker relations, and supervisor support.[3] Because most employee referrals involve a two-way interaction (e.g., an in-person conversation), a prospective recruit has the opportunity to ask questions of an employer (e.g., inquire about topics that are of personal relevance to the individual). Second, employee referrals are thought to be effective because they promote prescreening. That is, because of a concern for their own reputation, current employees typically will only refer persons they believe to be suitable for the job opening. This prescreening can be advantageous for an organization because a current employee may have insight into personal characteristics (e.g., work ethic) of a potential new hire that are difficult to assess with an employee selection system. Yet another reason that employee referrals are likely to have beneficial outcomes is because they are more likely to attract the attention of targeted individuals (e.g., referrals can be an ideal method of reaching individuals who are not currently looking for a job). One reason for this is individuals making referrals are likely to be seen as a credible information source (Breaugh, 2013), and credible sources have been shown to capture the attention of the intended audience (Wyer & Adaval, 2003).

Studies by Collins and his associates (e.g., Collins & Han, 2004; Collins, 2007) have investigated whether recruitment practices used by an employer prior to visiting a college campus influenced student views of the employer, their application intentions, and whether job applications were submitted. Three practices that increased an organization's visibility on campus had beneficial recruitment effects: sponsorship activities, recruitment advertisements, and word-of-mouth endorsements. For example, having heard that an organization sponsors scholarships and/or that faculty describe it as a good place to work, many students are likely to form a positive first impression of the employer and, in turn, submit applications.

Recently, many employers rely on their Web site as a recruitment method. Such a strategy for communicating information about job openings is most beneficial when certain conditions are met (Allen, Mahto, & Otondo, 2007). For example, it is imperative that an organization has high visibility to the audience targeted for recruitment. Web site aesthetics (e.g., an attractive design) and ease of use (e.g., navigation around the site) have been found to be important (Uggerslev et al., 2012). Web sites also should convey information about a job opening that is specific and realistic. The credibility of the information contained on a Web site may be enhanced by including employee testimonials and information concerning awards an organization has won (Walker, Field, Giles, Armenakis, & Bernerth, 2009).

The use of job boards (e.g., Monster.com) is another popular method for making individuals aware of job openings (job boards typically involve a third party providing an Internet site on which for a fee employers can post job listings; many boards allow job seekers to post resumes). A job board can bring a job opening to the attention of several individuals quickly and often inexpensively. These are advantages that can be especially beneficial for small employers and/or those that have less visibility to the type of individual targeted for recruitment. In addition to general job boards (i.e., those that post a wide variety of jobs with no limitations on location), there are boards that focus on a given industry, profession, or geographic area. Being geared to a more specific audience, these job boards are likely to generate fewer job applicants but ones that better fit an employer's needs.

Little research has been published on job boards. In one study, Jattuso and Sinar (2003) investigated differences in the type of applicants generated by general job boards and boards focused on specific industries and professions. They found that recruits generated by means of more targeted job boards had a higher level of education and skill but less work experience. Backhaus (2004) analyzed job advertisements placed on Monster.com. He found that most employers' job postings presented extremely positive information and failed to provide information that would help a recruit differentiate one employer from another.

Social media is increasingly being used as a recruitment method. Although they have some attributes in common with job boards and employer Web sites, important distinctions exist. For example, an employer using a Twitter account may reach an individual who is not looking for a job who would not have been made aware of a job opening through a job board or employer Web site. Social media have other potential benefits for an employer (Dineen & Allen, 2014), including the capability to target certain individuals (e.g., individuals who list education on a Facebook page that is sought by an employer); the ability to customize the information shared (e.g., use a Twitter account to inform a targeted person who is going to school that an employer offers a tuition-reimbursement program); the means to provide prompt feedback to information requests; and the potential to signal to a message recipient that it is a modern organization that has adapted to new technology.

Although discussions of social media frequently emphasize potential benefits, a few potential problems may also arise. One issue that should be considered is the possibility that inconsistent recruitment messages may be disseminated (e.g., an individual may receive different information from an employer's Web site than from a current employee communicating via Twitter). Such inconsistency can raise questions about the credibility of information that is shared. A second issue is whether an employer will receive more job applications than desirable. Finally, adverse impact may arise leading to legal charges concerning employment discrimination if an employer's reliance on social media resulted in individuals in certain protected classes being less likely to hear about job openings (Hansen, 2009).

Despite the attention given to social media in the popular press, research on their use is lacking. However, studies by Dineen, Ash, and Noe (2002) and Dineen and Noe (2009) that involved students taking part in simulation studies in which they received feedback concerning person–organization fit are suggestive. Although their focus was on an employer's Web site rather than social media, these researchers showed that providing feedback to individuals concerning how well they fit a job opening affected students' ratings of job attractiveness and applicant pool quality. The information conveyed to applicants concerning person–organization fit only will be useful if the information provided by the applicant is factual (applicants sometimes provide information that is exaggerated to make themselves look attractive to employers). In this regard, an employer may be able to make use of information available via social media (e.g., a Facebook page) to confirm the accuracy of recruit-supplied information.

To provide a sense of the creative recruitment methods that employers have used to reach prospective job applicants, the experience of Quicken Loans is informative. Unhappy with the number of qualified applicants it attracted via job fairs and its company Web site, Quicken Loans decided to undertake more assertive recruiting (Taylor, 2006). The company decided to have its recruiters visit stores and restaurants in the role of customers in order to identify other customers who exhibited high levels of enthusiasm and customer service orientation (the type of person it had targeted for recruitment). Those individuals that Quicken Loans' recruiters encountered who impressed them were encouraged to apply for positions.

Recruitment Media

The topic of recruitment media (i.e., the means of communicating a recruitment message) per se has received little attention from researchers. This is unfortunate given that media should differ in terms of their effectiveness for communicating a recruitment message. Recruitment media may not have been studied extensively because it is difficult to standardize the message communicated in order to study media effects. For example, consider a researcher who wanted to investigate media effects involving a face-to-face conversation versus a written text. Such a researcher would want to be certain that the same message was communicated in both conditions. However, it is difficult to ensure that a recruiter discussing a position opening with a job seeker (e.g., at a job fair) communicates only the information included in a recruitment brochure and nothing more. With the exception of Allen, Van Scotter, and Otondo's (2004) research described in the following, most studies that have involved the use of different media also have examined different recruitment methods. Consequently, recruitment media and recruitment method effects are confounded in these studies.

In Allen et al.'s (2004) study of college students, the same message was presented via one of four media (i.e., face-to-face, video, audio, and text). Based on media richness theory (Daft & Lengel, 1984), it was hypothesized that rich media would be more effective in communicating the complex messages inherent in recruitment. The results reported by Allen et al. largely reflect the predictions of media richness theory.

The research results on recruitment media suggest that employers would be wise when planning communications with prospective recruits to consider the ability of a particular media to adequately convey the information it intends to transmit. In this regard, it makes sense to consider that even a two-way conversation may be limited for communicating certain types of information. For example, an organization that is interested in accurately communicating information that is sensory in nature (e.g., unpleasant odors or extreme heat in a workplace) might be advised to consider a tour of the work site in order to provide direct experience with the work environment.

The Recruitment Message

A key element of an effective communication process is the content of the message that is sent. Several aspects of a recruitment message's content have been investigated. For example, studies have demonstrated the beneficial effects (e.g., increased job attractiveness) of recruitment messages that provide greater amounts of information about a job (Allen, Mahto, & Otondo, 2007) and more specific information (Stevens & Szmerekovsky, 2010). For example, Mason and Belt (1986) reported that a job advertisement that included specific information about the type of personal characteristics desired in an applicant (e.g., work experience or education) reduced the number of unqualified individuals who applied for a position. Studies also have shown that providing specific information can result in greater attention being given to a message by potential job applicants (Roberson, Collins, & Oreg, 2005).

Because recruits frequently have inflated (i.e., inaccurate) job expectations that can result in employee turnover (Phillips, 1998), researchers have investigated methods for improving the accuracy of job expectations (e.g., the use of employee referrals). The most popular method studied is the realistic job preview (RJP), which involves "the presentation by an organization of both favorable and unfavorable job-related information to job candidates" (Phillips, 1998, p. 673).[4]

The logic underlying the use of an RJP is as follows. Because most recruits possess inflated job expectations, providing realistic information about a job opening enables an applicant to make a more informed choice about whether to accept a job offer (i.e., self-select out of job consideration if a position is not perceived as a good fit). New hires who have received an RJP should be less likely to experience unmet expectations (i.e., be disappointed in a new job). Having their expectations met, they should experience greater job satisfaction and be less likely to experience turnover.

Traditionally, RJPs have presented job information either by means of a video or a booklet. However, media richness theory suggests there are advantages of communicating an RJP in a face-to-face conversation with a knowledgeable party (e.g., a coworker) and via a tour of the work site (i.e., direct experience of the work environment). RJPs are most effective when the open job is not highly visible to the public (i.e., unrealistic job expectations are likely), the RJP is presented early in the recruitment processes to allow for self-selection (i.e., in some studies, the RJP was provided after job offers had been accepted), and the individuals targeted have other employment options (e.g., are currently employed or have other job offers), thereby permitting them to decline less desirable job offers (Breaugh, 2008).

An employer should expect some attractive candidates for a position to withdraw from the applicant pool after receiving an RJP. Although this may appear to be a reason not to use an RJP, such withdrawal is generally preferred over having an uninformed individual accept a job offer and then quit a few months later (e.g., after the organization has incurred the costs of training). Another factor to consider is that RJPs typically cause employers to be perceived as trustworthy, which, in turn, should result in an employer having greater credibility with respect to other information it conveys during the recruitment process.

Recruitment messages also should be considered from the standpoint of workforce diversity. In attempting to create a diverse applicant pool, employers generally fashion messages that convey that they are an attractive place to work for ethnic minorities and women (in some cases, efforts are also made to recruit older individuals). In order to do so, many employers include photographs of minorities and women in recruitment brochures or on their Web site. Researchers have found such pictures to be effective, especially if some of the individuals portrayed are in supervisor positions (Avery, Hernandez, & Hebl, 2004). In creating recruitment communication geared toward minorities and women, it is important that they convey an accurate message. In this regard, McKay and Avery (2005) found that many black students reported that the information they received concerning an employer's commitment to diversity during the recruitment process did not reflect what they experienced once they became employees.

A final issue that should be addressed regarding the recruitment message involves audience analysis. Research on this topic has shown the merits of tailoring a message to different groups targeted for recruitment. Among the factors that Albers (2003) suggested be considered in customizing a recruitment message are: what knowledge the audience already possesses; how much detail the audience desires about a topic; and, the level of ability the audience has to comprehend the message. Failure to consider such audience characteristics in designing a recruitment message can result in a less effective recruitment message.

Recruiters

In many recruitment efforts (e.g., campus recruiting), recruiters play an important role. Because they typically have face-to-face interactions with job applicants (i.e., high media richness) and may be able to provide a recruitment message that is specific and realistic, theory suggests that recruiters should have a sizable impact on recruits. To date, several studies have examined the effects of recruiter characteristics (e.g., demographic characteristics, amount of experience). A meta-analysis by Chapman, Uggerslev, Carroll, Piasentin, and Jones (2005) documented that, with the exception of recruiter behaviors, recruiter characteristics are not associated with recruitment outcomes.

With respect to recruiter behavior, job applicants who rated recruiters as being personable, competent, trustworthy, and informative also rated a job opening as being more attractive and stated they were more likely to accept a job offer (Uggerslev et al., 2012). Viewed from the perspective of a communication process, these findings are not surprising. For example, in order for a recruitment message to positively influence a recruit, the recruit must perceive the message as informative and believable. It is hard for recruiters to be informative if they are not familiar with the job opening. In terms of being personable, applicants are inclined to view the way they are treated during the recruitment process as a signal of how they will be treated after being hired (Dineen & Soltis, 2011).

The Timing of Recruitment Communications

It is not sufficient to reach a targeted audience with a well-crafted message. The timing of the message also is important. For example, in a study with graduating college students, Turban and Cable (2003) found that organizations that interviewed later in the academic year received fewer applications, and those that were received were from poorer quality applicants. Rynes, Bretz, and Gerhart (1991) and Boswell, Roehling, LePine, and Moynihan (2003) reported that for their samples, delays in responding to applicants resulted in employers being viewed as less attractive and in some cases being eliminated from consideration as an employer. More recently, Becker et al. (2010) found that the shorter the time lag between a recruit's final interview and a job offer being extended, the greater the probability that the offer would be accepted.

Two explanations have been offered for the effects of recruitment timing. First, individuals may find the job search process stressful and want to end the uncertainty by securing a job offer (Becker et al., 2010). If this explanation is valid, it is likely that when an employer begins the recruitment process is less important if it is trying to recruit individuals who are currently employed. Second, applicants may view delays as a signal that they are not highly sought after by the employer and/or that the organization is not professional in how it treats individuals (not only recruits but also its employees).

The U.S. Internal Revenue Service provides an example of the importance of recruitment timing (Matthews, 2006). Having been relatively unsuccessful in recruiting law students, the IRS concluded that it was starting its recruitment efforts late in the year compared to the law firms against which it competed for students (i.e., good students had already accepted jobs). When it started recruiting earlier in the academic year, the IRS found that it was able to fill job openings more easily and with better applicants.

Conclusion

In this chapter, I have addressed key aspects of the recruitment process. From the information presented, the complexity of the communication challenges involved in designing a recruitment campaign should be apparent. For example, in deciding what type of individuals to target for recruitment, consideration should be given to such issues as these: Will targeted individuals be attracted to positions with an employer? Will they have the personal attributes (e.g., skills, values) needed in employees? Will these individuals be likely to accept job offers? Once a decision has been made concerning whom to recruit, an employer can intelligently address relevant communication issues, including how to reach these targeted individuals, what message to convey, and when to begin recruiting.

Before concluding, it is important to emphasize two issues that do not receive sufficient attention in the recruitment process. Research has shown that when making decisions about a job opening, two key factors for a job applicant are one's prospective boss and one's prospective coworkers (e.g., Uggerslev et al., 2012). Given the impact these individuals can have on a new hire (e.g., types of assignments, mentoring, peer support), their influence on the job offer acceptance decision is not surprising. What is surprising is that information on a supervisor and coworkers frequently is not communicated during the early stages of the recruitment process (Breaugh, 2009).

The second issue concerns the distinction between a "sent" and a "received" message. As noted by political consultant Frank Luntz (*Colbert Report*, August 16, 2011), "It's not what you say; it's what they hear." This statement certainly holds for recruitment communications. In terms of increasing the connection between a "sent" versus a "received" message, several actions can be important. For example, individuals with experience working a night shift are more likely to grasp what working such hours means than are individuals lacking such relevant experience (i.e., the importance of who is targeted). Similarly, a tour of a warehouse (i.e., direct experience) may better convey the visceral experience of working in a noisy environment (e.g., headaches) than simply being told a work environment is loud (i.e., the importance of recruitment media). In situations in which targeting individuals with relevant experience or providing a tour of the work site is not feasible, an organization can still improve the likelihood that a "sent" message is "received" by carefully considering how messages are expressed. Meglino, DeNisi, and Ravlin (1993) describe the careful development of an RJP and the procedure to substantiate the realism of messages received by its viewers (i.e., prospective prison guards).

To end where I began, the recruitment of employees is the first step in hiring and developing a quality workforce. Done well, employee recruitment provides an organization with a pool of job applicants who possess the skills, ability, values, motivation, interests, and so on to help an organization succeed. Done poorly, recruitment greatly limits an employer's potential success. Obviously, good communication is necessary for good recruitment.

Notes

1 As used in this chapter, the term *communication* includes personal conversations (e.g., between a recruit and a recruiter) as well as more formal information exchanges (e.g., e-mail).
2 See Cable and Yu (2013) for more detailed coverage of recruitment methods.
3 Discussion of issues such as employee benefits is better left to a representative from the HR department.
4 See Breaugh (2008) for a detailed discussion of RJPs.

Bibliography

Albers, M.J. (2003). Multidimensional audience analysis for dynamic information. *Journal of Technical Writing and Communication, 33*(3), 263–279.

Allen, D.G., Mahto, R.V., & Otondo, R.F. (2007). Web-based recruitment: Effects of information, organizational brand, and attitudes toward a Web site on applicant attraction. *Journal of Applied Psychology, 92,* 1696–1708.

Allen, D.G., Van Scotter, J.R., & Otondo, R.F. (2004). Recruitment communication media: Impact on pre-hire outcomes. *Personnel Psychology, 57,* 143–171.

Avery, D.R., Hernandez, M., & Hebl, M.R. (2004). Who's watching the race? Racial salience in recruitment advertising. *Journal of Applied Social Psychology, 34,* 146–161.

Backhaus, K.B. (2004). An exploration of corporate recruitment descriptions on Monster.com. *Journal of Business Communication, 41,* 115–136.

Becker, W.J., Connolly, T., & Slaughter, J.E. (2010). The effect of job offer timing on offer acceptance, performance, and turnover. *Personnel Psychology, 63,* 223–241.

Boswell, W.R., Roehling, M.V., LePine, M.A., & Moynihan, L.M. (2003). Individual job-choice decisions and the impact of job attributes and recruitment practices: A longitudinal field study. *Human Resource Management, 42,* 23–37.

Breaugh, J.A. (2008). Employee recruitment: Current knowledge and important areas for future research. *Human Resource Management Review, 18,* 103–118.

Breaugh, J.A. (2009). Recruiting and attracting talent: A guide to understanding and managing the recruitment process. *SHRM Foundation's Effective Practice Guidelines Series.* Alexandria, VA: Society for Human Resource Management.

Breaugh, J.A. (2013). Employee recruitment. *Annual Review of Psychology, 64,* 10.1–10.28.

Cable, D., & Turban, D. (2003). The value of organizational reputation in the recruitment context: A brand equity perspective. *Journal of Applied Social Psychology, 33,* 2244–2266.

Cable, D., & Yu, K.Y. (2013). *Oxford handbook of employee recruitment.* New York: Oxford University Press.

Castilla, E.J. (2005). Social networks and employee performance in a call center. *American Journal of Sociology, 110,* 1243–1283.

Chapman, D.S., Uggerslev, K.L., Carroll, S.A., Piasentin, K.A., & Jones, D.A. (2005). Applicant attraction to organizations and job choice: A meta-analytic review of the correlates of recruiting outcomes. *Journal of Applied Psychology, 90,* 928–944.

Collins, C.J. (2007). The interactive effects of recruitment practices and product awareness on job seekers' employer knowledge and applicant behaviors. *Journal of Applied Psychology, 92,* 180–190.

Collins, C.J., & Han, J. (2004). Exploring applicant pool quantity and quality: The effects of early recruitment practices, corporate advertising, and firm reputation. *Personnel Psychology, 57,* 685–717.

Daft, R.L., & Lengel, R.H. (1984). Information richness: a new approach to managerial behavior and organizational design. *Research in Organizational Behavior, 6,* 191–233.

Devendorf, S.A., & Highhouse, S. (2008). Applicant-employee similarity and attraction to an employer. *Journal of Occupational and Organizational Psychology, 81,* 607–617.

Dineen, B.R., & Allen, D. G. (2014). Internet recruiting 2.0: Shifting paradigms. In K.Y.T.Yu & D. M. Cable (Eds.). *The Oxford handbook of recruitment* (pp. 382–401). New York: Oxford University Press.

Dineen, B.R., Ash, S.R., & Noe, R.A. (2002). A web of applicant attraction: Person-organization fit in the context of Web-based recruitment. *Journal of Applied Psychology, 87,* 723–734.

Dineen, B.R., & Noe, R.A. (2009). Effects of customization on application decisions and applicant pool characteristics in a web-based recruitment context. *Journal of Applied Psychology, 94,* 224–234.

Dineen, B.R., & Soltis, S.M. (2011). Recruitment: A review of research and emerging directions. In S. Zedeck (Ed.), *APA handbook of industrial and organizational psychology, Vol. 2* (pp. 43–66). Washington, DC: American Psychological Association.

Dunning, D. (2007). Prediction: The inside view. In A.W. Kruglanski & E.T. Higgins (Eds.), *Social psychology: A handbook of basic principles* (pp. 69–90). New York: Guilford Press.

Hansen, F. (2009, September). Discriminatory twist in networking sites puts recruiters at peril. *Workforce Management Online.*

Harold, C., Uggerslev, K.L., & Kraichy, D. (2013). Recruitment and job choice. In D. Cable & K.Y.Yu (Eds.), *Oxford handbook of employee recruitment.* New York: Oxford University Press.

Highhouse, S., Thornbury, E., & Little, I.S. (2007). Social-identify functions of attraction to organizations. *Organizational Behavior and Human Decision Processes, 103,* 134–146.

Jattuso, M.L., & Sinar, E.F. (2003). Source effects in Internet-based screening procedures. *International Journal of Selection and Assessment, 11,* 137–140.

Mason, N.A., & Belt, J.A. (1986). The effectiveness of specificity in recruitment advertising. *Journal of Management, 12,* 425–432.

Matthews, R.G. (2006, October 10). It's taxing to tap top law grads to IRS, but a new push betters returns. *Wall Street Journal,* B1.

McKay, P.F., & Avery, D.R. (2005). Warning! Diversity recruitment could backfire. *Journal of Management Inquiry, 14,* 330–336.

Meglino, B.M., DeNisi, A.S., & Ravlin, E.C. (1993). Effects of previous job exposure and subsequent job status on the functioning of a realistic job preview. *Personnel Psychology, 46*(4), 803–822.

Phillips, J.M. (1998). Effects of realistic job previews on multiple organizational outcomes: A meta-analysis. *Academy of Management Journal, 41,* 673–690.

Roberson, Q.M., Collins, C.J., & Oreg, S. (2005). The effects of recruitment message specificity on applicant attraction to organizations. *Journal of Business and Psychology, 19,* 319–339.

Rynes, S.L., Bretz, R.D. Jr., & Gerhart, B. (1991). The importance of recruitment in job choice: A different way of looking. *Personnel Psychology, 44,* 487–521.

Stevens, C.D., & Szmerekovsky, J.G. (2010). Attraction to employment advertisements: Advertisement wording and personality characteristics. *Journal of Managerial Issues, 22,* 107–126.

Taylor, W.C. (2006, April 23). To hire sharp employees, recruit in sharp ways. *New York Times,* B3.

Turban, D.B., & Cable, D.M. (2003). Firm reputation and applicant pool characteristics. *Journal of Organizational Behavior, 24,* 733–751.

Uggerslev, K.L., Fassina, N.E., & Kraichy, D. (2012). Recruiting through the stages: A meta-analytic test of predictors of applicant attraction at different stages of the recruiting process. *Personnel Psychology, 65,* 597–660.

Walker, H.J., Field, H.S., Giles, W.F., Armenakis, A.A., & Bernerth, J.B. (2009). Displaying employee testimonials on recruitment web sites: Effects of communication media, employee race, and job seeker race on organizational attraction and information credibility. *Journal of Applied Psychology, 94,* 1354–1364.

Wyer, R.S. Jr., & Adaval, R. (2003). Message reception skills in social communication. In J.O. Greene & B.R. Burleson (Eds.), *Handbook of communication and social interaction skills* (pp. 291–355). Mahwah, NJ: Lawrence Erlbaum Associates.

Yakubovich, V., & Lup, D. (2006). Stages of the recruitment process and the referrer's performance effect. *Organizational Science, 17,* 710–723.

4

THE ROLE OF COMMUNICATION IN INTUITIVE AND ANALYTICAL EMPLOYEE SELECTION[1]

Robert L. Dipboye

The mission of human resource management (HRM) as an area of scholarship and application is achieving a good fit between people and their work, and employee selection is a primary means of doing this. Organizational agents must induce job seekers to apply, evaluate the relative qualifications of applicants, and then choose among them. Selection decisions range from initial screening in which applicants are moved to the next stage of scrutiny (e.g., the decision of a recruiter to recommend inviting for an in-house interview) to the final offer of employment. Employee selection is arguably the area of research in HRM and industrial and organizational psychology that has made the most progress in research and theory and has had the greatest impact on HRM practice. The psychometric approach is the dominant paradigm and tends to treat selection as a set of scales, inventories, and tests to be administered, scored, and then plugged into selection decisions. However, selection is a dynamic process in which job seekers and various agents of the organization exchange information and construct meaning in the pursuit of their individual objectives. This has not been ignored in communication research, which has produced an impressive body of findings on the employment interview (e.g., Jablin, 2001). Yet, selection involves more than interviewing. This chapter explores possible ways that an understanding of communication can contribute to the understanding and improvement of selection in organizations.

I begin by providing a brief review of contributions stemming from what I call analytical selection. Although this psychometrically based approach yields more valid and reliable decisions, selection as practiced tends to stray from the analytical approach. Figure 4.1 depicts analytical versus intuitive selection at the level of the core selection process as shaped by conflicts and pressures originating within the HRM function, the organizational culture, and the organizational environment.

The Core Selection Process

In the core selection process, organizational agents define the requirements of the position, gather and evaluate information on job applicants, choose the applicants providing the best fit to the position, and then evaluate the outcomes of that decision. Organizational agents and job seekers approach the core selection process with expectations, beliefs, needs, and intentions that influence

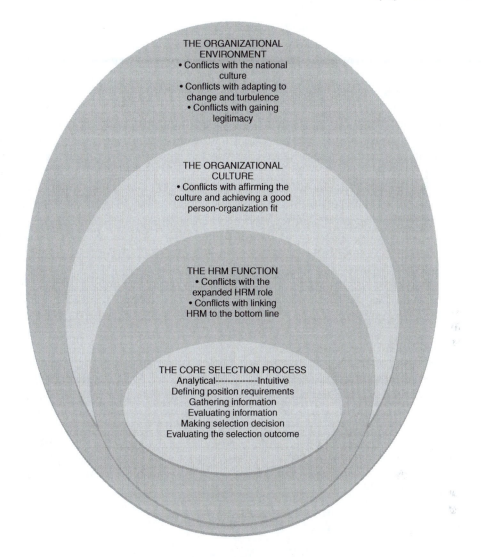

THE ORGANIZATIONAL
ENVIRONMENT
• Conflicts with the national
culture
• Conflicts with adapting to
change and turbulence
• Conflicts with gaining
legitimacy

THE ORGANIZATIONAL
CULTURE
• Conflicts with affirming the
culture and achieving a good
person-organization fit

THE HRM FUNCTION
• Conflicts with the
expanded HRM role
• Conflicts with linking
HRM to the bottom line

THE CORE SELECTION PROCESS
Analytical---------------Intuitive
Defining position requirements
Gathering information
Evaluating information
Making selection decision
Evaluating the selection outcome

FIGURE 4.1 Conflicts between analytical selection and pressures on the core selection process at the levels of the HRM function, the organizational culture, and the organizational environment.

their subsequent interaction and the processing of information. Before, during, and after the selection process, both are engaged in information processing, judgment, and decision making (Dipboye & Johnson, 2013). All this culminates in final decisions that can be evaluated using standards of reliability, validity, fairness, and usefulness.

Analytical Versus Intuitive Selection

The distinction between these two approaches is adapted from dual process models of information processing and decision making (e.g., Hammond, 1996). These approaches are presented as prototypes or ideals, with most selection processes found somewhere between these extremes.

1. **Position specifications:** In the intuitive approach, organizational agents are guided by personal, often idiosyncratic, and undifferentiated views of what is required in the position (Adkins, Russell, & Werbel, 1994). Such intuitive conceptions of the position contrast with the analytical approach in which a detailed set of personnel specifications of the knowledge, skills, abilities, and other characteristics of the job (KSAOs) are generated from an objective work analysis.

2. **Information gathering:** The intuitive approach to gathering information is characterized by unstandardized, casual observations; unstructured interviews; global impressions; and instruments based on clinical judgment (e.g., projective tests). By contrast, the analytical approach relies on data gathered with validated, objective instruments that limit the organizational agent to collecting information on the KSAOs relevant to the position.

3. **Judgment of applicant fit to the position:** In the intuitive approach, the organizational agent judges the general fit of the job seeker's characteristics to the KSAOs. An analytical approach provides rules for translating the information gathered into KSAO judgments. These translations are often facilitated with anchored scales that provide examples of answers that deserve each rating.

4. **Decision making:** In the intuitive approach, selection decisions occur quickly, in an effortless manner, and are based on holistic impressions. The analytical approach requires more effortful decision making based on predetermined rules with consideration of the costs and benefits of each alternative. Taken to the analytical extreme, the decisions are guided by a statistical model untouched by human judgment.

5. **Evaluation of the selection process:** The intuitive approach involves little systematic evaluation of how well the final decision achieved organizational objectives. At best, evaluations are based on memories of chosen applicants who subsequently succeeded and failed on the job. In the analytical approach, there is a systematic, quantitative, and rigorous validation based on scientific principles such as set forth in the Society for Industrial and Organizational Psychology (SIOP, 2003) *Principles for the Validation and Use of Selection Procedures*. Similarly, Boxell, Purcell, and Wright (2008) define analytical HRM as an approach that is concerned with assessing why HRM practices work or do not work and the best tactics for making them work.

What Have We Learned?

A century of quantitative research on employee selection by psychologists and HRM scholars produced a set of highly useful and scientifically sound conclusions, including an impressive body of evidence on the relative success of selection procedures and constructs as predictors of job performance. At the top of the list are paper-and-pencil tests of mental ability. Schmidt and Hunter (1998) summarize the meta-analyses of 85 years of validation research on 19 selection procedures and conclude that general mental ability had the highest validity, the lowest cost, and the strongest theoretical foundation of any of the other procedures or constructs. Although the evidence for other predictors is not as impressive as that of mental ability tests, there is also support for biographical or background questionnaires on past behaviors and experiences (Schmidt & Hunter, 1998), assessment centers (Arthur, Day, McNelly, & Edens, 2003), work samples (Roth, Bobko, & MacFarland, 2005), and structured interviews (Huffcutt & Arthur, 1994). After correcting for artifacts such as unreliability in the criteria, validities in the 0.50s are found for mental ability tests, whereas validities in the 0.30s are found for biodata, assessment centers, work samples, and structured interviews. Validities in the 0.20s are typically found for other procedures such as situational judgment tests (Christian, Edwards, & Bradley, 2010), grades (Roth, BeVier, Switzer, & Shippmann, 1996), work experience (Quinones, Ford, & Teachout, 1995), and personality tests measuring conscientiousness (Barrick & Mount, 1991). Validities in 0.10s and 0.20s typify integrity tests (Van Iddekinge, Roth, Raymark, & Odle-Dusseau, 2011), personality tests other than conscientiousness (Morgeson et al., 2007), unstructured interviews (Huffcutt & Arthur, 1994), and educational level (Ng & Feldman, 2009). Despite the differences in validity among selection procedures, even the least valid can be useful where there is a large number of applicants and relatively few positions.

Continuing Issues

The research on human judgment and decision making (Dawes, Faust, & Meehl, 1989), as well as the research on employee selection, provides strong support for the superiority of an analytical over an intuitive approach at every step of the core selection process. Although the analytical model is uncontested when evaluated against psychometric criteria, controversies continue among psychologists and HRM scholars with regard to several issues.

1. **Confusion of method and construct:** Confounding exists between the method of assessment and the psychological construct assessed for some selection procedures (Arthur & Villado, 2008). For instance, the high predictive validities of mental ability tests clearly reflect the general and specific components of intelligence that are the focus of these tests. It remains unclear what psychological constructs account for the relatively high validities obtained with assessment centers, structured interviews, and situational judgment tests, each of which have been used to measure a wide variety of KSAOs.
2. **Adverse impact of some procedures:** There are large ethnic differences on mental ability tests that can disadvantage the members of some groups in hiring decisions (Ployhart & Holtz, 2008). The reasons for these subgroup differences and ways to reduce them continue to be debated.
3. **Impact on recruiting:** Some selection procedures, such as biographical data, personality tests, and integrity tests, are not well received by job seekers and have the potential to adversely affect recruitment (Hausknecht, Day, & Thomas, 2004).
4. **Statistical issues:** There are disputes over the most appropriate quantitative approaches to estimating reliability and validity of selection procedures (Van Iddekinge & Ployhart, 2008). For instance, debates continue over whether there are alternatives to a full-scale, predictive validation design in estimating validity. The disputed alternatives include concurrent validation designs (Barrett, Phillips, & Alexander, 1981; Guion & Cranny, 1982), synthetic validity models (Scherbaum, 2005), and validity generalization theory (Van Iddekinge & Ployhart, 2008).
5. **The criterion problem:** The criterion used to validate selection processes typically is a single performance rating by a supervisor. There have been numerous calls to expand the criterion domain to include a broader, multidimensional model of performance criteria (Campbell, McCloy, Oppler, & Sager, 1993).
6. **Banding:** The practice of treating scores within given ranges as equivalent (i.e., banding) has been debated as an alternative to traditional top-down selection and as a means of reducing adverse impact against minorities (Campion et al., 2001).
7. **Adjustments for artifacts:** Controversy persists regarding the appropriate corrections to make for measurement error and range restriction in observed validities to provide estimates of operational or "true" validities (Van Iddekinge & Ployhart, 2008).

8. **Alternative approaches to utility:** The correct approach to estimating the utility of selection procedures remains a matter for debate (Winkler, König, & Kleinmann, 2010).
9. **The prevalence and impact of faking:** Whether faking has an adverse impact on the validity and fairness of self-report selection procedures (e.g., personality tests) remains a subject of debate (Morgeson et al., 2007; Ones, Dilchert, Viswesvaran, & Judge, 2007).
10. **Effects of selection at the level of the unit or organization:** Most research evaluating selection procedures has been conducted at the level of the individual employee. A selection procedure that is beneficial at this level, however, is not necessarily beneficial in allowing the firm to achieve sustained corporate success in competition with other firms. Ployhart (2012) refers to this as the "sustained competitive advantage paradox" (p. 671) and calls for validation at the organizational and unit levels.
11. **The underutilization of analytical selection:** Given the evidence in favor of an analytical approach, one would expect organizations to passionately embrace analytical selection. Just the opposite seems true. Organizational agents still appear to rely on unstandardized, subjective procedures that perform poorly against traditional psychometric standards (Carless, Rasiah, & Irmer, 2009; Colarelli & Thompson, 2008; Highhouse, 2008; Nowicki & Rossi, 2002; Rynes, Colbert, & Brown, 2002; Wilk & Cappelli, 2003). Nowicki and Rossi (2002) found the following:

> when managers attributed successful hiring outcomes to their own actions, the most common explanations had to do with intuition, gut feelings, luck, or chance. Despite decades of research, many managers continue to view hiring as a mysterious, almost random process. (p. 163)

Even when valid structured selection procedures are implemented, organizational agents appear prone to follow their intuitive inclinations (see Latham & Saari, 1984, for an example).

Conflicts That Lead to Deviations From Analytical Selection

The aforementioned underutilization of the analytical model and the need to address multiple levels will serve as foci for the remainder of the chapter. I will discuss the barriers to analytical selection originating at the HRM, organizational, and environmental levels.

Conflicts at the Level of the HRM Function

Although they often espouse analytical selection, HRM specialists rarely can devote themselves solely to selection or any other traditional HRM function (e.g., training or appraisal). The HRM role has expanded to include strategic management, entrepreneurial, championing, and change agent roles (Ulrich, 1997). In the attempt to fulfill these multiple roles, practitioners fall back on imitation of the latest fads and fashions rather than pursuing a lengthy and costly process of scientific research. The failure to fully implement an analytical model is not an irrational choice by the HRM specialist, who is expected to perform the expanded role and not just the core selection process.

Practitioners are pressured to link HRM practices to the bottom line of the organization. This expectation can work against thorough, scientifically rigorous evaluations of long-term benefits associated with analytical selection. An analytical approach is time-consuming, costly, and often slow in yielding results. In contrast, downsizing, layoffs, restructurings, dismantling pension plans, scaling down benefits plans, using temporary employees and outsourcing, and other solutions are relatively inexpensive and can yield quick, visible results (Kochan, 2008; Osterman, 2000). Again, the choice of quick fixes involving short-term cost reductions is not an irrational decision from the perspective of HRM practitioners attempting to demonstrate tangible results for upper management unfriendly to long-term investments in an analytical model.

Conflicts at the Level of the Organizational Culture

The core selection process and the HRM function are embedded within an organizational culture, defined by widely shared values, norms, and expectations for how things are done in an organization (Schein, 1985). The selection process is an important means of communicating and maintaining the values of the organizational culture (Dandridge, Mitroff, & Joyce, 1980; Trice & Beyer, 1984). In a strong organizational culture defined by visible, shared values, there is likely to be pressure to bring selection practices in line with these values (Robert & Wasti, 2002). HRM practices can have "a symbolic or signaling function by sending messages that employees use to make sense of and to define the psychological meaning of their work situation" (Bowen & Ostroff, 2004, p. 206). The value of selection practices in communicating the culture explains why selection practices in some organizations are more akin to rites, ceremonies, and rituals than rigorous assessments. Examples include the use of brain teasers and bizarre questions (e.g., "Approximately how many garbage men are there in California?" or "If you were a superhero, who would you be?"), offering cash incentives to turn down the offer, evaluating applicants on the basis of their social media postings, speed interviewing requiring a decision based in three minutes or less, observing how well applicants play poker, and a host of other bizarre practices.

Conflicts at the Level of the Organizational Environment

Organizations are located within environmental contexts that are often multinational, competitive, and rapidly changing. Organizational agents may deviate from analytical selection in coping with environmental factors. For one, most analytical selection procedures were developed in the United States and may not fit other national cultures (Hofstede, 2001). Structured interviews, for instance, appear to be more compatible with masculine, individualistic cultures than feminine, collectivist cultures (Spence & Petrick, 2000), with universalistic more than particularistic cultures (Nyfield & Baron, 2000), and with cultures high on uncertainty avoidance more than cultures low on this dimension (Ryan, McFarland, Baron, & Page, 1999).

Analytical selection is probably best suited to relatively stable environments. In a highly unstable, turbulent, changing environment, selection techniques that are unstructured and intuitive are quicker and more adaptable (Hausknecht & Wright, 2012; Taylor, 2006). For example, in assessing applicants for a position with well-defined KSAOs, a stable technology, and a hierarchical organization having clear reporting relationships, analytical selection makes sense. In contrast, when assessing applicants for a position with poorly defined KSAOs, a rapidly changing technology, and a flat organization with fluid relationships, an unstructured approach may make more sense by allowing for the rich communication needed to make sense of the situation and reach a shared understanding (Daft & Lengel, 1986).

Institutional theory suggests that organizational agents mimic the practices of large, successful firms (DiMaggio & Powell, 1983; Meyer & Rowan, 1977). Such mimicry may extend to hiring practices (Williamson & Cable, 2003), although it is inherently antithetical to an analytical approach in which procedures are adopted because they have the highest reliabilities and validities, generate the highest monetary benefits, and cost the least. For example, firms increasingly followed the lead of high reputation corporations to select out "surplus" employees. This decision is often guided by attempts to communicate to shareholders and stock analysts that the firm is efficient and attempting to reduce costs rather than providing a rational analysis of long-term benefits and costs (Budros, 2004; Day, Armenakis, Feild, & Norris, 2012). Another example is the imitation of the unvalidated interview procedures of some successful high-tech firms that have captured the imagination of the business press (e.g., "How many golf balls would fit in a school bus?" or "How much would you charge to wash all the windows in Seattle?"). Successful firms probably are not greatly harmed by such procedures because of the presence of other less visible but more valid procedures (e.g., prescreening applicants for GPA or caliber of educational program) and the large number of applicants that high reputation firms can attract. More harm is likely to occur for the less successful firms that unwisely mimic bizarre selection practices rather than using a rational/analytic approach.

The Role of Communication in the Core Selection Process

Psychometric research on selection tends to ignore the influence of language and conversation on assessment, whereas communication research tends to ignore the impact of communication processes on the validity and reliability of judgments. Research is needed to explore the links between communication processes and the psychometric quality of assessments. Here are a few suggestions.

1. **Intuitive selection may prove superior due to the mediating role of communication:** An interesting possibility is that judgments on some attributes, such as many personality traits, might require a less constrained conversation between the applicant and assessor than found in the structured assessments of analytical selection. Support comes from Blackman (2002), who found that unstructured interviews yielded more accurate assessments of personality traits than structured interviews as the result of the interviewees talking more and providing a richer mix of information.
2. **The relation of the quality of conversation in assessments to the quality of judgments:** The assumption underlying much interviewer training is that a high-quality conversation characterized by rapport and synchronicity enhances the reliability and validity of interviewer judgments. Few attempts have been made to examine this linkage (e.g., Collins, Lincoln, & Frank, 2002; Powell & O'Neal, 1976).
3. **Responses to self-report items as private conversations and negotiations of identity:** Psychometric research on personality inventories and other self-report assessment procedures assumes that in responding to a statement such as "I like to attend wild parties," the respondent recalls past parties, determines what type of parties were enjoyed, and then decides to tell the truth or fake the answer. In some cases, as Hogan (1991, p. 902) observes, "item endorsements reflect ... efforts on the part of test-takers to negotiate an identity with an anonymous interviewer (the test author)." Using think-aloud procedures to explore the private conversations involved in answering self-report measures can provide insight into the meaning of the scores on these measures (Robie, Brown, & Beaty, 2007).
4. **The antecedents and consequences of trust in the core selection process:** Personnel selection is a signaling game, and the primary determinant of the reliability of information exchanges is the sense of trust emerging between the organization and the applicant (Bangerter, Roulin, & König, 2012). Jablin (2001) and others recommend exploring how a sense of mutual trust emerges from interactions between interviewer and applicant and the

impact of this trust on judgments. Some research, for instance, suggests that transparency increases the validity of assessment (Melchers et al., 2009). It seems quite likely that the nature of the communication between applicant and assessor mediates these effects.

The Role of Communication in Implementing Analytical Selection

Communication plays a crucial role in managing the boundaries between the core process and the HRM function, the organizational culture, and the organizational environment. Research areas relevant to the management of these boundaries follow.

1. **Communication of analytical selection to increase implementation:** Communication theory and research can contribute to an understanding of how the analytical approach can be communicated so as to facilitate implementation (Gelade, 2006; Hodgkinson, 2006; Tsui, Pearce, Porter, & Tripoli, 1997; Wasti & Robert, 2004). One frequent suggestion is that analytical selection should be communicated in language that is understandable and relevant to administrators rather than in technical language. An interesting paradox of this solution is that the use of administrative terms may lead to decay and slippage as users drift into more intuitive procedures (Roulin & Bangerter, 2012). Research is needed on how these two conflicting tendencies can be resolved. Communication research and theory provide obvious sources of ideas on how to proceed.

2. **The intended and unintended messages sent by selection practices:** The technology of selection not only serves the instrumental function of providing a good fit to the position but also serves a symbolic function by constituting "communication from the employer to the employee" about what is valued and appropriate (Bowen & Ostroff, 2004, p. 207). For instance, a highly structured and rigorous process may communicate that only the most skilled are hired and that working in the organization is a privilege. Another example would be an organization that values innovation and creativity and uses a casual, unstructured selection procedure to communicate these values. Knowing more about the signals sent by selection procedures would help HRM practitioners retain psychometric rigor while communicating what is important and unique about the organization.

3. **Monitoring and feedback mechanisms to increase implementation:** Most organizations install selection procedures and then walk away. Implementation of an analytical approach would benefit from research on the design and use of mechanisms to monitor how well selection procedures are achieving objectives at multiple levels of the organization and provide feedback on needed adjustments. Monitoring and feedback are especially crucial in leaderless teams or where HRM has been decentralized to the unit levels of the firm. The well-established tendency of groups to drift toward homophily and increasing uniformity would seem to be a powerful force acting against implementation of an analytical approach. How such self-managed units and teams can be induced to adhere to analytical procedures without violating self-determination remains unexplored.

4. **Exploring communication networks:** Rather than an isolated activity, selection is almost always embedded within a social process. The social nature of selection is seen not only in the interactions between interviewers and applicants, but in the numerous conversations among organizational agents that punctuate the phases of the selection process. Those involved in selection are embedded in networks of relationships that can determine the outcome and effectiveness of the selection process. One example is provided by Bozionelos (2005) in a case study of how faculty attempted to further the interests of their power networks in filling a faculty position.

5. **The communication of conflicting role expectations as a source of stress:** From the perspective of role theory, the extent to which HRM practitioners adopt intuitive or analytical selection procedures is an attempt to cope with conflicting expectations for how they should approach selection, as well other stressors such as job insecurity, time pressure, and scarce resources. Research in other settings (e.g., health care) shows that stress discourages analytical approaches while encouraging less effortful intuitive decision making (Hammond, 1996). Similar research is needed on how conflicting expectations are communicated to HRM practitioners and how their attempts to deal with stressors influence their adoption of intuitive and analytical selection procedures.

A Sociotechnical Perspective on Selection and the Role of Communication

In contrast to Hausknecht and Wright (2012), who emphasized the choice that must be made among selection models, I would suggest something akin to a sociotechnical strategy in which the conflict between analytical selection and pressures to adopt intuitive approaches are resolvable. This could involve designing the core selection process so that it allows psychometrically sound assessments while also serving legitimate goals at the levels of the HRM function, the organizational culture, and the environment. One simple solution is to segregate rigorous assessment from other phases of the selection process involving unstructured, two-way communication. Another solution is to bundle psychometrically rigorous assessment with procedures that allow communication and affirmation of the values of the organization. Still another solution is to split the roles of HRM practitioners so that some focus on structured assessment and others focus on objectives better achieved through unstructured means.

HRM managers should engage users and decision makers as partners in the design, implementation, monitoring, and evaluation of the core selection process. This implies that HRM specialists cannot serve solely as technicians but must become change agents and politicians. They must acquire skills in negotiating, forming alliances, networking, and using a variety of formal information vehicles, including written, computer-mediated, teleconferenced, and face-to-face communications (Yost et al., 2011). In short, the creative integration of the technology of analytical selection with concerns originating at other levels of the organization will require a reframing that explicates the linkages between assessment and communication at multiple levels of the organization.

Note

1 The author wishes to acknowledge the assistance of Lindsay Dhanani in the preparation of this chapter.

Bibliography

Adkins, C.L., Russell, C.J., & Werbel, J.D. (1994). Judgments of fit in the selection process: The role of work value congruence. *Personnel Psychology, 47*(3), 605–623.

Arthur, W., Day, E.A., McNelly, T.L., & Edens, P.S. (2003). A meta-analysis of the criterion-related validity of assessment center dimensions. *Personnel Psychology, 56*(1), 125–154.

Arthur, W.J., & Villado, A.J. (2008). The importance of distinguishing between constructs and methods when comparing predictors in personnel selection research and practice. *Journal of Applied Psychology, 93*(2), 435–442.

Bangerter, A., Roulin, N., & König, C.J. (2012). Personnel selection as a signaling game. *Journal of Applied Psychology, 97*(4), 719–738.

Barrett, G.V., Phillips, J.S., & Alexander, R.A. (1981). Concurrent and predictive validity designs: A critical reanalysis. *Journal of Applied Psychology, 66*(1), 1–6.

Barrick, M.R., & Mount, M.K. (1991). The big five personality dimensions and job performance: A meta-analysis. *Personnel Psychology, 44*(1), 1–26.

Blackman, M.C. (2002). Personality judgment and the utility of the unstructured employment interview. *Basic and Applied Social Psychology, 24*(3), 241–250.

Bowen, D.E., & Ostroff, C. (2004). Understanding HRM-firm performance linkages: The role of the "strength" of the HRM system. *Academy of Management Review, 29*(2), 203–221.

Boxall, P., Purcell, J., & Wright, P. (2008). Human resource management: Scope, analysis, and significance. In P. Boxall, J. Purcell, & P. Wright (Eds.), *The Oxford handbook of human resource management* (pp. 1–19). Oxford: Oxford University Press.

Bozionelos, N. (2005). When the inferior candidate is offered the job: The selection interview as a political and power game. *Human Relations, 58*(12), 1606–1631.

Budros, A. (2004). Causes of early and later organizational adoption: The case of corporate downsizing. *Sociological Inquiry, 74*(3), 355–380.

Campbell, J.P., McCloy, R.A., Oppler, S.H., & Sager, C.E. (1993). A theory of performance. In N. Schmitt & W.C. Borman (Eds.), *Personnel selection in organizations* (pp. 35–70). San Francisco: Jossey-Bass.

Campion, M.A., Outtz, J.L., Zedeck, S., Schmidt, F.L., Kehoe, J.F., Murphy, K.R., & Guion, R.M. (2001). The controversy over score banding in personnel selection: Answers to 10 key questions. *Personnel Psychology, 51*(1), 149–185.

Carless, S.A., Rasiah, J., & Irmer, B.E. (2009). Discrepancy between human resource research and practice: Comparison of industrial/organizational psychologists and human resource practitioners' beliefs. *Australian Psychologist, 44*(2), 105–111.

Christian, M.S., Edwards, B.D., & Bradley, J.C. (2010). Situational judgment tests: Constructs assessed and a meta-analysis of their criterion-related validities. *Personnel Psychology, 63*(1), 83–117.

Colarelli, S.M., & Thompson, M. (2008). Stubborn reliance on human nature in employee selection: Statistical decision aids are evolutionarily novel. *Industrial and Organizational Psychology: Perspectives on Science and Practice, 1*(3), 347–351.

Collins, R., Lincoln, R., & Frank, M.G. (2002). The effect of rapport in forensic interviewing. *Psychiatry, Psychology, and Law, 9*(1), 69–78.

Daft, R.L., & Lengel, R.H. (1986). Organizational information requirements, media richness and structural design. *Management Science, 32*(5), 554–571.

Dandridge, T.C., Mitroff, I., & Joyce, W.F. (1980). Organizational symbolism 1986: A topic to expand organizational analysis. *Academy of Management Review, 5*(1), 77–82.

Dawes, R.M., Faust, D., & Meehl, P.E. (1989). Clinical versus actuarial judgment. *Science, 243*(4899), 1668–1674.

Day, K., Armenakis, A.A., Feild, H.S., & Norris, D.R. (2012). Other organizations are doing it, why shouldn't we? A look at downsizing and organizational identity through an institutional theory lens. *Journal of Change Management, 12*(2), 165–188.

DiMaggio, P.J., & Powell, W.W. (1983). The iron cage revisited: Institutional isomorphism and collective rationality in organizational fields. *American Sociological Review, 48*(2), 147–160.

Dipboye, R.L., & Johnson, S.K. (2013). Understanding and improving employee selection interviews. In K.F. Geisinger, B.A. Bracken, J.F. Carlson, J.C. Hansen, N.R. Kuncel, S.P. Reise, & M.C. Rodriguez (Eds.), *APA handbook of testing and assessment in psychology, Vol. 1: Test theory and testing and assessment in industrial and organizational psychology* (pp. 479–499). Washington, DC: American Psychological Association.

Gelade, G.A. (2006). But what does it mean in practice? The *Journal of Occupational and Organizational Psychology* from a practitioner perspective. *Journal of Occupational and Organizational Psychology, 79*(2), 153–160.

Guion, R.M., & Cranny, C.J. (1982). A note on concurrent and predictive validity designs: A critical reanalysis. *Journal of Applied Psychology, 67*(2), 239–244.

Hammond, K.R. (1996). *Human judgment and social policy: Irreducible uncertainty, inevitable error, unavailable injustice.* New York: Oxford University Press.

Hausknecht, J.P., Day, D.V., & Thomas, S.C. (2004). Applicant reactions to selection procedures: An updated model and meta-analysis. *Personnel Psychology, 57*(3), 639–683.

Hausknecht, J.P., & Wright, P.M. (2012). Organizational strategy and staffing. In N. Schmitt (Ed.), *The Oxford handbook of personnel assessment and selection* (pp. 147–155). New York: Oxford University Press.

Highhouse, S. (2008). Stubborn reliance on intuition and subjectivity in employment selection. *Industrial and Organizational Psychology: Perspectives on Science and Practice, 1*(3), 333–342.

Hodgkinson, G.P. (2006). The role of *JOOP* (and other scientific journals) in bridging the practitioner-researcher divide in industrial, work and organizational (IWO) psychology. *Journal of Occupational and Organizational Psychology, 79*(2), 173–178.

Hofstede, G. (2001). *Culture's consequences: Comparing values, behaviors, institutions, and organizations across nations* (2nd ed.). London: Sage.

Hogan, R. (1991). Personality and personality measurement. In M.D. Dunnette & L.M. Hough (Eds.), *Handbook of industrial and organizational psychology, Vol. 2* (2nd ed., pp. 873–919). Palo Alto, CA: Consulting Psychologists Press.

Huffcutt, A.I., & Arthur, W. Jr. (1994). *Hunter & Hunter* revisited: Interview validity for entry-level jobs. *Journal of Applied Psychology, 79*(2), 184–190.

Jablin, F.M. (2001). Entry, assimilation, disengagement/exit. In F.M. Jablin & L.L. Putnam (Eds.), *The new handbook of organizational communication: Advances in theory, research, & methods* (2nd ed., pp. 732–818). Newbury Park, CA: Sage.

Kochan, T. (2008). Social legitimacy of the HRM profession: A US perspective. In P. Boxall, J. Purcell, & P.M. Wright (Eds.), *The Oxford handbook of human resource management* (pp. 599–621). New York: Oxford University Press.

Latham, G.P., & Saari, L.M. (1984). Do people do what they say? Further studies on the situational interview. *Journal of Applied Psychology, 69*(4), 569–574.

Melchers, K.G., Klehe, U., Richter, G.M., Kleinmann, M., Konig, C.J., & Lievens, F. (2009). "I know what you want to know": The impact of interviewees' ability to identify criteria on interview performance and construct-related validity. *Human Performance, 22*(4), 355–374.

Meyer, J.W., & Rowan, B. (1977). Institutionalized organizations: Formal structure as myth and ceremony. *American Journal of Sociology, 83*(2), 340–363.

Morgeson, F.P., Campion, M.A., Dipboye, R.L., Hollenbeck, J.R., Murphy, K., & Schmitt, N. (2007). Reconsidering the use of personality tests in personnel selection contexts. *Personnel Psychology, 60*(3), 683–729.

Ng, T.W.H., & Feldman, D.C. (2009). How broadly does education contribute to job performance? *Personnel Psychology, 62*(1), 89–134.

Nowicki, M.D., & Rossi, J.G. (2002). Managers' views of how to hire: Building bridges between science and practice. *Journal of Business and Psychology, 17*(2), 157–170.

Nyfield, G., & Baron, H. (2000). Cultural context in adapting selection practices across borders. In J.F. Kehoe (Ed.), *Managing selection strategies in changing organizations* (pp. 242–268). San Francisco, CA: Jossey-Bass.

Ones, D.S., Dilchert, S., Viswesvaran, C., & Judge, T.A. (2007). In support of personality assessment in organizational settings. *Personnel Psychology, 60*(4), 995–1027.

Osterman, P. (2000). Work reorganization in an era of restructuring: Trends in diffusion and effects on employee welfare. *Industrial and Labor Relations Review, 53*(2), 179–196.

Ployhart, R.E. (2012). Multilevel selection and the paradox of sustained competitive advantage. In N. Schmitt (Ed.), *The Oxford handbook of personnel assessment and selection* (pp. 667–685). New York: Oxford University Press.

Ployhart, R.E., & Holtz, B.C. (2008). The diversity-validity dilemma: Strategies for reducing racioethnic and sex subgroup differences and adverse impact in selection. *Personnel Psychology, 61*(1), 153–172.

Powell, R.S., & O'Neal, E.C. (1976). Communication feedback and duration as determinants of accuracy, confidence, and differentiation in interpersonal perception. *Journal of Personality and Social Psychology, 34*(4), 746–756.

Quinones, M., Ford, K.J., & Teachout, M.S. (1995). The relationship between work experience and job performance: A conceptual and meta-analytical review. *Personnel Psychology, 48*(4), 887–910.

Robert, C., & Wasti, S. (2002). Organizational individualism and collectivism: Theoretical development and an empirical test of a measure. *Journal of Management, 28*(4), 544–566.

Robie, C., Brown, D.J., & Beaty, J.C. (2007). Do people fake on personality inventories? A verbal protocol analysis. *Journal of Business and Psychology, 21(4)*, 489–509.

Roth, P.L., BeVier, C.A., Switzer, F.S. III, & Shippmann, J.S. (1996). Meta-analyzing the relationship between grades and job performance. *Journal of Applied Psychology, 81*(5), 548–556.

Roth, P.L., BeVier, C.A., Switzer, F.S., & Shippmann, J.S. (1996). Meta-analyzing the relationship between grades and job performance. Journal of Applied Psychology, 81, 548–556.

Roth, P.L., Bobko, P., & McFarland, L.A. (2005). A meta-analysis of work sample test validity: Updating and integrating some classic literature. *Personnel Psychology, 58*(4), 1009–1037.

Roulin, N., & Bangerter, A. (2012). Understanding the academic-practitioner gap for structured interviews: "Behavioral interviews diffuse, structured interviews do not." *International Journal of Selection and Assessment, 20*(2), 149–158.

Ryan, A.M., McFarland, L., Baron, H., & Page, R. (1999). An international look at selection practices: Nation and culture as explanations for variability in practice. *Personnel Psychology, 52*(2), 359–391.

Rynes, S.L., Colbert, A.E., & Brown, K.G. (2002). HR professionals' beliefs about effective human resource practices: Correspondence between research and practice. *Human Resource Management, 41*(2), 149–174.

Schein, E.H. (1985). *Organizational culture and leadership.* San Francisco: Jossey-Bass.

Scherbaum, C.A. (2005). Synthetic validity: Past, present, and future. *Personnel Psychology, 58*(2), 481–515.

Schmidt, F.L., & Hunter, J.E. (1998). The validity and utility of selection methods in personnel psychology: Practical and theoretical implications of 85 years of research findings. *Psychological Bulletin, 124*(2), 262–274.

Society for Industrial and Organizational Psychology (SIOP). (2003). *Principles for the validation and use of personnel selection procedures* (4th ed.). College Park, MD: Author. Retrieved from www.siop.org/_Principles/principlesdefault.aspx.

Spence, L.J., & Petrick, J.A. (2000). Multinational interview decisions: Integrity capacity and competing values. *Human Resource Management Journal, 10*(4), 49–67.

Taylor, S. (2006). Acquaintance, meritocracy and critical realism: Researching recruitment and selection processes in smaller and growth organizations. *Human Resource Management Review, 16*(4), 478–489.

Trice, H.M., & Beyer, J.M. (1984). Studying organizational cultures through rites and ceremonials. *Academy of Management Review, 9*(4), 653–669.

Tsui, A.S., Pearce, J.L., Porter, L.W., & Tripoli, A.M. (1997). Alternative approaches to the employee-organization relationship: Does investment in employees pay off? *Academy of Management Journal, 40*(5), 1089–1121.

Ulrich, D. (1997). *Human resource champions: The next agenda for adding value and delivering results.* Cambridge, MA: Harvard Business School Press.

Van Iddekinge, C.H., & Ployhart, R.E. (2008). Developments in the criterion-related validation of selection procedures: A critical review and recommendations for practice. *Personnel Psychology, 61*(4), 871–925.

Van Iddekinge, C.H., Roth, P.L., Raymark, P.H., & Odle-Dusseau, H.N. (2011). The criterion-related validity of integrity tests: An updated meta-analysis. *Journal of Applied Psychology, 97*(3), 499–530.

Wasti, S.A., & Robert, C. (2004). Out of touch? An evaluation of the correspondence between academic and practitioner concerns in IHRM. In J.L.C. Cheng & M. Hitt (Eds.), *Managing multinationals in a knowledge economy: Economics, culture and human resources.* London: JAI Press.

Wilk, S.L., & Cappelli, P. (2003). Understanding the determinants of employer use of selection methods. *Personnel Psychology, 56*(1), 103–124.

Williamson, I.O., & Cable, D.M. (2003). Organizational hiring patterns, interfirm network ties, and interorganizational imitation. *Academy of Management Journal, 46*(3), 349–358.

Winkler, S., König, C.J., & Kleinmann, M. (2010). Single-attribute utility analysis may be futile, but this can't be the end of the story: Causal chain analysis as an alternative. *Personnel Psychology, 63*(4), 1041–1065.

Yost, P.R., McLellan, J.R., Ecker, D.L., Chang, G.C., Hereford, J.M., Roenicke, C.C., & Winberg, Y.L. (2011). HR interventions that go viral. *Journal of Business and Psychology, 26*(2), 233–239.

5

EFFECTIVE NEW EMPLOYEE SOCIALIZATION

A Review of the Critical Role of Communication

Talya N. Bauer, Berrin Erdogan, and Lauren Simon

New employee socialization (NES) is a process of a *newcomer* moving from being an organizational outsider to an insider (Louis, 1980). It is a process of reciprocal influence (Reichers, 1987), with both the organization, through its structures, procedures, and employees, and the newcomers, through their perceptions, attitudes, and behaviors, affecting one another. Given its interactional nature, the socialization process is dependent upon and embedded within a constellation of communication among organizational insiders and newcomers. We adopt this perspective.

Researchers and human resource management (HRM) professionals have taken a strong interest in NES in the last few decades using both communication and noncommunication approaches. Organizational representatives have emphasized and formalized socialization under the umbrella of *new employee onboarding*, even devoting conferences to the topic. Interest in socialization may stem from its profoundly positive outcomes. By creating more effective onboarding programs, organizations can save considerable sums of money when factoring in productivity increases and lower turnover costs. Better job attitudes and job performance result from employees who are more confident, report less ambiguity, and feel more connected to organizational insiders (Bauer, Bodner, Erdogan, Truxillo, & Tucker, 2007). Further, given that individuals likely transition jobs and organizations an average of ten times or more in their lifetime, NES continues to be important for HRM.

Successful socialization is manifest in both the early stages and the later stages of new employees' tenure with an organization. Early indicators of success include feeling accepted by the group, having role clarity, and confidence in one's role (Bauer, Morrison, & Callister, 1998). Later indicators of successful socialization include more positive job satisfaction and organizational commitment, better performance, more innovative behavior, better organizational and job fit, lower levels of stress, and remaining with the organization longer. The specific goals of this chapter are to describe the manner in which organizational programs used to socialize new employees currently rely on effective communication and to suggest expansion of these HR activities based on new streams of communication research.

NES: A Special Time for HRM

During the first year of employment, new employee learning is substantial (Berlew & Hall, 1966), with the first 90 days being especially salient (Bauer & Erdogan, 2010). Although some roles, jobs, and individuals may socialize more rapidly or more slowly, the adjustment process is especially intense at entry. NES is most important early on but continues well beyond the first year of employment in a given organization.

HRM is key for successful socialization (Wanous, 1980). By paying attention to the signals the organization sends forward during recruitment in the pre-entry phase, job applicants attempt to reduce their uncertainty regarding their fit with the organization and the job and determine how they will be treated (Walker et al., in press). Signals sent during the recruitment process about organizational life, how organizational representatives act, how organized they appear, and how well they communicate expectations spill over to affect organizational entry, and the adjustment process is set in motion on a given trajectory. An ineffective recruitment process that leads to mismatched expectations rarely can be overcome with an onboarding program (Wanous & Colella, 1989). Similarly, perceptions of the organization are created by the choices made in selecting new members, and this affects the relative ease or difficulty of successful socialization. Other traditional HRM functions contribute to the socialization process, including formal and on-the-job training, performance feedback, and job descriptions. Similarly, Baker and Feldman (1991) discussed the interrelated roles that strategic HRM and socialization play in identifying, selecting, and developing the right type of employees for an organization's chosen strategy.

The HRM function that individuals most strongly associate with NES is the orientation process. Orientation programs are intended to establish the relationship between the organization, organizational insiders, and newcomers (Wanous & Reichers, 2000). Most medium- to large-sized organizations have formal orientation programs that begin the first days or weeks of a new employee's tenure. These orientations (and the entire socialization process) vary in terms of how formal they are, how long they take, and how much they involve organizational insiders (Louis, Posner, & Powell, 1983). Research shows that orientation programs may help newcomers become more comfortable with their team (Klein & Weaver, 2000). In general, effective onboarding programs include an orientation that is welcoming, does not overwhelm newcomers with too much information, and communicates appreciation for the newcomers.

The expansion of technology in the field of HRM has spawned research on the differences and similarities of conducting an orientation program in person versus online. For example, individuals undergoing a computer-based orientation were shown to have lower understanding of their job and the company (Wesson & Gogus, 2005), indicating that different formats of orientations may not substitute for each other. In a study of organizational socialization and communication technology use, Waldeck, Seibold, and Flanagin (2004) found that face-to-face communication was the most effective strategy followed by advanced communication and information technologies such as e-mail, the Internet, and videoconferencing. The least useful were the traditional technologies such as handbooks, memos, and one-to-one telephone conversations. Researchers should continue this stream by examining the efficacy of communication technology use on understanding specific topics and employee identification prior to and during organizational entry.

Successful Socialization: It Takes Two to Tango

Successful socialization is an interactive process that depends on both new employees and key insiders (Settoon & Adkins, 1997). While the socialization literature has examined many factors beyond the role of communication, the communication process can truly help new employees and organizational insiders create a successful environment for socialization.

New Employee Behaviors and Successful Socialization

Newcomers may engage in a variety of proactive behaviors to assist their own adjustment into a new organization. As indicated in Figure 5.1, several employee-initiated behaviors play a role in the newcomer adjustment process, including proactive behaviors and information seeking. The more that organizational insiders encourage greater proactive communication from newcomers and provide information to them via written and oral communication, the better.

Proactive Newcomer Behaviors

It is important to understand that newcomers' behavior influences the socialization process. Gruman and Saks's (2011) examination of the relationship between employee personality and newcomer proactive behaviors found that individuals who were high on extraversion and proactive personality reported stronger intentions to be proactive when they began a new job. Additionally, working students who are more proactive have higher self-efficacy (Gruman, Saks, & Zweig, 2006). Likewise, Ashforth, Sluss, and Saks (2007) found that proactive behavior was related to newcomer learning among recent business and engineering college graduates. Kammeyer-Mueller and Wanberg (2003) and Wanberg and Kammeyer-Mueller (2000) found that individuals with higher proactive personalities reported better work adjustment than those with lower proactivity. Finally, research indicates an interaction between how organizations approach newcomer socialization and employee personality. Formalized socialization systems in which newcomers are subjected to a set of structured activities were more helpful for employees who did not demonstrate proactive behaviors (Kim, Cable, & Kim, 2005). Important potential future research areas include examining how HRM should design orientations and training with proactive versus non-proactive employees and whether there are ways for HRM to assess proactive inclinations of newcomers.

Information Seeking

It is well established in the socialization literature that newcomers seek information and feedback to help them lower their uncertainty about what is expected of them within their new work

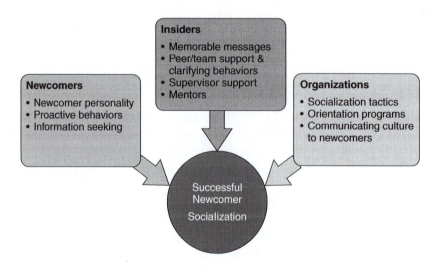

FIGURE 5.1 Summary of key factors contributing to the NES process.

context (Bauer et al., 2007). Information sought may include referent information that relates to the function of the job, appraisal information relating to how well the newcomer is doing at learning his or her job, and relational information, which refers to their relationship with organizational insiders (Miller & Jablin, 1991). These three types of information map onto the adjustment outcomes of role clarity, self-efficacy, and acceptance by insiders (Bauer et al., 2007).

The context in which newcomers find themselves matters in terms of their information-seeking behaviors. Insiders as well as HRM professionals are in an important position to leverage the role of communication to enhance the effectiveness of socialization. Sias, Kramer, and Jenkins (1997) found that the information-seeking behaviors of temporary and non-temporary employees differed in that temporary employees were less focused on impression management and sought information less frequently. Similarly, Major, Kozlowski, Chao, and Gardner (1995) found that newcomers who were low on self-efficacy engaged in greater information seeking when task interdependence and accessibility were high. Thus, whether employees seek information or not depends on the job and organizational context.

Individual differences appear to influence information seeking as well. Harrison, Sluss, and Ashforth (2011) found that newcomer curiosity was related to information-seeking behavior for a sample of new telemarketing employees. Tidwell and Sias (2005) found that among new university employees, extraversion was related to covert relational information seeking. However, perceived relational costs mediated this relationship. Mignerey, Rubin, and Gordon (1995) examined the communication behavior of newcomers and found that socialization tactics as well as communication traits, attitudes, and values influenced information-seeking behaviors. Those who were able to become more deeply embedded within the organization early on were more innovative. It is important to note that not all information seeking is overt because information seeking is inherently a risky activity, revealing individual vulnerability and lack of knowledge (Miller & Jablin, 1991). As a result, newcomers may find more subtle ways of gaining access to the desired information. For example, Miller (1996) found that newcomers employed different tactics depending on the information they were seeking as well as their perception of the sources of information and the potential social costs of gathering the information. A majority of the research to date has focused on this specific newcomer behavior, which is squarely situated in the communication as well as socialization domain. Therefore, it is important to extend this line of research by examining actionable ways in which HRM professionals can use this information to enhance the development of socialization and training programs. Research is needed to take this information one step further so that HRM could use insights into newcomer information seeking to assist with socialization.

Insider Behaviors and Successful Socialization

Examining only the behaviors of new employees is not enough to create a full picture of the factors related to NES success. Helping new employees adjust to their new organization and roles is often accomplished in partnership with organizational insiders, including peers, supervisors, and mentors. Research shows that insiders play a critical role during newcomer socialization by communicating regularly with newcomers at consistent, predetermined time intervals (Bauer & Erdogan, 2010), as sources of information (e.g., Miller & Jablin, 1991; Morrison, 1993a, 1993b; Ostroff & Kozlowski, 1992), and as role models and mentors for newcomers (e.g., Filstad, 2004; Green & Bauer, 1995; Holton & Russell, 1997; Major, Kozlowski, Chao, & Gardner, 1995; Weiss, 1977). Future research questions include the following: To what extent do HR professionals seek feedback from new hires about their adjustment and create training materials for supervisors or units? To what extent do

HR managers train incumbents in formal and informal mentoring roles? And finally, how should mentors be trained to best facilitate effective socialization during a newcomer's first year?

Memorable Messages

In a study of communication content during socialization, newcomers recalled receiving messages about a number of key dimensions during organizational entry. These memorable messages included information (presented here in order of the number of times mentioned by newcomers) regarding professional behavior, work expectations and rules, work ethic, office politics, customer service, and welcoming messages that indicated the newcomer was valued and her/his input was requested. These memorable messages were most frequently received within the first week of the newcomer joining the organization, and they came predominantly from insiders such as managers, trainers, and peers. Men were twice as likely as women to send such messages. Of the respondents, 82% felt the messages were given for helpful reasons. While 25% of the messages were given during training, fully 63% were during informal conversations. Face-to-face communication was the medium 98% of the time (Barge & Schlueter, 2004).

Peers and Teams

Peer influence, usually in the form of mentoring, affects the degree to which employees adjust to their roles, teams, and organizations. Mentors can help new employees adjust by teaching them the ins and outs of their jobs and how the company really operates. Similar to what was found in studies of memorable messages, Nelson and Quick (1991) found that daily interactions with peers were both the most available and most helpful practice that newcomers encountered (Saks & Gruman, 2012). In a study of engineers, Korte (2010) found that building positive relationships with one's peers and managers helped newcomers socialize successfully. Kammeyer-Mueller, Wanberg, Rubenstein, and Song (in press) conducted a 14-wave study of over 200 new employees. They examined the role of both supporting and undermining behaviors of peers and supervisors. They found that the first 90 days were indeed critical because the support received during this period was more predictive of important socialization outcomes than support (or undermining) received later. Their findings suggest that while insiders matter throughout a new employee's first year, the critical window for support is earlier rather than later. Chen (2005) found that performance was higher for newcomers who integrated into their team earlier in their adjustment process. Similarly, Chen and Klimoski (2003) found that in order for newcomers to integrate successfully, team members needed to communicate their expectations, goals, and role requirements clearly.

Supervisors/Leaders

Leaders have a key influence over the socialization process. The information and support leaders provide determine how quickly employees learn important aspects of their company such as its politics and culture. After controlling for leader behavior, information seeking by newcomers was not significantly related to newcomer adjustment (Bauer & Green, 1998). Supervisors delegate tasks to new employees as their relationship develops. Those employees who responded with high performance on the delegated tasks were more likely to report successful relationships with their supervisors at later points in time (Bauer & Green, 1996). Jokisaari and Nurmi (2009) found that during the first 21 months on the job, newcomers perceived less supervisor support after 6 months than before. This is a concern as this decrease in support was related to higher rates of role ambiguity and lower job satisfaction as well as slowing down the rate of salary growth for newcomers.

Mentors

An effective mentor provides an employee with career-related advice and support. Although a mentor can be any employee or manager who has insights that are valuable to the new employee, mentors tend to be more experienced than their protégés. Newcomers who have mentors report having learned and internalized their organization's culture more than those who do not (Chatman, 1991). Mentoring can occur naturally between two interested individuals, or organizations can facilitate this process by having formal mentoring programs. These programs may successfully bring together mentors and protégés who would not come together otherwise (Cawyer & Friedrich, 1998). However, having a mentor is the practice least available to newcomers (Nelson & Quick, 1991), and not all such programs are successful. Nonetheless, certain program characteristics may make them more effective (Allen, Eby, & Lentz, 2006). For example, when mentors and protégés feel that they have input into the mentor-protégé matching process, they tend to be more satisfied with the arrangement. Additionally, when mentors receive training beforehand, the outcomes of the program tend to be more positive. Because mentors may help newcomers interpret and understand the company's culture, organizations may benefit from selecting mentors who personify its values. Thus, organizations need to design these programs carefully. Further, critical questions center around the intersection of HRM, communication, and socialization. For example, we do not clearly know the respective roles played by of HRM professionals and line managers during socialization. Which roles do each play? Which roles should they play? How do these respective roles align with organizational strategies and resources? How is communication featured in these roles?

Organizational Socialization Tactics and Successful Socialization

Socialization tactics refer to the approaches an organization takes to orienting newcomers. These may range from institutionalized tactics to individualized tactics (Jones, 1986). Institutionalized tactics include set time lines, clear roles, and information provided to newcomers. When organizations utilize institutionalized tactics, newcomers are subjected to experiences as a cohort and are given a clear time line for their socialization process. Conversely, individualized tactics are more unpredictable in terms of timing. The process varies by the individual, is less structured, and relies more on informal learning opportunities on the job. Hart, Miller, Johnson, and Johnson (2003) studied new mortgage insurance employees and found that newcomers reported changes in their perceptions of socialization tactics during an organizational restructuring. This was one of the earliest time-lagged studies on the topic. In another longitudinal study, Scott, Montes, and Irving (2012) found that trust mediated the relationship between institutionalized tactics and job satisfaction and commitment. They argued that socialization serves as an early signal to newcomers regarding how they will be treated, with structured approaches yielding greater levels of trust in the organization.

Ashforth et al. (2007) found that individualized tactics were related to newcomer on-the-job learning. When individualized approaches are used, newcomers have more opportunities to customize the socialization process, which should facilitate learning. In general, however, past research finds that employees who encounter more institutionalized tactics have lower role ambiguity and turnover, more positive job attitudes, and more positive perceptions regarding their level of fit with the organization (e.g., Bauer et al., 2007; Hart & Miller, 2005; Saks, Uggerslev, & Fassina, 2007). This relationship also seems to be more prevalent among new college graduates compared to more seasoned job changers (Cable & Parsons, 2001; Saks et al., 2007). At the same time, institutionalized tactics are not without their limitations. While they are associated with more positive attitudes, Allen and Meyer (1990) and Hart and Miller (2005) found that institutionalized tactics were negatively related to role innovation. In other words, the structure inherent in institutionalized approaches may reduce ambiguity and create comfort, but also may communicate that there is a narrow range of acceptable behaviors on their new jobs, limiting the potential for adopting an innovative approach to their work. Future research on tactics should consider the role of communication in both institutionalized and individualized tactics. For example, we know many newcomers, especially those with less experience, report liking institutionalized tactics more, but we do not truly understand why. Could they interpret information relayed to them as indicating great concern for their well-being? This and other questions seem of paramount importance to propelling HRM, communication, and socialization research forward.

A Key Socialization Outcome: Communicating Culture to Newcomers

New employees need to learn many things that organizations and insiders wish to convey, none more important than learning about an organization's culture. Organizational culture is the social glue that holds organizations together, defining the range of acceptable and unacceptable behaviors and values that guide action. Culture is maintained or changed by many factors, but one of the most powerful is the socialization process. As newcomers enter the organization, they are able to change it in fundamental ways or help preserve it. Successfully learning an organization's culture is related to better newcomer adjustment as well as important socialization outcomes such as higher organizational commitment, job satisfaction, and lower turnover (Chao, O'Leary-Kelly, Wolf, Klein, & Gardner, 1994; Klein, Fan, & Preacher, 2006; Klein & Weaver, 2000). However, research into how HRM professionals may best facilitate these important outcomes is sorely needed.

An important indicator of successful adjustment is the degree to which newcomers fit with the organization's culture. Helping ensure that newcomers share the unique values of the organization results in more positive attitudes and behaviors, as well as perpetuation of the culture of the organization. Cooper-Thomas, van Vianen, and Anderson (2004) found that receiving social support from organizational insiders during organizational entry was positively related to the degree to which employee values were aligned with organizational values post-entry. In considering the link between culture and socialization, future investigations should examine these questions: To what extent can HRM professionals influence newcomers person-organization fit at the organizational level? To what extent can HRM professionals influence supervisors and unit leaders to facilitate newcomer person–unit fit? Given that social support has been identified as a critical feature of newcomer adjustment, what research might shed light into how HRM professionals may best influence the social support that newcomers receive (or the conveyance of social support)?

Future Research Directions

Although organizational scholars typically identify learning as the primary mechanism through which effective newcomer adjustment occurs, recent theoretical and empirical research has emphasized that social exchange processes are also crucial for effective newcomer adjustment (Fang, Duffy, & Shaw, 2011; Kammeyer-Mueller et al., in press; Sluss & Thompson, 2012). For example, Fang et al.'s (2011) promising social capital model suggests that socialization tactics and newcomer proactivity influence both newcomers' access to social resources (e.g., important organizational insiders) and their effective use in facilitating early adjustment processes and long-term career success. Central to this model is the notion that early efforts on the part of the newcomer and the organization influence how newcomers become connected to insiders and their access to information essential for adjustment.

Given that relationship building is fundamental for adjustment and career success, it would be fruitful for researchers to thoroughly examine how positive and negative relationships among newcomers and organizational insiders emerge and develop over time. To accomplish this goal, multi-wave, longitudinal studies that observe communication patterns among employees would be particularly useful. A newcomer who attempts to communicate with a particular insider only to receive an ill-mannered response might react by avoiding further communication with that insider. This avoidance, in turn, can serve to reinforce the newcomer's initial negative impression; avoidance will naturally decrease exposure to the insider, preventing the newcomer from obtaining additional information to counter his or her initial judgment (Denrell, 2005) and, thus, from forming a more positive impression of the insider. This line of reasoning suggests that when newcomers start off on the "wrong foot," it can be especially detrimental to the formation of high-quality relationships. Because information is unlikely to flow easily, if at all, in low-quality relationships, newcomers who fail to develop high-quality relationships with powerful, well-connected insiders are at risk for isolation from information crucial for effective job performance. Such a dynamic may help explain why, for example, supervisor undermining behaviors (experienced on the earliest days on the job) predict subsequent employee turnover (Kammeyer-Mueller et al., in press).

Due to the critical nature of early interactions for newcomers, a second important area for future research involves gaining a more detailed understanding of the types of events that are most meaningful for new employees. Lundberg and Young (1997) used a critical incident technique to determine which events "made impressions" on new hospitality employees. Using content analysis, they found that critical incidents spanned several categories including both interpersonal (e.g., supportiveness and care from others, welcoming experiences) and information-based (e.g., training, events regarding company values) categories. However, these researchers did not link event categories to relational trajectories or future adjustment outcomes. By identifying meaningful events and their potential impact on newcomers, HRM professionals can better recognize situations that are likely to be especially troubling for newcomers in general as well in specific units and, thus, empower supervisors to intervene when such events occur. This fine-grained understanding of early organizational communication processes should facilitate the development of more effective, communication-focused socialization interventions by HRM professionals.

A final future research area involves examining how newly established socialization interventions (Cable, Gino, & Staats, 2013) that influence certain adjustment outcomes also affect communication among organizational insiders and newcomers. Recent research demonstrated that having organizational entrants focus on their best selves (e.g., by having them participate in short exercises such as choosing three words that best describe them as individuals and identifying unique features that led to their happiest times and best performance at work) rather than on identifying with the organization leads to greater customer satisfaction and lower turnover after six months. In a second lab study, Cable et al. found that a similar intervention led to increased job satisfaction, performance, and attendance and that authentic self-expression mediated these intervention–outcome relationships.

Conversely, Kammeyer-Mueller, Simon, and Rich (2012) found that early career lawyers who were encouraged to behave *counter* to their own sense of right and wrong during the organizational socialization process experienced increased feelings of ethical conflict and emotional exhaustion as well as a decreased sense of career fulfillment. This suggests that there are detrimental effects to discouraging authenticity during the socialization process. Given the profound effects of early interventions that facilitate authentic self-expression—and the detrimental effects of certain tactics that may impede it—HRM professionals and line managers would be well-served by learning more about how such interventions influence communication patterns and relationship development over time. Because employees who undergo interventions similar to those proposed by Cable and his colleagues are more likely to express themselves authentically, perhaps feelings of social connectedness emerge more rapidly than they would otherwise, resulting in the formation of higher quality relationships among colleagues. These high-quality relationships should, in turn, facilitate favorable outcomes including the efficient flow of information and a willingness among employees to help one another. The low cost and high potential rewards of such interventions make them promising and attractive candidates as levers HRM professionals can build upon for improving communication during the organizational socialization process and beyond.

Conclusion

HRM activities such as recruitment, selection, onboarding, and orientation programs are highly visible during the newcomer socialization process. While the importance of communication during this process is implicitly recognized, specific studies examining how communication processes influence this process and how the socialization process can be structured more effectively to facilitate effective communication of the intended goals should be conducted.

Bibliography

Allen, N.J., & Meyer, J.P. (1990). Organizational socialization tactics: A longitudinal analysis of links to newcomers' commitment and role orientation. *Academy of Management Journal, 33*(4), 847–858.

Allen, T.D., Eby, L.T., & Lentz, E. (2006). Mentorship behaviors and mentorship quality associated with formal mentoring programs: Closing the gap between research and practice. *Journal of Applied Psychology, 91*(3), 567–578.

Ashforth, B.E., Sluss, D.M., & Saks, A.M. (2007). Socialization tactics, proactive behavior, and newcomer learning: Integrating socialization models. *Journal of Vocational Behavior, 70*(3), 447–462.

Baker, H.E., & Feldman, D.C. (1991). Linking organizational socialization tactics with corporate human resource management strategies. *Human Resource Management Review, 1*(3), 193–202.

Barge, K.J., & Schlueter, D.W. (2004). Memorable messages and newcomer socialization. *Western Journal of Communication, 68*(3), 233–256.

Bauer, T.N., Bodner, T., Erdogan, B., Truxillo, D.M., & Tucker, J.S. (2007). Newcomer adjustment during organizational socialization: A meta-analytic review of antecedents, outcomes, and methods. *Journal of Applied Psychology, 92*(3), 707–721.

Bauer, T.N., & Erdogan, B. (2010). Organizational socialization: The effective onboarding of new employees. In S. Zedeck, H. Aguinis, W. Cascio, M. Gelfand, K. Leung, S. Parker, & J. Zhou (Eds.), *APA handbook of I/O psychology, Vol. 3* (pp. 51–64). Washington, DC: APA Press.

Bauer, T.N., & Green, S.G. (1996). Development of leader-member exchange: A longitudinal test. *Academy of Management Journal, 39*(6), 1538–1567.

Bauer, T.N., & Green, S.G. (1998). Testing the combined effects of newcomer information seeking and managerial behavior on socialization. *Journal of Applied Psychology, 83*(1), 72–83.

Bauer, T.N., Morrison, E.W., & Callister, R.R. (1998). Organizational socialization: A review and directions for future research. In G.R. Ferris (Ed.), *Research in personnel and human resources management, Vol. 16* (pp. 149–214). Greenwich, CT: JAI Press.

Berlew, D.E., & Hall, D.T. (1966). The socialization of managers: Effects of expectations on performance. *Administrative Science Quarterly, 11*(2), 207–223.

Cable, D.M., Gino, F., & Staats, B.R. (2013). Breaking them in or eliciting their best? Reframing socialization around newcomers' authentic self-expression. *Administrative Science Quarterly, 58*(1), 1–36.

Cable, D.M., & Parsons, C.K. (2001). Socialization tactics and person-organization fit. *Personnel Psychology, 54*(1), 1–23.

Cawyer, C.S., & Friedrich, G.W. (1998). Organizational socialization: Processes for new communication faculty. *Communication Education, 47*(3), 234–245.

Chao, G.T., O'Leary-Kelly, A.M., Wolf, S., Klein, H.J., & Gardner, P.D. (1994). Organizational socialization: Its content and consequences. *Journal of Applied Psychology, 79*(5), 730–743.

Chatman, J.A. (1991). Matching people and organizations: Selection and socialization in public accounting firms. *Administrative Science Quarterly, 36*(3), 459–484.

Chen, G. (2005). Newcomer adaptation in teams: Multilevel antecedents and outcomes. *Academy of Management Journal, 48*(1), 101–116.

Chen, G., & Klimoski, R.J. (2003). The impact of expectations on newcomer performance in teams as mediated by work characteristics, social exchanges, and empowerment. *Academy of Management Journal, 46*(5), 591–607.

Cooper-Thomas, H.D., van Vianen, A., & Anderson, N. (2004). Changes in person-organization fit: The impact of socialization tactics on perceived and actual P-O fit. *European Journal of Work and Organizational Psychology, 13*(1), 52–78.

Denrell, J. (2005). Why most people disapprove of me: Experience sampling in impression formation. *Psychological Review, 112*(4), 951–978.

Fang, R., Duffy, M.K., & Shaw, J.D. (2011). The organizational socialization process: Preview and development of a social capital model. *Journal of Management, 37*(1), 127–152.

Filstad, C. (2004). How newcomers use role models in organizational socialization. *Journal of Workplace Learning, 16*(7), 396–409.

Green, S.G., & Bauer, T.N. (1995). Supervisory mentoring by advisers: Relationships with Ph.D. student potential, productivity, and commitment. *Personnel Psychology, 48*(3), 537–561.

Gruman, J.A., & Saks, A.M. (2011). Socialization preferences and intentions: Does one size fit all? *Journal of Vocational Behavior, 79*(2), 419–427.

Gruman, J.A., Saks, A.M., & Zweig, D.I. (2006). Organizational socialization tactics and newcomer proactive behaviors: An integrative study. *Journal of Vocational Behavior, 69*(1), 90–104.

Harrison, S.H., Sluss, D.M., & Ashforth, B.E. (2011). Curiosity adapted the cat: The role of trait curiosity in newcomer adaptation. *Journal of Applied Psychology, 96*(1), 211–220.

Hart, Z.P., & Miller, V.D. (2005). Context and message content during organizational socialization. *Human Communication Research, 31*(2), 295–309.

Hart, Z.P., Miller, V.D., Johnson, J.R., & Johnson, J.D. (2003). Socialization, resocialization, and communication relationships in the context of an organizational change. *Communication Studies, 54*(4), 483–495.

Holton, E.F. III, & Russell, C.G. (1997). The relationship of anticipation to newcomer socialization processes and outcomes: A pilot study. *Journal of Occupational and Organizational Psychology, 70*(2), 163–172.

Jokisaari, M., & Nurmi, J.E. (2009). Change in newcomers' supervisor support and socialization outcomes after organizational entry. *Academy of Management Journal, 52*(3), 527–544.

Jones, G.R. (1986). Socialization tactics, self-efficacy, and newcomers' adjustments to organizations. *Academy of Management Journal, 29*(2), 262–279.

Kammeyer-Mueller, J.D., Simon, L.S., & Rich, B.L. (2012). The psychic cost of doing wrong: Socialization, ethical conflict, and burnout. *Journal of Management, 38*(3), 784–808.

Kammeyer-Mueller, J.D., & Wanberg, C.R. (2003). Unwrapping the organizational entry process: Disentangling multiple antecedents and their pathways to adjustment. *Journal of Applied Psychology, 88*(5), 779–794.

Kammeyer-Mueller, J.D., Wanberg, C., Rubenstein, A., & Song, Z. (in press). Support, undermining, and newcomer socialization: Fitting in during the first 90 days. *Academy of Management Journal.*

Kim, T., Cable, D.M., & Kim, S. (2005). Socialization tactics, employee proactivity, and person–organization fit. *Journal of Applied Psychology, 90*(2), 232–241.

Klein, H.J., Fan, J., & Preacher, K.J. (2006). The effects of early socialization experiences on content mastery and outcomes: A meditational approach. *Journal of Vocational Behavior, 68*(1), 96–115.

Klein, H.J., & Weaver, N.A. (2000). The effectiveness of an organizational-level orientation entry program in the socialization of new hires. *Personnel Psychology, 53*(1), 47–66.

Korte, R. (2010). "First, get to know them": A relational view of organizational socialization. *Human Resource Development International, 13*(1), 27–43.

Louis, M.R. (1980). Surprise and sense making: What newcomers experience in entering unfamiliar organizational settings. *Administrative Science Quarterly, 25*(2), 271–298.

Louis, M.R., Posner, B.Z., & Powell, G.N. (1983). The availability and helpfulness of socialization practices. *Personnel Psychology, 36*(4), 857–866.

Lundberg, C.C., & Young, C.A. (1997). Newcomer socialization: Critical incidents in hospitality organizations. *Journal of Hospitality & Tourism Research, 21*(2), 58–74.

Major, D.E., Kozlowski, S.W.J., Chao, G.T., & Gardner, P.D. (1995). A longitudinal investigation of newcomer expectations, early socialization outcomes, and the moderating effects of role development factors. *Journal of Applied Psychology, 80*(3), 418–431.

Mignerey, J.T., Rubin, R.B., & Gordon, W. (1995). Organizational entry: An investigation of newcomer communication behavior and uncertainty. *Communication Research, 22*(1), 54–85.

Miller, V.D. (1996). An experimental study of newcomers' information seeking behaviors during organizational entry. *Communication Studies, 47*(1), 1–24.

Miller, V.D., & Jablin, F.M. (1991). Information-seeking during organizational entry: Influences, tactics, and a model of the process. *Academy of Management Review, 16*(1), 92–120.

Morrison, E.M. (1993a). Longitudinal study of the effects of information-seeking on newcomer socialization. *Journal of Applied Psychology, 78*(2), 173–183.

Morrison, E.M. (1993b). Newcomer information-seeking. Exploring types, modes, sources, and outcomes. *Academy of Management Journal, 36*(3), 557–589.

Nelson, D.L., & Quick, J.C. (1991). Social support and newcomer adjustment in organizations: Attachment theory at work? *Journal of Organizational Behavior, 12*(6), 543–554.

Ostroff, C., & Kozlowski, S.W.J. (1992). Organizational socialization as a learning process: The role of information acquisition. *Personnel Psychology, 45*(4), 849–874.

Reichers, A.E. (1987). An interactionist perspective on newcomer socialization rates. *Academy of Management Review, 12*(2), 278–287.

Saks, A.M., & Gruman, J.A. (2012). Getting newcomers on board: A review of socialization practices and introduction to socialization resources theory. In C. Wanberg (Ed.), *The Oxford handbook of organizational socialization.* New York: Oxford University Press.

Saks, A.M., Uggerslev, K.L., & Fassina, N.E. (2007). Socialization tactics and newcomer adjustment: A meta-analytic review and test of a model. *Journal of Vocational Behavior, 70*(3), 413–446.

Scott, K.A., Montes, S.D., & Irving, P.G. (2012). Examining the impact of socialization through trust. *Journal of Personnel Psychology, 11*(4), 191–198.

Settoon, R.P., & Adkins, C.L. (1997). Newcomer socialization: The role of supervisors, coworkers, friends and family members. *Journal of Business and Psychology, 11*(4), 507–516.

Sias, P.M., Kramer, M.W., & Jenkins, E. (1997). A comparison of the communication behaviors of temporary employees and new hires. *Communication Research, 24*(6), 731–754.

Sluss, D.M., & Thompson, B.S. (2012). Socializing the newcomer: The mediating role of leader-member exchange. *Organizational Behavior and Human Decision Processes, 119*(1), 114–125.

Tidwell, M., & Sias, P. (2005). Personality and employee information-seeking: Understanding how traits influence information-seeking behaviors. *Journal of Business Communication, 42*(1), 51–78.

Waldeck, J.H., Seibold, D.R., & Flanagin, A.J. (2004). Organizational assimilation and communication technology use. *Communication Monographs, 71*(2), 161–183.

Walker, H.J., Bauer, T.N., Cole, M., Bernerth, J., Feild, H., & Short, J. (in press). Is this how I will be treated? Reducing uncertainty through recruitment interactions. *Academy of Management Journal.*

Wanberg, C.R., & Kammeyer-Mueller, J.D. (2000). Predictors and outcomes of proactivity in the socialization process. *Journal of Applied Psychology, 85*(3), 373–385.

Wanous, J.P. (1980). *Organizational entry: Recruitment, selection, and socialization of newcomers.* Reading, MA: Addison-Wesley.

Wanous, J.P., & Colella, A. (1989). Organizational entry research: Current status and future directions. In G. Ferris & K. Rowland (Eds.), *Research in personnel and human resource management, Vol.* 7 (pp. 59–120). Greenwich, CT: JAI Press.

Wanous, J.P., & Reichers, A.E. (2000). New employee orientation programs. *Human Resource Management Review, 10*(4), 435–451.

Weiss, H.M. (1977). Subordinate imitation of supervisor behavior: The role of modeling in organizational socialization. *Journal of Organizational Behavior and Human Performance, 19*(1), 89–105.

Wesson, M.J., & Gogus, C.I. (2005). Shaking hands with a computer: An examination of two methods of newcomer orientation. *Journal of Applied Psychology, 90*(5), 1018–1026.

6

PROMOTIONS AND TRANSFERS

Michael W. Kramer and Carrisa S. Hoelscher

Climbing the corporate ladder through promotions and transfers has been part of the American dream for decades. Yet, despite its importance to individual careers and organizational success, research on promotions and transfers is quite limited compared to the extensive research on new employees (Hill, 2003). We address this important topic by summarizing existing research that explores communication during the processes of promotions and transfers, both domestic and international.

Goals of Career Opportunities

Individuals generally have two primary goals when seeking career opportunities via promotions and transfers: economic gain and career development. Management has somewhat different goals: (1) offering incentives by encouraging employees to seek long-term, career payoffs rather than short-term gains that may hurt the organization; (2) rewarding certain individuals to communicate to other organizational members characteristics of desirable employees; (3) providing employees on-the-job training so they develop a broad organizational understanding; and (4) placing individuals in positions that match the skills and talents they develop during their careers (Baron & Kreps, 1999). These sometimes competing individual and organizational goals drive career development through promotions and transfers. We discuss the unique characteristics of promotions, domestic job transfers, and international job transfers separately before examining issues associated with all these career development opportunities.

Communication and Promotions

Selecting Individuals for Promotions

Selecting individuals for promotions creates challenges for management. According to Katz's (1974) classic article, supervisory personnel need to excel in three skills: (1) technical skills including specialized knowledge, analytic skills, and physical ability to produce occupational outputs; (2) human skills to interact and manage people in effective and productive ways; and (3) conceptual skills to understand the larger picture of how individual organizational units function together as a whole. Organizational leaders agree on the importance of these three skills while recognizing that they vary in significance according to organizational position. Furthermore, textbooks reify these categories' importance although they sometimes are divided into subcategories (Peterson & Van Fleet, 2004). This scholarship seems to accurately identify skills needed to manage routine supervisory activities such as making resource decisions, exchanging information, networking, and managing conflict and change; unfortunately, it tends to overlook competencies needed to manage emergent, complex, and nonroutine activities in a changing environment (Kanungo & Misra, 1992). Leaders need competencies, not just related to specific tasks, but also general intra-organizational and industry-wide competencies (Nordhaug, 1998).

Despite recognizing that individuals should be carefully selected for promotions, individuals are frequently promoted in less optimal manners. Although some human resource management (HRM) departments have extensive programs that identify individuals for promotions, often those with the greatest technical skills in their current positions or with the longest tenure at a particular level are promoted regardless of their human and conceptual skills. In many organizations, individuals promoted to supervisory roles receive little or no training with the assumption that they will develop the necessary conceptual and interpersonal skills on the job (Kramer & Noland, 1999). Consequently, some people may be promoted to their level of incompetence (i.e., the Peter Principle). If they fail to develop the needed skills and management is reluctant to stigmatize them by demoting them (Peter & Hull, 1969), these individuals continue in positions for which they lack the necessary technical, interpersonal, or conceptual skills. Despite this familiar, but likely exaggerated, potential pitfall, most organizations manage their promotion process adequately, if not maximally.

Types of Promotions

Research on CEO succession suggests three ways in which new leaders are promoted that likely apply to managerial positions at all organizational levels (Shen & Cannella, 2002). An *heir apparent succession* involves an insider who is expected to be promoted. There are no surprises in these cases because organizational members anticipated the person would be promoted either because he/she was the most skilled, had the longest tenure, or had insider connections with management. In *contender successions*, an individual who differs from the prior manager is selected to bring change to the unit. This person may be welcomed if the unit's employees also want change or face opposition if they prefer maintaining the status quo. *Outsider succession* involves hiring from outside the unit or organization. This creates a different dynamic and may not involve a promotion for the individual. When the unit has been unsuccessful, the outsider is likely seen as a welcome opportunity for change. However, if the unit has been successful, the outsider may be viewed suspiciously as potentially disruptive to its success (Moreland & Levine, 1982). In any case, the new leader's origin and the former leader's position (remains in the group or not) influence the unit's future success (Worchel, Jenner, & Hebl, 1998). HRM departments can be instrumental in making it clear whether the selection process is open or predetermined and in communicating expectations for the type of promotion involved.

Communication and the Promotion Process

The importance of communication in the promotion process is revealed in Kramer and Noland's research (1999) on individuals being promoted and Ballinger and Schoorman's (2007) study of the experiences of workgroups in which promotions occurred. Successfully moving from one organizational role to another transpires according to a three-phase process akin to Lewin's (1951) familiar model of change: unfreezing, moving, and freezing. During the *pre-promotion phase*, individuals learn of promotion opportunities, either through formal communication channels or via the grapevine, and communicate interest in positions. When it is not an heir apparent situation, individuals apply and compete for the position by demonstrating the skills necessary to succeed. Simultaneously, the workgroup learns that the current leader is leaving. Those who were in close relationships with the outgoing supervisor may express concern over whether they will lose the insider relationship that likely benefitted them, while those with outsider relationships may discuss opportunities for improving their work situation (Graen & Uhl-Bien, 1995; Kramer, 2010). Without an heir apparent, the workgroup may experience reduced productivity due to extensive discussions concerning who might be selected. Alternatively, individuals competing for the position may increase their productivity.

During the *changeover phase*, the promoted individual assumes the new role and the workgroup begins transitioning with the new leadership. Communication relationships are altered as former supervisors become peers and former peers become subordinates. New supervisors report a number of potential communication issues (Kramer & Noland, 1999). For example, former peers may expect special privileges from their former coworker, and new peers may relegate the former subordinate to peripheral roles instead of treating him or her as an equal. New supervisors must learn to manage communication for the unit and make decisions about confidential information to which they now have access. They likely need to develop new communication skills as ambassadors who promote their group, guards who protect it from outside interference, and coordinators and scouts who enable the group to acquire resources and complete tasks (Ancona & Caldwell, 1992). We are unaware of any formal training programs designed to assist supervisors in handling these communication issues. Rather, existing training programs seem to focus on the needed technical skills (e.g., budgeting, scheduling) and conceptual skills (e.g., understanding the unit's relationships to others).

During the *adjustment to stabilization phase*, promoted individuals and workgroups reach a new normal. This is most likely a gradual process in which promoted individuals develop new identities as managers having addressed three main problems: (1) reconciling their own expectations with the reality of their new positions; (2) handling various conflicts between subordinates as their manager instead of their peer; and (3) making sense of often conflicting expectations of subordinates who were former peers, peers who were former supervisors, and new supervisors who were former second-level supervisors (Hill, 2003). Workgroups may attempt to socialize new supervisors to maintain the status quo and resist implementation of changes, particularly if they have previous successes, or readily adapt to changes if previously unsuccessful. New supervisors should have developed some competencies as their group's formal representative (Ancona & Caldwell, 1992). Promoted individuals typically experience a mixture of positive outcomes, such as increased authority, challenge, and freedom, and negative ones, such as increased stress and difficulty integrating family, recreational, and social activities (Nicholson & West, 1988). If a new equilibrium is created, it is probably a temporary state as additional personnel changes are likely to affect the group.

Critical Issues for Promotions

It seems imperative that scholars and practitioners create promotion processes that more completely consider the combination of technical, interpersonal, and conceptual skills required to perform the new job and provide training to address deficiencies. In particular, training is needed on managing communication within and between units, including when either open communication or withholding information may be appropriate. Finally, it would be valuable to understand how employees make sense of the intentional and unintentional messages communicated about what the organization values in managerial personnel by promoting particular individuals who possess and display certain traits and behaviors instead of other personnel.

Communication and Domestic Job Transfers

In multisite organizations, job transfers or relocations from one geographic location to another within the same country are common. Although occasionally organizations relocate entire divisions, which involves a unique set of issues (e.g., Gross, 1981), most domestic job transfers involve moving individual employees, the focus here. Management uses domestic transfers to fill positions vacated due to retirements, resignations, or promotions because it is often less expensive to move qualified internal candidates from one location to another than to hire and train new employees. Additionally, transferred employees develop skills and a broader organizational understanding while increasing organizational commitment (Stroh, 1999). Ambitious individuals often accept domestic transfers because they perceive that doing so increases opportunities for future advancement, particularly higher in the organization (Brett, Stroh, & Reilly, 1993), and avoids perceived negative career consequences from rejecting one (Brett & Werbel, 1980). They also seek transfers for less career-oriented reasons, such as moving to more desirable locations that are closer to family, have more amenable climates, or simply offer new work environments (Kramer, 2010). The most significant deterrent to employees' willingness to relocate is their partners' willingness to relocate, particularly when dual careers are involved (Challiol & Mignonac, 2005).

Domestic Job Transfer Selection Process

Individuals may initiate their own transfers, or management may encourage or initiate the process. When management initiates transfers, the HRM department has often already determined which individual has the necessary technical and supervisory skills to fill a vacant or new position at another location. Earlier research indicates that management initiates approximately 80% of transfers (Pinder, 1977). Employees initiating transfers likely heard of a desirable opening either through formal communication channels such as listings of openings supplied by the HRM department (perhaps a Web page) or through informal communication contacts. In these cases, there may be competition between transfer applicants via interviews and other testing methods where contenders attempt to convey that they are the most qualified applicant. Employees who requested job relocations were significantly more satisfied with their new positions, as were those who viewed their transfers as promotions (Pinder, 1977).

Communication and the Domestic Job Transfer Process

A series of studies by Kramer (1989, 1993a, 1993b, 1995, 1996) suggest the importance of supervisor and peer communication throughout the job transfer process. During the *pre-transfer phase*, individuals gather information to make decisions on accepting job transfers. After accepting a position, the individual attempts to wrap up current projects, withdraw from other projects in anticipation of leaving, and convey important confidential information to others.

Colleagues respond similarly by withdrawing job-specific communication as they recognize the person is a "short-timer" who will be unavailable after a particular date. They typically maintain social contacts until the end, when they engage in departure ceremonies possibly including final informal lunches together, formal events in rented halls, or conferral of plaques on a wall of fame recognizing people who transferred. Communication with future supervisors is uncommon but advantageous when it occurs; new technologies are making this easier to accomplish.

Employees enter the *changeover phase* when they leave their old positions. This is not always clear cut if they began working on new projects prior to relocating or continued finishing projects after moving. Communication may continue to the old location for some time, but it gradually trails off even with close friends if there are no formal work relationships to maintain. Although transferees already know the general organizational culture, they must learn the subculture, norms, and politics of their new locations. The transition is different for transferees than for newcomers. Ongoing supervisor communication is important for newcomers' adjustment (Ostroff & Kozlowski, 1992). For transferees, supervisors had a long-term influence on transferees' adjustment only if they communicated support and feedback to transferees during their initial months on the job, but not if they waited until later (Kramer, 1995, 1996). These differences suggest supervisors should assist transferees immediately upon their arrival when they are in a deep learning mode; transferees become reliant on other communication sources, such as peers, if supervisors wait.

An important part of the transition involves spouses and families. Transferees average an eight-week separation from when they move to new locations to when their families arrive (Brett, 1982). New technology likely has made it easier for families to stay in touch, but it still is difficult to feel settled in new locations during separations even if work is going well. Organizations vary widely in the support they provide for families during relocations. The more they do to shorten the separation period and assist with finding community services (e.g., schools, doctors, affordable day care), and not just with moving logistics, the more quickly transferees will work up to speed in their new jobs due to fewer family-related concerns.

The *adjustment to stabilization phase* is reached when transferees have developed routine communication relationships with supervisors, peers, and subordinates, as well as network linkages at their new locations. Even though new technologies make it easier for transferees to contact former colleagues, these interactions typically become infrequent unless work-related projects require interaction. At this point, transferees feel that they have adjusted to their new positions; they are more satisfied when their spouses and families have settled into routines, found jobs and schools, and are no longer focused on the transition (Brett, 1982; Stroh, 1999). However, a sense of stability is often elusive as workgroup membership continues to change, organizational changes affect the work setting, or individuals consider transferring to another location.

Effects of Domestic Job Transfers on Workgroups

Although most research focused on transferees, transfers influence other workgroup members. Kramer (1989) found that transferring one individual caused others to communicate to make sense of the organization and their own career trajectories. For example, while preparing to relocate, transferees were often contacted by other organizational members from close colleagues to infrequent associates or even total strangers. These individuals typically wanted to know the reason for the transfer and sometimes wondered if they should explore transfer opportunities because the move indicated a problem at the organizational location, such as future layoffs or department shutdowns. At their new locations, transferees create uncertainty for new colleagues (Gallagher & Sias, 2009). New colleagues must include transferees in communication networks and socialize them into workgroup norms that may differ from those of the previous location. The transferee's success may motivate both former and new colleagues to update their résumés and apply for transfers for themselves (Kramer, 1989). In this way, one employee's transfer potentially communicated information about the organization, the type of employees it valued, and the career development opportunities available for employees in both locations.

Critical Issues in Domestic Job Transfers

Communication issues need additional examination throughout the transfer process. It is important to explore how to communicate that transfers are career development opportunities without implying there are penalties for those rejecting them due to other considerations, such as family. Too often, HRM departments focus on assisting transferees with physical moves and work transitions with limited assistance to families. It is imperative to determine which family services have the greatest impact and then to effectively communicate those options to them. In addition to broader concerns, such as communicating supervisor and peer feedback and social support, it would be valuable to explore how specific communication behaviors, such as interpersonal introductions and asking questions, are central to the adjustment process. For example, given the reluctance of many individuals to ask questions in learning environments (Butler, 1998) and transferees' impression management concerns (Callister, Kramer, & Turban, 1999), communication research on asking questions in work environments in a face-saving manner would be useful. Finally, focus on how transfers influence communication in workgroups at both ends of the transfer can likely improve the transition for transferees and workgroups.

Communication and International Job Transfers

As business becomes increasingly globalized, organizations often transfer employees to international locations (Black, Mendenhall, & Oddou, 1991; Stohl, 2001). Research has examined the experiences of expatriates, or individuals residing and working in countries different from their native country (Black, Gregersen, & Mendenhall, 1992; Harvey, Speier, & Novicevic, 1999). Although there are parallels between domestic and international transfers, important differences exist due primarily to the amount of change individuals experience in both work and nonwork contexts when transferring internationally. Such differences are discussed here.

Reasons for International Job Transfers

Management uses international job transfers for various reasons. These include filling vacant positions, developing specialized skills, training individuals for management or other positions, helping create or maintain continuity across branches, and developing organizational loyalty (Kostova & Roth, 2003; Stroh, 1999).

Individuals often accept expatriate assignments hoping to advance their careers. Bolino's (2007) model of expatriate assignments identified four key components that potentially have an impact on whether an expatriate's career is negatively or positively affected. These components are: (1) the overall expatriate experience, including whether the assignment is successfully completed, whether the assignment was developmental, and the expatriate's prior international experience; (2) the context of the parent organization, such as whether the organization has a global strategic posture and management with international experience; (3) career development practices including how connectivity tools and training are utilized, if any adjustment assistance is provided, and whether career development plans are implemented; and (4) certain organizational or individual outcomes such as the willingness of other employees to accept expatriate assignments and the turnover rate after repatriation.

Kraimer, Shaffer, and Bolino (2009) examined expatriates' career paths and advancement opportunities and organizations' ability to retain them following repatriation. Findings indicated that individuals who completed one international assignment showed the best career advancement. Interestingly, those who completed two or more assignments were either less likely to advance or did not improve their prospects for advancement. Employees who were not promoted upon completing their international assignments were more likely to seek employment opportunities outside of their current organization. As might be expected, organizations that provided career support throughout were most likely to retain repatriates.

In sum, how an organization manages these key components and their impact on expatriates' careers communicates a powerful message to employees involved and other organizational members concerning the value of accepting expatriate assignments. Communicating the appropriate message influences an organization's ability to achieve its goals while simultaneously encouraging employees to achieve their own.

Selecting Individuals for International Job Transfers

As with domestic transfers, international transfers may be initiated by management or the individual. Organizations typically consider only job-related factors as the most important for selection of individuals for international job transfers. However, research indicates that other factors, such as flexibility, previous international experience, or the family's adaptability, ought to be considered throughout the selection process (Gertsen, 1990). The ability to communicate competently in a variety of cultural and intercultural settings, as well as host country language fluency in some instances, should also be given consideration for international transfers (Gacho Segumpan, Christopher, & Rao, 2007; Shaffer, Harrison, & Gilley, 1999).

Communication Prior to International Job Transfers

After individuals are selected for international transfers, but prior to the actual move, certain communicative practices should take place. Although not investigated empirically within the context of expatriate assignments, the importance of communication during international transfers likely resembles what is suggested by Kramer's (1989, 1993a, 1993b, 1995, 1996) studies regarding domestic transfers. International transferees likely begin the shift from one location to another by changing their communicative practices with supervisors and peers.

Unique to expatriate assignments, however, is the probable need for cross-cultural training. The amount of change an individual experiences in both work and nonwork environments when transferring abroad often demands such training to ease the adjustment process after the move. Black and Mendenhall's (1990) comprehensive overview of research on cross-cultural training indicated that such training is generally very effective, affecting employees' development of skills, cross-cultural adjustment, and job performance in cross-cultural settings. Mendenhall,

Dunbar, and Oddou (1987) also stressed the importance of offering cross-cultural training to employees' family members to assist with nonwork adjustment. Ultimately, however, the goal of expatriate training should be to increase communicative competence in the new environment by providing both culture-specific and general intercultural training focusing on a variety of verbal and nonverbal behaviors that might assist expatriates in communicating competently in their new locations (Gertsen, 1990).

Communication After International Job Transfers

After individuals transfer abroad, communication remains important as they adjust to new work and nonwork environments. Regular communication with new supervisors and peers with different cultural backgrounds often is necessary. An inability to both effectively and appropriately communicate in the new environment can negatively affect the expatriate's success. For example, recent research found that increasing communication and interaction with host country nationals (HCNs) in the same branch improved and accelerated expatriate adjustment. This increased interaction is made possible and more likely if HCNs are willing to fulfill liaison roles, offering social support and sharing important information with expatriates (Toh, DeNisi, & Leonardelli, 2012; Vance, Vaiman, & Andersen, 2009).

To provide ongoing assistance, many organizations have instituted mentoring programs for international transferees. These programs can be formal or informal, and mentors can be in the expatriate's same branch or in the expatriate's home country. Feldman and Bolino (1999) investigated the relationships between on-site mentoring of expatriates, expatriate socialization, and the outcomes of such socialization. This study measured host-country culture according to Hofstede's (2001) cultural dimensions, the amount of on-site mentoring expatriates received, expatriate socialization, and socialization outcomes. Findings indicated that small power distance cultures, weak uncertainty avoidance cultures, and individualistic cultures provided more on-site mentoring; there was no relation between masculine/feminine cultures and amount of mentoring. As expected, on-site mentoring was positively related to expatriate socialization, which led to higher job satisfaction, a greater intention to finish the assignment, and a deeper understanding of international business issues. Similar to findings in communication literature, communicative support and feedback were necessary early in a transferee's experience (e.g., Kramer, 1995, 1996).

A similar study of 299 expatriates working for one multinational corporation with branches in ten countries examined mentors' roles in expatriate situations (Carraher, Sullivan, & Crocitto, 2008). Results indicated that home-country mentors had significant positive effects on promotability, job performance, and organizational knowledge. Host-country mentors, however, had significant positive effects on a greater number of outcomes: perceptions of teamwork, promotability, job performance, organizational knowledge sharing, and organizational knowledge. This greater impact is likely due to the ability of host-country mentors to provide more frequent and effective (e.g., face-to-face) communication with mentees than are home-country mentors.

Critical Issues in International Job Transfers

While some prior research has found no significant differences among job adjustment experiences for expatriates, repatriates, and domestic geographical relocators (Feldman & Tompson, 1993), there are certain unique challenges for both organizations and individuals involved in international transfers. Research needs to explore how to improve training for expatriates who confront the difficulty of adjusting to new work and nonwork environments simultaneously and must manage the dichotomy between maintaining allegiance to the home organization or developing a new loyalty to the international branch (Black & Gregersen, 1992).

However, the most prominent and unique challenge faced by individuals transferring internationally is the surprising rate of unsuccessful expatriate assignments. Past research indicates that expatriates return home prior to completing their international assignments at rates as high as 40% (Black et al., 1991). The most often cited reason for these high failure rates is the expatriate's inability to adapt to the new environment, thus further emphasizing the need for intercultural communication training prior to international transfers (Toh et al., 2012).

Prior communication research on international job transfers has highlighted key issues for expatriates such as adjustment concerns and requisite intercultural communication training. However, a better understanding of international transfers and their implications for organizations from a communication perspective is necessary. For example, Kramer's (1989, 1993a, 1993b, 1995, 1996) studies suggested the importance of supervisor and coworker communication throughout domestic job transfers. Future research should investigate whether or not the role of communication in international job transfers is similar to the process of domestic transfers. Additional emphasis on the communicative practices of expatriates such as social support and information sharing with supervisors and coworkers in both their previous and new locations also would be beneficial.

General Issues With Promotions and Transfers

Although promotions and transfers are perceived as positive career development opportunities, a number of unintended consequences may occur. For example, individuals promoted or transferred may face acceptance problems with new workgroups. Transferees sometime report that employees take a "wait and see" attitude of expecting them to prove themselves before offering the support and assistance they need to be successful (Kramer, 1996). New supervisors report that workgroup members, especially those who unsuccessfully competed for the same positions, sometimes created tests to see if they deserved the promotion or even hazed them in an effort to make them appear incompetent (Kramer & Noland, 1999). During the stressful time when they are assuming new jobs and positions, these employees sometimes are treated in ways that undermine their potential for success instead of receiving social support and acceptance that would help them succeed in their new jobs.

Management must decide on the type of career development to encourage. During work transitions, employees may be encouraged to imitate and replicate role behaviors of predecessors or to explore and create changes in their new roles (Nicholson, 1984). Management can communicate which career development plan is preferred by the amount of discretion and novelty that is provided. Too often, contradictory messages that encourage innovation while simultaneously rejecting new ideas as "not how we do things here" lead to role ambiguity and discouragement rather than employee development.

Focusing only on promoted or transferred employees overlooks the potential negative effects these opportunities can have on individuals who were unsuccessful in vying for the same positions. A message may inadvertently be conveyed that there are two groups of employees, those with the potential to rise in the organization and those without it; the latter may become unmotivated in their work (Baron & Kreps, 1999). The subjective perception of having reached a career plateau influences worker satisfaction and perceptions of inequity, even if management attempts to convey that future career advancement opportunities exist (Tremblay, Roger, & Toulouse, 1995). Some negative outcomes can be alleviated by communicating that passed-over employees are valued. For example, providing opportunities for new assignments, special (high-profile) projects, mentoring others, or developing new technical expertise increases their satisfaction, commitment, and effort, while allowing negative responses such as blaming the organization, reduced effort, and substance abuse has opposite effects (Rotondo & Perrewé, 2000). However, repeated unsuccessful career advancement attempts or regular promotion of younger, less experienced individuals may cause employees to perceive that their career has stagnated. Offering opportunities after that point may be insufficient to prevent turnover as they seek opportunities elsewhere.

Finally, those who fail to move laterally or upward can become roadblocks for aspiring employees who become de-motivated waiting for someone to retire or leave (Baron & Kreps, 1999). Sometimes management may be able to console blocked individuals by making them aware when future advancement opportunities will occur. However, most organizations' pyramid-shaped hierarchies provide fewer opportunities for advancement, thereby making it impossible for everyone to continue to advance their careers beyond certain points. For some this is not a problem as they focus instead on interests outside their career; others seek employment elsewhere.

Conclusion

Successful management of promotions and transfers can benefit organizations and individuals. Individuals who are successful develop managerial resourcefulness; affective competence, the ability to regulate their own and others' emotional reactions; intellectual competence, the ability to problem solve and conduct goal analysis from a broader perspective; and action-oriented competence, the ability to move tasks and people toward goal achievement and interpersonal relationship development and maintenance (Kanungo & Misra, 1992). Unsuccessful management of promotions and transfers can result in some people rising to their levels of incompetence (Peter & Hull, 1969) or in others feeling undervalued and looking for employment elsewhere when they are not promoted (Rotondo & Perrewé, 2000). Employees no longer seem to expect lifetime employment in the same organization. Given the disparate potential outcomes from satisfied, fulfilled employees to disgruntled ones leaving, it behooves management and HRM personnel to carefully consider the processes they use to promote and transfer employees.

Bibliography

Ancona, D.G., & Caldwell, D.F. (1992). Bridging the boundary: External activity and performance in organizational teams. *Administrative Science Quarterly, 37*, 634–665.

Ballinger, G.A., & Schoorman, F.D. (2007). Individual reactions to leadership succession in workgroups. *Academy of Management Review, 32*, 118–136.

Baron, J.N., & Kreps, D.M. (1999). *Strategic human resources: Frameworks for general managers.* New York: Wiley.

Black, J.S., & Gregersen, H.B. (1992). Serving two masters: Managing the dual allegiance of expatriate employees. *Sloan Management Review, 33*, 61–61.

Black, J.S., Gregersen, H.B., & Mendenhall, M.E. (1992). *Global assignments: Successfully expatriating and repatriating international managers.* San Francisco: Jossey-Bass.

Black, J.S., & Mendenhall, M. (1990). Cross-cultural training effectiveness: A review and a theoretical framework for future research. *Academy of Management Review, 15*, 113–136.

Black, J.S., Mendenhall, M.E., & Oddou, G. (1991). Toward a comprehensive model of international adjustment: An integration of multiple theoretical perspectives. *Academy of Management Review, 16*, 291–317.

Bolino, M.C. (2007). Expatriate assignments and intra-organizational career success: Implications for individuals and organizations. *Journal of International Business Studies, 38*, 819–835.

Brett, J.M. (1982). Job transfer and well-being. *Journal of Applied Psychology, 67*, 450–463.

Brett, J.M., Stroh, L.K., & Reilly, A.H. (1993). Pulling up roots in the 1990s: Who's willing to relocate? *Journal of Organizational Behavior, 14*, 49–60.

Brett, J.M., & Werbel, J.D. (1980). The effect of job transfer on employees and their families. Washington, DC: Employee Relocation Council.

Butler, R. (1998). Determinants of help seeking: Relations between perceived reasons for classroom help-avoidance and help-seeking behaviors in an experimental context. *Journal of Educational Psychology, 90*, 630–643.

Callister, R.R., Kramer, M.W., & Turban, D.B. (1999). Feedback seeking following career transitions. *Academy of Management Journal, 42*, 429–438.

Carraher, S.M., Sullivan, S.E., & Crocitto, M.M. (2008). Mentoring across global boundaries: An empirical examination of home- and host-country mentors on expatriate career outcomes. *Journal of International Business Studies, 39*, 1310–1326.

Challiol, H., & Mignonac, K. (2005). Relocation decision-making and couple relationships: A quantitative and qualitative study of dual-earner couples. *Journal of Organizational Behavior, 26*, 247–274.

Feldman, D.C., & Bolino, M.C. (1999). The impact of on-site mentoring on expatriate socialization: A structural equation modelling approach. *International Journal of Human Resource Management, 10*, 54–71.

Feldman, D.C., & Tompson, H.B. (1993). Expatriation, repatriation, and domestic geographical relocation: An empirical investigation of adjustment to new job assignments. *Journal of International Business Studies, 24*, 507–529.

Gacho Segumpan, R., Christopher, A.A., & Rao, R. (2007). Cross-cultural communication styles in multinational companies in Malaysia. *Human Communication, 10*, 1–19.

Gallagher, E.B., & Sias, P.M. (2009). The new employee as a source of uncertainty: Veteran employee information seeking about new hires. *Western Journal of Communication, 73*, 23–46.

Gertsen, M.C. (1990). Intercultural competence and expatriates. *International Journal of Human Resource Management, 1*, 341–362.

Graen, G.B., & Uhl-Bien, M. (1995). Relationship-based approach to leadership: Development of a leader-member exchange (LMX) theory of leadership over 25 years—Applying a multi-level multi-doman perspective. *Leadership Quarterly, 6*, 219–247.

Gross, T.S. (1981). Blueprint for a group move. *Personnel Journal, 60*, 546–546.

Harvey, M., Speier, C., & Novicevic, M.M. (1999). The role of inpatriation in global staffing. *International Journal of Human Resource Management, 10*, 459–476.

Hill, L.A. (2003). *Becoming a manager: How new managers master the challenges of leadership.* Boston: Harvard Business School Press.

Hofstede, G. (2001). *Culture's consequences: Comparing values, behaviors, institutions, and organizations across nations.* Thousand Oaks, CA: Sage.

Kanungo, R.N., & Misra, S. (1992). Managerial resourcefulness: A reconceptualization of management skills. *Human Relations, 45*, 1311–1332.

Katz, R.L. (1974). Skills of an effective administrator. *Harvard Business Review, 52*, 90–102.

Kostova, T., & Roth, K. (2003). Social capital in multinational corporations and a micro-macro model of its formation. *Academy of Management Review, 28*, 297–317.

Kraimer, M.L., Shaffer, M.A., & Bolino, M.C. (2009). The influence of expatriate and repatriate experiences on career advancement and repatriate retention. *Human Resource Management, 48*, 27–47.

Kramer, M.W. (1989). Communication during intraorganization job transfers. *Management Communication Quarterly, 3*, 219–248.

Kramer, M.W. (1993a). Communication after job transfers: Social exchange processes in learning new roles. *Human Communication Research, 20*, 147–174.

Kramer, M.W. (1993b). Communication and uncertainty reduction during job transfers: Leaving and joining processes. *Communication Monographs, 60*, 178–198.

Kramer, M.W. (1995). A longitudinal study of superior-subordinate communication during job transfers. *Human Communication Research, 22*, 39–64.

Kramer, M.W. (1996). A longitudinal study of peer communication during job transfers: The impact of frequency, quality, and network multiplexity on adjustment. *Human Communication Research, 23*, 59–86.

Kramer, M.W. (2010). *Organziational socialization: Joining and leaving organizations.* Cambridge, UK: Polity.

Kramer, M.W., & Noland, T.L. (1999). Communication during job promotions: A case of ongoing assimilation. *Journal of Applied Communication Research, 27*, 335–355.

Lewin, K. (1951). *Field theory in social science.* New York: Harper & Row.

Mendenhall, M.E., Dunbar, E., & Oddou, G.R. (1987). Expatriate selection, training and career-pathing: A review and critique. *Human Resource Management, 26*, 331–345.

Moreland, R.L., & Levine, J.M. (1982). Socialization in small groups: Temporal changes in individual-group relations. In B. Leonard (Ed.), *Advances in Experimental Social Psychology, Vol. 15* (pp. 137–192). New York: Academic Press.

Nicholson, N. (1984). A theory of work role transitions. *Administrative Science Quarterly, 29*, 172–191.

Nicholson, N., & West, M.A. (1988). *Managerial job change: Men and women in transition.* New York: Cambridge University Press.

Nordhaug, O. (1998). Competence specificities in organizations: A classificatory framework. *International Studies of Management & Organization, 28*, 8–29.

Ostroff, C., & Kozlowski, S.W.J. (1992). Organizational socialization as a learning process: The role of information acquisition. *Personnel Psychology, 45*, 849–874.

Peter, L.J., & Hull, R. (1969). *The Peter Principle: Why things always go wrong.* New York: William Morrow.

Peterson, T.O., & Van Fleet, D.D. (2004). The ongoing legacy of R.L. Katz: An updated typology of management skills. *Management Decision, 42*, 1297–1308.

Pinder, C.C. (1977). Multiple predictors of post-transfer satisfaction: The role of urban factors. *Personnel Psychology, 30*, 543–556.

Rotondo, D.M., & Perrewé, P.L. (2000). Coping with a career plateau: An empirical examination of what works and what doesn't. *Journal of Applied Social Psychology, 30*, 2622–2646.

Shaffer, M.A., Harrison, D.A., & Gilley, K.M. (1999). Dimensions, determinants, and differences in the expatriate adjustment process. *Journal of International Business Studies, 30*, 557–581.

Shen, W., & Cannella, A.A.J. (2002). Revisiting the performance consequences of CEO succession: The impacts of successor type, postsuccession senior executive turnover, and departing CEO tenure. *Academy of Management Journal, 45*, 717–733.

Stohl, C. (2001). Globalizing organizational communication. In F.M. Jablin & L.L. Putnam (Eds.), *The new handbook of organizational communication: Advances in theory, research, and methods* (pp. 323–375). Thousand Oaks, CA: Sage.

Stroh, L.K. (1999). Does relocation still benefit corporations and employees? An overview of the literature. *Human Resource Management Review, 9*, 279–308.

Toh, S.M., DeNisi, A.S., & Leonardelli, G.J. (2012). The perspective of host country nationals in socializing expatriates: The importance of foreign-local relations. In C.R. Wanberg (Ed.), *The Oxford handbook of organizational socialization* (pp. 230–249). New York: Oxford University Press.

Tremblay, M., Roger, A., & Toulouse, J.M. (1995). Career plateau and work attitudes: An empirical study of managers. *Human Relations, 48*, 221–237.

Vance, C.M., Vaiman, V., & Andersen, T. (2009). The vital liaison role of host country nationals in MNC knowledge management. *Human Resource Management, 48*, 649–659.

Worchel, S., Jenner, S.M., & Hebl, M.R. (1998). Changing the guard: How origin of new leader and disposition of ex-leader affect group performance and perceptions. *Small Group Research, 29*, 436–451.

7

DISCLOSURE AND DECEPTION

Communication Issues in Organizational Disengagement

Michael E. Gordon

The exit interview (EI) is an exchange of information between an institutional representative and a departing employee that "is a critical responsibility shared by every organization" (Buhler, 2011, p. 11). The involvement of personnel managers in employment policy began in the 1920s when they assumed responsibility for the EI to determine the causes and costs of labor turnover. Today, 80% of surveyed companies report using EIs (Exit interviews provide feedback, 2012). Originally a face-to-face conversation about organizational disengagement, EIs are conducted today with paper-and-pencil questionnaires, telephone surveys, and computer-mediated surveys.

The EI is a high-stakes exchange that is freighted with the problems of self-report measures that seek sensitive information. Sensitive questions are perceived as intrusive. Because they elicit responses that may be considered socially unacceptable, sensitive questions raise fears about the consequences of giving truthful answers, thus lowering response rates and reducing response accuracy (Tourangeau & Yan, 2007). The sensitive questions that characterize the EI affect the willingness of departing employees to disclose their reasons for leaving and may undermine the authenticity of their responses. Trade publications contain plenty of advice on making the EI more successful. However, "there is very little empirical exploration of the effectiveness of these techniques" (Wood & Karau, 2009, p. 520; see also Gordon, 2011).

In this chapter I address central issues for HRM professionals and employees in the EI, with special attention given to research that deals with self-disclosure and deception.[1] The paucity of research on upward organizational communication in general, and on authentic EIs specifically, made it necessary to consider studies that bear faint resemblance to the EI, thereby raising concerns about the generalizability of the findings. Although most of these studies do not involve the EI, they nonetheless suggest communication practices that can improve its effectiveness. And, unlike the practitioner literature intended to make the EI more effective, the ideas reviewed herein are based on published empirical work that is subject to scrutiny and replication. Importantly, these studies identify avenues for communication research on the EI itself.

Rationale for Conducting the EI

Organizations undertake EIs for two reasons. First, EIs address a variety of administrative matters associated with an employee's departure. Termination paperwork must be checked for completeness, including assuring that the employee has submitted a letter of resignation. Arrangements for delivering the employee's final paycheck also may be completed, and information about outplacement services may be offered. The EI affords the opportunity to retrieve all organizational property issued to the employee and, should they exist, to offer reminders about intellectual property and noncompete agreements.

Second, the EI can be a channel for upward communication that offers most departing employees the opportunity to discuss why they are leaving and their impressions of the organization.[2] Feedback from departing employees may be used to detect sources of job satisfaction and/or dissatisfaction, to identify training needs, to reveal opportunities for productivity enhancements, and to offer warning signs about organizational practices that could result in litigation claims. Importantly, the EI provides a forum for articulated dissent in which employees are encouraged to describe any disagreements with, or contradictory opinions about, workplace issues directed to an audience empowered to undertake organizational change (Kassing, 2008). Designed originally as a check on the practice of arbitrary discharge, it was assumed that foremen would be less willing to fire arbitrarily knowing that employees would be interviewed prior to their leave taking (Miller, 1926/1927). Concerns about foreman misfeasance coincided with attempts by employers to stem the tide of unionism in the United States by addressing sources of job dissatisfaction, primarily those resulting from the actions of immediate supervisors.

Departing Employee Self-Disclosure

"A communication act is considered self-disclosing if it has the self as content, is intentionally directed at another person, and contains information generally unavailable from other sources" (Rosenfeld & Kendrick, 1984, p. 326). Departing employees must decide whether to divulge the actual reasons underlying their decision to leave the organization or to mask their real motives for disengagement. Therefore, self-disclosure is determined by a revealing-concealing dialectic that is inherent in all social relationships, with one or the other pole of the dialectic dominating at different times (Petronio, 2002). Several factors determine the degree of access to or protection of private knowledge, feelings, and beliefs, thereby affecting the polarity of the reveal-conceal dialectic.

Context of the Conversation

In general, upward communication and dissent are muted in organizations (Kassing & Avtgis, 1999). A "climate of silence" often prevails among employees who perceive that "speaking up about problems and issues is futile and/or dangerous" (Morrison & Milliken, 2000, p. 708). This leaves a residue of official conversation that promotes unwarranted positive thinking and socially upbeat behavior (Argyris, 1994) and may deprive line and staff managers of information about potential organizational opportunities or problems. Organizations with open communication climates may be an exception to this rule; expression of varied perspectives and opinions are the norm, thereby offering fertile ground for greater disclosiveness (Morrison & Milliken, 2000). Research on communication climates is called for to verify familiar preachments that self-revelations obtained in EI reports often are issues that come to light during day-to-day conversations between employees and their supervisors (e.g., Giacalone & Duhon, 1991).

Risk/Benefits Ratio to the Departing Employee

Self-disclosures are tactical behaviors intended to attain extant social goals (Omarzu, 2000). Perceptions of felt vulnerability and of expected advantages from self-disclosure affect the polarity of the revealing-concealing dialectic (Petronio, 2002). Departing employees must estimate the subjective utility of goal attainment and the subjective risk of goal forfeiture before deciding whether to divulge the actual reasons for leaving.

Benefits

In general, the potential benefits stemming from self-disclosure in everyday conversation typically include expression, self-clarification, and social validation (Petronio, 2002). Specifically, departing employees reported that self-disclosure during the EI afforded the opportunity for personal catharsis (Giacalone, Elig, Ginexi, & Bright, 1995). It is also possible that valued employees may be able to correct misunderstandings as a consequence of self-disclosure and rescind their decision to quit.

Risks

Departing employees perceive numerous risks associated with self-disclosure during the EI. They may fear employer retribution against former colleagues who remain with the firm and/or reprisals exacted against themselves (e.g., unflattering references to potential future employers; Giacalone, Knouse, & Ashworth, 1991). Further, if they believe the EI to be a symbolic gesture that fails to use the collected information to improve organizational practices, departing employees may not accept even modest risk (Garretson & Teel, 1982). On the other hand, "if they believe that the company was so unfair that any potentially negative consequences are worth the disclosure of their information" (Giacalone, Knouse, & Montagliani, 1997, p. 445), departing employees may be completely candid.

Interviewer Behavior

The behavior of the interviewer has an important influence on the conversational partner's self-disclosure and may be especially pertinent to the EI. For example, certain individuals have a penchant for extracting private information from conversational partners (Colvin & Longueil, 2001). Individuals classified as "high-openers" present attentive facial expressions, and their relaxed and cheerful demeanor potentially encourages the interviewee's participation (Purvis, Dabbs, & Hopper, 1984). Although their verbal and affective prompts do not differ qualitatively from those of low-opener interviewers, high-opener interviewers tend to be perceived in a positive light by interviewees, perhaps because their prompts are more closely related to the intimacy of the information disclosed by the interviewee (Pegalis, Shaffer, Bazzini, & Greenier, 1994).

Research on openers suggests related findings about the shaping of verbal behavior with social reinforcement of speech, which increases the likelihood that a message will contain specific topics, figures of speech, or word usage (Greenspoon, 1955). Social reinforcers at the disposal of a conversational partner include attention, approval, affection, and praise (Pierce & Cheney, 2004). Systematically applied social reinforcement affects disclosures of private information. For example, by contrast with a continuous negative reinforcement schedule, experimental subjects' self-disclosures revealed more aspects of themselves (breadth), encouraged longer speech episodes (duration), and divulged more intimate revelations (depth) when a continuous positive reinforcement schedule was employed (Taylor, Altman, & Sorrentino, 1969; see also Colson, as cited in Cozby, 1973). Hence, interviewers may be able to induce self-disclosures during an EI with nonverbal reinforcers, including smiles and nods of approval, or statements such as "that's really interesting" or "that's important to know."

Substantial evidence suggests that self-disclosure itself is an effective social reinforcer of self-disclosure; in other words, "disclosure begets disclosure" (Jourard, as cited in Petronio, 2002, p. 50). Reciprocity of self-disclosures increases the rewards and decreases the costs of revealing private information between conversants (see Dindia and Allen's meta-analysis as reported in Dindia, Fitzpatrick, & Kenny, 1997) and is the only factor that promotes self-revelation of private information in task/work relationships (Tardy & Dindia, 2006). This conclusion was based primarily on communication experiences during the socialization of new employees (Kramer, 1994) and maintenance communication patterns involving supervisors and their direct reports (Waldron, 1991). Research is obviously required to test the effectiveness of disclosure reciprocity in an EI. Particular attention should be given to the types of disclosures that spur revelations without influencing the departing employee's substantive comments regarding organizational matters.

Liking/Attraction

Trust and respect between the members of a dyad affect decisions about revealing-concealing (Eisenberg & Witten, 1987). For example, articulated dissent was more common among employees who reported higher quality relationships with their supervisors than among employees who reported lower quality relationships with their supervisors (Kassing, 2008). Lacking research on the EI, evidence was sought about the role of interpersonal attraction on self-disclosure in other conversations about disengagement. For example, communication researchers have investigated how the prior relationship between individuals intent on extricating themselves from a dating relationship affected the degree to which they revealed their reasons for ending the association. A series of studies confirmed that the greater the intimacy between the partners, the more likely that a justification strategy (i.e., complete explanation of the disengager's reasons for termination) would be used to end the relationship (Banks, Altendorf, Greene, & Cody, 1987) and the more likely that negative self-disclosures would occur (Gilbert & Horenstein, 1975). Research seems warranted about the relationship between the conversational partners in the EI, not just because of the potential for increasing self-disclosure on the part of departing employees, but also for the assessment of the authenticity of their remarks, to which I now turn.

Assessment of Authenticity

From its inception interviewers in the EI were forewarned to be on guard because "some people will not tell him the truth" (Miller, 1926/1927, p. 305). Concerns about authenticity inspired the first empirical research on the EI that compared employees' responses obtained at the time of their departure with their responses obtained six months or more afterward. Lefkowitz and Katz (1969) and Hinrichs (1975) found that 59% and 44% of departing employees, respectively, gave different reasons for leaving on the two occasions. Both studies found that respondents gave few specific reasons for leaving during the initial EI, citing, instead, factors that were extra-organizational in origin (e.g., those out of management control) and that posed little threat of engendering recriminations when revealed. However, many organization-specific reasons for departing were provided during the follow-up EI (Lefkowitz & Katz, 1969).

Departing employees' approach to the EI has changed very little over the years; 64% of departing nurses changed their EI responses on a follow-up interview. And of these respondents, almost 90% of those who attributed their leaving to "pull" factors (e.g., the attraction of a new job) on the first EI changed their story by mentioning "push" factors (e.g., dissatisfaction with various aspects of the job) during a follow-up interview (Wilkinson & Taylor, 2005). None of the respondents changed their response from a "push" to a "pull" reason.

Little confidence can be placed in people's ability to detect deceit, whether they are professional lie catchers (e.g., police, federal law enforcement agents, and customs inspectors; Aamodt & Custer, 2006) or laypersons, especially when the sender is highly motivated to lie (Burgoon, Blair, & Hamel, 2006). Bond and DePaulo's (2006) meta-analysis concluded that individuals correctly identified the veracity of messages 54% of the time, accuracy that is better than chance statistically but that is practically unimportant. Nonverbal behavior is only weakly and inconsistently related to source authenticity. Beliefs about verbal cues of deception probably are more accurate than beliefs about nonverbal cues (Reinhard, Sporer, Sharmach, & Marksteiner, 2011). Deceptive statements are more recognizable in terms of verbal content that makes less sense, is less plausible and logically structured, and contains fewer details, thereby creating the impression of greater ambivalence (DePaulo et al., 2003).

The usefulness of the EI to HRM professionals is dependent on being able to differentiate between truthful—in other words, authentic—and deceitful—in other words, inauthentic—reports of departing employees. Unfortunately, specific clues that always identify deception in every liar do not appear to exist. Hence, a normative approach to deceit detection that compares markers present in a person's conversation to a distribution of similar behaviors obtained from other people is likely to be unproductive.[3] However, several factors have been identified that can improve deceit detection and that suggest an alternative to the normative approach.

Familiarity Between the Conversational Pair

Lamiell (1988) suggested that impression formation may be described better in terms of a dialectical process rather than normative considerations. "Smith's conception of *who Jones is* is grounded fundamentally not in Smith's conception of who others are, but rather in his conception of *who Jones is not* but might otherwise be" (p. 14, italics in original). In the normative approach, Smith's mental images of interactions with others are the bases for defining "not Jones." By contrast, Jones is the referent for Smith's notions of the authentic "Jones" and the inauthentic "not Jones" with a dialectical approach. Predictions of people's reported impressions of others were more accurate using the dialectical model than the normative model.

The accuracy of a subjective impression appears to depend upon the interviewer's opportunity to form an impression of "who Jones might otherwise be." Research has confirmed that when circumstances permit observers to employ a dialectical approach based on their knowledge of Jones's normal expressive behavior—in other words, "who Jones might otherwise be"—their judgments of whether "Jones" is being deceptive are more accurate. For example, deceit detection improves when judges are given the opportunity to familiarize themselves with "who Jones might otherwise be" by viewing her/him engaged in honest conversation (e.g., O'Sullivan, Ekman, & Friesen, 1988). Bond and DePaulo (2006) confirmed that "judges achieve better lie-truth discrimination if they have a baseline exposure to the sender" (p. 231). Deviations from a person's normal communicative patterns hint at something being amiss (Burgoon, 2005). The stark juxtaposition of "Jones" and a different "who Jones might otherwise be" shifts the polarity of the dialectic toward inauthentic.

These results suggest that interviewers selected to conduct the EI should have interacted with the departing employees previously and, therefore, can rely on earlier conversational patterns for determining "who Jones might otherwise be." However, the tendency to exaggerate

the authenticity of others' communication is a robust finding (Burgoon, 2005) that is exacer-
bated by greater friendship between sender and receiver (DePaulo, Charlton, Cooper, Lindsay, &
Muhlenbruck, 1997). Hence, the degree of familiarity between the conversants in the EI should
be considered by HRM professionals and represents an important question to be answered by
communication researchers.

Familiarity With the Situation

Social actors outside of the deception lab typically have some limited, but useful, knowledge of
the situation that improves the accuracy of their judgments of the authenticity of another's statements. Contextual information may contradict deceptive statements (e.g., "President Obama is a
Muslim"), or it may offer perspective on exaggerated claims by providing data on what is normal
or possible in a situation (e.g., amateur marathoners like former vice presidential candidate Paul
Ryan don't run the 26-plus miles in under three hours). Judges perform significantly better than
chance when given meaningful contextual information before making assessments of deception
(Blair, Levine, & Shaw, 2010). Primarily because they relied on verbal rather than nonverbal dis-
plays as the basis for deceit detection, observers who had actual knowledge of, or believed that
they were at least familiar with, the situation about which a subject spoke were better able to
identify the authenticity of the statements than were unfamiliar observers (Reinhard et al., 2011).

Absent previously gathered information about the departing employee and/or the situation,
interviewers may expand the profile of the interviewee and explore the context of her/his leaving by interrogative probing. Probes encourage interviewees to substantiate their claims with
specific work situations.[4] However, probing may cause stress, putting interviewees on guard and
causing them to manage their behavior more carefully. Further, the simple act of probing, or
witnessing a source being probed, enhances source believability, regardless of the actual authenticity of the messages presented (Levine & McCornack, 2001). Because these effects are robust,
interviewers who rely on probes during the EI should be alerted to their predilection for forming
authentic impressions.

Self-Administered EIs

Like many other HRM functions, the EI has been automated to permit self-administration by the
departing employee, and many templates are available online (see Stephens, Waters, & Sinclair's
chapter 19 for a broader discussion of media and information systems management). Computer-
mediated EIs have several virtues, including avoidance of problems encountered in scheduling
interviews, elimination of data entry, automatic scoring, and "point-and-click access to reports
that can reveal important patterns related to employee attrition and other issues" (Carvin, 2011,
p. 6). Although computer-mediated EIs are discussed frequently in practitioner literature, research
has not substantiated whether departing employees are more willing to disclose opinions about
their employment experiences in an online environment and whether the information derived
is less beset by deception.

Claims that computer-mediated EIs reduce deception (e.g., Carvin, 2011) find support in
people's beliefs that computers can access other information about them with which to check
the authenticity of their answers (i.e., a bogus pipeline) and/or that computers can serve as lie
detectors (Feigelson & Dwight, 2000). On the other hand, by comparison with a face-to-face
interview, deception is easier in computer-mediated channels because nonverbal cues need not

be managed when sending messages electronically (e.g., it is unnecessary to force a smile or to summon appropriate paralinguistic cues to feign enthusiasm when conveying an inauthentic positive message).

It also is alleged that disclosure is greater using computer-mediated EIs. Absent direct evidence, support for this assertion may be found in the voluminous literature dealing with social media that indicates that people are less reticent about self-disclosure in electronic environments (Jiang, Bazarova, & Hancock, 2011). Because the communication contexts are quite dissimilar, generalizing about the willingness to self-disclose in the EI from findings about social media may not be appropriate.

More to the point, the effectiveness of computer-mediated EIs may be inferred from research that has assessed the degree to which people respond candidly when surveyed about other sensitive topics (e.g., alcohol and drug use, attitudes on cohabitation and separation, and various public health issues) using different self-report mediums. The findings are neither consistent nor strong. "The most striking trend in the research literature, especially in recent years, is the large number of studies that found essentially *no difference* in socially desirable responding due to survey administration mode" (Boothe-Kewley, Larson, & Miyoshi, 2007, p. 465, italics in original). Feigelson and Dwight's (2000) meta-analysis found that computer-mediated surveys had a small positive effect on candidness compared to interviews and paper-and-pencil channels but qualified their findings as having practical importance only in situations involving "massed" (p. 253) administrations of the measures. Computer-mediated self-reports do not provide more candid responses than a paper-and-pencil method: "There are relatively few studies that find large differences in reporting across different methods of self-administration" (Couper, Singer, & Tourangeau, 2003, p. 392).

For want of hard data on the effectiveness of computer-mediated EIs, it is necessary to consider research on other sensitive issues using computer-mediated surveys. Further, misrepresenting about sensitive topics, though common, "is largely situational" (Tourangeau & Yan, 2007, p. 859), and many variables are in play when an individual decides whether to provide accurate responses to online surveys (Rogelberg, Spitzmueller, Little, & Reeve, 2006). Consequently, it is important that research be undertaken to verify the claims about the quality of information provided by computer-mediated EIs.

Limitations of Cited Research

Gordon (2011) identified a number of serious shortcomings of research on the EI. There is little empirical study of the EI itself, and almost no attempt has been made within the HRM community to use well-researched areas of communication such as self-disclosure and deceit detection to address the problems inherent in conversations about organizational disengagement. Perhaps the reluctance to consider these bodies of work stems from concerns about ecological validity (Shadish, Cook, & Campbell, 2002). For example, studies of deceit detection employed observers passively watching and evaluating videotaped conversations of strangers rather than interacting with their targets face-to-face (Feeley & Young, 1998). Further, most disengagement studies involved termination of personal relationships, not organizational relationships, and personal rather than professional matters provided the social context for research on self-disclosure. Finally, the experimental subjects almost invariably were college students, a practice that typically does not produce responses that characterize those of actual organizational samples, at least in context-centered (i.e., particularistic) inquiry (Gordon, Slade, & Schmitt, 1986).

Contrarily, because the cited research was intended to reveal certain regularities in behavior by documenting lawful relations among variables (i.e., universalistic inquiry; Kruglanski, 1975), the findings may generalize to the EI. The specific characteristics of the experimental subjects may be inconsequential when the abstract meaning of empirical data is derived exclusively from theoretical relations among the variables under study. Confidence in the external validity of the relations uncovered in universalistic research is bolstered when similar relations are determined to exist in additional samples, and, hence, generalizability does not depend necessarily on detailed similarity across settings. Importantly, the generalizability of many of the propositions about disengagement, disclosure, and deception has been affirmed by meta-analyses across a variety of experimental contexts and subject populations.

Finally, many of the first studies of upward communication in organizations replicated the findings of earlier small group research, thereby supporting the generalizability of the experimental findings. For example, field studies of distortion in upward communication in various ongoing organizations (Athanassiades, 1973) replicated earlier findings observed in small group experiments (e.g., Cohen, 1958).

In particular, trust was a facilitator of upward communication in laboratory studies (Zand, 1972) and confirmed by survey research in four organizations (Roberts & O'Reilly, 1974). Hence, theoretical propositions generated in laboratory experiments about communication have proved to be useful for understanding communication in organizations.

Reliance on laboratory research is, in part, a consequence of the difficulties of studying naturally occurring discourse involving disengagement, disclosure, and deceit. Because of the risks inherent in the context of an EI, applied research must respect the rights of departing employees to privacy and confidentiality and assure the welfare of both EI participants. Additionally, data collection should minimize interference with administration of the EI. Given these constraints, future study of the EI might utilize conversation analysis, a methodology for studying naturally occurring talk in a variety of settings, including task- and organization-centered social interaction such as the performance appraisal interview (Asmuß, 2008). This method describes and explicates the collaborative practices of conversational partners engaged in intelligible discourse. A detailed transcription of an audio or video recording of the conversation is the basis for an inductive data-driven analysis intended to identify the sequential structuring of talk, especially recurring patterns of interaction. For example, examination of turn taking might be used to assess the influence of disclosure reciprocity in the EI.[5]

Conclusion

Despite the importance of debriefing departing employees, the EI has received little attention from researchers. Nonetheless, this chapter identified a number of ideas based on communication research about selecting the individual to conduct the EI and about the process of conversing with departing employees in ways that will increase the likelihood that the actual reasons for organizational disengagement will be disclosed and that interviewers will be better able to discern the authenticity of the information provided.

There is general agreement among HRM sources that someone other than the departing employee's immediate supervisor (who may have caused the problems that prompted leaving) should conduct the interview. Instead, an HRM professional, a manager from a different department, or an outside consultant is recommended to conduct the EI (Exit interviews provide feedback, 2012). Especially in large organizations, these potential interviewers are unlikely to be familiar with departing employees' circumstances or their pattern of day-to-day communication.

The findings reported in this chapter suggest that the problems that typify EIs may result from the interviewer's lack of familiarity with the departing employee and that a different approach to choosing a conversational partner may be advisable. Consideration of the dialectics underlying self-disclosure and deceit detection indicate the use of interviewers who are familiar with the departing employee. The closer the relationship between the conversants, the greater the amount of self-disclosure that may be expected to occur in the EI. Familiarity also provides the interviewer with samples of the departing employee's "who Jones might otherwise be" communication behavior. This enables the interviewer to assess the authenticity of the departing employees' statements during the EI by comparing "Jones" against the "otherwise Jones," noting differences in the enactment of particular verbal or nonverbal behaviors. Interviewers who are unfamiliar with the departing employee are likely to base assessments of authenticity on a single communication sample that is compared with normative profiles of inauthentic communication behavior that are unlikely to aid deceit detection.

Communication research offers support for some recommended procedures for conducting the EI. For example, especially in the case of interviewers who are unfamiliar with the departing employee, preparation is crucial to become acquainted with her/his situation. The interviewer should do some background checking on the departing employee, including talking to her/his immediate supervisor and relevant colleagues to get their thoughts on why the individual is leaving (Buhler, 2011). Clearly, knowledge of the environment in which deception occurs facilitates accurate judgments about deceit. When possible, the contents of the personnel file, including any information provided by the performance management system, should be examined prior to the EI.

Research ought to look into interviewers' use of social reinforcement as a means to increase the willingness of the departing employee to self-disclose. The effectiveness of different classes of nonverbal and verbal reinforcers, particularly interviewers' reciprocal self-disclosures, is a worthy subject of future study. Future research also ought to determine whether departing employees, like Greenspoon's (1955) experimental subjects, are unaware of the environmental event(s) on which their self-disclosures were conditioned, thereby giving some idea about the obtrusiveness of the conditioning process.

In sum, investigation of these ideas will connect the EI to more general conceptual bases in communication. Hopefully, such connections will suggest additional research, the results of which will assist in the creation of conversational contexts, strategies, and skills that HRM professionals can use to improve the EI.

Notes

1 Detailed information about appropriate communication practices in interviewing may be found in Stewart and Cash (2011).
2 In addition to voluntary departures and retirees, organizations differ with regard to whether involuntary leavers should be interviewed (e.g., those terminated due to a reduction in force or a disciplinary firing).
3 "Paying attention to cues promoted in police manuals (gaze aversion, fidgeting, etc.) actually hampers ability to detect truths and lies" (Mann, Vrij, & Bull, 2004, p. 137).
4 See Stewart and Cash (2011, chapter 3) for information about probing.
5 See Sidnell (2010) for more information regarding conversation analysis.

Bibliography

Aamodt, M.G., & Custer, H. (2006). Who can best catch a liar? *Forensic Examiner, 15*(1), 6–11.
Argyris, C. (1994). Good communication that blocks learning. *Harvard Business Review, 72*(4), 77–85.

Asmuß, B. (2008). Performance appraisal interviews: Preference organization in assessment sequences. *Journal of Business Communication, 45*(4), 408–429.

Athanassiades, J.C. (1973). The distortion of upward communication in hierarchical organizations. *Academy of Management Journal, 16*(2), 207–226.

Banks, S.P., Altendorf, D.M., Greene, J.O., & Cody, M.J. (1987, Winter). An examination of relationship disengagement: Perceptions, breakup strategies and outcomes. *Western Journal of Speech Communication, 51*, 19–41.

Blair, J.P., Levine, T.R., & Shaw, A.S. (2010). Content in context improves deception detection accuracy. *Human Communication Research, 36*(3), 423–442.

Bond, C.F. Jr., & DePaulo, B.M. (2006). Accuracy of deception judgments. *Personality and Social Psychology Review, 10*(3), 214–234.

Boothe-Kewley, S., Larson, G.E., & Miyoshi, D.K. (2007). Social desirability effects on computerized and paper-and-pencil questionnaires. *Computers in Human Behavior, 23*(1), 463–477.

Buhler, P.M. (2011). The exit interview: A goldmine of information. *Supervision, 72*(8), 11–13.

Burgoon, J.K. (2005). The future of motivated deception and its detection. In P.J. Kalbfleisch (Ed.), *Communication yearbook, 29* (pp. 49–92). Mahwah, NJ: Lawrence Erlbaum.

Burgoon, J.K., Blair, J.P., & Hamel, L. (2006, June). *Factors influencing deception detection: Impairment or facilitation?* Paper presented at the annual meeting of the International Communication Association, Dresden, Germany.

Carvin, B.N. (2011). New strategies for making exit interviews count. *Employment Relations Today, 38*(2), 1–6.

Cohen, A.R. (1958). Upward communication in experimentally created hierarchies. *Human Relations, 11*(1), 41–53.

Colvin, C.R., & Longueil, D. (2001). Eliciting self-disclosure: The personality and behavioral correlates of the Opener Scale. *Journal of Research in Personality, 35*(2), 238–246.

Couper, M.P., Singer, E., & Tourangeau, R. (2003). Understanding the effects of audio-CASI on self-reports of sensitive behavior. *Public Opinion Quarterly, 67*(3), 385–395.

Cozby, P.C. (1973). Self-disclosure: A literature review. *Psychological Bulletin, 79*(2), 73–91.

DePaulo, B.M., Charlton, K., Cooper, H., Lindsay, J.J., & Muhlenbruck, L. (1997). The accuracy-confidence correlation in the detection of deception. *Personality and Social Psychology Review, 1*(4), 346–357.

DePaulo, B.M., Lindsay, J.J., Malone, B.E., Mulenbruck, L., Charlton, K., & Cooper, H. (2003). Cues to deception. *Psychological Bulletin, 129*, 74–118.

Dindia, K., Fitzpatrick, M.A., & Kenny, D.A. (1997). Self-disclosure in spouse and stranger interaction: A social relations analysis. *Human Communication Research, 23*(3), 388–412.

Eisenberg, E.M., & Witten, M.G. (1987). Reconsidering openness in organizational communication. *Academy of Management Review, 12*(3), 418–426.

Exit interviews provide feedback. (2012). *Agri Marketing, 50*(4), 17.

Feeley, T.H., & Young, M.J. (1998). Humans as lie detectors: Some more second thoughts. *Communication Quarterly, 46*(2), 109–126.

Feigelson, M.E., & Dwight, S.A. (2000). Can asking questions by computer improve the candidness of responding? A meta-analytic perspective. *Consulting Psychology Journal: Practice and Research, 52*(4), 248–255.

Garretson, P., & Teel, K.S. (1982). The exit interview: Effective tool or meaningless gesture? *Personnel, 59*(4), 70–77.

Giacalone, R.A., & Duhon, D. (1991). Assessing intended employee behavior in exit interviews. *Journal of Psychology, 125*(1), 83–90.

Giacalone, R.A., Elig, T.W., Ginexi, E.M., & Bright, A.J. (1995). The impact of identification and type of separation on measures of satisfaction and missing data in the exit survey process. *Military Psychology, 7*(4), 235–252.

Giacalone, R.A., Knouse, S.B., & Ashworth, D.N. (1991). Impression management and exit interview distortion. In R.A. Giacalone & P. Rosenfeld (Eds.), *Applied impression management: How image-making affects managerial decisions* (pp. 97–107). Newbury Park, CA: Sage.

Giacalone, R.A., Knouse, S.B., & Montagliani, A. (1997). Motivation for and prevention of honest responding in exit interviews and surveys. *Journal of Psychology, 131*(4), 438–448.

Gilbert, S.J., & Horenstein, D. (1975). The communication of self-disclosure: Level versus valence. *Human Communication Research, 1*(4), 316–322.

Gordon, M.E. (2011). The dialectics of the exit interview: A fresh look at conversations about organizational disengagement. *Management Communication Quarterly, 25*(1), 59–86.

Gordon, M.E., Slade, L.A., & Schmitt, N. (1986). The "science of the sophomore" revisited: From conjecture to empiricism. *Academy of Management Review, 11*(1), 191–207.

Greenspoon, J. (1955). The reinforcing effect of two spoken sounds on the frequency of two responses. *American Journal of Psychology, 68,* 409–416.

Hinrichs, J.R. (1975). Management of reasons for resignation of professionals: Questionnaire versus company and consultant exit interviews. *Journal of Applied Psychology, 60*(4), 530–532.

Jiang, L.C., Bazarova, N.N., & Hancock, J.T. (2011). The disclosure-intimacy link in computer-mediated communication: An attributional extension of the hyperpersonal model. *Human Communication Research, 37*(1), 58–77.

Kassing, J.W. (2008). Consider this: A comparison of factors contributing to employees' expressions of dissent. *Communication Quarterly, 56*(3), 342–355.

Kassing, J.W., & Avtgis, T.A. (1999). Examining the relationship between organizational dissent and aggressive communication. *Management Communication Quarterly, 13*(1), 100–115.

Kramer, M.W. (1994). Uncertainty reduction during job transitions: An exploratory study of communication experiences of newcomers and transferees. *Management Communication Quarterly, 7*(4), 384–412.

Kruglanski, A.W. (1975). The human subject in the psychology experiment: Fact and artifact. In L. Berkowitz (Ed.), *Advances in experimental social psychology, 8,* 101–147.

Lamiell, J.T. (1988). Dialectical reasoning and the epistemology of impression formation. *Revue Internationale de Psychologie Sociale, 1,* 12–26.

Lefkowitz, J., & Katz, M.L. (1969). Validity of exit interviews. *Personnel Psychology, 22*(4), 445–455.

Levine, T.R., & McCornack, S.A. (2001). Behavioral adaptation, confidence, and heuristic-based explanations of the probing effect. *Human Communication Research, 27*(4), 471–502.

Mann, S., Vrij, A., & Bull, R. (2004). Detecting true lies: Police officers' ability to detect suspects' lies. *Journal of Applied Psychology, 89*(1), 137–149.

Miller, L.R. (1926/1927). Why employees leave: Company records and analysis of causes of exits. *Journal of Personnel Research, 5,* 298–305.

Morrison, E.W., & Milliken, F.J. (2000). Organizational silence: A barrier to change and development in a pluralistic world. *Academy of Management Review, 25*(4), 706–725.

Omarzu, J. (2000). A disclosure decision model: Determining how and when individuals will self-disclose. *Personality and Social Psychology Review, 4*(2), 174–185.

O'Sullivan, M., Ekman, P., & Friesen, W.V. (1988). The effect of comparisons on detecting deceit. *Journal of Nonverbal Behavior, 12*(3), 203–215.

Pegalis, L.J., Shaffer, D.R., Bazzini, D.G., & Greenier, K. (1994). On the ability to elicit self-disclosure: Are there gender-based and contextual limitations on the opener effect? *Personality and Social Psychology Bulletin, 20*(4), 412–420.

Petronio, S. (2002). *Boundaries of privacy: Dialectics of disclosure.* Albany: State University of New York Press.

Pierce, W.D., & Cheney, C.D. (2004). *Behavior analysis and learning* (3rd ed.). Mahwah, NJ: Lawrence Erlbaum.

Purvis, J.A., Dabbs, J.M. Jr., & Hopper, C.H. (1984). The "opener": Skilled user of facial expression and speech pattern. *Personality and Social Psychology Bulletin, 10*(1), 61–66.

Reinhard, M-A., Sporer, S.L., Sharmach, M., & Marksteiner, T. (2011). Listening, not watching: Situational familiarity and the ability to detect deception. *Journal of Personality and Social Psychology, 101*(3), 467–484.

Roberts, K.H., & O'Reilly, C.A. III (1974). Failures in upward communication in organizations: Three possible culprits. *Academy of Management Journal, 17*(2), 205–215.

Rogelberg, S.G., Spitzmueller, C., Little, I., & Reeve, C.L. (2006). Understanding response behavior to an online special topics organizational satisfaction survey. *Personnel Psychology, 59*(4), 903–923.

Rosenfeld, L.B., & Kendrick, L. (1984). Choosing to be open: An empirical investigation of subjective reasons for self-disclosing. *Western Journal of Speech Communication, 48*(4), 326–343.

Shadish, W. R., Cook, T. D., & Campbell, D.T. (2002). *Experimental and quasi-experimental designs for generalized causal inference.* Boston: Houghton-Mifflin.

Sidnell, J. (2010). *Conversation analysis: An introduction.* London: Wiley-Blackwell.

Stewart, C.J., & Cash, W.B. (2011). *Interviewing: Principles and practices* (13th ed). New York: McGraw-Hill.

Tardy, C.H., & Dindia, K. (2006). Self-disclosure: Strategic revelation of information in personal and professional relationships. In O. Hargie (Ed.), *The handbook of communication skills* (3rd ed., pp. 229–266). London: Routledge.

Taylor, D.A., Altman, I., & Sorrentino, R. (1969). Interpersonal exchange as a function of rewards and costs and situational factors: Expectancy confirmation-disconfirmation. *Journal of Experimental Social Psychology, 5*(3), 324–339.

Tourangeau, R., & Yan, T. (2007). Sensitive questions in surveys. *Psychological Bulletin, 133*(5), 859–883.

Waldron, V.R. (1991). Achieving communication goals in superior-subordinate relationships: The multifunctionality of upward maintenance tactics. *Communication Monographs, 58*(3), 289–306.

Wilkinson, K., & Taylor, S. (2005). Are exit interviews of any value—do leavers really tell the truth? *People Management, 11*(19), 58.

Wood, M.S., & Karau, S.J. (2009). Preserving employee dignity during the termination interview: An empirical examination. *Journal of Business Ethics, 86*(4), 519–534.

Zand, D.E. (1972). Trust and managerial problem solving. *Administrative Science Quarterly, 17*(2), 229–240.

8

HOW STAFFING FUNCTIONS COMMUNICATE TO ORGANIZATION MEMBERS AND THE PUBLIC

Neal Schmitt

I believe this book is unique in that it considers the role that communication plays as organizations manage and execute human resource management (HRM) functions. The chapters in this section of the book devoted to staffing consider aspects of communication to organizational members, in particular, and to customers and the general public. I never considered this issue directly before in the context of HRM functions. Apparently, neither do others. A search of several organizational psychology and human resource textbooks and handbooks (Boxall, Purcell, & Wright, 2007; Kozlowski, 2012; Landy & Conte, 2004; Noe, Hollenbeck, Gerhart, & Wright, 2012; Schmitt and Highhouse, 2012) revealed that not a single one had chapters devoted to organizational communication.

The five authors in this section of the book make a strong case for a specific consideration of the role of communication in HRM practice and research. In a few pages, each author also provides a very well-written and comprehensive review of the extant literature on the topics they address. The various aspects of communication (e.g., message, source, receiver, context, and the media used to send a message) vary in importance with the particular function, but it is clear that communication is central to the success of each of these HRM functions. The implementation and survival of good HRM practices depend on the effectiveness of the communication of these practices to employees. The way in which these functions are designed and operate also provides an implicit communication about what the organization values and how it treats its people.

In this chapter, I first provide a comparison of the chapters in terms of the aspect of communication each appears to stress. Then, I discuss the importance of the consistency of communication across staffing functions, a topic the authors do not address. This is followed by a discussion of the exit interview, which is very different from the other functions considered in this section. The need for clarity in terms of the purpose and content of communication is briefly mentioned. Finally, a set of important research questions stimulated by these chapters is presented.

Comparison of Communication Issues Across Human Resource Functions

Because the manner in which communication and the role it plays in organizational effectiveness were treated differently by each of these authors, I thought it would be useful to compare their orientations. Bauer, Erdogan, and Simon were concerned with the effectiveness of the communication by organizational personnel during the socialization phase of their employment. They were concerned with the communication received from mentors at this stage, how the organization communicated a concern for employee well-being, how organizational culture was communicated during newcomer socialization, and how early communication affected long-term employee outcomes such as commitment, turnover, absenteeism, and so forth.

For Breaugh, recruitment is all about communication with the applicant. During the recruitment process, the nature of the job and the organization as well as salary and benefits are communicated. Applicants, too, communicate their concerns and qualifications. The accuracy and attractiveness of these messages determine whether applicants are offered and accept positions and, presumably, affect applicants' subsequent adaptation and performance in the organization. Because his remarks focus on external recruitment, Breaugh, unlike the other chapters in this section, spends time considering the target of a communication and the media necessary to deliver a recruitment message to an individual who is not a member of the organization. In the case of the other authors, the audience is presumed to consist of organizational employees. Like the other authors, he also discusses the nature of the recruitment message and makes the interesting point (at least to me) that information about coworkers and supervisors is rarely communicated in recruitment messages. This is odd since peers and coworkers as well as supervisors are major components of job satisfaction (Smith, Kendall, & Hulin, 1969).

According to Dipboye, the way in which applicants are selected often results in unintended messages about selection procedures that are communicated to prospective employees. The selection process can be an important means of communicating and maintaining organizational values and culture, but this communication is often indirect. Applicants attribute certain values and culture to an organization based on their experiences during the selection process. These attributions, if they affect applicant behavior during the selection process, may have an impact on the validity and reliability of the selection procedures and may affect future applicant behavior, including the acceptance/rejection of a job offer. As a consequence, a great deal of the Dipboye chapter is spent contrasting analytical and intuitive approaches to selection and the unintended messages that may be sent to applicants exposed to these two approaches to selection.

Kramer and Hoelscher explore communication that occurs in the context of employee promotions and transfers. In the case of promotions, they highlight the importance of both unintended and intended communication on the part of organizational personnel. Further, they also mention the fact that in some instances management may not want to communicate its real intent in making a promotion. In the case of both promotions and transfers, Kramer and Hoelscher discuss the impact on the context of the communication (the other employees who are not promoted or transferred). Another context factor that requires attention in the case of these HRM decisions is the employee's family. Treatment of family issues in these cases may produce significant and long-term outcomes while communicating organizational values and culture. In the case of international transfers, communicating with both host nationals and the host company is critical for adjustment and career advancement. Concern for family issues serves a critical communication function in this latter case.

The Gordon chapter is different from the previous four chapters in that it deals with upward communication (i.e., the leaving employee to the organization) that occurs at the end of the employee's tenure rather than at the beginning. Gordon treats the exit interview as an instance of self-disclosure on the part of the departing employee. Hence, the characteristics, behavior, and relationship of the interviewer and interviewee are the topics most discussed in this chapter.

TABLE 8.1 Major Communication Concerns of Staffing Authors

	Message Content	Source	Target	Media	Context	Unintended Consequences
Breaugh: Recruitment	XXX	XXX	XXX	XXX		
Dipboye: Selection					XXX	XXX
Bauer, Erdogan, and Simon: Socialization	XXX	XXX	XXX			
Kramer and Hoelscher: Promotion and Transfer		XXX			XXX	XXX
Gordon: Exit Interview	XXX	XXX	XXX			

Interest in detecting deceit in these interviews focuses attention on the nature of the message and clues to the veracity of what is communicated during this interaction.

Table 8.1 was prepared to compare these five chapters. In this table, I have listed the various components of a communication situation across the top and then made a judgment of the major communication concerns articulated in each of these chapters. This may serve as a summary statement of the issues targeted by each author and may also serve to direct future communication research as to the most important issues for HRM professionals in the areas for which they have responsibility. They also may alert those responsible for the various HRM functions to those aspects of communication that deserve the greatest attention. I would suggest that components not identified as a major concern also should matter despite not receiving much attention by a particular author(s).

Consistency in Communication Across HRM Functions

Surprisingly, none of these five authors mention the need for consistency among the HRM practices that are addressed in the staffing section. Assuming these practices do communicate important information about how the organization views and treats people, it is equally important that the message is consistent across the various functions in an organization. This almost certainly requires some discussion and coordination of these functions and what objectives they serve in the organization. A recruitment function that is not coordinated with selection cannot be expected to produce job applicants who will possess the capabilities for which selection systems are designed. What is communicated to potential applicants about the organization must also be consistent with the manner in which those applicants are evaluated for positions in the organization. For example, recruitment messages that emphasize the openness and innovativeness of the organization may be jarringly inconsistent with the analytical approach to selection described by Dipboye. A selection system that is analytical coupled with a promotion system that is intuitive may communicate an unintended arbitrariness to those who later apply for promotions. It should also be the case that consistency should follow through the HRM programs discussed in the developing and conserving sections of this book. The point is that human resource managers must be concerned with adequate communication within their function, but they must also be concerned that what they do does not communicate intentionally or unintentionally something that will make the achievement of objectives elsewhere in the system more difficult. The bottom line is that there must be communication and consistency among those responsible for various staffing functions.

The Exit Interview

Exit interviews are radically different from the other staffing functions discussed in this section in the sense that one is now concerned with communicating to someone who is leaving the organization as opposed to joining it or moving to a different position in the organization. It seems that exit interviews could serve an important evaluation role with respect to each of the other functions mentioned. The interviewer could explore the degree to which those leaving the organization perceive the fairness of promotion and transfer decisions and whether the organization has clearly articulated its practices in these areas. These exit interviews could also be used to ascertain how consistent various human resource functions communicate the same message to employees. In this connection, they could be used to explore the manner in which employees were recruited and selected, what messages were received by the interviewees at that time, and whether those communications were or were not consistent with what they perceive happened to them in the organization. Obviously answers may be self-serving and the result of various perceptual distortions, but perception is reality for much human interaction. Further, if the exit interviewer gets the same message repeatedly, an evaluation of what is happening in recruitment, selection, and socialization as well as in subsequent personnel decisions would be appropriate.

A good part of the chapter on exit interviews by Gordon explores the possibility that what is said in the exit interview is deceptive—either intentional or unintentional. This does lead to some suggestions as to how and when an exit interview should be conducted and by whom. However, I don't think an organization should assume that communications received in exit interviews are deceptive. Rather, the organization should take comments seriously and then evaluate through other sources the degree to which exit interview communications are symptomatic of a problematic practice and lack of communication with employees. Even if such communications are self-deceptive, the perceptions of these people and others in the organization are likely guided by these perceptions. Hence, they are important factors that must be considered in any organizational reaction to information obtained in the exit interview.

Finally, it seems to me that communication in exit interviews will be very different depending on the circumstance of the exit. A long-term employee who is retiring after many productive years in an organization will certainly be motivated differently than one who is leaving because of a disciplinary issue or the organization's need to downsize its operations. The challenge of conducting a productive exit interview will be very different depending on the circumstances surrounding the exit. It would likely also be the case that the information gleaned from exit interviews in these two cases should be treated differently.

Need for Clear Articulation of Communication Content

Although important in my mind from the outset, I don't believe any of these authors directly addressed the following issues: What do these practices communicate? What are they meant to communicate and to whom? The answers to these questions will, of course, vary by organization as well as a host of other contingent factors. However, without a clear sense of the intended communication, it is not likely that the message delivered will be clear and consistent across those who are responsible for the communication. Again, it is crucial that various staffing functions be coordinated in providing communication to new employees.

Research Issues

As indicated at the outset of this chapter, effective communication in staffing has not been explicitly considered by researchers or, it seems, practitioners. Hence, there are many research issues that require attention. The following issues are those that seem important to me, some of which were stimulated or mentioned by the authors of the five chapters. Overall, I believe that there should be an examination of the degree to which the messages being sent and perceived by the targets of various staffing functions are (or are not) consistent. Obviously, researchers also should be interested in the outcomes associated with the level of consistency. Second, with technological advancements (e.g., online recruiting, assessment, and applicant tracking) the need for research evaluating communication in electronic venues is obvious.

In the area of socialization, the realistic job preview and preemployment expectations have been frequently investigated. Communication from current employees has not been studied frequently and may be different than that provided through organizational venues. I am reminded of a college visit with my daughter many years ago. In one session sons and daughters received a talk from current students while, in an adjacent room, parents were addressed by college admissions officials. The prospective students received a message containing information about student parties while the parents received a message about the maintenance of student discipline in the dorms and community. Current employees may be effective purveyors of the "real" organization, but they may not be sending the intended message. What impact such inconsistency might have on the socialization process and subsequent outcomes deserves research attention. Second, during the socialization process, some newcomers repeatedly seek information and advice. One question that has not been addressed is when this newcomer becomes a nuisance and what the fallout might be for this annoying employee's future in the organization. How do supervisors and coworkers handle these people effectively? Third, a potentially informative technique that may provide valuable information about the impact of events during socialization mentioned by Bauer and colleagues is the collection of critical incidents that may have occurred during the socialization phase of one's employment. I recall a graduate student asking me what research I was planning to undertake when I first began my academic career. I had been working on preparing my courses but promptly spent the next few weeks reviewing literature and outlining research studies. The realization that research and publication were of primary importance was a "critical incident" brought home by this very appropriate graduate student question. These critical incidents could serve as valuable sources of subsequent content in an organizational socialization.

In the recruitment area, I think a relatively neglected issue is the importance of delays in providing information to those being recruited. At least among graduate students, this has certainly been one of the most frustrating aspects of seeking employment. Having listened to many student attributions as to the meaning of such delays, it seems obvious that a long (long may actually be quite short to the employer) delay communicates something very important to recruits. A second issue recognized by Breaugh that has received little attention is the role of information about one's coworkers and supervisors. What, if any, information should be presented and by whom? Third, electronic recruiting is increasingly popular, and yet we know very little about its effectiveness as compared with other forms of recruiting. I suspect there will be major differences depending on the age of the people being recruited. Finally, information on recruiting in the military ought to be of value in civilian organizations as well (Sackett & Mavor, 2003, 2004). Different messages under differing circumstances from different sources to very different types of recruits have been a major concern for the military, and much research has been conducted. It is very rarely cited or discussed in our research literature.

In the case of exit interviews, I am not aware of any research that evaluates the agreement or validity of these interviews. As Gordon asserts, the motivation to intentionally or unintentionally deceive in the exit interview is almost always present. However, when similar comments are made in multiple exit interviews, the message being communicated gains credibility. Second, research designed to assess the extent of agreement across exit interviews as it relates to some organizational action (they finally got the message) would be interesting and might serve to guide future responses to exit interview comments. Third, the validity (or accuracy) of comments made in the exit interview can be assessed in some cases. If so, then an interesting practical question would be the type of person who is most effective in obtaining accurate information in this context. Finally, it would also be interesting to know how the exit interview affects the perceptions of those being interviewed. Are perceptions of the organization improved or worsened as a function of the interview, and what aspects of the communication serve to enhance or diminish these perceptions?

Selection presents a situation in which the applicant is communicating something about her/his qualification for a position. This would be indirect in the case of responses to assessments, but direct in the case of interviews. Unless selection is part of recruitment in an organization, the main message is directed to the organization, rather than the applicant, during the selection process. There is a rather large literature on the impressions that applicants attempt to manage in the selection interview (Dipboye, Macan, & Shabani-Denning, 2012) and the manner in which both parties gather and process information and make decisions in that context. However, there is far less literature on what is implicitly communicated (organization to applicant) by structured assessments that do not entail face-to-face communication. In addition, many organizations are now using online assessments. The simple use of online assessments as well as the content of those assessments must communicate to the applicant. What is being communicated and how that communication compares with other modes of test delivery should receive research attention. Research on applicant reactions may offer some leads in this context (Gilliland & Steiner, 2012). Second, we know that recruitment can affect the quality of an applicant pool and thus applicant test scores, as Dipboye mentions. However, the manner in which communication during recruitment is conducted may also affect the attitudes and test scores of the applicants. This issue has not been addressed in our literature to my knowledge. Third, on the basis of a study by Blackman (2002), Dipboye suggests that unstructured interviews might allow for more accurate assessments of personality variables because they allow the interviewee more time to communicate unconstrained by structured questions. This hypothesis is interesting, and the results reported by Blackman should be replicated under various circumstances. This suggestion certainly defies conventional wisdom. Finally, Dipboye highlights the importance of monitoring and feedback in implementation of selection procedures. This communication process is one that many personnel selection specialists do not examine. We often provide written and oral direction on the use of some procedure and then assume our job is complete. In one instance in which I proceeded in this fashion, I found one manager was changing test scores to percents before applying a suggested cut score for selection. Only after a year in which this manager found that no one ever came close to failing this component of the selection process did he question this finding. Since the test consisted of only 40 items, changing scores to percents involved multiplying them by 2.5, which meant no one would ever fail.

In the case of promotions, the impact of a promotion on those not promoted has not received the attention it deserves. Who does and does not get promoted certainly has the potential to send strong messages to employees. We know far too little about effective communication in this context. Kramer and Hoelscher acknowledge the importance of communication to family members when an employee is being transferred to another location, but there are few studies of the manner in which this is done effectively. Communication is even more important in the case of international transfers. The person being transferred must often be willing and able to learn to communicate in another language and culture, both verbally and nonverbally. During the time spent in an international assignment, communication with individuals in other locations of the organization is critical if one's career in the organization is to remain viable. Providing for transferees' families is also critical, and the manner in which that is accomplished can make a huge difference to the success of international assignments. The body of research by Kramer certainly highlights the importance of communication for domestic transfers, but communication problems and challenges in the case of international transfers must be more complicated and must generate additional communication challenges. This is an area in which good research is critical if globalization is to be successful.

Conclusions

The chapters on the staffing function are excellent brief descriptions of the research on five functions conducted by most organizations. Each is an appropriate description of the role communication plays in these functions and the available research literature in that area. Moreover, the book as a whole represents a needed emphasis on organizational communication, a topic that seems to get only passing, if any, attention in current HRM texts and handbooks. Perhaps more attention should be directed to the nature and content of the communication that organizations intend and the degree to which communication, both intentional and implicit, is consistent across HRM functions. Finally, there are many interesting and important research questions that should be addressed.

Bibliography

Blackman, M.C. (2002). Personality judgment and the utility of the unstructured employment interview. *Basic and Applied Social Psychology, 24,* 241–250.

Boxall, P., Purcell, J., & Wright, P. (2007). *The Oxford handbook of human resource management.* Oxford: Oxford University Press.

Dipboye, R.L., Macan, T., & Shabani-Denning, C. (2012). The selection interview from the interviewer and applicant perspectives: Can't have one without the other. In N. Schmitt & S. Highhouse (Eds.), *The Oxford handbook of personnel selection and assessment* (pp. 323–352). New York: Oxford University Press.

Gilliland, S.W., & Steiner, D.D. (2012). Applicant reactions to testing and selection. In N. Schmitt & S. Highhouse (Eds.), *The Oxford handbook of personnel selection and assessment* (pp. 629–666). New York: Oxford University Press.

Kozlowski, S.W.J. (2012). *The Oxford handbook of organizational psychology.* New York: Oxford University Press.

Landy, F.J., & Conte, J.M. (2004). *Work in the 21st century.* New York: McGraw-Hill.

Noe, R.A., Hollenbeck, J.R., Gerhart, B., & Wright, P.M. (2012). *Human resource management: Gaining a competitive advantage.* New York: McGraw-Hill/Irwin.

Sackett, P.R., & Mavor, A. (Eds.) (2003). *Attitudes, aptitudes, and aspirations of American youth: Implications for military recruitment.* Washington, DC: National Academies Press.

Sackett, P.R., & Mavor, A. (Eds.) (2004). *Evaluating military advertising and recruiting: Theory and methodology.* Washington, DC: National Academies Press.

Schmitt, N.W., & Highhouse, S. (2013). *Handbook of Psychology, Vol. 12: Industrial and Organizational Psychology.* New York: Wiley.

Smith, P.C., Kendall, L.M., & Hulin, C.L. (1969). *Job satisfaction in work and retirement: A strategy for the study of attitudes.* Chicago: Rand-McNally.

PART III
DEVELOPING

9

MEETING THE COMMUNICATION CHALLENGES OF TRAINING

Jeremy P. Fyke and Patrice M. Buzzanell

Training continues to be a priority in organizations and is vital for overall human resource management (HRM). Aligned with its charge to recruit, motivate, develop, and retain individuals, training provides one means by which HRM plays an important role in improving organizational processes and outcomes. Through training, HRM increases employee value for present and future opportunities and needs. Increasing employee value may be justified by assuming that individuals have the right to enrich their skill sets as part of their employment contracts and that organizations have obligations to their stakeholders, including clients and employees, to engage not only in continuous improvement of technical work but also of human assets. Consequently, academicians and practitioners continue to explore the dynamics, processes, and outcomes involved in training individuals. Although it is recognized that HRM personnel need various communication competencies (Rothwell, 1996), much less is known about communication approaches to training and the HRM function. Given that training literature rarely investigates its communicative content and activity, communication researchers have much to contribute to the improvement of this HRM process (Messersmith, Keyton, & Bisel, 2009).

We address central issues facing organizations and HRM professionals with respect to training, beginning with an explanation of the communication-as-constitutive-of-organizing perspective that forms the foundation of our chapter. Then, we consider the trainer, trainee, and training itself as three aspects that any organization must consider in training.

The Case for a Communicative Approach to Training

Given today's business realities of tighter career progression, budget constraints, hypercompetitive business environments, and market-driven philosophies, "training for training's sake" is a thing of the past (McGuire, Cross, & O'Donnell, 2005). Hence, this is an ideal moment for reappraising training theory and practice and for considering the central role that communication plays in creating and sustaining organizational viability. In this section we consider the important role of communication underlying instruction.

Training "is the process of developing skills in order to perform a specific job or task more effectively" (Beebe, Mottet, & Roach, 2013, p. 5). Training involves "the systematic approach to affecting individuals' knowledge, skills, and attitudes in order to improve individual, team, and organizational effectiveness" (Aguinis & Kraiger, 2009, p. 452). According to the most recent industry report from the American Society for Training and Development (ASTD), U.S. organizations spent approximately $156.2 billion on employee learning in 2011, amounting to $1,182 per individual learner (Miller, 2012). Of the $156.2 billion, $87.5 billion (56 percent) was spent internally on training employees, $46.9 billion (30 percent) on external services, and $21.9 billion (14 percent) on tuition reimbursement. Given that most funds are spent internally on training, this HRM function remains paramount and is perceived as critical in business.

Many of the skills involved in effective training are communicative. Trainers need to actively engage their adult learners for training to be successful and for commitment to practice to take place (Greene, 2003). Furthermore, training must be audience centered and is, therefore, a rhetorical process that requires trainers to adapt and adjust instruction to trainees' current capacities (Beebe et al., 2013). We argue that communication theory and practice stands to contribute greatly to understandings of the training function of HRM.

Overall, training theory and practice is premised on communication as a tool to transmit content in order to enhance successful outcomes. Training suffers from a reliance on the communication-as-transmission, or conduit, model (Axley, 1984). Regarding communication as merely the vehicle for disseminating information severely underestimates the influence of communication in organizational life and limits the potential of communication to simply a vehicle or tool for accomplishing other ends. In the training context, this means that communication is one of many organizational processes for which training could be provided, such as customer service, decision making, teamwork, and conflict management—all common foci of training efforts. Thus, the conduit perspective fails to recognize the central role that communication plays in all of the aforementioned organizational processes.

When the communication-as-constitutive-of-organizing (CCO; Fairhurst & Putnam, 2006; Putnam & Nicotera, 2009) approach, or, in our case, communication-as-constitutive-of-training approach, is adopted, the focus shifts to how training is formed and made sensible in context through communication. The difference between the communication-as-conduit and communication-as-constitutive approaches is theoretically and generally helpful for HRM and training specifically. For instance, the CCO perspective realizes that meanings are actively produced, reproduced, maintained, and resisted in and through interactions (Jian, Schmisseur, & Fairhurst, 2008). From needs assessments through training delivery, trainers can capitalize on the negotiation of meaning that is ongoing among organization members. For example, trainers do more than simply explain a process or procedure; through techniques such as narratives and framing, they can help trainees understand how their learning fits into their daily work lives.

Trainers could adopt audience-centered models that foreground the meaning-making efforts of trainees within the particular contexts for which they are trained as well as larger contexts (e.g., careers). If trainees are struggling to adopt new techniques learned in training, a communication-centered approach can tap into the lived experiences of workers and explore root causes of problems. Such an approach that asks questions such as "Why do you think that happened?" and "How did you respond?" and "Why are changes being implemented?" attends to members' sensemaking of training and of the communication that takes place about it (Mills, 2009). Furthermore, as CCO integrates organizing and communicating, it enables sustained focus on the ongoing process of creating, maintaining, and integrating training aspects in situ. As communication as constitutive of training, HRM can adapt more readily to changing needs and interests of trainers and trainees.

The Trainer

Despite much research on training outcomes at individual and organizational levels, few studies beyond simple self-report and retrospective measures examine the extent to which the personal qualities and skills of the trainer actually result in lasting change. Core interpersonal communication skills for successful trainers include relationship and team building, listening, questioning, and engaging in dialogue. Effective trainers view their roles as facilitating rather than teaching or instructing—pulling "a message out of people [rather] than . . . put[ting] one in them" (Beebe, 2007, p. 251), thereby drawing out issues most germane to clients' working lives. In this vein, listening skills are a core competency because trainers must "listen well enough to identify and address unasked questions based on dialogue during training" (Ricks, Williams, & Weeks, 2008, p. 603). Effective trainers use narratives, metaphors, and examples to enhance communication clarity, a key factor in learning (Daly & Vangelisti, 2003; Faylor, Beebe, Houser, & Mottet, 2008). From a CCO perspective, these various linguistic devices allow trainers to tap into "the symbols that make up the day-to-day life world of communicators" (Meyer, 2002) and help them not only connect content to their learning environments but (re)create their workplaces.

Effective trainers are adept at building relationships with trainees to establish partnerships and safe spaces for learning. One way of envisioning trainer-trainee relationships is through the working alliance (WA; Bordin, 1979). The WA stems from clinical psychology where mutual trust, acceptance, and openness enable (a) responding with empathy; (b) expressing genuine, spontaneous feelings expressions; and (c) reassuring clients that they are free to terminate the relationship when ready (Gelso & Hayes, 1998, as cited in Latham & Heslin, 2003). These three WA conditions can help constitute meaningful trainer-trainee relationships (Latham & Heslin, 2003). However, the WA has not been empirically tested, and specific ways to enhance trainer-trainee relationships have been largely ignored (Latham & Heslin, 2003). For example, research has yet to identify a method for training trainers to behave supportively (Latham & Heslin, 2003). Therefore, exploration of the communicative abilities requisite for establishing the WA would be useful. This would facilitate the adoption and testing of a communication social support framework (Albrecht, Burleson, & Goldsmith, 1994; Burleson, 2003) in training contexts to investigate the impact of supportive behaviors on constituting trainer-trainee alliances.

In sum, although research has explored and, in some cases, empirically validated behaviors of effective trainers, much literature tends to be anecdotal or based on retrospective accounts (i.e., "think of the last trainer from whom you received training"). In agreement with Faylor and colleagues (2008), we recommend research designs that involve direct observation of trainee-trainer interactions. Furthermore, as training platforms continue to evolve (e.g., interactive or online formats), research could explore evolutions of trainers' skills and sensemaking about the efficacy of such changes in light of training goals. For example, how are best practices in facilitating and providing client feedback constructed in online modes such as e-forums?

The Trainee

Training begins by considering the knowledge, skills, and abilities (KSAs) of trainees. Given the cost of training employees ($81 on average per learning hour in 2011; Miller, 2012), care must be taken to determine what trainees should understand, value, or be able to do upon completion of the training. As the problems facing organizations become more complex, training must scale up such that "the emphasis is on training the business rather than training individuals within it" (Talbot,

2011, p. 5). Training outcomes are dependent upon who receives the training—management or employee—as roles vary within organizations.

Management Training

Organizations believe that managers and leaders can be developed over time with quality experiences and focused learning, resulting in continual investment in management training (Allio, 2005). In 2011, managerial and supervisory training was in the top three in training content (Miller, 2012). Leading is a key component of managerial training because managers in various positions, including directors and entrepreneurs, need to be trained to not only do their jobs effectively, but also to train others to be most effective (Saks, Tamkin, & Lewis, 2011). Although communication is a core leadership competency, many training programs lack a firm grounding in communication theory (Ayman, Adams, Fisher, & Hartman, 2003). Alarmingly, ASTD survey data reveal that "interpersonal skills" were in the bottom three in terms of content focal area for Fortune 500 companies (Miller, 2012).

Training employees at any level is expensive, but it is especially so for managers when the cost of their time is considered (Collins & Holton, 2004). Organizations seek to reduce training costs by incorporating e-learning, in-house training, and episodic event-based training (Saks et al., 2011). Although promising, research has not explored whether these types of training can meet the challenges of developing leaders in today's environment. For example, do virtual training episodes afford the contexts and materials that develop the ethical and legal competencies necessary today?

Scholars predict shortages of leadership talent required to meet the changing needs of businesses affected by technology, globalization, and hypercompetition. DeRue and Myers (in press) argue that scholarly literature has failed to produce results that can adequately address this talent shortage. One reason for this shortcoming includes a primary focus on individual leader development (e.g., KSAs) without exploring dynamic leader-follower processes. Communication-centered approaches to leadership see leadership as relational. For instance, Fairhurst's (2007, 2011) work on discursive leadership and framing advocates moving past predispositional and trait-based approaches to view leadership as enacted communicatively in leader-follower relationships and as essential to sensemaking about organizational events. Scholars could design studies using Fairhurst's (2007, 2011) scholarship as a framework considering leadership as relational and communicative.

Lastly, managerial training efforts often involve mentoring (Dominguez, 2012). Former General Electric chief executive officer Jack Welch introduced an interesting twist on classical mentoring, viz., a practice in which junior employees mentor older, experienced workers (Murphy, 2012). The purpose of reverse mentoring is knowledge sharing, typically focused on technical expertise (e.g., the use of Twitter for business purposes), as well as sharing generational perspectives (Murphy, 2012). Organizations increasingly use reverse mentoring to facilitate leadership development and help leaders connect with employees at all levels. Yet research is needed to get past anecdotal evidence supporting the merit of reverse mentoring. Research shows that high-performing companies are ones where leadership development is embedded culturally (Bersin, 2012) and leaders and employees are mentored at all levels.

Employee Training

Ostroff and Bowen (2000) provide a scheme to represent various HRM attributes that are targets of training efforts. These attributes include attitudes and motivation (e.g., greater employee morale), performance-related behaviors (e.g., increased sales), and human capital (e.g., higher workforce KSAs). Training focused on these key areas should lead to higher organizational performance, although scant research demonstrates connections between individual and organizational outcomes of training (Aguinis & Kraiger, 2009).

Research mostly confirms that trainees can experience cognitive, behavioral, and affective outcomes as training results. *Cognitive* outcomes are those that demonstrate increases in both declarative knowledge (i.e., basic ability to recall) and procedural knowledge (i.e., knowledge of how, what, and why; Ford, Kraiger, & Merritt, 2010). *Behavioral* outcomes relate to skills that are demonstrable (i.e., employees perform learned tasks more effectively). *Affective* outcomes are those that relate to levels of motivation, evaluations of the training content, and the value of training in general.

Finally, metacognition—in other words, knowledge about cognition and awareness of one's cognition (Ford et al., 2010)—offers still another outcome of training. Employees high in metacognition understand the connection between task demands and skills and can match task strategies to specific contexts (Ford et al., 2010). For instance, employees high in metacognitive abilities would be able to discontinue failing decision-making processes and opt for more effective strategies. The development of metacognition is especially important given the speed with which decisions are made in today's environment and the needs for continued experience and skill acquisition (Greene, 2003). This self-regulatory process can be developed through trainers' use of questioning, dialogue, and other communication-based strategies, a topic ripe for further research (Ford et al., 2010). Through dialogue, questioning, and reflection, trainers can stimulate a communicative environment co-constructed with trainees (Beebe, 2007) and dependent on sensemaking and mindful processing of instruction and information (Bushe & Marshak, 2009). Further research is needed to test how dialogue strategies may facilitate continual, adaptive change so employees may better be able to tap into and use their metacognitive skills in their daily work.

The Training Process

As the nature of work continues to change, workers are expected to develop broad, agile skill sets that are crucial for their own and their organization's success (Grossman & Salas, 2011). The challenge confronting HRM is to identify whether workers possess these skills, provide learning experiences that will develop these skills, and then assure that what trainees have learned actually improves the manner in which they perform their jobs.

Pre-Training: Assessing Training Needs

The training process should begin by identifying the skills and abilities required of workers to perform organizational jobs and an assessment of whether the workforce actually possesses these requisite characteristics. Laird, Naquin, and Holton (2003) explain the various sources for revealing individual needs, including new hires, promotions, transfers, performance appraisals, new positions, and job descriptions. In terms of organizational training needs, routine management reports, changes in standards, new policies, and new products and/or services can be used along with systematic analyses of organizations' strengths, weaknesses, opportunities, and threats (SWOT; Beebe et al., 2013).

Whether assessing individual or organizational needs, a communication-centered approach proposes that training should be audience centered because training is constituted and deployed relationally (Duck & McMahan, 2010). Whether training is conducted in-house or external to the organization, HRM professionals must understand the various needs of audience members receiving training. For example, Gordon and Miller (2012), in their discussion of audience-centered performance appraisals, note that several factors should be taken into consideration: distinct characteristics of employees (e.g., cultural backgrounds); type of feedback and method of delivery (e.g., e-mail, phone) preferred by employees; and past history of interactions with employees. HRM professionals should also note that audience analysis and adaptation must be ongoing throughout training processes (Beebe et al., 2013). At an organizational level, training settings and cultural dynamics influence success. Given that training is a meaning-making process, something as simple as the room arrangement can send messages about training goals and can influence the levels of audience participation (Beebe et al., 2013; Laird et al., 2003).

Communication research contributes insights into the methods for audience analysis important for HRM professionals and researchers. Audience analysis can provide information on preferred delivery styles and methods, participation levels to be expected from audience members, organizational time investments, whether or not trainees have special needs (e.g., visual or audio impairment), and trainees' experience with particular technologies or various mediums used in the training. For the latter, the social information processing model (SIP; Fulk, Steinfield, Schmitz, & Power, 1987) identifies various factors that affect technology use, including experience with the technology and others' sensemaking about technology through interactions with coworkers. The development of models of procedural discourse—in other words, "written and spoken discourse that guides people in performing a task"—has identified a "consistent logic" that underlies the preparation of material intended to assist individuals in the adoption of new technology (Farkas, 1999, p. 42). For example, procedural discourse could be used as the basis for preparing explanations for a university professor about how to upload grades to a new course management system. Research applying SIP and procedural discourse can affect training content, discourse, and materialities through adaptations to trainee needs and contributions to HRM theory.

Finally, HRM researchers and practitioners should consider time and resource constraints that affect audience analysis. With necessary time and resources, trainers have the luxury of conducting complete analyses using questionnaires, interviews, and focus groups (Beebe, 2007). Often, trainers make on-the-spot analyses. Questioning techniques that can be used to help tailor message content by soliciting information about trainee needs, interests, and experiences (e.g., "What would you like to learn?") assists in on-the-spot audience analysis (Beebe, 2007). Research could study the efficacy of such questioning in training programs.

Training: Methods and Practices

Although trainers have many delivery methods at their disposal, most prefer to use combinations of techniques (Miller, 2012). In general, methods vary along a continuum of participation—lectures and demonstrations are low on participation; panel discussions, question-and-answer sessions, and behavioral modeling require midlevel participation; and brainstorming, case studies and role-playing necessitate active participation (Laird et al., 2003). Communication research has shown that comprehension of material in educational settings increases through the use of questions by teachers and students (Daly & Vangelisti, 2003). Trainers can facilitate this process by requiring that trainees develop the questions and facilitate discussion. Given that training in corporate settings is different from learning in classroom settings, additional research could explore the outcomes and processes of adult learners' use of questions for training material comprehension and application.

Incorporating questioning techniques allows HRM professionals to get past seeing training as disseminating information. Trainers use discourse to generate meaning as to why changes are needed based upon the various means of engaging users (e.g., training manuals, advanced work-shops, including pros and cons of new technologies; Hovde, 2010). Further, Hovde's research demonstrates the importance of understanding the audience's expressed desires for the technical training. Yet the incorporation of said desires into training content has not received sufficient attention in HRM literature. Further research could expand Hovde's study of content genera-tors by exploring user reactions to how discourse creates meaning and with what effect. Other research in technical communication includes strategies for explaining information (e.g., eluci-dating, quasi-scientific, and transformative; see Rowan, 2003), yet research is needed to test the applicability of these strategies in training-specific contexts. Some research considerations include the following: how training content can be modified to help less experienced users become accli-mated to technology, how HRM professionals can best gauge the most effective means to design and deliver information and training, and how various discursive techniques facilitate learning and affect on-the-job performance.

Furthermore, research on technological advances could assess recent trends in training deliv-ery. E-learning is a key cost-cutting method (Saks et al., 2011). However, little is known about the constitution of the training/learning environment in e-learning contexts. Trainers can use an online platform to monitor and track trainees' progress through various training phases. Addi-tionally, techniques such as dialogue and questioning can be leveraged in online formats through e-journals and listservs where trainees reflect on training content. Encouraging participation using asynchronous methods gives learners the opportunity to carefully reflect and apply the material.

Another way to enhance participation is to form accountability groups where trainees team up with fellow organization members to track each others' progress. Teams can even compare their progress to those of other teams, which can lead to social facilitation that is productive for learning. Research could delve into the extent to which online methods such as e-journaling can affect training transfer to the organization and how sensemaking about training aspects (e.g., trainer skills at questioning) might differ in online contexts.

Post-Training: Evaluation and Transfer

Training Evaluation

Two issues of utmost importance are evaluation and transfer of training content. Despite the importance of evaluation in terms of return on investment, and despite entreaties over many years to conduct assessments of training effects, trainers typically fail to perform systematic evaluations of what trainees learned and whether such learning affected their job performance (Spitzer, 1999; Wang & Wilcox, 2006). Training evaluation most often relies on reaction measures about the pro-gram to make improvements in content—known as formative feedback. Formative feedback—in other words, information that trainers can use to alter training or instructional programs—may be provided to trainees as ways to modify their thinking or behavior and thus enhance their learning (Shute, 2008). For example, trainers teaching strategies for managing conflict at work can observe trainees practicing various techniques and provide specific communicative recommendations for how to reach collaborative solutions. Similarly, trainees can be provided feedback on their incor-poration of active listening techniques (e.g., eye contact, paraphrasing).

As these examples might indicate, training evaluation can be especially difficult for human resource development (HRD) personnel. As opposed to the types of investments and monetary assessments that occur in the accounting and financial worlds, training evaluation in HRD is difficult given that many skills and outcomes being measured are intangible (e.g., listening, feedback, mentoring, employee satisfaction) and, therefore, cannot be easily calibrated in terms of dollars and cents (Wang, Dou, & Li, 2002). At a broader level, HRD evaluation is tricky given that learning outcomes interact with organizational and environmental factors (e.g., organizational culture and mission, business market, market circumstances, competition; see Wang, 2000, as cited in Wang et al., 2002).

The evaluation of training often is compromised by the evaluation mind-set of trainers. This mind-set is symptomatic of a preoccupation with fairness (e.g., when judging training outcomes as effective/ineffective or individual abilities as low/high skill) and fears of making discriminatory judgments about training outcomes. For Swanson (2005), a trainer may bypass evaluation for fear of an imperfect discrimination or lack of courage to stand behind an evaluation that discriminates. Failure to provide feedback can be antithetical to trainee progress by limiting trainees' abilities to apply skills from training to work settings. To improve outcomes and provide feedback, training could incorporate supportive communication such as appraisal feedback (e.g., "You're really improving how you complete those reports. Nice job!"; see Cheney, Christensen, Zorn, & Ganesh, 2011). Constructive feedback precisely describes the situational requirements, subsequent behavior, and processes of trainees' skill development. Research linking feedback to training outcomes and formative changes to training programs is warranted.

Training Transfer

"Without transfer, training fails" (Laird et al., 2003, p. 207). Scholars and practitioners have written about the "transfer problem" (e.g., Baldwin & Ford, 1988; Burke & Hutchins, 2007; Grossman & Salas, 2011; Laird et al., 2003; Talbot, 2011). For training to have an impact on individuals, teams, and organizations, what is learned in training must be applied by trainees in their job settings. Training content must be *generalizable* to the context in which the training takes place, and workers must *maintain* the learning, skills, and attitudes over time (Blume, Ford, Baldwin, & Huang, 2010).

One way that trainers can attempt to ensure training transfer is through the use of the functional context approach (Philippi, 1996). The functional approach begins with a task analysis during which trainers interview and observe workers completing tasks to familiarize themselves with actual job-related scenarios (e.g., relevant steps needed for greeting customers in customer service–related tasks). The task analysis affords the trainer the opportunity to ensure that training materials are connected to actual work processes.

Studies have identified factors that affect the success of transfer (Grossman & Salas, 2011). Many factors are based on Baldwin and Ford's (1988) model of trainee characteristics, training design, and work environment. In terms of *trainees*, the greatest predictors of transfer are cognitive ability (i.e., intelligence, understanding complex ideas), self-efficacy (i.e., the belief that one is capable of enacting the desired training), motivation (i.e., persistence in goal setting and attainment), and perceived utility or value of the training being offered (i.e., cost-benefit ratio). The greatest factors in terms of training *design* are behavior modeling (i.e., observing and practicing desired behaviors), error management (i.e., learning about common errors and how to correct/avoid them), and a realistic training environment (i.e., mirroring the environment in which competencies will be applied). Finally, in terms of work *environment*, factors include the transfer climate (i.e., organizations that facilitate or inhibit transfer—by means of positive reinforcement, organizational culture, feedback, and so on), support (from peers and supervisors), opportunity to perform (i.e., ability to apply what they have learned), and follow-up (e.g., after action reviews). Further research is needed on the various factors that lead to transfer (Blume et al., 2010). Moreover, attention to how communication during training creates an environment more conducive to training transfer is warranted.

For example, aligned with our communication-as-constitutive-of-training approach is an alternative to common transfer assessment, viz., narrative/interpretive approaches. These approaches involve eliciting stories, myths, values, and metaphors, collectively known as organizational culture (Beebe et al., 2013; Meyer, 2002). These communication-centered techniques afford access to the "symbols that make up the day-to-day life world of communicators in organizations [which] is crucial for assessment because they represent the key sensemaking actions of organizational members" (Meyer, 2002, p. 472). Acknowledging that established norms and practices reveal themselves whenever new practices are taught or new routines are being established, various methods could be used to tap into these factors to reveal how they affect training transfer. Research employing systematic methods to study organizational politics that emerge, for example, during performance appraisals (Latham & Dello Russo, 2008) might take a meaning-centered approach. Further, a meaning-centered approach affords insight into interpersonal power dynamics and organizational history, including history with training programs and subcultures (Weick, 2007). These considerations are potentially valuable to the development of training content but are explored rarely in extant training literature in communication or HRM fields.

Conclusion

We have reviewed key issues, trends, and practices related to training. Our aim was to stimulate interest in avenues for further research so that scholars and practitioners can begin to adopt communication-centered approaches, particularly the communication as constitutive of training. As greater demands are placed on organizations in an increasingly complex and global environment, the study and practice of training must respond to these challenges. We believe that communication-centered approaches are poised to play a central role in ensuring the health and long-term viability of organizations. For this reason, communicative content and competencies (e.g., interpersonal and intercultural) of training warrant further attention (Rothwell, 1996). Furthermore, the mechanisms through which training takes place—in other words, communication—need to be more fully explored (Messersmith et al., 2009).

Indeed, despite recognition that communication competencies play an important role in training, and are often the target of training efforts (e.g., listening, conflict management, public speaking), it remains unclear how communication is conceptualized by HRM practitioners. It appears that a transmission or informational view of communication is the dominant viewpoint. For example, Hovde (2010) argues that the dominant viewpoint in technical communications is that communication transmits information. In apparently simple situations such as training on a new process—for example, uploading grades to a course management site—it appears all that is required is a message about how to upload the information. However, if the user is skeptical of the merits of posting information to a site, then a more complex perspective on communication is needed. Techniques such as questioning and framing then can be used to tap into how users make sense of the changes and training.

Thus, we wish to widen the viewpoint to propose that communication is central to training. Further, whether training is in-house or external, trainers and trainees are constantly in the process of creating and negotiating meaning. We propose that rather than see communication as one of many skills to develop in training, HRM theory and practice could benefit from seeing training *as* communication. What we have provided here are a number of questions and avenues for future research that can explore further how communication is conceptualized by HRM professionals. In the end we hope to encourage conversation about the ways that a CCO perspective might inform HRM theory and practice.

Bibliography

Aguinis, H., & Kraiger, K. (2009). Benefits of training and development for individuals, teams, organizations, and society. *Annual Review of Psychology, 60,* 451–474.

Albrecht, T.L., Burleson, B.R., & Goldsmith, D. (1994). Supportive communication. In M.L. Knapp & G.R. Miller (Eds.), *Handbook of interpersonal communication* (2nd ed., pp. 419–449). Thousand Oaks, CA: Sage.

Allio, R.J. (2005). Leadership development: Teaching versus learning. *Management Decision, 43*(7/8), 1071–1077.

Axley, S.R. (1984). Managerial and organizational communication in terms of the conduit metaphor. *Academy of Management Review, 9,* 428–437.

Ayman, R., Adams, S., Fisher, B., & Hartman, E. (2003). Leadership development in higher education institutions: A present and future perspective. In S.E. Murphy & R.E. Riggio (Eds.), *The future of leadership development* (pp. 201–222). Mahwah, NJ: Lawrence Erlbaum Associates.

Baldwin, T.T., & Ford, J.K. (1988). Transfer of training: A review and directions for future research. *Personnel Psychology, 41,* 63–105.

Beebe, S.A. (2007). Raising the question #6: What do communication trainers do? *Communication Education, 56,* 249–254.

Beebe, S.A., Mottet, T.P., & Roach, K.D. (2013). *Training and development: Communicating for success* (2nd ed.). Boston: Pearson.

Bersin, J. (2012, July 30). It's not the CEO, it's the leadership strategy that matters. *Forbes.* Retrieved from http://www.forbes.com/sites/joshbersin/2012/07/30/its-not-the-ceo-its-the-leadership-strategy-that-matters/.

Blume, B.D., Ford, J.K., Baldwin, T.T., & Huang, J.L. (2010). Transfer of training: A meta-analytic review. *Journal of Management, 39,* 1065–1105.

Bordin, E.S. (1979). The generalizability of the psychoanalytic concept of the working alliance. *Psychotherapy: Theory, Research, and Practice, 16,* 252–260.

Burke, L.A., & Hutchins, H.M. (2007). Training transfer: An integrative literature review. *Human Resource Development Review, 6,* 263–296.

Burleson, B.R. (2003). Emotional support skills. In J.O. Greene & B.R. Burleson (Eds.), *Handbook of communication and social interaction skills* (pp. 551–594). Mahwah, NJ: Lawrence Erlbaum Associates.

Bushe, G.R., & Marshak, R.J. (2009). Revisioning organization development: Diagnostic and dialogic premises and patterns of practice. *Journal of Applied Behavioral Science, 45*(3), 348–68.

Cheney, G., Christensen, L.T., Zorn, T.E., & Ganesh, S. (2011). *Organizational communication in an age of globalization* (2nd ed.). Long Grove, IL: Waveland Press.

Collins, D.B., & Holton, E.F. (2004). The effectiveness of managerial leadership development programs: A meta-analysis of studies from 1982 to 2001. *Human Resource Development Quarterly, 15,* 217–248.

Daly, J.A., & Vangelisti, A.L. (2003). Skillfully instructing learners: How communicators effectively convey messages. In J.O. Greene & B.R. Burleson (Eds.), *Handbook of communication and social interaction skills* (pp. 871–908). Mahwah, NJ: Lawrence Erlbaum Associates.

DeRue, D.S., & Myers, C.G. (in press). Leadership development: A review and agenda for future research. In D.V. Day (Ed.), *Oxford handbook of leadership and organization.* Oxford: Oxford University Press.

Dominguez, N. (Ed.). (2012). *Proceedings of the Fifth Annual Mentoring Conference: Facilitating developmental relationships for success.* Albuquerque, NM: Mentoring Institute.

Duck, S., & McMahan, D.T. (2010). *Communication in everyday life.* Los Angeles, CA: Sage.

Fairhurst, G.T. (2007). *Discursive leadership: In conversation with leadership psychology.* Los Angeles, CA: Sage.

Fairhurst, G.T. (2011). *The power of framing: Creating the language of leadership.* San Francisco, CA: John Wiley & Sons.

Fairhurst, G.T., & Putnam, L. (2006). Organizations as discursive constructions. *Communication Theory, 14,* 5–26.

Farkas, D.K. (1999). The logical and rhetorical construction of procedural discourse. *Technical Communication, 46*(1), 42–54.

Faylor, N.R., Beebe, S.A., Houser, M.L., & Mottet, T.P. (2008). Perceived differences in instructional communication behaviors between effective and ineffective corporate trainers. *Human Communication, 11,* 145–156.

Ford, J.K., Kraiger, K., & Merritt, S.M. (2010). An updated review of the multidimensionality of training outcomes: New directions for training evaluation research. In S.W.J. Kozlowski & E. Salas (Eds.), *Learning, training, and development in organizations* (pp. 135–165). New York: Taylor & Francis.

Fulk, J., Steinfield, C.W., Schmitz, J., & Power, J.G. (1987). A social information processing model of media use in organizations. *Communication Research, 14,* 529–552.

Gordon, M.E., & Miller, V.D. (2012). *Conversations about job performance: A communication perspective on the appraisal process.* New York: Business Expert Press.

Greene, J.O. (2003). Models of adult communication skill acquisition: Practice and the course of performance improvement. In J.O. Greene & B.R. Burleson (Eds.), *Handbook of communication and social interaction skills* (pp. 51–92). Mahwah, NJ: Lawrence Erlbaum Associates.

Grossman, R., & Salas, E. (2011). The transfer of training: What really matters. *International Journal of Training and Development, 15,* 103–120.

Hovde, M.R. (2010). Creating procedural discourse and knowledge for software users: Beyond translation and transmission. *Journal of Business and Technical Communication, 24,* 164–205.

Jian, G., Schmisseur, A.M., & Fairhurst, G.T. (2008). Organizational discourse and communication: The progeny of Proteus. *Discourse and Communication, 2,* 299–320.

Laird, D., Naquin, S.S., & Holton, E.F. (2003). *Approaches to training and development* (3rd ed.). Cambridge, MA: Perseus.

Latham, G.P., & Dello Russo, S. (2008). The influence of organizational politics on performance appraisal. In S. Cartwright & C.L. Cooper (Eds.), *The Oxford handbook of personnel psychology* (pp. 388–410). Oxford: Oxford University Press.

Latham, G.P., & Heslin, P.A. (2003). Training the trainee as well as the trainer: Lessons to be learned from clinical psychology. *Canadian Psychology, 44,* 218–231.

McGuire, D., Cross, C., & O'Donnell, D. (2005). Why humanistic approaches in HRD won't work. *Human Resource Development Quarterly, 16,* 131–137.

Messersmith, A.S., Keyton, J., & Bisel, R.S. (2009). Training practice as a communication medium: A throughput model. *American Communication Journal, 11*(2), 1–20.

Meyer, J.C. (2002). Organizational communication assessment: Fuzzy methods and the accessibility of symbols. *Management Communication Quarterly, 15,* 472–479.

Miller, L. (2012). *State of the industry, 2012: ASTD's annual review of workplace learning and development data.* Alexandria, VA: ASTD.

Mills, C. (2009). The case of making sense of organizational communication. In O. Hargie & D. Tourish (Eds.), *Auditing organizational communication* (pp. 370–390). London: Routledge.

Murphy, W.M. (2012). Reverse mentoring at work: Fostering cross-generational learning and developing millennial leaders. *Human Resource Management, 51,* 549–574.

Ostroff, C., & Bowen, D.E. (2000). Moving HR to a higher level: HR practices and organizational effectiveness. In K.J. Klein, & S.W. Kozlowski (Eds.), *Multilevel theory, research, and methods in organizations* (pp. 211–266). San Francisco, CA: Jossey-Bass.

Philippi, J.W. (1996). Basic workplace skills. In R.L. Craig (Ed.), *The ASTD training and development handbook* (pp. 819–843). New York: McGraw-Hill.

Putnam, L.L., & Nicotera, A.M. (Eds.). (2009). *Building theories of organization: The constitutive role of communication*. New York: Routledge.

Ricks, J.M., Williams, J.A., & Weeks, W.A. (2008). Sales trainer roles, competencies, skills, and behaviors. *Industrial Marketing Management, 37,* 593–609.

Rothwell, W.J. (1996). Selecting and developing the HRD staff. In R.L. Craig (Ed.), *The ASTD training and development handbook* (pp. 48–76). New York: McGraw-Hill.

Rowan, K.E. (2003). Informing and explaining skills: Theory and research on informative communication. In J.O. Greene & B.R. Burleson (Eds.), *Handbook of communication and social interaction skills* (pp. 403–438). Mahwah, NJ: Lawrence Erlbaum Associates.

Saks, A.M., Tamkin, P., & Lewis, P. (2011). Management training and development. *International Journal of Training and Development, 15,* 179–183.

Shute, V.J. (2008). Focus on formative feedback. *Review of Educational Research, 78,* 153–189.

Spitzer, D.R. (1999). Embracing evaluation. *Training, 36,* 42–47.

Swanson, R.A. (2005). Evaluation, a state of mind. *Advances in Developing Human Resources, 7,* 16–21.

Talbot, J. (2011). *Training in organizations: A cost-benefit analysis.* Surrey, UK: Gower.

Wang, G.G., Dou, Z., & Li, N. (2002). A systems approach to measuring return on investment for HRD interventions. *Human Resource Development Quarterly, 13,* 203–224.

Wang, G.G., & Wilcox, D. (2006). Training evaluation: Knowing more than is practiced. *Advances in Developing Human Resources, 8,* 528–539.

Weick, K.E. (2007). The generative properties of richness. *Academy of Management Journal, 50,* 14–19.

10

THE APPRAISAL INTERVIEW

Finding the Right Words

Michael E. Gordon and Vernon D. Miller

> The only task more difficult than receiving performance feedback is giving performance feedback.
>
> —Cleveland, Lim, & Murphy, 2007, p. 170

The statement by Cleveland and her associates has been a truism for almost as long as performance appraisal has been an essential management activity. A survey cosponsored by Sibson Consulting and WorldatWork of 750 senior-level human resource management (HRM) professionals revealed that the top challenge confronting organizations is managers' lack of courage to have difficult performance discussions (Sibson Consulting, 2010). Because managers routinely fail to devote sufficient time to the preparation of appropriate comments regarding their subordinates' job performance, and are often reluctant to conduct candid performance reviews, the appraisal interview (AI) is the "Achilles' heel" of performance management (Kikoski, 1998, p. 491). Despite the institutional character of the task—for example, organizations make managers responsible for providing corrective feedback following poor subordinate job performance—there is an orientation to critical feedback as a socially problematic action (Asmuß, 2008). Indeed, the prevalence of this problem, viz., "dysfunctional performance appraisals," was deemed sufficiently noteworthy for inclusion in the *Blackwell Encyclopedia of Management* (Longnecker, 2005), a comprehensive compilation of the most significant concepts, terminology, and techniques of management theory and practice. Nevertheless, because the consequences of not conducting AIs can be dire, performance feedback remains a staple of HRM. There is increasing attention in the literature to performance management and appraisal programs, in part due to their relationship to organizational performance (Posthuma, Campion, Masimova, & Campion, 2013).

It is understandable that a problem as pervasive and serious as dysfunctional performance appraisal has engendered advice and recommended systems for evaluating employee performance. Many of these suggestions pertain to the conduct of the AI, most of which have yet to be tested empirically. "Although there are numerous books giving advice on the handling of the appraisal session, little content could claim to a strong research base" (Fletcher, 2001, p. 478). It is ironic, however, that so little communication research has been devoted to resolving a problem that, reduced to its essentials, is a conversation about performance. For example, only 5 of the 109 references in the bibliography of Tourish's (2006) chapter on performance appraisal in the *Handbook of Communication Skills* were published either in a communication journal or in a book devoted to communication.

Recently, there has been an uptick in literature on the AI based on communication research (e.g., Gordon & Miller, 2012; Gordon & Stewart, 2009). The purpose of this chapter is to deepen these earlier findings by examining how consideration of communication principles can improve the AI and to suggest several existing streams of communication research with the potential to produce further insight into useful procedures for providing performance feedback. Following a brief presentation on the history of performance appraisal, we will address three communication issues pertinent to the AI: appropriate subject matter for and structure of a conversation about performance; trust, an important contextual factor that influences the willingness of the participants to produce a meaningful exchange during the AI; and conversation analysis as a way of examining the discourse characteristic of successful and unsuccessful performance feedback.

History of Performance Appraisal

Early in the 20th century, performance appraisal relied on an "old method of hiring all sorts of people and trying them out in jobs, keeping them if they 'make good' and discharging them if they do not" (Snow, 1930, p. 428). Judgments of suitability in the old method were based on nothing more than casual observation that was considered to provide all the facts and skills necessary for dealing with human problems. Resistance to newer methods of performance appraisal was based on the assumption that "the experienced foreman, manager, or worker has acquired a fund of common sense to which no addition may be made by the researches of those who frequently have limited contact with industry" (Jenkins, 1935, p. 16).

More systematic methods of performance appraisal became an accepted personnel practice about the time that rating scales were developed to determine the validity of employment tests. The scales also "proved valuable in determining progress in training, in indicating specific needs for self-improvement, and in solving questions of promotion or salary readjustment" (Bingham & Freyd, 1926, p. 122). Given this realization, periodic appraisals of employees using the latest rating instruments were recommended in order to remove "the fog of uncertainty which beclouds the mental processes of workers with respect to their status in their companies" (Scott & Clothier, 1925, p. 117).

Performance appraisal methods were used first in military organizations. However, the rating methods developed for the armed services were generally considered too cumbersome and time-consuming for business organizations (Scott & Clothier, 1925). It was not until after World War I that rating systems became popular for the evaluation of hourly workers in private industry and soon were "closely related to arrangements for systematic promotions" (Yoder, 1938, p. 347). Managers in the lower tiers of the organizational hierarchy became subject to performance appraisal after World War II. Most large U.S. organizations had adopted formal performance appraisal programs by the early 1950s, although the methodologies were, by today's standards, not particularly sophisticated.

Performance of a majority of jobs does not lend itself to objective measurement, and, consequently, most research on performance appraisal focused on the development of subjective measures that could assist managers to make reliable judgments about employee performance. The focus on instrumentation afforded industrial psychologists an inside track on the development of performance appraisal. We will discuss the shortcomings of these rating scales and the reasons they were not particularly useful for providing performance feedback. As a result, managers have long opined that conducting conversations with their subordinates about performance is the biggest hurdle in the performance management process (Sibson Consulting, 2010). The development of feedback procedures that managers believe will assist them with their responsibilities for conducting AIs is a task well suited for communication researchers and is where we begin.

Feedback

Feedback sharing and seeking involve complex dynamics (Gordon & Miller, 2012). Managers are eager to share good news but reluctant to share bad news (e.g., the MUM effect; Dibble & Levine, 2010). In turn, employees have different motives for seeking feedback. They are likely to inquire about their performance when they expect the feedback they receive will be positive and when they believe they are capable of making meaningful changes (Cleveland et al., 2007; see chapter 20 by Schneper and Von Glinow for a discussion of differences in response to performance appraisal among dissimilar age and cultural groups).

Suggestions abound in the practitioner and academic literature regarding the proper manner in which to construct and deliver performance feedback. We will address two problematic issues that can be mitigated by attention to the communication requirements for conducting an AI.

Describing the Appraisee's Performance

More than half of the respondents to the Sibson Consulting (2010) survey reported that their organizations relied on five-point rating scales to measure performance; we assume these also serve as the foundation for providing feedback. Unfortunately, these ratings often evaluate personal characteristics of the appraisee and, consequently, draw upon nomenclature derived from academic jargon (e.g., temperament such as assertiveness or reliability, or abilities that underlie work-related competencies such as analytical thinking or business acumen). Such terminology is likely to be misunderstood (Rabey, 2001), thereby "introducing a great deal of distortion into the measurement process" (Woehr & Huffcutt, 1994, p. 189) and complicating the feedback process.

The scale anchors of many ratings scales also engender confusion. "If supervisors and subordinates at least spoke a common language and knew what phrases such as 'average performance' or 'acceptable performance' actually meant, the potential value of performance feedback would probably increase" (Cleveland et al., 2007, p. 182). Without common understanding of the ratings that emerge from these scales, a meaningful conversation about performance often is beyond the reach of the AI participants. The extent to which HRM professionals actually train those with supervisory responsibility to avoid rating errors and then follow up on their training remains unclear. Equally important for future research, investigations should continue to explore the extent to which HRM training fosters understanding of understanding in rating error (Woehr & Huffcutt, 1994).

Performance feedback cast in personal terms such as traits is not only likely to be misunderstood and difficult to communicate successfully, it probably will undermine the attainment of the conversational purposes of the AI. Feedback intervention theory (Kluger & DeNisi, 1996) suggests that feedback will be less effective to the extent that it focuses appraisees' attention on themselves rather than on their job performance. Feedback has actually resulted in a diminution of performance when the AI concentrates on personal rather than task issues.

Rather than focusing on personal traits, performance feedback should concentrate on behavior, although such recommendations often are at odds with HRM practice.[1] "The question is not what kind of guy he is but how he goes about doing the job" (Grote, 1996, p. 44). Gordon and Miller (2012) described an appraisal system that incorporates work activities that managers and employees believe represent an appropriate basis for discussing job performance. They create a shared semantic net that identifies specific behaviors ("point-at-ables") with commonly accepted meanings within a particular organizational unit. AI participants are able to situate the specific behaviors within the appraisee's job that constitute starting points for the performance feedback. By creating a common language that grows out of existential organizational service, feedback is audience centered, contextually appropriate, credible, and detailed, thereby establishing a foundation for clear and accepted understanding of performance feedback.

Creating the shared semantic net is a time-consuming, iterative task of identifying specific work behaviors, eliminating duplicates, and grouping the remainder into meaningful categories. HRM professionals are likely to be involved in this process. Communication researchers can assist them in the development of shared semantic nets by virtue of their long history of creating taxonomies of verbal concepts by means of content analysis (e.g., Berelson, 1952). Research that examines the extent to which HRM formally and informally fosters the use of shared semantic nets is an important initial step in the development of credible AI language throughout the organization.

Separate Discussions of Performance From Discussions of Salary

Eighty percent of HRM managers indicated that merit increases in their organizations were linked to the performance management system (Sibson Consulting, 2010). However, it is unclear from the report whether consideration of these increases was incorporated in the AI. The rationale for the linkage is a belief that tying performance appraisal results to compensation decisions is an effective way to motivate employee performance and, ultimately, to enhance the effectiveness of HRM and boost the fortunes of the entire organization. Although there is not much research on these linkages, senior HRM managers from 102 companies strongly endorsed the idea that it is unwise to separate the determination of pay changes from performance appraisal (Lawler, Benson, & McDermott, 2012). Although they believed that performance management systems were more effective when appraisal results were connected to salary determination, the respondents provided no direct evidence that AIs addressed both issues during the same conversation. However, the report contained the following introductory remarks:

> When an appraisal is "just for feedback purposes," managers may see it as a system that "fires blanks" rather than as a potentially vital piece of their management system that can alter the direction of behavior and motivate performance. Individuals being appraised may also see the appraisal as "relatively unimportant" if it does not have consequences. (p. 2)

Decoupling the developmental and administrative purposes of the AI by separating discussions of performance and salary was proposed initially at General Electric (Meyer, Kay, & French, 1965). Armstrong and Appelbaum (2003) assert that the AI should focus on performance in relation to organizational goals and be "distinct from talk about compensation" (p. 14). From a communication's standpoint, restricting the AI to a conversation about performance only is important for many reasons.

- When the AI serves both developmental and administrative purposes, managers are placed in the incompatible roles of judge and counselor (Meyer et al., 1965), thereby complicating their communication task and lessening their enthusiasm for conducting the discussion.
- AIs that include discussions of both developmental and administrative matters are likely to be permeated by concerns about salary adjustments and/or promotions (Gordon & Miller, 2012). Such preoccupations are natural, but also significant distractions during a conversation also intended to review past performance and plan future activities.
- Appraisal ratings intended for administrative purposes are one-third of a standard deviation higher than those gathered for development purposes (Jawahar & Williams, 1997), suggestive of rating errors that will sully the basis of the performance feedback.
- Effective conversations address only a limited number of topics (Gordon & Stewart, 2009). Given the communication difficulties stemming from performance ratings and the typical confusion about compensation programs (see Fulmer's chapter 15 on compensation), both topics are likely to require discussion that is more extended than anticipated and difficult to conclude in a single meeting.[2]

Fortunately, the decoupling strategy is bolstered by practical arguments as well.

- In any given year, salary increases may *not* be highly correlated with job performance. For example, some high performing employees with salaries that are close to the tops of their rate ranges only may be eligible for small increases unless they are promoted. Similarly, when funds for merit increases are in short supply, all individuals may be awarded a small salary increase, thereby ignoring differences in performance (Mani, 2002).
- Compensation decisions typically must receive the approval of managers several organizational levels removed from the appraiser. Therefore, it may be premature to discuss salary during the AI because any recommendations are advisory only to higher management or a compensation committee.
- To serve administrative purposes AIs must address an employee's overall performance in order to identify relatively stronger and weaker employees. Conversations intended for developmental purposes require attention to the distinct strengths and weaknesses of a single employee's performance (Kavanaugh, 1989).

In sum, because of the significance of both compensation and performance feedback, the AI should be confined to the latter and a separate discussion should be scheduled to deal with the former. Communication researchers potentially have much to offer HRM about meeting strategy (e.g., Argenti, 1998), particularly if different approaches and discursive resources are appropriate for the administrative and the developmental conversations.

Trust

A second issue affecting AIs is trust, the "willingness of a party to be vulnerable to the actions of another party based on the expectation that the other will perform a particular action important to the trustor, irrespective of the ability to monitor or control that other party" (Mayer, Davis, & Schoorman, 1995, p. 712). Trust is a social dynamic that is nonrecursively intertwined with communication; in other words, trust affects people's willingness to communicate and communication is the basis for developing trust. We first consider the interaction between trust and communication and then discuss the role of HRM in this manager-employee dynamic.

Trust Influences Communication

It has long been recognized that trust has a profound impact on interpersonal and group behavior (Golembiewski & McConkie, 1975). Organizational communication is among the social behaviors most affected by trust (e.g., Read, 1962), particularly conversations about performance, and notably the messages produced by the appraisal process. Years ago, Lawler (1971) warned that the validity and usefulness of performance appraisals was undermined by organizational climates characterized by low trust. In fact, he recommended that performance appraisals should not be conducted in such social environments in the absence of objective data. It is especially problematic to provide negative feedback when "trust in supervisors and in the performance appraisal system is low" (Cleveland et al., 2007, p. 178). Only 30 percent of HRM managers reported that employees in their organizations trusted the performance appraisal system (Sibson Consulting, 2010).

Heeding Lawler's (1971) warning, industrial and organizational (I/O) psychologists examined the effects of trust on the psychometric properties of performance ratings, the output of a large majority of appraisal systems. Bernardin, Orban, and Carlyle (1981) developed the Trust in the Appraisal Process Survey (TAPS) to gather perceptions of the rating behavior of the "typical" supervisor in the department. The more that appraisers lacked trust in the manner in which their peers evaluated their subordinates' performance, the greater their tendency to produce lenient appraisals of their own direct reports. Additional research confirmed that the TAPS measure accounted for a significant amount of nonperformance-related variance in performance ratings (Bernardin & Orban, 1990).

Not only does trust in the appraisal system affect performance ratings, but it is a predictor of ratees' reactions to appraisals and intention to improve on performance weaknesses. Pichler's (2012) meta-analysis found that the quality of the relationship between the supervisor and the subordinate, notably trust, was closely related to both appraisal characteristics and outcomes. Specifically, the better the relationship between the co-interactants, the higher the level of joint participation in, and the more favorable the reaction to, the appraisal process, including perceptions of appraisal accuracy, utility, fairness, satisfaction with the process, and motivation to improve performance. "Ratees react more positively to their appraisals, regardless of how favorable they were in an instrumental sense, when they have a good working relationship with their supervisor—which is a relatively novel contribution in the performance appraisal literature" (p. 726).

According to these findings, organizations should be concerned primarily with employee relationships with their managers when it comes to reactions to performance appraisal systems. Therefore, HRM research on performance feedback interventions and training should address productive communications between managers and their employees both before and after the AI. Numerous commercially available programs that link trust development with leadership might assist HRM professionals to create a supportive social context for performance appraisal.

Communication Influences Trust

"Open communication, in which managers exchange thoughts and ideas freely with employees, enhances perceptions of trust" (Whitener, Brodt, Korsgaard, & Werner, 1998, p. 517). Although empirical research is scarce on the link between communication and trust in the workplace (Willemyns, Gallois, & Callan, 2003), it is, nonetheless, an article of faith that trust is strongly influenced by the communication climate of an organization (Cleveland et al., 2007). Day-to-day conversation can create an atmosphere of trust. Roberts and O'Reilly (1974) operationally defined communication that inspires trust with a single item: "How free do you feel to discuss with your immediate superior the problems and difficulties you have in your job without jeopardizing your position or having it 'held against' you later?"

Given that communication can engender trust, further exploration is invited into how managers might alter their discourse in order to create and maintain more trusting relationships with their employees. For example, Whitener et al.'s (1998) literature review found that the accuracy of information provided by supervisors has the strongest relationship with their trustworthiness in the eyes of their subordinates. Further, the adequacy of their explanations and timeliness of their feedback also influence supervisors' perceived trustworthiness. These findings are supported by Thomas, Zolin, & Hartman's (2009) analysis of communication audit data for approximately 200 oil company employees. The quality of information (i.e., its accuracy, timeliness, and usefulness) was important for developing trust among coworkers and supervisors, and the quantity of information (i.e., organizational members' perception that they are adequately informed) was particularly important for developing trust in top management. Finally, Willemyns et al. (2003) content analyzed narratives prepared by employees to describe a satisfactory and an unsatisfactory interaction with their manager or supervisor. Communication behaviors were identified that built and maintained trust, particularly relational strategies that emphasized awareness of face and emotional needs of the interactants (see also Jo & Shim, 2005).

Communication literature provides little guidance for managers on how to use language as a means to increase levels of trust. By focusing on the structural categories of communication associated with trust (e.g., "gives instruction" or "questions") rather than at the word level, the actual nuances of conversation have been neglected. Communication accommodation theory (CAT; Giles, Coupland, & Coupland, 1991) represented an important first step in examining how people negotiate social distance from others by means of their conversational tactics, including using convergent linguistic, paralinguistic, and noverbal cues. CAT also recognized that people employ stylistic convergence in which dialects, idioms, accents, and code-switching are made similar to those of the co-interactant. For example, Maddux, Mullen, and Galinsky (2008) demonstrated that trust (as measured by joint gains for the participants in a negotiation simulation) could be altered by behavioral mimicry—in other words, copying the mannerisms of the other party led to better outcomes. This implies that the greater the interactive convergence between two speakers, the greater the solidarity, the smaller the social distance, and the greater the level of trust.

Because CAT did not emphasize word use, sociolinguistic approaches were developed to identify conversational strategies that proved useful for understanding a variety of organizational phenomena and group dynamics that are embedded in everyday speech (e.g., organizational status or power; Mourand, 1996).[3] One such approach, linguistic style matching (LSM), examines the tendency of participants to use a common vocabulary and similar sentence structures. LSM measures conversational accommodation at the specific, verbatim level during which co-interactants engage in linguistic mimicry by repeating the words or word phrases uttered by their conversational partner. By measuring the degree to which co-interactants address concepts with related meanings (e.g., "unhappy" and "sad"), LSM also assesses accommodation at the semantic level.

LSM metrics are related to various social dynamics, including group cohesiveness (Gonzales, Hancock, & Pennebaker, 2010). The level of verbal mimicry (i.e., the degree to which participants produced similar rates of function words in their dialogue) was related to the cohesiveness that emerged among the members of experimental groups engaged in an information search task in both face-to-face and text environments.[4] Although trust was not measured directly, it was assumed that the groups were unlikely to become highly cohesive without at least a modicum of trust. Scissors, Gill, and Gergle (2009) operationalized trust in terms of the number of defections during an experiment with the Day Trader task paradigm in which investors must cooperate to perform well. Better group performance indicative of high levels of interpersonal trust was associated with "good" accommodation characterized by linguistic mimicry and similarity in the use of positive and task-related words.

> To summarize, at a verbatim level, trusting pairs show similarity in their use of noun phrases and emoticons. At a semantic level, similarity in words relating to positive emotion and the task processes is associated with trust. (p. 22)

What may be concluded about how HRM managers might use words to engender trust to facilitate the performance appraisal process? First, because matching linguistic style has demonstrated effectiveness in facilitating complex interpersonal interactions where the stakes are high and limits on time are apparent (e.g., negotiations and investing), communication scholars ought to extend sociolinguistic research to the AI. Investigators are urged to rely on field studies (e.g., those employing conversation analysis as described in the following) as well as experimental methodologies given the ineluctable questions that arise regarding the generalizability of laboratory investigations. Second, attempts at implementing the conversational behaviors associated with the development and maintenance of trust should not be attempted without a broader commitment to the establishment of genuinely sincere relationships with subordinates. Employing these linguistic devices in a Machiavellian manner is unlikely to be successful. Subordinates will detect the pretense, and this will "result only in greater mistrust of the manager in the long term" (Willemyns et al., 2003, p. 125).

Third, trusting relationships are based on linguistic accommodation focused on the task that relies on expressions that minimize ambiguity and aid understanding. These recommendations for creating trust are consistent with Gordon and Miller's (2012) development of a shared semantic net that provides a specialized vocabulary of terms chosen for their relevance to the subordinate's job and that permit participants in the AI to be confident that they already share certain knowledge related to the concepts and issues that will be addressed. "Mutual agreement or concurrence about the definitions of the terms used to discuss performance is a very important, but often overlooked, starting point for a useful conversation" (p. 56). Future research should explore ways that shared semantic nets are implemented in AI systems and evaluate both their implementation and the nature of their shared semantic nets to assess the promotion of trust between the participants.

Conversation Analysis

Much of the literature dealing with the AI consists of either experimental studies of simulated performance reviews (e.g., Kacmar, Wayne, & Wright, 2009) or self-reports of individuals' recollections of their experiences as participants in the process (e.g., Linna et al., 2012). By contrast, there is only limited research on authentic AIs (Downs, 1992).

Conversation analysis can provide a fine-grained analysis of in situ communication behavior. Having emerged from the ethnomethodology tradition that influenced the pioneering work of Sacks (1992), conversation analysis is now an established discipline that can be brought to bear on any set of data where language is used in interaction (e.g., institution-centered discussions) in order to reveal subtleties in the co-interactants' use of discursive resources to generate interactional contributions and make sense of the inputs of others. Conversation analysis can provide "a thick description of what actually goes on inside the black box [i.e., the AI] and this could be used to offer practitioners advice on which concrete discursive strategies to adopt" (Clifton, 2012, p. 286).

Illustrating conversational analysis' value to understanding AIs, Asmuß (2008) found that supervisors who orient the AI as a socially problematic activity inadvertently complicate the process of providing negative feedback. That is, if supervisors launch the AI in a negative manner, the conversation lasts longer, limits the appraiser's opportunity to gain insights into the subordinate's understanding of the problem(s), and restricts focus on proposals for solving the problem(s). The findings suggest that a direct interactional approach will assist the appraiser to produce negative feedback in a nonproblematic way by utilizing discursive resources that make it clear that this type of communicative activity is an integral part of the AI. Clifton (2012) used conversation analysis to reveal the communicative strategies employed by the co-interactants to build solidarity and, thereby, minimize threats to face during the AI. Although the use of face-saving tactics to help deal with delicate situations is not a new finding, the fine-grained analyses demonstrated that facework is achieved as a joint accomplishment. Obviously, more research employing this methodology is required to substantiate these findings.

Conversation analysis holds great potential for HRM because it may be used to examine the validity of the prescriptive theories of interaction found in practitioner literature devoted to the AI and, where appropriate, amplify this material conceptually and/or descriptively (Peräkyliä & Vehviläinen, 2003). Popular prescriptive books (e.g., Grote, 1996) propose linguistic advice for appraisers intended to assist in managing repeated communicative situations that take the form of decontextualized, simplified scripts rather than recommendations that are cast in terms of specific discursive strategies. Conversation analysis could reveal dialogic communication strategies derived from actual AIs, including the interactional function of positive feedback and the discursive resources necessary to effect meaningful joint participation (Asmuß, 2008).

Conversation analysis of the AI has thus far been limited by small data sets that are group and place specific and by somewhat narrow foci on a small subset of crucial communicative activities. Hence, although the explanatory power of this methodology is substantial, its generalizability is questionable. Effort ought to be made to create a database of transcribed AIs that would encourage and broaden the use of conversational analysis to investigate workplace interaction.[5] Certain professional organizations associated with the broader HRM discipline have the potential to be a useful partner in the creation of such a database and might be able to support this endeavor by assisting with entrée to various organizations in order to collect transcribed AIs. At the same time, these organizations could be primary beneficiaries of the findings of this work that might be incorporated into educational programs for HRM professionals.

Notes

1 Only 11 percent of 156 HRM professionals surveyed indicated that behavior was the primary focus of their performance appraisal systems (Freedman, 2006).
2 Communication research dealing with explanatory discourse might be able to provide assistance to HRM professionals in structuring more understandable explanations of wage and benefit programs (e.g., see Huang & Reiser, 2012, on worked examples; Inoue, 2009, on explanatory instruction).
3 Sociolinguistics is based on the notion that conversation is managed jointly—in other words, the co-interactants' language is coordinated and reciprocal (i.e., the words spoken by one conversational participant prime the other participant to respond in a particular way). "When two people are talking, their

communicative behaviors are patterned and coordinated, like a dance" (Niederhoffer & Pennebaker, 2002, p. 338).
4 Function words (e.g., articles and prepositions) do not contain semantic information, are context independent and frequently occurring, and are non-consciously produced, making it difficult to manipulate one's function-word patterns.
5 Earlier, Goia, Donnelion, and Sims (1989) created a database of 96 videotaped simulated performance appraisals that was used in a series of studies involving interpretive analyses of the speech acts on which the interactions were based.

Bibliography

Argenti, P.F. (1998). Strategic employee communications. *Human Resource Management, 37,* 199–206.
Armstrong, S., & Appelbaum, M. (2003). *Stress-free performance appraisals.* Franklin Lakes, NJ: Career Press.
Asmuß, B. (2008). Performance appraisal interviews: Preference organization in assessment sequences. *Journal of Business Communication, 45*(4), 408–429.
Berelson, B. (1952). *Content analysis in communication research.* Glencoe, IL: Free Press.
Bernardin, H.J., & Orban, J.A. (1990). Leniency effect as a function of rating format, purpose for appraisal, and rater individual differences. *Journal of Business and Psychology, 5*(2), 197–211.
Bernardin, H.J., Orban, J.A., & Carlyle, J.J. (1981). Performance rating as a function of trust in appraisal and rater individual differences. *Academy of Management Proceedings,* 311–316.
Bingham, W.V.D., & Freyd, M. (1926). *Procedures in employment psychology: A manual for developing scientific methods for vocational selection.* New York: A.W. Shaw.
Cleveland, J.N., Lim, A.S., & Murphy, K.R. (2007). Feedback phobia? Why employees do not want to give or receive performance feedback. In J. Langan-Fox, C.L. Cooper, & R.J. Klimoski (Eds.), *Research companion to the dysfunctional workplace: Management challenges and symptoms* (pp. 168–186). Northampton, MA: Edward Elgar.
Clifton, J. (2012). Conversation analysis in dialogue with stocks of interactional knowledge: Facework and appraisal interviews. *Journal of Business Communication, 49*(4), 283–311.
Dibble, J.L., & Levine, T.R. (2010). Breaking good and bad news: Direction of the MUM effect and senders' cognitive representations of news valence. *Communication Research, 37*(5), 703–722.
Downs, T.M. (1992). Superior and subordinate perceptions of communication during performance appraisal interviews. *Communication Research Reports, 9*(2), 153–159.
Fletcher, C. (2001). Performance appraisal and management: The developing research agenda. *Journal of Occupational & Organizational Psychology, 74*(4), 473–488.
Freedman, A. (2006, August). Balancing values, results in reviews. *Human Resource Executive, 20,* 62–63.
Giles, H., Coupland, J., & Coupland, N. (1991). Accommodation theory: Communication, context, and consequence. In H. Giles, J. Coupland, & N. Coupland (Eds.), *Contexts of accommodation: Developments in applied sociolinguistics* (pp. 1–68). Cambridge: Cambridge University Press.
Goia, D.A., Donnelion, A., & Sims, H.P. (1989). Communication and cognition in appraisal: A tale of two paradigms. *Organization Studies, 10*(4), 503–530.
Golembiewski, R.T., & McConkie, M. (1975). The centrality of interpersonal trust in group processes. In C.L. Cooper (Ed.), *Theories of group processes* (pp. 131–185). New York: John Wiley.
Gonzales, A.L., Hancock, J.T., & Pennebaker, J.W. (2010). Language style matching as a predictor of social dynamics in small groups. *Communication Research, 37*(1), 3–19.
Gordon, M.E., & Miller, V.D. (2012). *Conversations about job performance: A communication perspective on the appraisal process.* New York: Business Expert Press.
Gordon, M.E., & Stewart, L.P. (2009). Conversing about performance: Discursive resources for the appraisal interview. *Management Communication Quarterly, 22*(3), 473–501.
Grote, D. (1996). *The complete guide to performance appraisal.* New York: AMACOM Books.
Huang, X., & Reiser, R.A. (2012). The effect of instructional explanations and self-explanation prompts in worked examples on student learning and transfer. *International Journal of Instructional Media, 39*(4), 331–344.

Inoue, N. (2009). Rehearsing to teach: Content-specific deconstruction of instructional explanations in pre-service teacher training. *Journal of Education for Teaching, 35*(1), 47–60.

Jawahar, I.M., & Williams, C.R. (1997). Where all the children are above average: The performance appraisal purpose effect. *Personnel Psychology, 50*(4), 905–925.

Jenkins, J.G. (1935). *Psychology in business and industry: An introduction to psychotechnology.* New York: John Wiley & Sons.

Jo, S., & Shim, S.W. (2005). Paradigm shift of employee communication: The effect of management communication on trusting relationships. *Public Relations Review, 31*(2), 277–280.

Kacmar, K.M., Wayne, S.J., & Wright, P.M. (2009). Subordinate reactions to the use of impression management tactics and feedback by the supervisor. *Journal of Managerial Issues, 21*(4), 498–517.

Kavanaugh, M.J. (1989). How'm I doin'? I have a need and a right to know. In C.A.B. Osigweh (Ed.), *Managing employee rights and responsibilities* (pp. 175–185). New York: Quorum Books.

Kikoski, J.F. (1998). Effective communication in the performance appraisal interview: Face-to-face communication for public managers in the culturally diverse workplace. *Public Personnel Management, 27*, 491–513.

Kluger, A.N., & DeNisi, A. (1996). The effects of feedback intervention on performance: A historical review, a meta-analysis, and a preliminary feedback intervention theory. *Psychological Bulletin, 119*(2), 254–284.

Lawler, E.E. (1971). *Motivation in work organization.* Monterey, CA: Brooks/Cole.

Lawler, E.E., Benson, G.S., & McDermott, M. (2012). *Performance management and reward systems.* [Publication G 12–10 (617)]. University of Southern California, Center for Effective Organizations. Retrieved from http://ceo.usc.edu/pdf/G12-10.pdf.

Linna, A., Elovainio, M., Van den Bos, K., Kivimäki, M., Pentti, J., & Vahtera, J. (2012). Can usefulness of performance appraisal interviews change organizational justice perceptions? A 4-year longitudinal study among public sector employees. *International Journal of Human Resource Management, 23*(7), 1360–1375.

Longnecker, C.O. (2005). Dysfunctional performance appraisals. In S. Cartwright (Ed.), *Blackwell encyclopedia of management* (2nd ed., p. 102). Oxford: Blackwell.

Maddux, W.W., Mullen, E., & Galinsky, A.D. (2008). Chameleons bake bigger pies and take bigger pieces: Strategic behavioral mimicry facilitates negotiation outcomes. *Journal of Experimental Social Psychology, 44*(2), 461–468.

Mani, B.G. (2002). Performance appraisal systems, productivity, and motivation: A case study. *Public Personnel Management, 31*(2), 141–159.

Mayer, R.C., Davis, J.H., & Schoorman, F.D. (1995). An integrative model of organizational trust. *Academy of Management Review, 20*(3), 709–734.

Meyer, H.H., Kay, E., & French, J.R.P. (1965). Split roles in performance appraisal. *Harvard Business Review, 43*(1), 123–129.

Mourand, D. (1996). Dominance, deference, and egalitarianism in organizational interaction: A socio-linguistic analysis of power and politeness. *Organization Science, 7*(5), 544–556.

Niederhoffer, K., & Pennebaker, J.W. (2002). Linguistic style matching in social interaction. *Journal of Language & Social Psychology, 21*(4), 337–360.

Peräkyliä, A., & Vehviläinen, S. (2003). Conversation analysis and the professional stocks of interactional knowledge. *Discourse & Society, 14*(6), 727–750.

Pichler, S. (2012). The social context of performance appraisal and appraisal reactions: A meta-analysis. *Human Resource Management, 51*(5), 709–732.

Posthuma, R.A., Campion, M.C., Masimova, M., & Campion, M.A. (2013). A high performance work practices taxonomy: Integrating the literature and directing future research. *Journal of Management, 39*(5), 1184–1220.

Rabey, G. (2001). Tracking performance. *New Zealand Management, 48*(4), 60–61.

Read, W. (1962). Upward communication in industrial hierarchies. *Human Relations, 15*(1), 3–16.

Roberts, K.H., & O'Reilly, C.A. III. (1974). Measuring organizational communication. *Journal of Applied Psychology, 59*(3), 321–326.

Sacks, H. (1992). *Lectures on conversation, Volumes I and II.* Edited by G. Jefferson. Oxford: Blackwell.

Scissors, L., Gill, A., & Gergle, D. (2009, May 22). "You can trust me," "I can trust you": Linguistic accommodation and trust in text based CMC. Paper presented at the Annual Conference of the International Communication Association, Chicago, IL.

Scott, W.D., & Clothier, R.C. (1925). *Personnel management: Principles, practices, and point of view.* New York: A.W. Shaw.

Sibson Consulting. (2010). *Results of the 2010 study of the state of performance management.* Retrieved from www.sibson.com/publications-and-resources/surveys-studies/?id=1537.

Snow, A.J. (1930). *Psychology in business relations.* New York: McGraw-Hill.

Thomas, G.F., Zolin, R., & Hartman, J.L. (2009). The central role of communication in developing trust and its effect on employee involvement. *Journal of Business Communication, 46*(3), 287–310.

Tourish, D. (2006). The appraisal interview reappraised. In O. Hargie (Ed.), *Handbook of communication skills* (3rd ed., pp. 505–530). London: Routledge.

Whitener, E.M., Brodt, S.E., Korsgaard, M.A., & Werner, J.M. (1998). Managers as initiators of trust: An exchange relationship framework for understanding managerial trustworthy behavior. *Academy of Management Review, 23*(3), 513–530.

Willemyns, M., Gallois, C., & Callan, V.J. (2003). Trust me, I'm your boss: Trust and power in supervisor-supervisee communication. *International Journal of Human Resource Management, 14*(1), 117–127.

Woehr, D.J., & Huffcutt, A.I. (1994). Rater training for performance appraisal: A quantitative review. *Journal of Occupational and Organizational Psychology, 67*(3), 189–205.

Yoder, D. (1938). *Personnel and labor relations.* New York: Prentice-Hall.

11

LEADERSHIP, INGRATIATION, AND UPWARD COMMUNICATION IN ORGANIZATIONS

Dennis Tourish

The idea of leadership has long been extolled as "the" solution to competitive disadvantage and the need for further economic growth. Human resource management (HRM) departments in many organizations encourage senior managers to invest huge sums in leadership development—up to $50 billion annually throughout the world, according to at least one estimate (Day, 2012). The premise is that this will improve the practice of leadership and so enhance the effectiveness of the organizations concerned. Surprisingly, however, there is precious little evidence that development does have these effects, and few organizations attempt to assess its impact on their performance, as opposed to the satisfaction levels of those participating in it. Rather, there is plentiful evidence to suggest that the actual practice of leadership often falls short of what is required. A survey of 1,500 managers in the UK found that almost a third rated the quality of leadership in their organizations as "poor." International studies follow a similar pattern. A survey of Canadian CEOs found 70% of them asserting that leaders in their companies were only "fair to weak" in building strong teams, securing employee commitment, and making employees feel valued (Tourish, 2012).

More generally, confidence in leaders, whether in business, politics, or elsewhere, is low. The concentration of power in leadership hands over recent decades did not save us from the recent recession and, indeed, may well have contributed to both it and many associated business scandals. We have not yet emerged from the shadow of Enron's corrupt collapse in 2001; the bankruptcy of Lehman Brothers in 2008; the spectacular mishaps of those who led General Motors, Ford, and Chrysler to ruin; the sluggish response of European leaders to the Euro crisis; or the near paralysis of the political system in the United States.

Recognizing this, I suggest that leadership, at least as it has been traditionally envisaged, is a key part of the problems that many organizations now face, rather than the solution. Less may be best. Drawing on process-based (Langley & Tsoukas, 2010) and communication-based (Putnam & Nicotera, 2009) theories of organization, I challenge dominant frames of reference within the debates about leadership. In particular, I argue that transformational leadership (Bass & Riggio, 2006)—the dominant approach in leadership studies over recent decades—suffers from an implicit model that puts "the leader" at the center of more or less solid hierarchies and stable networks in which greater agency is attached to the leader than to followers. Although space prevents a detailed exploration of this issue, I suggest that this bias is widespread within leadership studies. It extends to those approaches that express a more emancipatory intent and that acknowledge a greater role for followers—including notions of servant leadership, authentic leadership, spirituality leadership, and the Vroom-Jago-Yetton contingency model. These continue to affirm the power of leaders to declare where the boundaries should be imposed around such concepts as participation and organizational justice, though they sometimes suggest that employees might be "consulted" about these issues. Although much less starkly and with more caveats than can be found with transformational models, differential power relations between leaders and followers are still legitimized, confirming the concentration of decision making and its associated privileges in the hands of managerial elites (Tourish, 2013). Such concentration contradicts and undermines the emphasis on empowerment, engagement, and participation by employees that we also find in the HRM literature. Accordingly, more challenges to the dominant transformational model are now emerging. One authoritative overview has concluded that "the concept is seriously flawed" (Van Knippenberg and Sitkin, 2013, p. 45), with imprecise definitions of key terms, poor or invalid statements of causality, insufficient theorization of its claimed effects, and fatally flawed measurement problems with the main survey instrument used to probe its effectiveness. We can and must do better.

Utilizing the analytic lens of dissent in organizations, I conceptualize leadership in terms of networks of interaction between organizational actors. This suggests that such networks are likely to reach more effective decisions when follower dissent is institutionalized into the theory and practice of leadership (Zoller & Fairhurst, 2007). It follows that the premium often placed on organizational consensus is misplaced since it tends to view follower dissent as "resistance to be overcome" rather than useful feedback. This encourages excessive leader agency, even when the perspective in question appears to advocate the opposite. A more process- and communication-oriented perspective of leadership yields theoretical and applied possibilities beyond what the field has so far offered.

Accordingly, I explore the extent to which transformational theories of leadership give undue emphasis to leader agency at the expense of other organizational actors. My argument is that this focus is inconsistent with communication perspectives that emphasize how multiple organizational actors co-construct organizational realities and any higher purposes to which they give rise. Having problematized leadership in this way, I then consider how communication-based perspectives can provide a useful rejoinder to the widespread calls that we face for "better" and more "effective" leadership.

Leader Agency (at Expense of) Followers

Extant models of leadership tend to unreflexively privilege leader agency over that of other organizational actors. As Banks (2008, p. 11) puts it:

> Conventionally, leaders show the way, are positioned in the vanguard, guide and direct, innovate, and have a vision for change and make it come to actuality. Followers on the other hand conventionally track the leader from behind, obey and report, implement innovations and accept leaders' vision for change.

It tends to be assumed that visionary leadership is powerful, exciting, and necessary, with leaders acting as a force for good whose efforts invariably produce positive outcomes

(Collinson, 2012). Much of this attributional process is vested in the persona of the CEO. Their charisma, reputation, and symbolic power are assumed to impact positively on corporate reputation (Cravens, Oliver, & Ramamoorti, 2003) and firm performance (Pollach & Kerbler, 2011). Influential practitioner journals such as *Harvard Business Review* regularly devote space to the need for "better" leadership. They provide forums in which influential CEOs proclaim their business "secrets" and methods of doing management as models that should be more universally applied. Transformational leadership theory, in particular, stresses how charismatic leaders can inspire, intellectually stimulate, and radically reorder the values and actions of others (Bass, 1999). It is an approach that has long been criticized for seeing organizational influence in unidirectional terms (that is, flowing from leaders to more or less compliant followers, who are expected to applaud rather than challenge what is on offer), advocating the achievement of corporate cohesion and a monocultural environment to the detriment of internal dissent and exaggerating the role of charismatic visionaries in the achievement of corporate goals (Tourish & Pinnington, 2002).

Hansen, Ibarra, and Peyer (2010) provide a typical example. They surveyed 2,000 CEOs world-wide to identify, in their article's title, "The best-performing CEOs in the world." The key question this seeks to address is, "Who led firms that, on the basis of stock returns, outperformed other firms in the same country and industry?" (p. 107). The point here is not whether—or to what extent—leadership makes a difference to organizational performance, however narrowly such performance is defined. Rather, total agency is here invested in the leader. Is this really accurate or wise? However brilliant a leader may be, he or she can only accomplish marvelous things with the help of many others. We cannot present leaders as miracle workers who must have absolute power and still create organizations of turned on, motivated, and involved workers who believe they too can make a difference. If leaders are all-powerful magicians, there is little need for anyone else to take much responsibility for ensuring organizational success. There is also little need for leaders to pay serious attention to the input of others, if any is offered. Rather, the assumption remains largely intact that organizational leaders need "to do the same things they always have done—demand compliance from those in less powerful positions" (Stohl & Cheney, 2001, p. 387).

Impact of Leadership Theory on Practice

The theories of leadership discussed here see agency primarily in terms of the behaviors of leaders—what might be viewed as a bias toward omnipotence. But if some people in organizations are omnipotent, it tends to follow that others are impotent. I suggest here that there is a relationship between such theories and the world of practice, with largely destructive consequences. The idea that theories can influence human behavior is well documented. For example, it has been found that after studying economics, however briefly, students become greedier. They then develop positive views of their own greedy behavior (Wang, Malhotra, & Murnighan, 2011).

I suggest here that the dominant approach to leadership theory discussed earlier can have a similar harmful effect on practice. Tourish, Craig, and Amernic (2010) discussed how many leading business schools prioritize transformational models of leadership in their MBA programs. This encourages them to over-promise how well developed as leaders their graduates will be and thus risks incubating hubris. Delves Broughton's (2010) account of his two years as an MBA student at Harvard Business School (HBS) offers support for this analysis, documenting in fine detail how students are persistently assured of their elite status as future business leaders who will transform the world. Many of them arrive already primed with this conviction. The HBS approach seems likely to elevate their self-belief to even greater heights, thus penalizing humility—arguably, a key requirement for the more participatory and effective styles of decision making that are promoted in the HRM literature and popularized in a number of influential practitioner-oriented texts (e.g., Collins, 2001). This relative neglect is all the more remarkable given the volume of work that has documented the prevalence of hubristic leadership practices and chronicled its effects on individuals (Aasland, Skogstad, Notelaers, Nielsen, & Einarsen, 2010), whole organizations (Tourish & Vatcha, 2005), and wider economic systems (Kerr & Robinson, 2012). It is difficult to reconcile such work with the mainstream emphasis on unbounded leader agency, generally regarded in an unproblematic manner. Moreover, when inflated expectations of agency collide with the messy reality of a complex world that refuses to conform to the norms of HBS case studies, the strain for stressed followers and anxious leaders is likely to be considerable.

The Liberating Potential of Followership?

One response to these tensions has been an increased focus on the notion of "followership." However, there is little conceptual clarity on what this means and how it might offset excessive leader agency in organizations. While there has been some suggestion that followership is consistent with the notion of "participants" or "collaborators" (Uhl-Bien, 2006), in practice the term remains little more than a synonym for "subordinate" (Crossman & Crossman, 2011). Subordinates are conceived as those "who have less power, authority and influence than do their superiors and who therefore usually, but not invariably, fall into line" (Kellerman, 2008, p. xix). Thus, scholars frequently invoke the term "followership," but do so in a manner that continues to reify and naturalize hierarchy, thereby reaffirming leader agency. Accordingly:

> Followership is a relational role in which followers have the ability to influence leaders and contribute to the improvement and attainment of group and organizational objectives. It is primarily a hierarchically upwards influence. (Carsten, Uhl-Bien, West, Patera, & McGregor, 2010, p. 559)

Here, asymmetrical power is taken for granted. It is simply assumed that "group" and "organizational," as opposed to sectional, objectives exist and that leaders are the prime arbiters of what they should be—albeit while remaining open to an unspecified degree of influence. Moreover, followership is viewed as being what *assists* in the "improvement" and "attainment" of such objectives, rather than what might fundamentally interrogate them. It follows that dissent, critical upward feedback from employees to organizational leaders, and resistance are likely to be dysfunctional and are viewed as somehow incompatible with the notion of "good" followership.

Thus, a tendency to downplay the value of dissent remains deeply ingrained. For example, Agho (2009) explored the perspective of senior business directors on what they thought would be desirable behaviors for followers and leaders. While they found that honesty and competence were highly valued for both, they also found that the directors felt that it was even more important for followers to show dependability, loyalty, and cooperation. This is a typically subordinate conception of followership, with it evidently being viewed in terms of how well people translate the visions/orders of leaders into practice. Notions of challenge and independent follower agency are, once more, conspicuous by their absence.

All this suggests that discourse around leadership is fraught with contradiction. This has led some to question the extent to which it is a useful analytical concept at all. But, while there may be no "essence" of leadership, and while there may be a tendency to label many "mundane" day-to-day managerial activities as leadership for various reasons (Alvesson & Sveningsson, 2003), my primary purpose in this chapter is not to add to the general burden of critique. Rather, it is to explore the degree to which process and communication perspectives can move the field on from a largely futile search for the essence of leadership and reveal rather more about how leadership is coproduced through the linguistic and other interactions of organizational actors. This may make it possible to develop ideas about leadership theory and practice that reveal a more nuanced picture of leadership in which it is neither completely emancipatory nor wholly repressive of widespread agency within organizations. This can help rebalance our view of agency in leader-follower interactions and, therefore, contribute to forms of organizing that are less likely to inflict social, organizational, and economic harm.

Toward a Process and Communication Perspective of Leadership

Process perspectives recognize that "the organization is constituted by the interaction processes among its members" (Langley & Tsoukas, 2010, p. 4). Consistent with this view, some communication theorists have suggested that we replace the notion of organization as a single entity by one in which it is constituted "by its emergence as an actor in the texts of the people for whom it is a present interpreted reality" (Robichaud, Giroux, & Taylor, 2004, p. 630). Interlocking patterns of communication can therefore be viewed as the driving force behind many organizational phenomena, including leadership.

The study of dissenting or critical communication from followers to leaders is a useful illustration. Much of the literature on employee "voice" focuses on those forms of expression most calculated to assist in the implementation of goals that, although determined by managers, are assumed to express a unitarist interest (Morrison, 2011). When a broader approach is adopted, scholars often report that nonleaders typically find their opportunities for dissent from leaders constrained (Kassing, 2011). This has been described as the "hierarchical mum effect" (Bisel, Messersmith, & Kelley, 2012, p. 128) and can be seen as a situation in which "moments of contestation are precluded by power imbalances" (Deetz & McClellan, 2009, p. 446). But to stress only this misses crucial processes of co-construction that also occur. For example, ingratiating behavior by followers, in which they exaggerate how much they agree with the opinions of leaders, contributes to exaggerated self-belief, narcissism, and the adoption of ultimately destructive forms of leader action (Tourish & Robson, 2006). In essence, leaders who receive too much positive feedback tend to develop an unrealistic sense of how well their organizations are doing and how well they are performing as leaders. They also experience personally negative outcomes from the dynamic of ingratiation. One study, among many similar studies, has found compelling evidence that poor performance, resulting from the behavior of CEOs who have internalized the overly positive feedback delivered by their followers, increases the likelihood of them being fired (Park, Westphal, & Stern, 2011).

We can see here that the identity (and fates) of leaders as leaders, and that of followers as followers, is the result of a mutually constitutive interaction between the two. For followers, the decision not to offer critical feedback is a demonstration of agency manifest in silence, based on an often justified calculation of self-interest. But silence remains a form of communication and, hence, has a co-constructive impact on its recipients in formal positions of leadership. Organizational actors can never fully relinquish the power to manage meaning since any attempt to abstain from communication itself becomes a form of communication. In Fairhurst's (2007) terms, drawing on a Foucauldian perspective, this would recast leaders as the subjects of influence attempts by others, rather than, for example, "change masters" who make things happen to other people. In essence, this approach suggests that organizational phenomena, including leadership, are regarded "as (re)created through interacting agents embedded in sociomaterial practices, whose actions are mediated by institutional, linguistic, and objectual artefacts" (Langley & Tsoukas, 2010, p. 9). Leadership style is thus often the product of the behaviors adopted by subordinates—a finding reported by leadership psychologists many years ago (Lowin & Craig, 1968).

The view of leadership that emerges from a processual communication perspective is more inclined to see it as an unstable, continuously evolving social construction embedded in what Gergen (2010) has characterized as "turbulent streams or conversational flows" (p. 57). Once leadership is conceived in these terms, it ceases to be a discrete "event," an observable interaction within organizational structures or a unidirectional flow of influence in which A has a causal impact on B. Rather, it is a communicatively organized, fluid process of co-orientation and co-construction between myriad organizational actors; its "essence" varies of necessity between each occasion of its occurrence. There is no essence of leadership waiting to be discovered and then summarized in formal definitions or lists of competencies and desired behaviors that are torn from particular social, organizational, and temporal contexts. It follows that discursive closure is neither a desirable outcome of leadership practice nor of leadership theorizing. Leadership is inherently protean if it is anything: a shape-shifting phenomenon that is highly sensitive to context, actor agency in its widest possible sense, and the discursive resources we employ to generate sensemaking in ourselves and others.

This suggests that leadership theories and practices should place more stress on the promotion of dissent, difference, and the facilitation of alternative viewpoints than the promotion of an organizational view wholly originating in the perspectives and values of formal leaders. In turn, followership is conceived in terms of differentiation and alternative positioning while leadership is seen as those practices that facilitate such creative expression. Overt consensus is likely to mark covert dissent since it is unlikely that followers will ever feel completely free to express the full range of their disagreements with leaders. The illusion of such consensus can therefore be held to denote leadership practices that are insufficiently sensitive to follower feedback, rather than a rational endpoint of healthy information exchange processes. While leadership actions that only facilitate the creative expression of divergent viewpoints would be likely to undermine cohesion in a manner at least as destructive as that delivered by excessive conformity, *the approach outlined here simply argues that leadership should be rebalanced so that more (but not exclusive) emphasis is placed on communication processes that validate dissent.* This has profound implications for both practice and further research, to which I now turn.

Implications for Practice and Research

Among the major implications for practice of this approach, I would highlight the following key points.

Experiment With Both Upward and 360-Degree Appraisal

Such practices are no longer regarded as revolutionary and are commonly employed in many leading corporations, including AT&T, the Bank of America, Caterpillar, GTE, and General Electric.

They are a powerful means of institutionalizing feedback. Moreover, there is growing evidence to suggest that they genuinely stimulate more focused self-development activities (Mabey, 2001). It is of course vital that the underlying organizational culture is genuinely supportive and that the feedback obtained is utilized to shape changes in behavior. Otherwise, both sides grow discouraged and give up on their relationship. Disappointment is more likely to occur when such efforts are freighted with overoptimistic expectations and the need to transform the wider organizational culture is not recognized. But, implemented with a realistic grasp of what can be achieved and a determination to tackle whatever obstacles arise, both upward and 360-degree appraisal can make a major contribution to the creation of a more open and honest communication climate between leaders and others (Tourish, 2005).

Managers Should Familiarize Themselves with the Basics of Ingratiation Theory

Senior managers, in particular, should recognize that they will be on the receiving end of too much feedback that is positive and too little that is critical, whatever their intentions. While increased awareness never solves a problem by itself, it is an essential first step. Managers at all levels need to become more aware of ingratiation dynamics, of their own susceptibility to its effects, and of the most effective responses to adopt in dealing with it. Such awareness forms part of the ABCs of emotional literacy. Managers without it risk building catastrophically imbalanced relationships with their people.

Research here is crucial. A great deal of communication research is available on direct ingratiation tactics (e.g., complimenting others). However, there are also promising avenues of research that focus on indirect tactics such as associating the target of ingratiation with other obviously successful individuals (Tal-Or, 2010). Given the increasing structural reliance on teams in organizations and the consequent greater familiarity of employees with each other's work, communication researchers might well examine the effects of such indirect tactics in these social environments. In turn, this can inform further improvements in practice.

Positive Feedback Should Be Subject to the Same, or Greater, Scrutiny Than Negative Feedback

Because positive feedback tends to predominate, managers will give it undue attention, and they will then go on to develop a dangerously rose-tinted view of the climate within their own organizations. In turn, this means that key problems remain off the agenda and, therefore, will grow worse. Managers should adopt a thoroughly questioning attitude to all feedback from those with a lower status and should treat feedback that is unremittingly positive in tone with considerable skepticism. Management meetings should combat the tendency to bask in positive feedback and instead should focus on a regular agenda of questions such as the following:

- What problems have come to our attention recently?
- What criticisms have we received about the decisions we are taking?
- Are the criticisms valid, partially or completely? What should we change in response to them?
- How can we get more critical feedback into our decision-making processes?

Flattery is best thought of as a nonmonetary bribe. It preys on similar weaknesses. This may be gratifying—most of us are more vulnerable to the seductive power of flattery than we like to think. But it poses a serious problem. What happens when strategies wrought by managers are seriously in error, as many of them inevitably are? Flattery constitutes a perfumed trap for decision makers. Managers should therefore ask themselves: What does this person have to gain by flattering me? And what do they have to lose by disagreeing with me? Empirical research into all these issues, including how managers can improve their resistance to overly positive feedback, is clearly required.

Managers Should Seek Out Opportunities for Regular Formal and Informal Contact With Staff at All Levels

This should replace reliance on official reports, written communiqués, or communication mediated through various management layers. Informal interaction is more likely to facilitate honest, two-way communication; provide managers with a more accurate impression of life and opinions at all levels of their organization; and open up new opportunities for both managers and staff to influence each other. "Back to the Floor" initiatives are increasingly recognized as a useful means of achieving this. A key focus during such contact should be the search for critical feedback. As a rule of thumb, the more reliant a manager is on official channels of communication, the more likely it is that he or she will be out of touch with the mood of his or her people.

This is a fertile area for further investigation. The "law of N-squared" proposes that with more and more people in a given organization, the number of potential links in a network organization increases geometrically and soon exceeds everyone's capacity for communicative action (Krackhardt, 1994). While the need for more frequent and informal communication between those with greater authority and those with less is obvious, there is a pressing need for more research into how this can be accomplished in the time-starved environments in which most of us work. We need to know more about precisely how much of such communication is effective, what forms it takes, and how managers can balance it against the other conflicting demands on their resources.

Promote Systems for Greater Participation in Decision Making

Participation involves the creation of structures that empower people and enables them to collaborate in activities that go beyond the minimum coordination efforts characteristic of much work practice (Stohl & Cheney, 2001). In general, people should be encouraged to make more decisions on their own. Open, information-based tactics are critical for success. It is important that employees are fully involved in such efforts, rather than simply presented with senior management's vision of the systems it thinks are required to produce it. Lessons can be drawn from General Electric's famous "Work Out" program, where a series of assemblies brought together large cross-sections of a business unit to identify ways to dismantle bureaucracy (Sull, 2003). Its techniques could be adapted to address the communication issues identified in this chapter.

Create "Red Flag" Mechanisms for the Upward Transmission of Information That Cannot Be Ignored

Organizations rarely fail because they have inadequate information. But they will fail if vital information either does not reach the top or is ignored when it gets there. To prevent such a state of affairs, it is important to create the type of mechanisms proposed in this paper. In Box 1

I give an example of a communication system that achieved its aim of facilitating clear upward communication and thus ensured that important information reached the ears or desks it needed to reach. Organizations need to develop similar mechanisms, appropriate for their own circumstances, and rigorously pursue their implementation.

Creating Systems for Information Flow That Cannot Be Ignored

During the 1960s, while Werner von Braun was director of the Marshall Space Flight Center, Tompkins (2005) interviewed engineers about communication within the organization. "Monday notes" were the medium clearly favored by the respondents. These notes originated as a response to a request by von Braun of 24 key managers across several administrative units to prepare a one-page weekly memorandum concerning the problems and progress experienced. Von Braun read the submitted memos, initialed them, and added his own questions, suggestions, and praise. The managers' responses were arranged alphabetically in a package that was returned to all contributors.

Interestingly, a parallel communication practice was found to exist among the key managers, many of whom compiled their own version of Monday notes. Based on information supplied by their direct reports, some of which was collected in organized meetings, managers' "Friday reports" focused on important unit activities. Von Braun's reports were circulated down the line in a number of units. In short, a simple request had triggered a robust mechanism for the transmission of information and ensured that whatever was contained in the Monday notes was acted upon rather than ignored.

In a cautionary coda, the disasters involving NASA's two space shuttles, the Challenger and the Columbia, engendered serious study by various investigative bodies that produced several explanations for these mission failures. One of these placed the blame for the two catastrophes in part on the fact that systems such as the Monday notes had fallen into disuse. Without systems to generate the kind of critical feedback provided by the Monday notes, an overly optimistic perspective about the chances for mission success was created among senior managers, thus making NASA more willing to take risks.

Existing Communication Processes Should Be Reviewed to Ensure That They Include Requirements to Produce Critical Feedback

With few exceptions, team briefings emphasize the transmission of information from the top to the bottom. This is akin to installing an elevator capable of traveling only in one direction—downward. Team briefings should also include a specific requirement that problems and criticisms be reported up. Again, balance is vital. As already noted, exclusively critical feedback may be as damaging as exclusively positive feedback and may create a fearful climate dominated by the expectation of imminent catastrophe. No one can innovate, or even work with minimal effectiveness, if they confidently expect the imminent arrival of the four horsemen of the apocalypse. Nevertheless, with that proviso in mind, most organizations are a long way from having to worry about the risk of too much critical feedback disturbing the tranquility of those in top positions.

Train Supervisors to Be Open, Receptive, and Responsive to Employee Dissent

When supervisors behave in such a manner, they are signaling receptiveness to entire workgroups. However, training in the appropriate skills is often lacking. As with many other vital communication skills, it is frequently just assumed that managers will have access to the right tool kit. This optimistic assumption is unwarranted. The lack of appropriate communication skills on the part of top managers is one of the main reasons for the disconnect so frequently noted between the inspiring rhetoric of strategic visions and the mundane operational reality. We need more work by communication researchers into what skill sets most facilitate receptivity to critical feedback and what interventions help managers to best acquire the skills in question.

Power and Status Differentials Should Be Eliminated or, Where That Is Impossible, at Least Reduced

Status differentials can be reduced by blitzing some of the most visible symbols of privilege, such as reserved parking, executive dining rooms, and percentage salary increases far in excess of those obtained by other employees. A growing body of research suggests that excessive executive privilege undermines organizational cohesion and effectiveness. In particular, it promotes an "us versus them" mentality rather than one of "us against the competition" (Pfeffer, 1998). The risks with addressing this question are few, but the potential gains are immense.

The CEO, in Particular, Needs to Openly Model a Different Approach to the Receipt of Critical Communication and Ensure That Senior Colleagues Emulate This Openness

Organizations that take communication seriously are led by CEOs who take communication seriously. CEOs who are defensive, uncertain, closed to feedback, and dismissive of contrary opinions may indeed get their way—in the short term. At the very least, they will be gratified by effusive public statements of compliance. But coerced compliance is usually combined with private defiance. Ultimately, it produces a fractious relationship between senior managers and their staff. And organizations where managers and employees are at war with each other, rather than the competition, cannot conquer new markets. Without a clear lead on communication at the level of the CEO, it is unlikely that progress on the issues discussed here will be made.

All these points constitute a fertile field for further research. They view leadership as "an act of transmission *and* negotiated meaning" (Fairhurst & Connaughton, in press). We need a richer understanding of followership and the role of leadership development in promoting an acceptance of dissent in decision making. In these and other areas, communication scholars have much to do and much to offer.

Conclusion

Much has been promised by traditional models of leadership. But, as the Great Recession attests, little has been delivered. Yet this does not mean that the potency of leader-centric visions has diminished. As Lipman-Blumen (2008) observes, the following is often the case:

> crisis provokes followers to turn to God or human leaders willing to play God ... Followers, shaken to their foundations by a crisis for which they have no ready answers, seek protection from an all-knowing, strong leader. (p. 40)

The dangers are considerable and include the potential for a swing to authoritarian forms of leadership in both organizations and wider societies.

A different view of agency is central to any reimagining of leadership that can help avert such destructive outcomes and would better position the field of HRM to intervene positively in organizational debates about how to make productive and positive use of leadership. It is one that challenges the preoccupation with leader agency, including the hope that a leader will emerge who can offer a transcendental sense of purpose, save the planet—while, on the eighth day, doubling GDP. In doing so, it also recognizes how crucial agency is when it is vested in non-leaders, acknowledges the productive potential of dissent, and sees leadership and followership as co-constructed phenomena embedded in fluid social structures we have barely begun to understand.

Bibliography

Aasland, M., Skogstad, A., Notelaers, G., Nielsen, B., & Einarsen, S. (2010). The prevalence of destructive leadership behavior. *British Journal of Management, 21*, 438–452.

Agho, A. (2009). Perspectives of senior-level executives on effective followership and leadership. *Journal of Leadership and Organizational Studies, 16*, 159–166.

Alvesson, M., & Sveningsson, S. (2003). The great disappearance act: Difficulties in doing leadership. *Leadership Quarterly, 14*, 359–381.

Banks, S. (2008). The problems with leadership. In S. Banks (Ed.), *Dissent and the failure of leadership* (pp. 1–21). London: Edward Elgar.

Bass, B. (1999). Two decades of research and development in transformational leadership. *European Journal of Work and Organizational Psychology, 8*, 9–26.

Bass, B., & Riggio, R. (2006). *Transformational leadership.* London: Psychology Press.

Bisel, R., Messersmith, A., & Kelley, K. (2012). Supervisor-subordinate communication: Hierarchical mum effect meets organizational learning. *Journal of Business Communication, 49*, 128–147.

Carsten, M., Uhl-Bien, M., West, B., Patera, J., & McGregor, R. (2010). Exploring social constructions of followership: A qualitative study. *Leadership Quarterly, 21*, 543–562.

Collins, J. (2001). *Good to great: Why some companies make the leap . . . and others don't.* New York: Harper Business.

Collinson, D. (2012). Prozac leadership and the limits of positive thinking. *Leadership, 8*, 87–108.

Cravens, K., Oliver, E., & Ramamoorti, S. (2003). The reputation index: Measuring and managing corporate reputation. *European Management Journal, 21*, 201–212.

Crossman, B., & Crossman, J. (2011). Conceptualising followership—a review of the literature. *Leadership, 7*, 481–497.

Day, D. (2012). Leadership development. In A. Bryman, D. Collinson, K. Grint, B. Jackson, & M. Uhl-Bien (Eds.), *The Sage handbook of leadership* (pp. 37–50). London: Sage.

Deetz, S., & McClellan, J. (2009). Communication. In M. Alvesson, T. Bridgman, & H. Willmott (Eds.), *The Oxford handbook of critical management studies* (pp. 433–453). Oxford: Oxford University Press.

Delves Broughton, P. (2010). *What they teach you at Harvard Business School: My two years inside the cauldron of capitalism.* London: Penguin.

Fairhurst, G. (2007). *Discursive leadership.* London: Sage.

Fairhurst, G., & Connaughton, S. (in press). Leadership. In L. Putnam & D. Mumby (Eds.), *The Sage handbook of organizational communication.* London: Sage.

Gergen, K. (2010). Co-constitution, causality, and confluence: Organizing in a world without entities. In T. Hernes & S. Maitlis (Eds.), *Process, sensemaking and organization* (pp. 55–69). Oxford: Oxford University Press.

Hansen, M., Ibarra, H., & Peyer, U. (2010). The best-performing CEOs in the world. *Harvard Business Review, 88*, 104–113.

Kassing, J. (2011). *Dissent in organizations.* Cambridge: Polity.

Kellerman, B. (2008). *Followership: How followers are creating change and changing leaders.* Boston: Harvard Business Press.

Kerr, R., & Robinson, S. (2012). From symbolic violence to economic violence: The globalising of the Scottish banking elite. *Organization Studies, 33,* 247–266.

Krackhardt, D. (1994). Constraints on the interactive organization as an ideal type. In C. Heckscher & A. Donnellon (Eds.), *The post-bureaucratic organization: New perspectives on organizational change* (pp. 211–222). Thousand Oaks, CA: Sage.

Langley, A., & Tsoukas, H. (2010). Introducing "Perspectives on process organization studies." In T. Hernes & S, Maitlis (Eds.), *Process, sensemaking and organization* (pp. 1–26). Oxford: Oxford University Press.

Lipman-Blumen, J. (2008). Dissent in times of crisis. In S. Banks (Ed.), *Dissent and the failure of leadership* (pp. 37–52). London: Edward Elgar.

Lowin, A., & Craig, J. (1968). The influence of level of performance on managerial style: an experimental object lesson in the ambiguity of correlational data. *Organizational Behavior and Human Performance, 3,* 440–458.

Mabey, C. (2001). Closing the circle: participant views of a 360 degree feedback programme. *Human Resource Management Journal, 11,* 41–53.

Morrison, E. (2011). Employee voice behavior: Integration and directions for future research. *Academy of Management Annals, 5,* 373–412.

Park, S., Westphal, J., & Stern, I. (2011). Set up for a fall: The insidious effects of flattery and opinion conformity toward corporate leaders. *Administrative Science Quarterly, 56,* 257–302.

Pfeffer, J. (1998). *The human equation.* Boston: Harvard Business School Press.

Pollach, I., & Kerbler, E. (2011). Appearing competent: A study of impression management in U.S. and European CEO profiles. *Journal of Business Communication, 48,* 355–372.

Putnam, L., & Nicotera, A. (Eds.). (2009). *Building theories of organization: The constitutive role of communication.* London: Routledge.

Robichaud, D., Giroux, H., & Taylor, J. (2004). The metaconversation: The recursive property of language as a key to organizing. *Academy of Management Review, 29,* 617–634.

Stohl, C., & Cheney, G. (2001). Participatory processes/paradoxical practices. *Management Communication Quarterly, 14,* 349–407.

Sull, D. (2003). *Revival of the fittest.* Boston: Harvard Business School Press.

Tal-Or, N. (2010). Indirect ingratiation: Pleasing people by associating them with successful others and by praising their associates. *Human Communication Research, 36,* 163–189.

Tompkins, P. (2005). *Apollo, Challenger, Columbia—The decline of the space program: A study in organizational communication.* Los Angeles: Roxbury.

Tourish, D. (2005). Critical upward communication: Ten commandments for improving strategy and decision making. *Long Range Planning, 38,* 485–503.

Tourish, D. (2012). Developing leaders in turbulent times: Five steps towards integrating soft practices with hard measures of organizational performance. *Organizational Dynamics, 47,* 23–31.

Tourish, D. (2013). *The dark side of transformational leadership: A critical perspective.* London: Routledge.

Tourish, D., Craig, R., & Amernic, J. (2010). Transformational leadership education and agency perspectives in business school pedagogy: A marriage of inconvenience? *British Journal of Management, 21,* S40–S59.

Tourish, D., & Pinnington, A. (2002). Transformational leadership, corporate cultism and the spirituality paradigm: An unholy trinity in the workplace? *Human Relations, 55,* 147–172.

Tourish, D., & Robson, P. (2006). Sensemaking and the distortion of critical upward communication in organizations. *Journal of Management Studies, 43,* 711–730.

Tourish, D., & Vatcha, N. (2005). Charismatic leadership and corporate cultism at Enron: The elimination of dissent, the promotion of conformity and organizational collapse. *Leadership, 1,* 455–480.

Uhl-Bien, M. (2006). Relational leadership theory: Exploring the social processes of leadership and organizing. *Leadership Quarterly, 17,* 654–676.

Van Knippenberg, D., & Sitkin, S. (2013). A critical assessment of charismatic-transformational leadership research: Back to the drawing board? *Academy of Management Annals, 7*, 1–60.

Wang, L., Malhotra, D., & Murnighan, J. (2011). Economics education and greed. *Academy of Management Learning & Education, 10*, 643–660.

Zoller, H.M., & Fairhurst, G.T. (2007). Resistance leadership: The overlooked potential in critical organization and leadership studies. *Human Relations, 60*, 1331–1360.

12

CHANGE MANAGEMENT

Laurie Lewis

Implementing change in organizations is a widespread practice and a common topic of scholarship. Change may be heralded as inevitable and good or decried as something "everyone hates."

> Change can serve as means to address many important challenges . . . Change can also be wrong-headed, faddish, unnecessary, and a waste of resources. (Lewis, forthcoming, p. 1)

Bringing about change in practice, technology, process, or even the meanings associated with organizational activity or roles involves oftentimes complex and sophisticated practice, behaviors, and routines of many stakeholders. Those responsible for implementing change and countering intentional or unconscious resistance are expected to address stakeholders' reactions. Communication is an important means by which change implementers introduce, describe, persuade, support, and evaluate changes and change processes. It is also the chief means by which those opposed to or uncertain about changes resist, question, challenge, and seek support. Lewis's (2000) study of an international sample of organizational implementers found that implementers rated communication problems as among the most severe they encountered.

Human resource management (HRM) professionals are often tasked with the "people side" of change. They are expected to develop training, share information, facilitate learning of new skills and responsibilities, realign feedback and appraisal systems with new expectations brought on by change, and manage or forestall resistant attitudes of employees. HRM professionals may have little say in the adoption of new ideas, technologies, and processes and frequently are only consulted about implementation after the major decisions about changing have been made through budget, production schedules, and other bottom-line outcomes. Frequently, top-level managers view HRM professionals as having appropriate people skills to execute the decisions of upper management. And, given this bias in many organizations, HRM professionals may feel pressure to resolve such problems or feel hesitant to surface "people problems" up the chain of command since doing so might diminish their perceived competence by others (Lewis & Russ, 2012). When change management is delegated to HRM professionals, they are likely to feel pressure from upper management to make a change happen and pressure from employees to listen to their complaints, concerns, and questions about a change that they may not understand or necessarily view as worthwhile. This is a classic double-bind position of HRM change implementers: to make change happen while respecting concerns of employees.

This chapter focuses on three critical aspects of HRM professionals' communication with employees during change: (1) soliciting employee input about change; (2) disseminating information and contending with alternate framing of change; and (3) the importance of creating ways to surface and resolve perceived problems with change initiatives. These are critical roles for any change implementer—especially those who are focused on the "people side" of change.

Soliciting Input and Early Involvement

A significant and accumulating body of evidence suggests the importance of early, dispersed, and frequent solicitation of input during change processes (cf. Edmondson, Bohmer, & Pisano, 2001). Scholars and practitioners generally agree that asking for opinions, feedback, and reactions, as well as developing empowering strategies to involve stakeholders in decision making, is critically important throughout a change process (Lewis, Schmisseur, Stephens, & Weir, 2006). Reducing resistance is frequently cited as a rationale for soliciting early input. Some have argued that unaddressed negative attitudes about change will manifest in lack of change readiness, cynicism, poor coping, and resistance (Bouckenooghe, 2010). In addition to the potential for reducing resistance to change, scholars have documented other benefits of soliciting input, including increasing satisfaction of participants and increasing stakeholders' feelings of control (Bordia, Hobman, Jones, Gallois, & Callan, 2004; Bordia, Hunt, Paulsen, Tourish, & DiFonzo, 2004; Russ, 2011; Sagie, Elizur, & Koslowsky, 2001). Evidence also exists about the potential downside of forcing change without input solicitation (Lewis, 2006; Lines, 2007; Russ, 2008, 2009).

Armenakis and colleagues have explored "what change recipients consider when making their decision to embrace and support a change effort or reject and resist it" (Armenakis & Harris, 2009, p. 128). They define "readiness" as "organizational members' beliefs, attitudes, and intentions regarding the extent to which changes are needed and the organization's capacity to successfully make those changes" (Armenakis, Harris & Mossholder, 1993, p. 681). This suggests that the most beneficial practice for implementers is "creating readiness for change rather than waiting to reduce resistance" (Armenakis & Harris, 2009, p. 129). They argue that early communication—during the formative stages of a change initiative—is an ideal time to affect five key beliefs of stakeholders that (1) the change is necessary, (2) the change is the correct one for the situation, (3) the organization is capable of executing this change, (4) high-level decision makers are committed to this change, and (5) this change is good for the individual stakeholder. In early solicitation of input from employees (and other stakeholders), HRM professionals may build these five beliefs by discussing the evidence and decision processes that led decision makers to undertake the change.

So, for example, if employees engage in a discussion about problems and/or opportunities and provide their own assessments and input, they contribute to the decision makers' understandings of what goals and obstacles are related to the change initiative. They both are informing decisions and being informed by the discussion. A firmer belief in the "need for change" may arise than if employees were merely provided a rationale much later in the implementation process. Similarly, early communication and solicitation of employee input can have an impact on the other four beliefs.

Despite the potential usefulness of widespread input solicitation, many organizations emphasize downward dissemination of information over soliciting stakeholder input (Doyle, Claydon, & Buchanan, 2000; Lewis, 1999, 2006; Lewis, Richardson, & Hamel, 2003). Doyle et al. (2000) studied UK managers' reflections on past change efforts in their own organizations. They found that only 50% of respondents agreed with the following: "We have remained faithful to the principle of participative change management" (p. S65). Typically, in cases where input is sought, opportunities to participate are unequal across employees and other stakeholders (Lewis et al., 2003; Lewis & Russ, 2012). Implementers who are committed to involving the voices of stakeholders find it challenging to determine whom to invite to the conversation (Barge, Lee, Maddux, Nabring, & Townsend, 2008). Further, some stakeholders will find that they are invited "to the table," but their input may not be used in any instrumental way to affect the path or shape of the change effort. Neumann (1989) argued that employees' participation typically exhibits no direct influence over the primary organizational decision-making process. Further, Graetz and Smith (2010) note that a typical response to the voices of non–implementer stakeholders "is not to listen to, but to silence, dissident voices" (p. 137). Lewis and Russ (2012) argue the following:

> participatory methods are typically used to clarify, emphasize, and energize the predetermined path of the process . . . In using participative methods, implementers likely hope to alleviate misgivings, fears, and misinformation. However, implementers are rarely advised . . . actually to adopt suggestions, reconsider the wisdom to change, or empower stakeholders to adapt change in ways that depart from the implementers' original plans. (p. 272)

Scant research has addressed the manner in which HRM professionals or other implementers process input or the value they place on it. We know that some practice advice books stress the importance of creating channels for employees' "venting" (Lewis et al., 2006) but rarely articulate a means to analyze or consider input that is gathered. There are numerous potential models for soliciting input from stakeholders. Lewis (2011) argued that participation may be direct (individuals represent themselves) or indirect (through a representative), forced (role prescribed) or voluntary (individuals have choice of voice or silence), and formal (committees or task forces) or informal (water-cooler moments), with varying degrees of intentions. Additional factors such as timing and duration of participation (e.g., before or after major decision making) may have important influences on how participants' view these opportunities, how the input is received, and to which outcomes it leads for the organization, the stakeholders, and the change effort.

Lewis and Russ (2012) investigated ways in which HRM professionals utilized input solicitation during change. Symbolic- and resource-based models of input solicitation were explored. Symbolic participation creates an appearance of participation whereas a resource approach truly empowers stakeholders to have impact on the manner, rate, timing, and possibly even the wisdom of implementing a change (Lewis, 2011). The sense of "resource" that I (Lewis, 2011) and others advocate in organizational input solicitation aligns with Kuhn and Deetz's (2008) "ideal speech situation" (p. 188), which involves stakeholders in important decision making. This approach is characterized by (a) reciprocity for expression; (b) some equality in expression skills; (c) the setting aside of authority relations; (d) the open investigation of stakeholder positions and "wants" to ascertain their interests more freely; (e) open sharing of information and transparency of decision processes; and (f) the opening of fact and knowledge claims to redeterminization based on contestation of claims and advantaged modes of knowledge creation.

Lewis and Russ (2012) interviewed HRM professionals who were charged with change implementation in a variety of organizations. Interviewees were asked about their strategies for collecting and using stakeholder input and reported that employees who questioned or objected to the change tended to be characterized by the HRM professionals as self-motivated and/or emotionally opposed to the very idea of change. However, input of employees who were perceived as embracing the change was more welcomed. Lewis and Russ developed four models of approaches to soliciting and using input (open, restricted, political, and advisory) represented in their data. None of these models embraced Lewis's (2011) "widespread empowerment" model where solicitation of input involves stakeholders in important decision making, permits reciprocity in expression, and involves setting aside authority relations, open consideration of stakeholders' wants and interests, and open transparent processes. Rather, the dominant approach by the HRM professionals was the "restricted" model in which input was solicited from a narrow specific pool of stakeholders, with the chief goal of gaining support for the original change vision. At best, the advisory approach made use of input to forestall negative reactions or on occasion was used to alter the strategy of the change. Even in this approach, though, the HRM professionals reported avoiding "complainers."

The Lewis and Russ study is a first effort (as far as I am aware) to explore how HRM professionals or other change implementers regard input solicitation that is touted by many popular press advice books as a critical part of change communication. We should not conclude from these data that there are no existing healthy models of input solicitation in practice. However, future research should determine and document the methods, models, and approaches for gathering and using input during organizational change. Scholarship in organizational communication generally has accumulated a great deal of evidence suggesting the importance of early, ongoing, and empowering participative practices (cf. Kuhn, 2008; Kuhn & Deetz, 2008). Nonetheless, we understand very little about the pressures on HRM professionals and other implementers to listen to or ignore input that is offered; to incorporate suggestions or to forge ahead despite warning signs suggested by various stakeholders (including lower-level employees); or to reconsider change plans or to devote energy to persuading employees and others of the wisdom of original decisions. There is also great need to explore the ways in which potential providers of input might view invitations to participate.

> It is easy to imagine circumstances in which such participation could be politically risky or judged as strategically less effective . . . It might be viewed as more strategic to avoid calling out defects in a change and simply let the change fail and eventually be revoked. (Lewis & Russ, 2012, p. 288)

In related work, Kassing (2002, 2009), Garner (2009a, 2009b), and others examined the role of upward dissent in organizations in general and in the context of organizational change. Kassing (2009) studied multiple attempts at upward dissent. Subjects self-reported higher frequencies of direct factual appeals and solution presentation. They also reported that repeated attempts at dissent over time were more likely to involve face-threatening appeals of circumvention (i.e., going around their supervisor to speak to someone higher in the chain of command) and threatening resignation. Garner (2009a) found that the most frequently self-reported primary goals of dissent communication were obtaining information and getting advice on how to deal with a dissatisfying circumstance. This suggests that "resisting" change is not always what it appears to be at first glance. Some "resisters" may be attempting to make sense of the change or to merely cope with change.

There is a good deal of work left to do. Despite strong agreement about espoused philosophy that participative processes and input solicitation during change is beneficial, still to be determined is how to go about it and what contingencies predict the models that are adopted by practitioners with what results.

Disseminating Information and Framing Change

Dissemination of information is oftentimes the first task any HRM professional confronts in implementing change. Formally disseminating information has the potential to help clarify and explain the purpose and process of change, to create a common level of understanding about a change effort, and to help dispel inaccurate rumors (Lewis & Russ, 2012). Uncertainty is nearly always high during periods of change and typically involves strategic, structural, and job-related questions (Bordia, Hobman et al., 2004). HRM professionals typically become the "face" of change initiatives and are called upon to possess and disseminate appropriate types and amounts of information to relevant employee groups.

Typically, the initial information dissemination activity during change is the announcement of change—which may be "news" or may follow a good deal of rumor communication. Smeltzer and Zener (1994, 1995) investigated effective planned change announcements. Interviews with change implementers revealed that commonly perceived predictors of failure of change announcements are lack of a communication strategy, circulation of rumors, poor channel selection, lack of adapting a message to different audiences, use of euphemisms, and overly positive announcements (Smeltzer, 1991).

In general, the scholarly literature supports strategies by implementers to promote honesty and openness since it tends to engender more cooperativeness and enhanced ability of stakeholders to cope with change. For example, Schweiger and DeNisi (1991) examined the effect of realistic previews on the implementation of a merger. Early previews of the details of the merger and its process significantly lowered uncertainty, and they increased job satisfaction, commitment, perceived trustworthiness, honesty, and caring, as well as self-reported performance. These effects endured over time as the merger progressed. Evidence collected by Griffith and Northcraft (1996) suggests that messages that balanced positive and negative previews of a new technology significantly affected the performance of new users in a positive direction. Miller and Monge (1985) found that employees so valued information during change that they found even negative information more helpful than no information. Finally, other research established the importance of information sharing in the reduction of stress, uncertainty, and negative attitudes about change (Bird, 2007; Schweiger & DeNisi, 1991).

A primary reason to disseminate information is to provide insight and tactical knowledge so that employees understand new expectations, learn new procedures and practices, and have some sense of the purpose and direction of change. However, another reason for information sharing during change is to build trust. Communication plays a critical role in the development of trust in organizations (Thomas, Zolin, & Hartman, 2009). Lines, Selart, Espedal, and Johansen (2005) characterize organizational change as a "critical trust building or trust destroying episode in a long-term and ongoing relationship between the organization, represented by its management and non managerial employees" (p. 222). Lines et al. (2005) argue that the level of uncertainty and vulnerability experienced by organizational members during change may lead to an active processing of trust-relevant information and that openness matters in the determination of trust. Schoorman, Mayer, and Davis's (2007) model of organizational trust suggests that trust leads to risk taking. Thomas et al. (2009) found that both quality and quantity of information available in the organization enhances levels of employee trust.

An alternative to building trust is to create an environment where cynicism dominates. Cole, Bruch, and Vogel (2006, p. 463) define cynicism as "an evaluative judgment that stems from an individual's employment experiences." It is comprised of (1) a belief that the organization lacks integrity, (2) negative affect toward the organization, and (3) tendencies to use disparaging and critical behaviors toward organization. Cynicism can lead to pessimism about future change, particularly blaming management for one's pessimism or lack of success (Reichers, Wanuos, & Austin, 1997; Wanous, Reichers, & Austin, 2000).

Lewis, Laster, and Kulkarni's (in press) recent experiment examined the extent to which acknowledging some negative aspects of change in announcements heightens perceptions of implementers' honesty and trustworthiness and affects stakeholders' favorability toward the change. Previews of possible negatives did not increase *initial* favorability or *initial* judgments of the credibility of implementers. However, we speculate that the payoffs in credibility and trustworthiness may appear weeks or months later when previewed negatives show up in the experience of employees. Further, there was no evidence that previewing negatives harmed initial favorability toward the change. That is, recipients of the more negative announcement did not dislike the change more than those who received the more positive announcements (that did not acknowledge known downsides). Finally, high-risk change (perceived as potentially personally threatening to job security, personal relationships, and work productivity) created a challenging context for implementers to announce change.

Although change implementers should always consider the important strategies for information dissemination during change, they should not assume that more information is always the best or only solution to employee uncertainty. A few studies suggest that increasing information access is not the default strategy for all employees experiencing uncertainty during change. For example, Kramer, Dougherty, and Pierce (2004) examined uncertainty in the context of an airline acquisition. Their data revealed that individuals differed in the degrees to which they sought information. For some who were less active in seeking information, uncertainty was managed internally by discounting the available information that could have been sought as likely to be inaccurate, misleading, or unavailable and, therefore, not worth gathering. Further, a majority of the pilots sought information to create comfort, share rumors (even if they were thought to be false), and seek mutual support—which are not always the first purposes that practitioners may consider when designing outreach programs.

In crafting messages about change and selecting channels and means of disseminating information about change, HRM professionals also must become aware of competing sources of information and the framing around information that is provided by other stakeholders including employees. Following Weick (1979, 1995), organizations are socially constructed largely through the communicative interactions of internal and external stakeholders. The ways in which stakeholders talk about and frame the actions, purposes, practices, activities, systems, and structures of organizing come to define what the organization is and what it does. Similarly, organizational changes are subject to social construction through framing. Dewulf et al. (2009) distinguish between cognitive frames (which live in our heads) and interactional frames (which are dynamic processes of enacting and shaping meaning in ongoing interaction).

> Cognitive frames capture chunks of what people believe is external reality. From an interactional perspective, frames are co-constructions created by making sense of events in the external world. Framing thus constructs the meaning of the situations it addresses. (p. 164)

Scholars increasingly attend to the framing activities of managers and employees during change. For example, Cherim (2006) describes how managerial frames are appropriated by employees. Appropriation, in their conceptualization, constitutes acceptance of managers' frames and has implications for internalization of the values, goals, and means of achieving them. Employees' willing appropriation, reluctant appropriation, and partial appropriation are ways in which employees respond to managerial frames for change.

Framing may be achieved through storytelling. "Narratives are both about and become the change process" (Buchanan & Dawson, 2007, p. 669). Much of the interaction that follows a change announcement involves storytelling (Brown, Gabriel, & Gheradi, 2009; Brown & Humphreys, 2003). Employees use stories to capture the change experience, aid in creating a sense of change, influence reactions of others, and construct after-the-change accounts of what transpired. The potential power in employees' stories can "express the dominant concerns of employees (description), vent anxiety but also create stress (energy control), and garner support for collective action for or against organizational goals (system maintenance)" (Bordia, Jones, Gallois, Callan, & DiFonzo, 2006, p. 616). Research on change-related stories generally has focused on categorizing stories according to their elements and themes. This approach tends to consist of reports of the residual "sense made" of a change or the accounts given of "what is going on" at a particular point in time. In general, current research has not provided much insight into in situ creation and sharing of stories, the impact of the storyteller, and the contexts of storytelling, and/or impacts of repeatedly sharing a particular story.

The scholarship on dissemination of information and framing of change richly describes the themes, types of frames, and categories of stories. However, little is known about how stories, framing, and even dissemination of information are or can be used strategically to affect outcomes and understandings of changes. As various groups of managers, HRM professionals, and employees compete to create a reality of what change means in a particular organization, some perspectives will hold more power, will endure, and will affect actions taken. Just what dynamics direct such outcomes are largely unknown.

Surfacing and Facilitating Resolution to Perceived Problems

Resistance to change is presumed to be negative and dysfunctional in both the popular press and many scholarly publications. Scholars and practitioners alike often consider anything apart from enthusiastic endorsement and participation in change as a form of resistance. However, recent scholarship has noted the complexity associated with emotional, cognitive, and behavioral resistance. For example, we can array resistance from "subtler" forms to more "forceful" forms, including ambivalence, peer complaints, upward dissent, sabotage, and refusal to comply (Lewis, 2011). Probably the dominant characterization of resistance is that it constitutes an emotional "knee-jerk" reaction to change itself (just the idea of changing; Dent & Goldberg, 1999). Oreg (2003, 2006) and colleagues explored what they term "dispositional resistance," described as "an individual's tendency to resist or avoid making changes, to devalue change generally, and to find change aversive across diverse contexts and types of change" (Oreg, 2003, p. 680).

However, "often overlooked in the search for a personality-rooted explanation for resistance is focus on principled perspectives of stakeholders who value their organizations and stakes held by various stakeholders" (Lewis, forthcoming). An alternative is to consider that some "resistance" may be principled dissent—expression of dissatisfaction for reasons of justice, honesty, or organizational benefit (Graham, 1986). Some portion of what might be labeled as "resistance" may indeed represent valuable intelligence about potential flaws in change planning, the implementation of change, or the change itself offered with the best interests of the organization in mind.

Therefore, during change processes HRM professionals should help surface critiques and challenges of changes in order to guard the organization against making errors in the selection or implementation of a change. HRM professionals should *seek* principled dissent. In fact, regardless of the reasons for individual employees' objections or "resistance" to a change (even if rooted in selfish or political motives), they might be able to identify weaknesses, red flags, or problematic practices that deserve reconsideration. It is critical for HRM professionals to create a safe environment and channels to surface known or suspected issues, to consider them seriously, to facilitate discussion of problems and potential solutions, and to forward unsolvable issues up the chain. Unfortunately, as noted earlier, HRM professionals typically are considered more successful the fewer problems—especially unsolvable ones—that they upwardly share. Thus, they can be pressured, even rewarded, for discouraging the upward communication of identified objections or problems.

Lewis and Russ (2012) identified a tension between "fidelity" and "resource" goals as the main predictor of when HRM professionals embrace and value the input of employees or, alternatively, when they are more likely to seek only confirming input and disregard "negative" input. Fidelity is defined as the match between the design/intended use and actual use of a change (Lewis & Seibold, 1993). High fidelity is not always important to implementers of change. In some cases, implementers are interested in adapting a change to the local organization and may wish to promote innovative, creative, and individualized uses of a change. However, in other cases, implementers have strong desires for the use of a change program to match their own preconceived ideas. Such implementers are typically unwilling or highly reluctant to permit employees to alter or question the change. Simply put, they don't want anyone changing the change. A resource orientation embraces a philosophy that stakeholders' ideas, suggestions, objections, and contributions as change unfolds may make the change better—not merely increasing stakeholder receptiveness to the change or placating those invited to give input.

Lewis and Russ (2012) propose two dimensions—fidelity and resource orientation—as predictive of the approach to input solicitation that implementers will take. HRM professionals who are pressured to adopt a fidelity goal over resource orientation are unlikely to create systems for surfacing problems and raising critiques. In fact, the manner of soliciting input is often established to protect what has already been invested by the key decision makers, the commitments upper-level decision makers have already made to those in higher ranks, and the accumulated evidence that inspired the original plans.

A major communication function of HRM professionals is to ascertain from high-level decision makers their commitment to embracing a resource orientation. With such commitment, HRM professionals can design systems to encourage critical thinking, provide information that enables employees to better understand potential benefits and risks of the change, and assign all involved employees the task of evaluating the change against any reasonable standard that would yield useful information about the wisdom to maintain the change and/or change the change. Such an approach deemphasizes a focus on "resistance." Within this approach everyone becomes part of the evaluation team and is tasked to consider and report potential drawbacks or risks involved with change. Various employees and managers may differ in perspectives and conclusions, but the protests, complaints, concerns, and so forth are reframed as critical feedback that enhances the organization's odds of accomplishing its goals. In this model everyone is expected to play devil's advocate.

This is not to suggest that those who remain opposed to change will not engage in foot dragging, badmouthing, or sabotage. Those reactions and others are still possible. However, in an open environment where even critical feedback is embraced—in fact sought—the dysfunctional behaviors that can often be traced to feelings of powerlessness and lack of trust can be limited. This approach holds much promise for surfacing real problems with change. Those who might have withheld a valid critique for fear of being branded "resistor" will be more likely to be forthcoming. The new skill set of the HRM professional in such an environment would involve exploring and investigating concerns in collaborative ways in order to determine accuracy, level of risk, and possible solutions.

Communication scholars can make tremendous contributions to understanding how input solicitation can be transformed into utilization of new perspectives and information during change processes. Current scholarship provides few clues to the successful models for collaborative methods of problem identification, analysis, and solution generation. Examination of tools, skills, and processes for collective problem solving involving multi-stakeholder groups would prove to be a highly productive research agenda for future scholarship. We need to learn not only how to gather useful input, but how then to take that input (especially contradictory input) and generate solutions and useful decisions.

Conclusion

Change communication is fundamentally concerned with soliciting employee input, disseminating information about and framing change, and creating ways to surface and resolve perceived problems with change initiatives. HRM professionals, especially with the help of thoughtful research in communication, could promote understanding of these critical processes among top-level decision makers in order to explicate the dysfunction of traditional approaches to resistance and the potential usefulness of a resource orientation. Unfortunately, change scholarship has merely scratched the surface of change communication. Although research in the areas of collaborative communication (cf. Edmondson et al., 2001) among others may provide clues to best models for retiring a "resistance frame" and moving toward a collaborative problem-solving model, much is still unknown about the ways for HRM professionals to guide such processes during change.

Bibliography

Armenakis, A.A., & Harris, S.G. (2009). Reflections: Our journey in organizational change research and practice. *Journal of Change Management, 9*(2), 127–142.

Armenakis, A.A., Harris, S.G., & Mossholder, K. (1993). Creating readiness for organizational change. *Human Relations, 46*, 681–703.

Barge, J.K., Lee, M., Maddux, K., Nabring, R., & Townsend, B. (2008). Managing dualities in planned change initiatives. *Journal of Applied Communication Research, 36*(4), 364–390.

Bird, S. (2007). Sensemaking and identity: The interconnection of storytelling and networking in a women's group of a large corporation. *Journal of Business Communication, 44*(4), 311–339.

Bordia, P., Hobman, E., Jones, E., Gallois, C., & Callan, V. (2004). Uncertainty during organizational change: Types, consequences, and management strategies. *Journal of Business and Psychology, 18*(4), 507–532.

Bordia, P., Hunt, L., Paulsen, N., Tourish, D., & DiFonzo, N. (2004). Communication and uncertainty during organizational change: It is all about control. *European Journal of Work and Organizational Psychology, 13*(3), 345–365.

Bordia, P., Jones, E., Gallois, C., Callan, V.J., & DiFonzo, N. (2006). Management are aliens! Rumors and stress during organizational change. *Group and Organization Management, 31*(5), 601–621.

Bouckenooghe, D. (2010). Positioning change recipients' attitudes toward change in the organizational change literature. *Journal of Applied Behavioral Science, 46*(4), 500–531.

Brown, A.D., Gabriel, Y., & Gheradi, S. (2009). Storytelling and change: An unfolding story. *Organization, 16*(3), 323–333.

Brown, A.D., & Humphreys, M. (2003). Epic and tragic tales: Making sense of change. *Journal of Applied Behavioral Science, 39*(2): 121–144.

Buchanan, D., & Dawson, P. (2007). Discourse and audience: Organizational change as multi-story process. *Journal of Management Studies, 44*(5), 669–686.

Cherim, S. (2006). Managerial frames and institutional discourses of change: Employee appropriation and resistance. *Organization Studies, 27*(9), 1261–1287.

Cole, M.S., Bruch, H., & Vogel, B. (2006). Emotion as mediators of the relations between perceived supervisor support and psychological hardiness on employee cynicism. *Journal of Organizational Behavior, 27*(4), 463–484.

Dent, E.B., & Goldberg, S.G. (1999). Challenging "resistance to change." *Journal of Applied Behavioral Science, 35*(1), 25–41.

Dewulf, A., Gray, B., Putnam, L.L., Lewicki, R., Aarts, N., Bouwen, R., & van Woekum, C. (2009). Disentangling approaches to framing in conflict and negotiation research: A meta-analytic perspective. *Human Relations, 62*(2), 155–193.

Doyle, M., Claydon, T., & Buchanan, D. (2000). Mixed results, lousy process: The management experience of organizational change. *British Journal of Management, 11*, S59-S80.

Edmondson, A.C., Bohmer, R.M., & Pisano, G.P. (2001). Disrupted routines: Team learning and new technology implementation in hospitals. *Administrative Science Quarterly, 46*, 685–716.

Graham, J.W. (1986). Principled organizational dissent: A theoretical essay. In B.M. Staw & L.L. Cummings (Eds.), *Research in organizational behavior, Vol. 8* (pp. 1–52). Greenwich, CT: JAI Press.

Garner, J.T. (2009a). Strategic dissent: Expressions of organizational dissent motivated by influence goals. *International Journal of Strategic Communication, 3*, 34–51.

Garner, J.T. (2009b). When things go wrong at work: An exploration of organizational dissent messages. *Communication Studies, 60*(2), 197–218.

Graetz, F., & Smith, A.C.T. (2010). Managing organizational change: A philosophies of change approach. *Journal of Change Management, 10*(2), 135–154.

Griffith, T.L., & Northcraft, G.B. (1996). Cognitive elements in the implementation of new technology: Can less information provide more benefits? *MIS Quarterly, 20*, 99–110.

Kassing, J.W. (2002). Speaking up: Identifying employees' upward dissent strategies. *Management Communication Quarterly, 16*, 187–209.

Kassing, J.W. (2009). "In case you didn't hear me the first time": An examination of repetitious upward dissent. *Management Communication Quarterly, 22*(3), 416–436.

Kramer, M., Dougherty, D.S., & Pierce, T.A., (2004). Managing uncertainty during a corporate acquisition: A longitudinal study of communication during an airline acquisition. *Human Communication Research, 30*(1), 71–101.

Kuhn, T. (2008). A communicative theory of the firm: Developing an alternative perspective on intra-organizational power and stakeholder relationships. *Organization Studies, 29*, 1197–1224.

Kuhn, T., & Deetz, S.A. (2008). Critical theory and corporate social responsibility: Can/should we get beyond cynical reasoning? In A. Crane, A. McWilliams, D. Matten, J. Moon, & D. Siegel (Eds.), *The Oxford handbook of corporate social responsibility* (pp. 173–196). Oxford: Oxford University Press.

Lewis, L.K. (forthcoming). *Organizational change and innovation.* In L.L. Putnam & D.K. Mumby (Eds.), *The new handbook of organizational communication.* Thousand Oaks, CA: Sage.

Lewis, L.K. (1999). Disseminating information and soliciting input during planned organizational change: Implementers' targets, sources and channels for communicating. *Management Communication Quarterly, 13*, 43–75.

Lewis, L.K. (2000). "Blindsided by that one" and "I saw that one coming": The relative anticipation and occurrence of communication problems and other problems in implementers' hindsight. *Journal of Applied Communication Research, 28*(1), 44–67.

Lewis, L.K. (2006). Employee perspectives on implementation communication as predictors of perceptions of success and resistance. *Western Journal of Communication, 70*, 23–46.

Lewis, L.K. (2011). *Organizational change: Creating change through strategic communication*. Chichester, UK: Wiley-Blackwell.

Lewis, L.K., Laster, N., & Kulkarni, V. (in press). Telling 'em how it will be: Previewing pain of risky change in initial announcements. *Journal of Business Communication*.

Lewis, L.K., Richardson, B.K., & Hamel, S.A. (2003). When the stakes are communicative: The lamb's and the lion's share during nonprofit planned change. *Human Communication Research, 29*, 400–430.

Lewis, L.K., & Russ, T. (2012). Soliciting and using input during organizational change initiatives: What are practitioners doing? *Management Communication Quarterly, 26*(2), 267–294.

Lewis, L.K., Schmisseur, A., Stephens, K., & Weir, K. (2006). Advice on communicating during organizational change: The content of popular press books. *Journal of Business Communication, 43*(2), 113–137.

Lewis, L.K., & Seibold, D.R. (1993). Innovation modification during intraorganizational adoption. *Academy of Management Review, 18*, 322–354.

Lines, R. (2007). Using power to install strategy: The relationships between expert power, position power, influence tactics, and implementation success. *Journal of Change Management, 7*, 143–170.

Lines, R., Selart, M., Espedal, B., & Johansen, S.T. (2005). The production of trust during organizational change. *Journal of Change Management, 5*(2), 221–245.

Miller, K.I., & Monge, P.R. (1985). Social information and employee anxiety about organizational change. *Human Communication Research, 11*, 365–386.

Neumann, J.E. (1989). Why people don't participate in organizational change. In R.W. Woodman & W.A. Pasmore (Eds.), *Research in organizational change and development, Vol. 3* (pp. 181–212). Greenwich, CT: JAI Press.

Oreg, S. (2003). Resistance to change: Developing an individual differences measure. *Journal of Applied Psychology, 88*(4), 680–693.

Oreg, S. (2006). Personality, context, and resistance to organizational change. *European Journal of Work and Organizational Psychology, 15*(1), 73–101.

Reichers, A.E., Wanous, J.P., & Austin, J.T. (1997). Understanding and managing cynicism about organizational change. *Academy of Management Executive, 11*(1), 48–58.

Russ, T.L. (2008). Communicating change: A review and critical analysis of programmatic and participatory implementation approaches. *Journal of Change Management, 8*, 199–21.

Russ, T.L. (2009). Developing a typology of perceived communication challenges experienced by frontline employees during organizational change. *Qualitative Research Reports in Communication, 10*, 1–8.

Russ, T.L. (2011). An exploratory study of an experiential change program's impact on participants' affective outcomes. *Leadership & Organization Development Journal, 32*, 493–509.

Sagie, A., Elizur, D., & Koslowsky, M. (2001). Effect of participation in strategic and tactical decisions on acceptance of planned change. *Journal of Social Psychology, 13*(4), 459–465.

Schoorman, F.D., Mayer, R.C., & Davis, J.H. (2007). An integrative model of organizational trust: Past, present, and future. *Academy of Management Review, 32*(2), 344–354.

Schweiger, D.M., & DeNisi, A.S. (1991). Communication with employees following a merger: A longitudinal field experiment. *Academy of Management Journal, 34*(1), 110–135.

Smeltzer, L.R. (1991). An analysis of strategies for announcing organization-wide change. *Group and Organization Studies, 16*(1), 5–24.

Smeltzer, L.R., & Zener, M.F. (1994). Minimizing the negative effect of employee layoffs through effective announcements. *Employee Counseling Today, 6*(4), 3–9.

Smeltzer, L.R., & Zener, M.F. (1995). Organization-wide change: Planning for an effective announcement. *Journal of General Management, 20*(3), 31–43.

Thomas, G.F., Zolin, R., & Hartman, J.L. (2009). The central role of communication in developing trust and its effect on employee involvement. *Journal of Business Communication, 46*(3), 287–310.

Wanous, J.P., Reichers, A.E., & Austin, J.T. (2000). Cynicism about organizational change: Measurement, antecedents, and correlates. *Group & Organization Management, 25*(2), 132–153.

Weick, K.E. (1979). *The social psychology of organizing* (2nd ed.). New York: McGraw-Hill.

Weick, K.E. (1995). *Sensemaking in organizations*. Thousand Oaks, CA: Sage.

13

IMPLICATIONS OF COMMUNICATION RESEARCH FOR IMPROVING DEVELOPING POLICIES, PROCEDURES, AND FUNCTIONS

Patricia M. Sias

I am very pleased about the creation of this book and honored that I was invited to contribute to it. As a communication scholar who has worked as a manager, a consultant, a faculty member in a communication college, and now a faculty member and administrator in a business school, I have lived and worked in the nexus of communication and human resource management (HRM) throughout my career. I have always believed communication is central to human organizing processes. In fact, I've been persuaded by the theoretical developments that have played out over the past decade among organizational communication scholars that communication is not just central to organizing, it constitutes organizing (Cooren, 2000; Fairhurst & Putnam, 2006).

My theoretical, conceptual, and managerial tendencies are firmly grounded in the fact that Dr. Fredric Jablin was my doctoral advisor and mentor. As any of Fred's advisees will attest, he constantly asked the question, "What about communication?" By that he meant that, whatever the topic (e.g., leadership, decision making, sociaization, feedback, change, relationships, etc.), our job as communication scholars is to question, investigate, and reveal the communicative aspects, functions, and very nature of those processes. Not surprisingly, I find myself constantly asking the same question (sometimes out loud, sometimes not) in my research, teaching, and leadership responsibilities.

The question "What about communication?" guided my reading of the four chapters in this section of the book. These chapters address HRM practices and processes (training, appraisal, leadership, and organizational change) that are communicative at their core. However, as each of the authors deftly points out, saying the processes are communicative only gets us so far. Understanding how they are communicatively constituted, the effective and ineffective communicative processes associated with each, and the ways HRM practitioners can develop, and help their employees develop, such communication skills key. I begin by briefly establishing my theoretical grounding as an overall framework for discussing the chapters. I then address each chapter, discussing its contributions as well as insights for additional research development.

Communicative Constitution of Organizations (CCO)

The core concept of CCO theorizing is the notion that communicating *is* organizing (Cooren, 2000). Communication in a variety of forms (formal and informal messages, discourse, verbal, nonverbal, interpersonal, group, mass communication, etc.) constitutes our worlds (work, personal, professional, and public). When we communicate, we create and re-create social reality. CCO also acknowledges the importance of informal communication by theorizing the emergent nature of communication and organization. Rather than communication occurring *in* organizations, organizations *emerge through* communication. In this way, formal communication is not privileged over informal. Wherever and however organizational members communicate, they create and re-create the organization.

Of course, CCO theory is far more complex and nuanced than this (see Cooren, 2000; Fairhurst & Putnam, 2006; and chapter 9 of this volume for more detailed treatments of the theory). Yet this fundamental notion is powerful because it acknowledges the power of words, the power of language, the power of interaction, and, in a more critical vein, the power accorded to those who control or influence messages. When we communicate, we make sense of, or organize, our world for ourselves and others. Thus, the power of communication is the power of sensemaking.

As the four chapters in this section acknowledge, effective communication reflects the power to influence employee learning, performance, motivation, and organizational change. Communication is, therefore, fundamental to organizational processes and practices because communication constitutes organizational processes and practices. This section of the book addresses employee and organizational development. Specifically, it addresses HRM programs that prepare employees for their present or future roles. In essence the section addresses how HRM practitioners help employees make sense of their roles via training, feedback, leadership, and change communication.

Certainly management and human resource practitioners have long acknowledged the importance of communication. This acknowledgement, however, is often superficial and glossed over in research, training, and practice. Any business textbook, for example, will highlight the importance of providing feedback to employees. Communication scholars are uniquely qualified to "flesh out" the complexities of such communication. Communication scholars tell us what effective feedback "sounds like." That is our job, and the chapters in this section provide a number of interesting and useful suggestions for how communication scholars and practitioners can contribute to our understanding of what effective appraisal, leadership, training, and organizational change "sound like."

The chapters are somewhat limited, to varying extents, in two primary ways. First, the chapters explicitly or implicitly address communication that occurs primarily in formal contexts or channels. Although formal communication is crucial to the developmental functions addressed in this section, informal communication is also central. Better understanding of training, appraisal, leadership, and organizational change communication that occurs informally would go far in improving HRM practices. This requires research examining communication in the "white spaces" of the organizational chart, in the hallways, outside meeting rooms, over lunch, and even via texting and social media. It is in such spaces that much employee and organizational development occur.

Second, while Gordon and Miller do an excellent job highlighting the interactive nature of the appraisal interview and call for research that focuses on micro-level communication practices and processes, such conceptualizations and research would also be of great benefit to HRM practitioners seeking to improve training, leadership, and organizational change communication. Such studies incorporate communication, not communicators, as the unit of analysis. Rather than developing an understanding of how people can become more competent communicators, interactive research identifies the characteristics of *competent communication*. This is a very different research tradition than typically used in HRM, but very valuable. In fact, I would argue that without understanding what makes conversation competent and effective, individuals cannot learn to become competent and effective communicators.

I highlight these two issues as I discuss each of the four chapters in the following sections.

Organizational Training

Training is perhaps the most obvious and explicit area of employee development. When employees are hired, they must understand their tasks, expectations, and roles in the organization and unit. Veteran employees benefit from training in new knowledge and skills that promote professional growth and career progression. Veteran employees also must learn and adopt new skills and knowledge as organizations and units implement change. Such understanding is accomplished via formal and informal training.

Fyke and Buzzanell make a wonderful contribution in their chapter by conceptualizing training as a communicative act. They make a strong case for adopting a communicative approach to HRM training. Rather than focusing on what topics to train employees on, they center their chapter on how to more effectively train employees via more effective training *communication*. In fact, they ground their chapter in the CCO perspective, arguing that perhaps the most important training HRM professionals need is training in training communication. Their chapter provides a broad treatment of training, discussing trainees (managers and employees), the training process, training methods, training evaluation, and training transfer. For each of these elements of training, the authors note how research should more centrally focus on how communication influences the relative effectiveness of each.

A fundamental conceptual point the authors make throughout is that training communication is a process of creating and negotiating meaning. When trainers explain concepts and teach skills, they are making sense of those concepts and skills and how they apply to the trainee's experience, tasks, and roles. As the authors note, this can be accomplished via a variety of rhetorical and discursive means such as narratives, metaphors, and framing. And the authors provide a number of useful suggestions for research examining these issues and processes. Their chapter, however, focuses largely on formal training. I contend that much, if not most, important training occurs in less formal settings. Initial conversations between veterans and newcomers should, and often do, involve "training" the newcomer in his or her new tasks, roles, and the organizational culture. In fact, it is in informal conversation that employees "learn the ropes" so necessary to successful adjustment and performance. Informal communication may be especially relevant in training transfer. As trainees apply newly acquired skills and knowledge to their actual tasks and roles, informal conversations with coworkers likely play an integral role in the sensemaking of such practices in situ. Understanding how trainees talk about training topics as they do their work and talk with others at work would be very helpful in developing more effective training methods. Communication researchers would make very useful contributions to HRM training by unpacking and identifying effective communication in informal training contexts.

I also encourage communication scholars to engage in research examining training as an *interactive* event. Fyke and Buzzanell do note the importance of listening to effective training. And they highlight the potential usefulness of stories, metaphors, and other discursive tools in the training context. Many important insights can result, however, from considering such tools as *cocreated in interaction*. Along these lines, it would be useful to examine how trainers and trainees build stories together to co-manage and negotiate meaning during a training session. For example, the trainer may tell a story to illustrate how an employee has used a particular skill in her work. Trainees may build on that story by sharing their experiences, resulting in an altered, but potentially more illuminating, narrative. Similarly, I have often observed a metaphor "chain out" as interactants develop entailments of the metaphor to enhance its meaning. Research centering on how metaphors are co-developed through interaction among trainer and trainees would be important.

Employee Appraisal

Gordon and Miller's chapter addresses a crucial element of employee development—the appraisal interview. Providing employees with feedback about their performance is so important and so poorly done. In fact, effective feedback and appraisal is an ethical commitment. Knowingly withholding performance feedback and coaching, especially negative feedback, is unfair to the employee and to the organization. Such withholding hinders employee development and hurts organizational performance.

The authors begin their chapter with a brief, but very interesting, history of performance appraisal. This history indicates that, despite the fact that practitioners have conducted employee appraisals since the early 1930s, much research indicates supervisors continue to do a poor job discussing performance with employees (Dibble & Levine, 2010). This is for a variety of reasons, including problematic instruments and, in particular, a large preoccupation with face-saving and concerns about hurting the employee's feelings and otherwise avoiding uncomfortable conversations. The appraisal interview is, therefore, viewed by managers as an unpleasant organizational chore rather than a crucial development and learning opportunity. Not surprisingly, organizations typically must mandate employee appraisals, and supervisors conduct them with little enthusiasm and skill.

The strength of the Gordon and Miller chapter is its focus on conversation and interaction. Understanding the appraisal interview as an interactive event, the authors make a strong persuasive argument for the value of research adopting a conversation analytic approach. Such research would provide many insights into what effective appraisal interviews "sound like." Such research would highlight how the appraisal conversation (interview) takes on a life of its own and follows a path guided by both parties. Revealing conversational practices and patterns that characterize effective, functional, and rewarding appraisal interviews would be very useful in helping HRM practitioners welcome, rather than avoid, the feedback event.

While Gordon and Miller intentionally center their chapter on the formal appraisal interview, I encourage communication scholars to also examine feedback that occurs via informal communication, or at least outside the appraisal interview itself. In my view, informal feedback provided on an ongoing basis is, or should be, more important than the formal annual, semi-annual, or quarterly appraisal interview. This is especially true for negative feedback. One of the most important characteristics of effective feedback is timeliness. Feedback is most effective when it is provided as soon after the performance event as possible. Managers should not simply catalog a performance problem to bring it up later at the official appraisal interview. Doing so ensures that neither the supervisor nor the employee accurately recalls the event. It also ensures that the employee will likely repeat the problem performance, which cumulatively harms employee, unit, and organizational performance. Waiting until the formal appraisal interview to talk to an employee about problematic performance is like walking by a person flailing in a swimming pool and, instead of helping them at that point, saying, "I see you struggling and I can help you, but

I'll wait six months until our formal appointment." The futility and danger of such an approach is obvious. In fact, I tell my students that if you are providing effective informal feedback throughout the year, the formal appraisal becomes really just a formality and is nothing to fear. A sure sign you're doing a good job as a supervisor in providing informal feedback is when there are no surprises in the formal appraisal interview. That indicates you've been having the important informal conversations all along.

In sum, I encourage communication researchers to take Gordon and Miller's advice and begin studying interaction in the appraisal interview to help HRM practitioners develop useful and effective appraisal conversational practices. Beyond the bounds of the Gordon and Miller chapter, I also encourage more research attention to communication in informal feedback conversations.

Leadership

Relative to training and appraisal, leadership is a more global skill that spans organizational type, level, functions, and the like. Leadership is fundamental to employee motivation, productivity, and morale and is also foundational to the developmental functions addressed in the other chapters in this section. Effective training requires effective leadership. Effective appraisal and feedback require effective leadership. And leadership is central to the successful implementation of organizational change. Developing exceptional leadership skills is, therefore, foundational to all organizational processes.

Leadership is a communicative phenomenon, and communication scholars have done much to develop our understanding of the communicative nature of leadership. The Tourish chapter usefully conceptualizes leadership as interaction, and not simply the unidirectional transmission of information. Most importantly, leadership is a communication process that emerges through conversation among interactants. At the same time, Tourish problematizes the state of the art of leadership research and practice by noting that followership has been under-theorized and wrongly excludes dissent. Dissent is not the absence of followership, but in fact a sign of effective, quality followership. Followership, therefore, is actually leadership.

As noted earlier, communication is essentially the management and negotiation of meaning. Communication scholars have long established meaning management and sensemaking as the central functions of leadership (Fairhurst & Sarr, 1996). Incorporating dissent into leadership theory and practice highlights the *negotiated* nature of leadership. Dissent is essential to revealing aspects of a situation (e.g., an employee's performance, a new vision, etc.) that may otherwise go unnoticed and unattended. To the extent that those aspects are important and meaningful, ignoring or suppressing dissent can lead to serious organizational dysfunction.

The Tourish chapter identifies a number of useful avenues for research and practice directed toward better enabling and incorporating dissent into leadership interaction. Similar to the other chapters, however, the chapter and recommendations center largely on formal communication contexts such as the 360-degree review and formal employee participation systems and mechanisms. In addition, those recommendations that might apply to informal communication tend to address managers' *individual* cognitive and behavioral processes such as being open and receptive to employee dissent, understanding ingratiation theory, and seeking out opportunities for formal and informal contact with employees.

These are all useful suggestions and would greatly improve current HRM theory and practice. However, they tend to gloss over the communicative and interactive processes of leadership and dissent. Seeking out opportunities for informal contact with employees, for example, does not necessarily mean that one is an effective leader or that effective leadership *communication* will emerge in these conditions. Research incorporating conversation or discourse analysis would be very helpful in illuminating a number of important issues related to dissent and leadership, such as how effective dissent emerges and develops during a conversation, what communication practices and patterns hinder effective dissent, how leadership/followership emerge in conversation, and the like. Such studies would, in turn, provide useful advice to HRM practitioners about how to initiate and engage in conversations with employees when you have opportunities for formal and informal contact. Interactive research would also help practitioners communicatively elicit constructive dissent in informal conversation.

Change Management

Leadership and change management are closely entwined (Lewis, 2011). As with leadership, communication scholars have done much to elucidate the characteristics of effective change management. In fact, organizational change communication research incorporates a great deal from the leadership literature (e.g., framing). Lewis provides an excellent overview of the organizational change literature, particularly highlighting the importance of input, dissemination, and resistance in organizational change processes.

Because organizations are constituted in communication, organizational change must be accomplished communicatively. Consequently, the solicitation and incorporation of input from employees and other stakeholders are important organizational change communication processes. Closely related to the topic of dissent discussed earlier, organizational change implementers ignore employee input and resistance at their peril.

Unfortunately, as Lewis correctly notes, we know relatively little about the communication processes and practices associated with effective input solicitation, input sharing, and input incorporation. Lewis provides a number of interesting directions for communication research in the area of change communication and employee input. Particularly important is research regarding how and why implementers use or ignore input. Communication scholars would make important contributions to this area by acknowledging the *embedded* nature of change communication. Input solicitation mechanisms are embedded in larger organizational processes and cultural structures that influence the solicitation process itself. For example, in an organization in which strict hierarchy and information control are the cultural rule, solicitations for input are likely to be viewed with suspicion and ineffective due to such cultural norms and employee distrust. Even if employees in such organizations do provide substantive constructive input, implementers' choices about what to do with that input (e.g., incorporate it, amend it, ignore it, or forge ahead despite warning signs, etc.) are embedded in and influenced by the broader cultural milieu of the organization.

Lewis also discusses communication scholars' substantial contributions to our understanding of how implementers disseminate change messages via framing. This area is perhaps where communication scholarship has had the most impact. However, much of this research has centered on one-way dissemination of information. Communication scholars could make important contributions to HRM theory and practice by examining change *interaction* rather than information dissemination as it occurs in both formal and informal settings. Just as input solicitation is embedded in organizational structures and cultures, change communication is embedded in larger conversations. Communication research using an interactive frame (e.g., conversation or discourse analysis) could provide knowledge about the larger constellation of communication in which input, framing, and resistance are embedded (see Fairhurst & Sarr, 1996, for an excellent example of such an approach as it applies to leadership). Such research would reveal how change is introduced in an ongoing conversation; how "invitations" for input are most effectively embedded in conversation; how employees respond to such solicitations; how implementers and employees together manage and negotiate solicitation, resistance, and meaning of the organizational change; and so on.

In sum, I encourage change communication research to conceptualize such communication as embedded in broader organizational structures and cultures and as embedded in broader formal and informal conversations.

Conclusion

I very much enjoyed reading the four chapters in this section of the book. Each addresses communication central to employee and organizational development. Each chapter also clearly illustrates the usefulness of a communication perspective on HRM practices that often ignores or treats communication as the relatively simplistic and unproblematic act of transmitting information. The communication scholars who authored these chapters understand communication as anything but. In fact, communication is complex, dynamic, and embedded in and constitutive of organizational, cultural, and even relational structures. In other words, communication is messy, and effective communication is difficult and challenging, but also rewarding.

As I mentioned in the introduction, our job as communication scholars is to generate knowledge and understanding of the complexities of communication to aid and improve HRM practice. The authors of the chapters in this section do their jobs well, outlining a number of useful directions for research that more fully develop our understanding of the complexities of communication in the various employee development areas. I offer two primary suggestions to augment theirs. First, I encourage organizational communication scholars to give more attention to communication in informal settings and via informal channels. I fear we miss much important organizing when we center our efforts on formal communication systems and settings. I hasten to note that the four chapters do not ignore informal communication. But they also don't foreground it. I'm calling for research that explicitly centers on informal interaction as its focus. Second, and consistent with the framework provided by the Gordon and Miller chapter, I encourage communication research that positions communication, rather than communicators, as the unit of analysis. Research examining conversations and interaction is rare in HRM research and would provide many useful insights into what effective training, appraisal, leadership, and change management "sound like."

Bibliography

Cooren, F. (2000). *The organizing property of communication.* Amsterdam: John Benjamins.

Dibble, J.L., & Levine, T.R. (2010). Breaking good and bad news: Direction of the MUM effect and senders' cognitive representations of news valence. *Communication Research, 37,* 703–722.

Fairhurst, G.T., & Putnam, L. (2006). Organizations as discursive constructions. *Communication Theory, 14,* 5–26.

Fairhurst, G.T., & Sarr, R.A. (1996). *The art of framing: Managing the language of leadership.* San Francisco: Jossey-Bass.

Lewis, L.K. (2011). *Organizational change: Creating change through strategic communication.* Chichester, UK: Wiley-Blackwell.

PART IV
CONSERVING

14

ATTITUDE SURVEYS

Paul M. Leonardi, Jeffrey W. Treem, William C. Barley, and Vernon D. Miller

> *Employee surveys, used effectively, can be catalysts for improving employee attitudes and producing organizational change. This statement is based on two important assumptions, both supported by research . . .: first, that employee attitudes affect behavior and second, that employee attitudes are important levers of organizational performance.*
>
> —Saari & Judge, 2004, p. 402

The formal assessing of employee attitudes goes back at least to the early 1930s, beginning with attempts to understand the nature and source of employee job satisfaction and attitudes at Kimberly-Clark Corporation (Kornhauser & Sharp, 1932). Almost any textbook (e.g., Mathis & Jackson, 2010; Noe, Hollenbeck, Gerhart, & Wright, 2011) on human resource management (HRM) includes materials on attitude surveys or assessment. Notable scholarly critiques (e.g., Edwards & Fisher, 2004) on employee survey programs are also available. Indeed, there are many good reasons for investigating employee attitudes and perspectives. Surveys, interviews, observations, and the like can provide feedback regarding work conditions and policies to "monitor employee satisfaction and identify problem areas" (Blackburn & Rosen, 1993, p. 53), reveal trends over time regarding the favorableness or usefulness of policies and programs, identify strengths and weaknesses in operations, and reveal opportunities to improve work conditions and be a tool for innovative suggestions for improvement (Hargie & Tourish, 2009).

HRM efforts to assess employees' perspective on almost any topic have significant symbolic meaning. Efforts to learn what employees think about specific issues can be interpreted as a sign that the employer cares about its employees' well-being (Blackburn & Rosen, 1993). Yet surveying employee attitudes creates an obligation that the organization be seen as acting constructively on the information that employees provide. Employees are likely to cease sharing their true feelings and opinions in response to survey or interview questions if they perceive their input is lost in a "black hole," or, worse, they may develop cynical opinions regarding HRM specifically and management intentions generally (Reichers, Wanous, & Austin, 1997; Saari & Judge, 2004).

We examine the communicative issues facing HRM professionals and the roles they play related to surveying employee attitudes. The various methods used to assess employee attitudes are reviewed. We comment throughout on ways that more rigorous study of HRM professionals' communicative actions related to assessing employee attitudes could enhance their effectiveness and organizational operations.

Basic Terminology

To begin, we define several terms. HRM professionals, like all employees, accomplish their work by communicating with others. Communication may be conceptualized as the sufficient frequency, quality, and duration of the flow of information (Axley, 1984). This perspective has considerable value in terms of the fulfillment of role expectations and coordination of assignments at the individual and unit levels. However, as Poole (2011) states:

> *Communication* is a complex, mulitfaceted process through which people and organizations exchange information; form and dispute understandings; organize and coordinate activities; influence one another; create communities; and generate, maintain, and undermine beliefs, values, perspectives, symbols, and ideologies. (p. 249)

So, communication, in a broad sense, pertains to and enables many of the activities of HRM professionals.

Surveying has been used to refer to a number of methods by which employee attitudes can be assessed (e.g., interviewing, observation, and formal Likert-type scales). Employee attitudes (i.e., viewpoints, opinions, and beliefs) are subjective but can be measured through self-report surveys, statements in interviews, and behavioral actions. In each case, the aim is to discover the nature of employees' orientations and beliefs about their work satisfactions (Saari & Judge, 2004), but also their understandings of unit and organizational operations (Poole, 2011; Seibold, 2009).

The Roles of HRM Professionals in Assessing Employee Attitudes

The complexities of the HRM role are evident in the challenges of assessing employee attitudes. On one hand, by gathering and sharing information depicting employee attitudes, HRM professionals are agents or conduits who simply pass data along from one party to another (Axley, 1984). Yet HRM professionals also could be considered to be engaging in constitutive actions (Poole, 2011) when they identify information targets, create questions, and interpret responses as well as when they shape policies and programs. Finally, they must also address the concerns of multiple stakeholders (Lewis, 1999). In assessing employee attitudes, HRM professionals engage in three intertwined roles: explorer, advocate, and facilitator.

Explorer

The explorer role involves discovering (and sometimes confirming) employee attitudes. From a communicative perspective, HRM professionals may serve as agents or representatives of executive management, seeking to understand the actions and mind-sets of employees. In their study of Baldrige Award–winning organizations, Blackburn and Rosen (1993) found that these firms see attitude surveys, along with due process and quality circles, as central to the total quality management philosophy of promoting "employee voice and involvement" (p. 51).

Saari and Judge (2004) posed several questions to help organizations form their strategic orientation prior to conducting attitude surveys. Because it is vital that HRM professionals create survey content that is interesting to employees and is predictive of employee performance, they should ask themselves the following: "Do we have an employee attitude survey that measures areas *important* for employee job satisfaction as well as organizational success?" (p. 403, emphasis added). Unfortunately, we know of little documentation of such efforts. Saari and Judge also ask, "Is the survey a *respected source* of information about the people side of the business?" (p. 403, emphasis added). Resources devoted to attitude surveys will be wasted if HRM's intent or abilities lack credibility in the eyes of employees or management.

Advocate

In the HRM advocate role, strategic issues and concerns identified through data collection efforts are presented to executives and line management. Although considerable research exists with regard to employee upward influence (Kipnis, Schmidt, & Wilkinson, 1980; Waldron, 1991), little is known about communication strategies and conditions that are associated with HRM professionals as persuasive agents. However, greater knowledge of the dynamics related to "going to bat" on behalf of employees appears to warrant a high priority as such advocacy could serve as feedback or corrective mechanisms and could avert a sense of futility related to seeing acquired information go to waste.

Here, questions posed by Saari and Judge (2004) may again serve as guides for practice and research:

> *How do we* know this and *make this case* to *line management*? Can I discuss *these measures in light of other* key business measures? (p. 403, emphasis added)

For instance, different strategies may be necessary to present information effectively to executives and to line managers. While the former may be interested in the long-term costs associated with HRM professionals' arguments, line managers may be concerned primarily with disruptions to their units' processes and difficulties related to implementation. Again, knowledge of stakeholders' needs and priorities may be central to a successful persuasive strategy (Lewis, 1999).

Facilitator

What HRM professionals *do* with survey data is as important as the information's validity. One application of survey data is its use in employee training (see Fyke & Buzzanell's discussion in chapter 9). Feedback from employees and their managers can provide HRM professionals with relevant and timely issues around which to develop training materials. A second application pertains to the use of survey data in assisting with organizational change. A survey of HRM professionals identified "managing change" as one of their most important perceived organizational functions (Ulrich, Brockbank, Yeung, & Lake, 1995). In some respects, gathering information, presenting it, and working with managers of all ranks to enable change places HRM at the center of organizational development.

Though important, little research on the communicative role of HRM professionals' use of survey research to assist organizational change exists (see Lewis's discussion in chapter 12). Yet the extent to which data from HRM is presented to executives and line managers prior to, during, and following organizational change appears to be an obvious starting point. For example, Saari and Judge (2004) ask, "*Am I at the table with line management* using the survey insights *for needed action* and organizational change?" (p. 403, emphasis added). Hence, the characteristics that lend credibility to HRM professionals when interacting with line managers about change seem to be a critical factor. To truly help organizations implement change, researchers ought to inquire about HRM communicative activities beyond determining whether line managers are "holding feedback discussions and have action plans" (p. 403). Indeed, HRM professionals probably should be adept at coaching, negotiating, and/or applying political pressure.

In sum, although HRM has long been involved in employee surveys, little is known about their communicative roles in exploring, advocating, and facilitating. Consequently, it may be instructive to understand how HRM professionals see their role when engaging in employee attitude assessment. Moreover, researchers should inquire into the particular communication challenges associated with the roles of explorer, advocate, and facilitator and should investigate the extent to which HRM professionals believe they have been properly trained to assume these roles.

Methods of Assessing Attitudes

There are at least five data collection methods that have proven useful for understanding and diagnosing employee attitudes: questionnaires, interviews, network analysis, work observations, and textual analysis. Individuals trained through university HRM coursework probably are most familiar with scale questionnaire methodology (e.g., Edwards & Fisher, 2004; Noe et al., 2011), but they may be well acquainted with other techniques such as interviewing too (Schmitt & Klimoski, 1991).

Questionnaires

Attitude scales offer HRM professionals the ability to specify constructs that they wish to measure, identify the relationships of one construct to another, and test casual inferences (Miller, Poole, & Seibold, 2011). Questionnaire scales also enable HRM professionals to assess the direction and strength of relationships and compare their findings with previous surveys in their organization or in comparison to other organizations. Although the results obtained are only as good as the quality (i.e., reliability and validity) of the scales, there are numerous resources available to assist in the development and validation of these measures (Edwards & Fisher, 2004; Schmitt & Klimoski, 1991).

A number of multinational organizations annually assess relationships between supervisors and employees, the dynamics within work units, and employee attitudes on specific issues (e.g., Nordblom & Hamrefors, 2007). Relational or communicative aspects of supervisor-employee dynamics are regularly measured in concert with job satisfaction as a criterion variable (Hargie & Tourish, 2009; Muchinsky, 1977). Yet it is unclear to what extent HRM professionals assess unit-level or hierarchical effects in supervisory and work unit relationships, even though such differences or interdependencies are anticipated to exist and are becoming an important focus in organizational studies (Klein, Dansereau, & Hall, 1994; Klein & Kozlowski, 2000; Miller et al., 2011).

Over the years, two questionnaire scale approaches have been used for surveying how employees' perceptions of their own and others' communication behaviors relate to outcomes such as job satisfaction or unit effectiveness. One approach is the development of a spectrum of scales that cover a potpourri of interrelated perceptions of communication adequacy, message-receiving openness, and cooperativeness of work unit members (Greenbaum, Clampitt, & Willihnganz, 1988). At times, researchers go as far as to refer to these collections of scale instruments as an "audit" (Goldhaber, 1979; Hargie & Tourish, 2000, 2009). Another approach is the development of questionnaire scales to measure specific constructs as they relate to one another (e.g., Muchinsky, 1977; Seibold, 2009).

Interviews

Interviews are distinct from other data collection methods in their dependence upon social interaction between the interviewer and employee(s) (Millar & Tracey, 2009). Whereas other survey methods are an effective way to uncover employees' perceptions of organizational policies, supervisory and coworker behavior, and work conditions, interviews may be used to reveal why processes are unfolding in particular ways. Interviews allow employees to share stories regarding the ways they and others communicate and act. In the course of telling stories, employees reveal their own salient experiences and what is valued in the organization (Browning, 1992).

Audit interviews commonly take one of two forms, exploratory or focused (Millar & Tracey, 2009). Exploratory interviews usually are conducted at the outset of the audit and concentrate on learning about job functions and the organization. Alternatively, focused interviews examine specific issues that have been identified based on organizational or personal knowledge. While exploratory interviews are likely to be structured to provide comparable data, focused interviews may benefit from a semi-structured approach that allows interviewers to probe issues surfaced in discussions (Kvale, 1996). Additionally, conducting multiple rounds of interviews, or having discussions later in the audit process, allows HRM professionals to explore anomalies or contradictions that arise during the audit as well as to validate assumptions they might hold.

Regarding analysis, interviews lend themselves to both deductive, structured approaches, as well as more inductive, interpretive approaches. Interview responses often are subjected to content analysis to reveal the presence or absence of pre-identified themes in order to produce a quantitative analysis of messages (Clampitt & Downs, 1993). Alternatively, responses can be examined using a more inductive approach that searches for patterns and themes expressed in the data, and HRM professionals iteratively sort segments of responses into like categories (Glaser & Strauss, 1967; Miles & Huberman, 1994). Regardless of whether analysis takes a more quantitative or qualitative form, HRM professionals may want to include relevant segments of interviews in reports to capitalize on the descriptive power of these data (Downs & Adrian, 2004).

Network Analysis

Network analysis is useful for assessing organizational processes and relationships because it can both map communicative relationships in organizations and capture the flow of information among individuals and organizational media (Zwijze-Koning & De Jong, 2005). Network analysis moves the study of organizational processes beyond consideration of formal roles and examines the emergent, informal relationships in organizations (Brass, Galaskiewicz, Greve, & Wenpin, 2004; Monge & Contractor, 2003). Furthermore, while most survey methods focus on collecting data on individuals, the goal of network analysis is to consider the integrated and interconnected nature of organizational relationships.

A frequent form of network analysis is sociometric questioning, which asks employees to indicate the presence or frequency of communication with others in the organization (Goldhaber & Krivonos, 1977). The responses of each worker create an egocentric network that maps all of his or her direct relationships. The aggregate of each individual's responses creates a picture of the organizational network as a whole. Networks can also be constructed based on more specific types of communicative relationships such as to whom employees address questions (Borgatti & Cross, 2003; Cross & Sproull, 2004); with whom employees are friends (Feeley, Hwang, & Barnett, 2008; Krackhardt & Porter, 1985); or from whom, or from what technology, employees retrieve information (Su, Huang, & Contractor, 2010; Yuan, Fulk, & Monge, 2007).

Network analysis also provides a number of statistical measures respective to individuals, groups, and the organization as a whole (see Brass, 1995) that can inform the evaluation of organizational processes. For example, a network analysis can indicate individuals who bridge communication between other employees, a measure that has been linked to more innovative thinking by employees (Burt, 1992). At the group level, network analysis can identify the presence of cliques among employees, or departments that are isolated from each other, and suggest ways to alter communication to overcome existing barriers. Last, when looking at the whole organization, network analysis can indicate how dense, centralized, and connected relationships are among employees, which may be particularly useful in assessing potential or post hoc changes associated with downsizing and other organizational structural changes (Susskind, Miller, & Johnson, 1998). The use of online tools specifically designed to assist with organizational network analysis, such as C-IKNOW (e.g. Science of Networks in Communities Laboratory; Johnson, 2010), can aid HRM professionals to collect and analyze network data.

Work Observation

Observational methods afford HRM professionals a means to develop situated understandings of organizational activity (Becker, Geer, Hughes, & Strauss, 1961; Blau, 1955; Gouldner, 1954). Observations are a class of data-collection activities that require the researcher to watch the organization during its day-to-day operations. Techniques include: *fly-on-the-wall* (HRM professionals attempt to monitor activity from an unobtrusive vantage), *shadowing* (HRM professionals follow specific individuals as they work), and *participant observation* (HRM professionals temporarily join the work operation themselves). These techniques share an emphasis on producing findings inductively. Observation enables HRM professionals to uncover aspects of work that other methods, including interviews, often overlook (Van Maanen, 1979). Individuals often *do* things differently than they *say* they do them (Becker & Geer, 1957). Further, because work may be routinized, individuals may not recognize or be able to report important aspects of their daily activities (Polanyi, 1966). Put simply, observation permits HRM professionals to understand organizational actions and employee behaviors as they occur in the wild.

Engaging in observations may help HRM professionals move from a static understanding of organizational processes toward one that understands the interplay of policies, structures, individual behaviors, and communication as a continually evolving process (Salem, 2002). Clients may consider observational findings more engaging because they were situated in the specific practices present within the organization (Meyer, 2002).

Because HRM professionals often are constrained by other responsibilities, they may only be able to perform several observations during the data-collection process. This limitation can make it difficult to generalize observational findings to the larger organizational climate (Hogard &

Ellis, 2006). In our experience, engaging in even a few observations can provide value. During a multi-method assessment performed at the request of a professional service firm by some of the chapter's authors, observational data revealed that employees were not sticking to scripts during their sales calls. Although variances were minimal, they resulted in unintended deception of customers about the nature of the services that the organization provided.

Textual Analysis

Daily organizational operations produce a surprising amount of texts, including memos, Web pages, and mission statements. As one of the most visible and permanent instantiations of organizational communication and operations, texts serve as a powerful force for guiding organizational behavior (Ashcraft, Kuhn, & Cooren, 2009; Cooren, 2004) and developing organizational identity (Fairhurst, Jordan, & Neuwirth, 1997). Structured analysis of these texts can provide HRM professionals with a unique perspective on internal and external organizational communication, such as shared values and channels of influence throughout the organization (Meyer, 2002, p. 473).

Texts offer important traces of organizational policy, communication activity, and employee responses over time and across individuals. For instance, Clampitt and Berk (2009) examined employee publications, corporate reports, and bulletin boards. Inconsistencies were identified between upper management's intended messages and representations of those messages throughout the organization. Some bulletin boards were updated more often than others, making certain employees more likely to receive some managerial messages than others. This finding contradicted questionnaire findings suggesting that employees and management were satisfied with bulletin boards' functionality.

Computational tools can also aid in uncovering patterns in organizational texts. One such tool, Centering Resonance Analysis (CRA; Corman, Kuhn, McPhee, & Dooley, 2002), processes a corpus of texts to identify recurring patterns of noun phrases. Identifying these patterns permits tracking how organizational discourses change over time. For example, Kuhn and Corman (2003) used CRA to compare how subgroups in a community organization interpreted an organizational change. The method allowed the authors to identify differences in interpretation that were unapparent to management. By revealing underlying divisions, such tools can help managers reflexively address underlying operational and communication issues.

In sum, HRM professionals have a broad set of tools with which to understand the nature, sources, and consequences of employee experiences and perspectives. Given the stated importance of communication behaviors to organizational success (Poole, 2011), it would seem important for researchers to discover how HRM conceptualizes and measures aspects of communication. One approach relies on multiple data-collection methods to reveal a broader picture of the way that communication occurs between people in the organization and external stakeholders.

Example of a Multi-Method Investigation of Levers for Strategic Change

Considerable informative power comes from supplementing the analysis of one set of data collected through one source with a second source that may offer different insights (Jick, 1979; Patton, 2002). It is the combination of these stories that has potential for understanding how the organization operates and for identifying potential enablers and constraints on strategic changes planned by management.

A regional chapter of a large nonprofit consumer advocacy group (henceforth referred to as Advocacy) noticed declines in the number of consumers that requested its help on key issues. Management decided that the decline in consumer inquiries was due, in part, to internal operations that were not running as smoothly as earlier and to lower communication "morale" among employees, who were distributed throughout four office buildings in the metro area. Also, management hoped employees would come up with more innovative programs, announcements, and services for consumers instead of simply implementing the corporate office's ideas. Several of the authors administered a standard attitude questionnaire (e.g., scales assessing information sufficiency, helpfulness) akin to those included in most audit approaches (e.g., Goldhaber, 1979). The results were interesting though not instructive. Employees reported some discrepancy between their actual and desired levels of communication with various colleagues, but findings failed to reveal significant or discernible patterns.

In order to get a coordinated picture of the communication environment within Advocacy and help identify strategic levers for change, 41 of the 75 employees were interviewed and 32 hours of work observations were conducted of people split across the organization's three departments: Operations, Sales, and Communication. Sociometric (network) measures were administered to all members of the organization to assess actual communication flow (66 were returned). Textual analyses were performed on a random sample of 82 "consumer intake forms" completed by employees as well as 308 (100%) of the press releases produced by Advocacy over the previous five years.

Interviews revealed that employees in every department had little ongoing, planned interaction with employees in other departments. People reported that they did not often talk to others outside their departments, which countered the questionnaire findings. The sociometric analysis provided a more definitive understanding of the discrepancy between questionnaire and interview data. Mapping each employee's communication network revealed that workers rarely interacted with colleagues outside of their departments and physical locations and that this pattern was more pronounced for employees who worked away from the organization's central office. Furthermore, analysis of the communication network as a whole revealed that department heads were the main link between business units. Removing managers from the network made the communication silos even more apparent.

The interview and network analysis data showed that employees often had little insight into the information needs of others outside of their respective departments, and, perhaps more troubling, they failed to recognize the interdependence among units. As one Communications employee noted, "When I get an email about some change in Sales, like how [other units] are selling companies, I will just put it in a folder without reading it because it has nothing to do with what I work on." This pattern hindered the ability of Advocacy to change and learn. With limited exposure across units, employees had fewer opportunities to gain insights into the roles and responsibilities of their colleagues. When individuals turned to similar others in the organization for information, existing mistakes and inefficiencies were reinforced instead of challenged.

The data also revealed three additional challenges to the organization's operations. First, the communication network demonstrated that senior managers served as central points to deliver messages across the organization. However, the work observations suggested that their presence as go-betweens also prevented employees from gaining insight into the business practices of others. Moreover, messages were often lost or distorted as they moved up and down the organization, and both managers and employees were hesitant to communicate issues to superiors. Second, the communication silos at Advocacy meant that instead of acting as a single, connected unit, the organization operated as a collection of "small worlds." Although each department developed specialized knowledge, employees only saw what happened right around them. Work observations revealed that best practices generated in one area of Advocacy were unlikely to be shared.

Third, a textual analysis revealed that Advocacy's press releases, one of its main "products," were disproportionately targeted at the general public versus current and potential business clients, often modifying old releases only slightly to fit the current context, mostly warning the media of scams that either were currently in progress, seasonal in nature, or direct responses to news or weather-related events. The CEO frequently appeared on morning television programs to talk about consumer issues. Although such releases could be highly relevant and valuable, they failed to take advantage of the organization's marketing position with their business clients. The failure of Communications and Operations to collaborate was troublesome because the accredited business program was one of the few revenue-producing venues for the organization.

Advocacy received a report containing three suggestions: expand the brokerage roles at various levels of the organization, reduce barriers between distributed employees, and develop collaborative relationships between the Communications and Operations units to understand and act on trends. Senior management occupied nearly all of the go-between or brokerage roles within the organization and, as such, decided what was communicated and how it would be disseminated. This structure limited the exposure of employees to new ideas and also symbolically suggested that employees did not need to know about other areas of the organization. To reduce barriers between distributed employees, we suggested that Advocacy promote sharing of best practices by increasing regular formal and informal communication among individuals in different locations. Finally, to move away from press releases that were largely repetitive and reactive in nature, we recommended that Communications should work directly with Operations to understand trends by sending a Communications representative to any Operations staff meetings during which marketing data were to be discussed. One year after the completion of our report, management indicated that the changes made to the way people communicated had allowed them to improve their strategic vision of work processes, which, in their opinion, decreased employee turnover and increased the innovative use of data across the organization, especially in the Communications department.

This case illustrates the various ways that HRM can assess employee attitudes and their perspective of organizational operations. Yet it also raises a number of questions that, if investigated, might assist HRM professionals in their discovery, advocating, and facilitating roles. Specifically, when HRM professionals receive an internal or external (i.e., consultant's) report of employees' attitudes, what are the steps by which they disseminate the findings? What information do they typically, if at all, present to executive management? What do they present to line managers? How do their reports to managers differ from what they present to workers? If they are a regional unit of a larger national or international corporation, what information do they present to corporate HRM, and what feedback do they typically receive? These questions are rudimentary, but they highlight the role of HRM as communicative entities that may shape corporate action with the data they collect, how they share the data, and what is derived from their assessment efforts.

Conclusion

According to Blackburn and Rosen (1993), many highly touted companies use questionnaire scales to "encourage bottom-up communication to insure that employee voices are heard in the managerial and executive suites" (p. 53). Certainly, it is essential to conduct employee surveys to identify problems and address them (Kornhauser & Sharp, 1932; Saari & Judge, 2004). Yet assessing employee attitudes in general and their perspectives on communication in their unit and throughout the organization may enable HRM professionals to shift from reactive or post hoc assessments to a proactive orientation for diagnosing how and where the organization needs to change.

One objective of this chapter is to stimulate more research on communication issues faced by HRM professionals. There are relatively few investigations into HRM managers' use of attitude surveys in organizations from this perspective, but it is a strategy we believe would benefit organizations. We advocate that HRM professionals augment their use of questionnaires with other techniques such as network analysis, interviews, work observations, and textual analysis to develop deeper insights into the communication environment and organizational operations.

Bibliography

Ashcraft, K.L., Kuhn, T.R., & Cooren, F. (2009). Constitutional amendments: "Materializing" organizational communication. *Academy of Management Annals, 3*(1), 1–64.

Axley, S.R. (1984). Managerial and organizational communication in terms of the conduit metaphor. *Academy of Management Review, 9*(3), 428–437.

Becker, H.S., & Geer, B. (1957). Participant observation and interviewing: A comparison. *Human Organization, 16*(3), 28–32.

Becker, H.S., Geer, B., Hughes, E.C., & Strauss, A.L. (1961). *Boys in white*. Chicago: University of Chicago Press.

Blackburn, R., & Rosen, B. (1993). Total quality and human resources management: Lessons learned from Baldrige Award-winning companies. *Academy of Management Executive, 7*(3), 49–66.

Blau, P.M. (1955). *The dynamics of bureaucracy*. Chicago: University of Chicago Press.

Borgatti, S.P., & Cross, R. (2003). A relational view of information seeking and learning in social networks. *Management Science, 49*(4), 432–445.

Brass, D.J. (1995). A social network perspective on human resources management. In G. Ferris (Ed.), *Research in personnel and human resources management, Vol. 13* (pp. 39–79). Greenwich, CT: JAI Press.

Brass, D.J., Galaskiewicz, J., Greve, H.R., & Wenpin, T. (2004). Taking stock of networks and organizations: A multilevel perspective. *Academy of Management Journal, 47*(6), 795–817.

Browning, L.D. (1992). Lists and stories as organizational communication. *Communication Theory, 2*(4), 281–302.

Burt, R. (1992). *Structural holes: The social structure of competition*. Cambridge, MA: Harvard University.

Clampitt, P.G., & Berk, L. (2009). A communication audit of a paper mill. In O. Hargie & D. Tourish (Eds.), *Auditing organizational communication: A handbook of research, theory, and practice* (pp. 274–289). New York: Routledge.

Clampitt, P.G., & Downs, C.W. (1993). Employee perceptions of the relationship between communication and productivity: A field study. *Journal of Business Communication, 30*(1), 5–28.

Cooren, F. (2004). Textual agency: How texts do things in organizational settings. *Organization, 11*(3), 373–393.

Corman, S.R., Kuhn, T., McPhee, R.D., & Dooley, K.J. (2002). Studying complex discursive systems: Centering resonance analysis of communication. *Human Communication Research, 28*(2), 157–206.

Cross, R., & Sproull, L. (2004). More than an answer: Information relationships for actionable knowledge. *Organization Science, 15*(4), 446–462.

Downs, C.W., & Adrian, C. (2004). *Assessing organizational communication: Strategic communication audits*. New York: Guilford Press.

Edwards, J.E., & Fisher, B.M. (2004). Evaluating employee survey programs. In J.E. Edwards, J.C. Scott, and N.S. Raju (Eds.), *The human resources program-evaluation handbook* (pp. 365–386). Thousand Oaks, CA: Sage.

Fairhurst, G.T., Jordan, J.M., & Neuwirth, K. (1997). Why are we here? Managing the meaning of an organizational mission statement. *Journal of Applied Communication Research, 25*(4), 243–263.

Feeley, T.H., Hwang, J., & Barnett, G.A. (2008). Predicting employee turnover from friendship networks. *Journal of Applied Communication Research, 36*(1), 56–73.

Glaser, B., & Strauss, A.L. (1967). *The discovery of grounded theory: Strategies for qualitative research.* Chicago: Aldine.

Goldhaber, G.M. (1979). *Auditing organizational communication systems: The ICA communication audit.* Dubuque, IA: Kendall/Hunt.

Goldhaber, G. M., & Krivonos, P. D. (1977). The ICA audit: Process, status, critique. *Journal of Business Communication, 15*(1), 41–55.

Gouldner, A.W. (1954). *Industrial bureaucracy.* New York: Free Press.

Greenbaum, H.H., Clampitt, P., & Willihnganz, S. (1988). Organizational communication : An examination of four instruments. *Management Communication Quarterly, 2*(2), 245–282.

Hargie, O., & Tourish, D. (Eds.). (2000). *Handbook of communication audits for organisations.* Boston: Routledge.

Hargie, O., & Tourish, D. (Eds.). (2009). *Auditing organizational communication: A handbook of research, theory, and practice.* New York: Routledge.

Hogard, E., & Ellis, R. (2006). Evaluation and communication: Using a communication audit to evaluate organizational communication. *Evaluation Review, 30*(2), 171–187.

Jick, T.D. (1979). Mixing qualitative and quantitative methods: Triangulation in action. *Administrative Science Quarterly, 24*(4), 602–611.

Johnson, Z. (2010). *C-IKNOW complete documentation & workflow.* Sonic Laboratory 2010. Northwestern University, Evanston, IL. Retrieved from http://ciknow.northwestern.edu/downloads/web/docs/ciknow-guide-all.pdf

Kipnis, D., Schmidt, S., & Wilkinson, J. (1980). Interorganizational influence tactics: Explorations in getting one's way. *Journal of Applied Psychology, 65*(4), 440–452.

Klein, K.J., Dansereau, F., & Hall, R.J. (1994). Levels issues in theory development, data collection, and analysis. *Academy of Management Review, 19*(2), 195–229.

Klein, K.J., & Kozlowski, S.W.J. (2000). *Multilevel theory, research, and methods in organizations: Foundations, extensions, and new directions.* San Francisco: Jossey-Bass.

Kornhauser, A.W., & Sharp, A.A. (1932). Employee attitudes: Suggestions from a study in a factory. *Personnel Journal, 10*(6), 393–404.

Krackhardt, D., & Porter, L.W. (1985). When friends leave: A structural analysis of the relationship between turnover and stayer's attitudes. *Administrative Science Quarterly, 30*(2), 242–261.

Kuhn, T., & Corman, S.R. (2003). The emergence of homogeneity and heterogeneity in knowledge structures during a planned organizational change. *Communication Monographs, 70*(3), 198–229.

Kvale, S. (1996). *Interviews: An introduction to qualitative research interviewing.* Thousand Oaks, CA: Sage.

Lewis, L.K. (1999). Disseminating information and soliciting input during planned organizational change: Implementers' targets, sources and channels for communicating. *Management Communication Quarterly, 13*(1), 43–75.

Mathis, R.L., & Jackson, J.L. (2010). *Human resource management* (13th ed.). Independence, KY: South-Western Cengage Learning.

Meyer, J.C. (2002). Organizational communication assessment: Fuzzy methods and the accessibility of symbols. *Management Communication Quarterly, 15*(3), 472–479.

Miles, M.B., & Huberman, A.M. (1994). *Qualitative data analysis: A source book of new methods* (2nd ed.). Beverly Hills, CA: Sage.

Millar, R., & Tracey, A. (2009). The interview approach. In O. Hargie & D. Tourish (Eds.), *Auditing organizational communication: A handbook of research, theory, and practice* (pp. 78–102). New York: Routledge.

Miller, V.D., Poole, M.S., & Seibold, D.R., with Meyers, K., Park, H.S., Monge, P.R., Fulk, J., Frank, L., Margolin, D., Schultz, C., Cuihua, S., Weber, M., Lee, S., & Shumate, S. (2011). Advancing research in organizational communication through quantitative methodology. *Management Communication Quarterly, 25*(1), 1–43.

Monge, P.R., & Contractor, N.S. (2003). *Theories of communication networks.* Oxford: Oxford University Press.

Muchinsky, P.M. (1977). Organizational communication: Relationships to organizational climate and job satisfaction. *Academy of Management Journal, 20*(4), 592–607.

Noe, R.A., Hollenbeck, J.R., Gerhart, B., & Wright, P.M. (2011). *Fundamentals of human resource management.* New York: McGraw-Hill Irwin.

Nordblom, C., & Hamrefors, S. (2007). *Communicative leadership. Development of middle managers' communication skills at Volvo Group* (No. 2/07). Stockholm: Swedish Public Relations Association.

Patton, M.Q. (2002). *Qualitative evaluation and research methods.* Thousand Oaks, CA: Sage.

Polanyi, M. (1966). *The tacit dimension.* London: Routledge.

Poole, M.S. (2011). Communication. In S. Zedeck (Ed.), *APA handbook of industrial and organizational psychology, Vol. 3* (pp. 249–270). Washington, DC: American Psychological Association.

Reichers, A.E., Wanous, J.P., & Austin, J.T. (1997). Understanding and managing cynicism about organizational change. *Academy of Management Executive, 11*(1), 48–59.

Saari, L.M., & Judge, T.A. (2004). Employee attitudes and job satisfaction. *Human Resource Management, 43*(4), 395–407.

Salem, P. (2002). Assessment, change, and complexity. *Management Communication Quarterly, 15*(3), 442–450.

Schmitt, N.W., & Klimoski, R.J. (1991). *Research methods in human resource management.* Cincinnati, OH: South-Western.

Seibold, D.R. (2009). Measurement in organizational and group communication. In R.B. Rubin, A.M. Rubin, E.E. Graham, E.M. Perse, & D.R. Seibold (Eds.), *Communication research measures II: A sourcebook, Vol. 2* (pp. 18–35). New York: Taylor & Francis/Routledge.

Su, C., Huang, M., & Contractor, N. (2010). Understanding the structures, antecedents and outcomes of organisational learning and knowledge transfer: A multi-theoretical and multilevel network analysis. *European Journal of International Management, 4*(6), 576–601.

Susskind, A.M., Miller, V.D., & Johnson, J.D. (1998). Downsizing and structural holes: Their impact on layoff survivors' perceptions of organizational chaos and openness to change. *Communication Research, 25*(1), 30–65.

Ulrich, D., Brockbank, W., Yeung, A.K., & Lake, D.G. (1995). Human resource competencies: An empirical assessment. *Human Resource Management, 34*(4), 473–495.

Van Maanen, J. (1979). The fact of fiction in organizational ethnography. *Administrative Science Quarterly, 24*(4), 539–550.

Waldron, V.R. (1991). Achieving communication goals in superior-subordinate relationships: The multi-functionality of upward maintenance tactics. *Communication Monographs, 58*(3), 289–306.

Yuan, Y.C., Fulk, J., & Monge, P.R. (2007). Access to information in connective and communal transactive memory systems. *Communication Research, 34*(2), 131–155.

Zwijze-Koning, K.H., & De Jong, M.D.T. (2005). Auditing information structures in organizations: A review of data collection techniques for network analysis. *Organizational Research Methods, 8*(4), 429–453.

15

HOW COMMUNICATION AFFECTS EMPLOYEE KNOWLEDGE OF AND REACTIONS TO COMPENSATION SYSTEMS

Ingrid Smithey Fulmer and Yan Chen

Scholarly research on communication about pay issues, while somewhat limited, has generally found that the way organizations communicate about compensation matters in terms of how it affects employees' attitudinal and behavioral reactions to their pay (e.g., Card, Mas, Moretti, & Saez, 2012; Folger & Konovsky, 1989; Futrell 1978; Futrell & Jenkins, 1978). Textbooks and practitioner-oriented reports also remind us that communicating with employees about compensation is very important (e.g., Milkovich, Newman, & Gerhart, 2014). Yet, in a recent survey of compensation professionals, only 50% of respondents answered "strongly agree" or "agree" when asked whether their organizations were focused on increasing their pay communications with employees (WorldatWork, 2012b). Only 29% agreed or strongly agreed when asked whether their organizations were able to effectively communicate the value of compensation (total rewards) to line managers, and only 25% said they communicated this effectively to employees (WorldatWork, 2012b). This area of compensation practice would seemingly benefit from a more evidence-based approach to increasing the effectiveness of pay communication. But what does the research evidence say exactly?

In this chapter we provide an overview of the scholarly research on several key aspects of compensation communication. Where appropriate, we also provide data from organizational surveys conducted by WorldatWork, a professional organization primarily comprised of human resource practitioners working in the areas of compensation and benefits; these frequent and often large-sample surveys provide a useful supplement to the academic research. To highlight the areas where research has been most and least evident, we present in Figure 15.1 a schematic for thinking about the various ways pay communication has been or could be studied in organizations, with two pay communication constructs emphasized with a heavy outline. The first construct (labeled "Organization's information-sharing strategy") focuses on the organization's perspective and includes communication policies and practices of the organization as they relate to pay data availability, the explanations provided about pay, and the mechanisms for communicating with employees about pay (e.g., through managers, online communications, etc.). The second construct (labeled "Employee perceptions of information-sharing practices") considers how most research has captured employees' perceptions of pay communications; when asked, employees usually weigh in on the frequency or adequacy of pay communications, the clarity

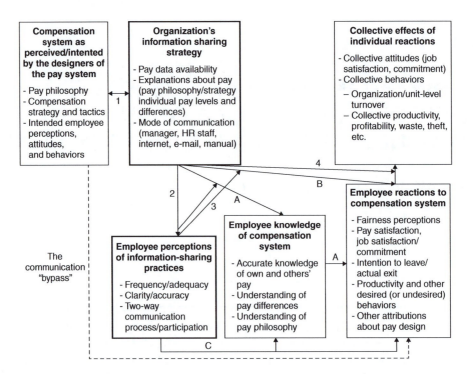

FIGURE 15.1 Role of communications in employee knowledge of and reactions to compensation systems.

of the information, and whether the process allows for two-way communication in the form of feedback, for example. In this review, we primarily consider two broad categories of employee outcomes—knowledge of the compensation system and attitudinal and behavioral reactions to the system.

Most research that seeks to understand the effectiveness of pay systems focuses on the effect of system design on employee reactions and typically does not take pay communication issues into account (the dashed line in Figure 15.1). This "bypass" approach risks mis-specifying the pay system–employee outcome relationship by effectively assuming that pay system outcomes are solely due to the good or bad design of the system itself, rather than to implementation issues (e.g., communication) that could enhance or diminish the effects of the system design.

Without attention to communication issues, it is conceivable that a researcher (or an organization) could conclude that a pay system is not working (and perhaps discontinue it), when in fact the problem is not with the system itself but with how it is communicated to and understood by employees. In what follows, we highlight what is currently known about pay communication, both from the organizational perspective and from the employee perspective, and how communication influences employee reactions to pay systems. From the organizational perspective, we consider the effects of pay openness and secrecy on pay data availability (the "what" of pay communication), of the explanations provided about pay (the "why" of pay communication), and of the mode of communication on employee knowledge of and reactions to pay (the "how"). These aspects of pay communication and their effects are reflected in paths A and B of Figure 15.1. Along the way, we also integrate research that has considered how employee perceptions about the pay communication process (which we treat as separate from knowledge of the pay system itself) affect pay knowledge and reactions to pay (path C). We conclude by highlighting areas where research is scarce (paths 1–4) in the hope of stimulating the curiosity of both scholars and organizational managers.

What: The Effects of Organizational Pay Openness Policies on Employee Pay Data Knowledge and Reactions

One dimension of communicating with employees about compensation involves the management of pay data itself. Employees know their own pay outcomes, of course, but most evaluate that information in light of what others make and as a consequence tend to seek information about relative pay and relative inputs that determine pay differences (Adams, 1965). This information seeking can take the form of guessing what other employees make, exchanging pay information with other employees, and/or referring to pay information provided by the organization (Colella, Paetzold, Zardkoohi, & Wesson, 2007). Organizations, in turn, vary in the degree to which they facilitate this information seeking. Organizations must decide whether to encourage or discourage employees from talking about pay, whether pay information will be released by the organization, and, if so, what type of pay information will be provided (basis of pay, pay range, or detailed pay information; Colella et al., 2007; WorldatWork, 2012a).

Some researchers (Burroughs, 1982) view pay communication policies as spanning a continuum, with pay openness and pay secrecy anchoring the opposite ends. At the more open end is the situation where organizations disclose detailed information such as a listing of each employee and his or her annual pay, with or without other information such as job title, seniority, and so forth; in the case of public sector workers, this information is often released to the public, and not just internally. Organizations that encourage or at least do not restrict discussion of pay among employees (e.g., Silverman, 2013) would also fall toward this end of the spectrum. At the closed end of the pay data spectrum are organizations that provide no official pay information to their employees about what others in the organization make and that may discourage discussion or even enforce rules prohibiting employees from discussing their pay with coworkers.[1] Surveys of compensation professionals suggest that organizations vary considerably along this continuum. In a recent WorldatWork survey, respondents indicated that 34% of organizations share "minimal pay information" with employees, while at the other end of the spectrum, 44% of organizations share the range of base salary for an employee's pay grade with the employee, 18% share this information for all pay grades, and 2% share actual pay levels for all employees (WorldatWork, 2012a).

Pay openness policies influence employee attitudes and behaviors through the effect they have on the accuracy of employees' perceptions about the pay of others and the resultant sensemaking to which this may lead. To date, the theoretical and empirical research has not provided a clear conclusion on the effects of pay secrecy and/or disclosure, and a relatively limited body of empirical research has been conducted on this topic. In a test of the relationships corresponding with path A in Figure 15.1, Lawler's seminal research (1965, 1967) found that in the absence of pay information, managers formed inaccurate perceptions of others' pay and pay differentials, which were related to dissatisfaction with pay and a weakening of the employees' perceptions of the link between performance and pay. Employees tend to systematically underestimate the pay of their superiors and overestimate the pay of their peers and subordinates. Findings from other empirical studies (Futrell 1978; Futrell & Jenkins, 1978; Thompson & Pronsky, 1975) were also generally consistent with Lawler's work. For example, two studies by Futrell and colleagues (Futrell 1978; Futrell & Jenkins, 1978) found that salespeople's job performance and sales managers' satisfaction with their pay and promotion policies increased after their units instituted a relatively open pay policy where employees were told of the low, high, and average merit raise amounts of their peers. (These studies correspond to path B in Figure 15.1 as they did not directly assess whether employees' perceptions of pay were accurate.)

Other research finds that the relationship between accuracy of compensation perceptions and employee satisfaction is more ambiguous. Milkovich and Anderson (1972) replicated Lawler's experiments (path C in Figure 15.1) in a firm that had a partially open policy where median salaries and pay ranges for one's own level were communicated. They again found that managers underestimated pay of superiors and overestimated pay of peers and subordinates. Even though 64% of employees said their manager had told them the median pay, and 79% had been told the range for salaries of their peers, less than 10% correctly estimated the average pay of their peers. In that study, managers with the most accurate perceptions were actually the most dissatisfied with their pay. In another study of an organization that made it a practice to disclose pay mid-points and ranges for managers' own and adjacent (higher and lower) managerial levels, Mahoney and Weitzel (1978) also found that managers systematically misperceived the pay of others and again found no evidence suggesting that satisfaction with compensation is related to accuracy of perceptions.

More recent evidence suggests that very open pay policies, where individual pay levels rather than medians and ranges are disclosed, may have different effects on different employees. For example, in a recent quasi-experimental study, researchers manipulated university employees' access to a public database where information on the salaries of others in the state university system was listed by name (Card et al., 2012). They found that employees whose actual salaries were below the median and who had access to peers' salary information were less satisfied and more likely to express intentions to search for a new job than those without that information. Interestingly, there was no corresponding positive effect (increased satisfaction or reduced job search intentions) among those paid above the median even when they had access to others' pay data to confirm their relatively higher position in the pay distribution. This asymmetric result is largely consistent with accumulated empirical research on equity theory (Adams, 1965), which tends to find that people do react negatively to unfavorable pay comparisons but do not always respond positively to favorable ("over-reward") pay comparisons (Pritchard, 1969; for a review see Gerhart & Rynes, 2003). However, it is inconsistent with the results of a study of turnover among university administrators by Pfeffer and Davis-Blake (1992) that found a more symmetrical positive/negative reaction among higher/lower paid workers, one that was expected to be enhanced under conditions of greater pay information. One key difference between Card et al.'s study and the Pfeffer/Davis-Blake study was that the latter assumed that administrators in public universities have greater access to pay data than those in private universities but did not actually evaluate the nature of that data (e.g., how detailed it might be) or the degree to which administrators in their study actually made use of the data. This is an important difference because one would surmise that in the early 1990s, even when pay data were technically publically available, they would not have been as readily accessible via online databases as they are today.

Moreover, researchers have found evidence that individual differences matter and that pay secrecy may lower motivation and adversely affect task performance for certain individuals while raising it for others. Using a lab-based simulation with students, Bamberger and Belogolovsky

(2010) found that pay secrecy has significantly negative effects on task performance for individuals with low inequity tolerance and that these adverse effects are partially explained by reduced performance-pay instrumentality perceptions. Participants with high tolerance for pay inequity actually performed better under pay secrecy conditions.

Despite social taboos that can affect pay discussions, given the opportunity to compare and share specific pay information, many people (but not all) will do so. Card et al. (2012) found that when they made people aware of the existence of the public employee pay database, it more than doubled the proportion of people who said they looked at it (50%), as compared to a control group, some of whom were already familiar with it (19%). And, as might be expected, employees who went to the pay database were most interested in the pay of their coworkers rather than of high-profile members of the organization. In Bamberger and Belogolovsky's (2010) study, participants in the pay openness condition were given a list of information about their own and their peers' pay, identified by a code number. When given the opportunity to talk about pay, 97% of people reportedly shared their code number at some point in the study, revealing their personal pay information (presumably in hopes of learning others' pay information). These differences in curiosity about pay among employees remind us that the effects of pay openness policies in organizations depend largely on the degree to which individuals care to look at the available pay information.

The effects of pay data communication policies are also likely contingent on factors related to the pay system itself, such as the basis used to evaluate individuals' performance and to determine differences in pay. For example, Thompson and Pronsky (1975) and others (Milkovich, Newman, & Gerhart, 2014) have noted that organizations allocating pay based on subjective performance evaluation may be more likely to see negative effects rather than benefits from an open pay system. In addition, the method used to disseminate pay data information to employees and the exact type of information may moderate the effects of pay openness. In most of the aforementioned studies that considered whether employees' perceptions of others' pay were accurate in organizations with open pay policies (path C in Figure 15.1), the employees' managers were the source of the pay information and it was provided in the form of pay level or pay raise midpoints and ranges. The consistently inaccurate perceptions of employees receiving information this way suggests either that employees do not trust the information received from managers or, perhaps, that it is not vivid enough to be memorable if it is not identified with specific other people. Unfortunately, in studies where actual pay data were available to employees in the form of a list of specific other employees' pay, the studies did not attempt to ascertain whether employees were accurate in their recollection of the information received.

Why: Communicating Explanations About Pay Systems and About Individual Pay

Besides providing data about pay levels themselves, organizations also provide information that helps employees interpret pay data, understand how their own current pay is determined, and understand how to increase their compensation in the future. This includes providing information about the organization's overall pay philosophy and strategy, the basis for pay differentials among organizational members, and the details and computations sometimes involved in understanding how various aspects of the compensation and rewards system work.

Organizations expend resources and design pay systems to motivate employee behavior in strategically important ways. However, if employees don't perceive or understand what the organization is providing and why, the organization will have a difficult time achieving its compensation objectives. For example, the accuracy of employees' understanding about their pay has been examined in the context of equity-based pay (i.e., stock options). Despite the growing use of employee stock options for nonexecutive employees, research suggests that many employees do not understand how to value them (Farrell, Krische, & Sedatole, 2011; Mulvey, LeBlanc, Heneman, & McInerney, 2002), and that many employees exercise them as soon as they can, reducing the potential value to be received from them (Huddart & Lang, 1996). In other words, organizations perceive they are giving something worth X, but, due to a lack of knowledge, employees feel they are being given something worth Y. The further apart X and Y are, and especially if Y is less than X, the less likely that this form of compensation will be appreciated and have the desired motivational effect on employees.

Effective pay communication is essential for ensuring that organizations are getting what they pay for when they spend money on compensation and that employees understand the value of what they are receiving. In addition, employees who understand their pay systems experience greater satisfaction with the administration of the system and greater perceptions of fairness regarding both the process of pay determination and the payouts from a pay plan (e.g., Brown & Huber, 1992; Dulebohn & Martocchio, 1998; Judge, 1993).

The communication of information about differences in pay among employees is usually not just about pay; rather, pay is often the byproduct or most visible manifestation of broader conversations about the organization's performance management system and about an individual's performance. In most organizations performance appraisal results are tied to salary increases and bonuses (Lawler, Benson, & McDermott, 2012; Lawler & McDermott, 2002; WorldatWork, 2012a). Consequently, the scholarly work that focuses on communication in performance management and performance appraisal obviously has implications for compensation communication. Since chapter 10 addresses communication in performance management/appraisal, we will focus on what we know about the communication of pay and pay system information other than what is typically discussed in the appraisal interview.

Recent surveys of compensation professionals suggest that even though most organizations have a written compensation philosophy, most practitioners believe that employees in their organizations do not understand it, with only 33% rating their organization as effective or very effective in communicating its philosophy and rewards strategy (Scott, Sperling, McMillen, & Bowbin, 2008; WorldatWork, 2012a). Less than half of organizational respondents said they communicated information regarding how an employee's individual pay fits with the overall pay strategy and how pay is tied to performance (WorldatWork, 2012a). Brief written notifications (e.g., memos, e-mails) and/or verbal discussions seem to be the preferred method for communicating annual pay increases to employees, with detailed messages (written or verbal) used less often (WorldatWork, 2012a).

This lack of detailed communication about an organization's pay philosophy and about how an employee's pay fits into the organization's overall pay strategy (and the resulting sense that employees do not understand these issues) may be attributable in part to compensation professionals' underestimating the ramifications of such knowledge. By and large, compensation professionals have an accurate understanding of academic research findings related to many pay issues. However, research suggests that many may not fully appreciate the linkage between an employee's knowledge of how his or her pay is determined and attitudinal outcomes such as pay satisfaction and commitment (WorldatWork, 2010). This stands in contrast to the substantial body of scholarly work that has found that both employees and organizations benefit when employees understand why and how their pay is set the way it is (e.g., Brown & Huber, 1992; Dulebohn & Martocchio, 1998; Judge, 1993).

We know relatively little about how employees come to understand the manner in which their pay systems work and what role organizations' information dissemination practices play in this understanding. Unlike the studies described earlier that compared what organizations disclose about pay levels and ranges with what employees perceive to be the pay levels of their coworkers (e.g., Mahoney & Witzel, 1978; Milkovich & Anderson, 1972), there have been few empirical studies that examined the accuracy of employees' knowledge about how their pay is determined as compared to what the organization has communicated to them.

Studies of employee reactions to pay systems typically do not focus on whether pay system information provided by the organization is actually effective in creating accurate knowledge in the employee, but rather focus on the organization's or the employee's perceptions of the adequacy of the information dissemination efforts. For example, one study asked HRM personnel to rate the amount of information provided to employees and whether employees understood what was required to get pay raises and then related this measure of pay communication to employee turnover in response to pay dispersion (Shaw & Gupta, 2007; this would be a path B study in our Figure 15.1 framework). Another study of profit-sharing plans assessed employees' perceptions of whether they received adequate information using a single item ("We discuss fund-related matters often enough.") and then compared that to employees' scores on a test that asked questions about how the plan worked (this would correspond to path C in our figure; Sweins & Kalmi, 2008). A positive relationship was found, but this does not establish conclusively which pay information practices were effective in creating profit-sharing system knowledge because we do not know exactly what was communicated in the discussions or whether the discussions were the sole source of information available to employees. It is possible that people learned about how the profit-sharing system worked from written materials or other sources. Other relevant information was provided by a study of performance appraisals (Williams & Levy, 1992). Researchers found that when employees self-report that they have more knowledge of their performance appraisal system, their self-appraisals of performance were more consistent with those of their supervisors; even this study did not directly test the accuracy of employees' knowledge, however.

While employee satisfaction with and organizational perceptions of the adequacy of pay communications are important for understanding the communication process, what is arguably more important is whether those information dissemination efforts improve the accuracy of employees' knowledge of how their pay is determined. Assuming the pay system itself is designed appropriately to achieve the worker attitudes and behaviors that the organization intends to foster, then the more knowledgeable employees are about the mechanics of how their pay is computed, the basis upon which their pay is determined, and how their pay fits into the overall compensation strategy of the organization, the more likely they are to react in the desired manner.

How: Modes of Communicating Pay Information

Organizations communicate about pay systems and about individual employees' pay using both impersonal and personal modes of communication. Respondents in a recent WorldatWork survey indicated that 44% said their organization utilized company Web sites, 37% communicated via e-mail, and 20% provided information about pay in employee handbooks and other written materials. But the personal touch still dominates the dissemination of information about pay: 79% of respondents said employees learned about pay from individual discussions with supervisors, and 29% said this information was communicated via individual discussions with someone in the HRM function (WorldatWork 2012a).

Although there is relatively little scholarly research that compares employee reactions to pay information conveyed through various channels, a survey of over 6,000 employees and managers across 26 organizations found that 63% of employees either somewhat agreed or strongly agreed that their managers were effective as sources of information about their pay systems, with similar ratings (58%) given to HRM staff (Mulvey et al., 2002). Other personal sources of information were rated less favorably, with only 42% of respondents voicing some level of agreement that fellow employees were effective sources, and formal training rated as such by only 22% of respondents. Similarly, all impersonal channels (written memos, handbooks, Web site, videos) were rated less favorably than managers and HRM staff; fewer than 50% of employees voiced agreement that any of these was effective.

One reason that employees may perceive managers and HRM staff to be more effective than many other channels is that, besides having legitimacy as authoritative sources of information, these types of interpersonal interactions afford more opportunity for two-way communication about pay. Employees' fairness perceptions are enhanced when they are able to provide feedback about or to appeal specific pay decisions that affect them (e.g., Folger & Konovsky, 1989; Folger, Rosenfield, Grove, & Corkran, 1979). When employees perceive that the pay system is fair, they tend to be more satisfied with pay outcomes, have greater trust in supervisors, and be more committed to the organization (e.g., Folger & Konovsky, 1989).

The manager's important role as a pay communication channel has also been studied from the manager's perspective via surveys (Mulvey et al., 2002). Managers indicated that employees' pay-related questions were relatively infrequent. They also indicated greater confidence in their ability to address performance-related questions than pay questions, with less than 50% saying they were completely or very confident in their ability to answer most specific pay questions, including questions about other employees' pay or about specific forms of pay. The lowest rated item? Not surprisingly, less than 31% said they were completely or very confident in their ability to answer employee questions about stock options (Mulvey et al., 2002), which is probably related to employees' own lack of understanding of options, as discussed earlier.

There is relatively little research directly comparing the accuracy of employees' pay knowledge resulting from different sources of pay information. Based on research described earlier in this chapter (e.g., Milkovich & Anderson, 1972), it would appear that even though employees may perceive their managers to be effective sources of information about pay, managers' information sharing about pay does not necessarily translate into pay knowledge accuracy among employees. We would surmise that this disconnect likely varies across managers and also across employees. Managers' ability to give accurate information is a function of how managers themselves are trained to communicate with employees about compensation, but we have little information from either the practitioner literature or from the academic literature on this type of training. Future research should strive to shed light on this question, as it is a significant aspect of pay communication, particularly given employees' confidence in their managers as sources of pay information.

Toward a More Evidence-Based Approach to Pay Communications: Future Research Directions

Communication issues, despite their obvious importance to the successful implementation of any compensation system, have received less attention relative to other aspects of pay system design and implementation. This omission is unfortunate for several reasons. First, it affects research on the effectiveness of pay system design. When communication issues are ignored in pay system effectiveness research, we are apt to conclude that any failure of a pay system to deliver desired results is a function of that pay system's design, when perhaps it is employees' lack of or inaccurate knowledge about the pay system that is to blame. A second, more direct consequence of the failure to study pay communication practices is that we cannot advise organizations on which practices best shape employees' accurate knowledge of their own and others' pay, which approaches are the best for communicating information about the organization's pay philosophy/strategy, or which are best for explaining why one person's pay differs from that of another.

Thus far in this overview, we have already highlighted the need for more research that directly examines whether organizations' information dissemination efforts result in accurate employee perceptions about pay, particularly when it comes to an understanding of why and how one's own pay is determined, as well as the basic mechanics of how certain complex compensation elements (e.g., stock options) work. A second area where research is sorely needed is comparative work that considers the relative effectiveness of different modes of communication (managers versus online sources, for example) for creating accurate pay knowledge in employees.

In Figure 15.1, we highlight several other research areas that have not received much scholarly attention and hence present opportunities for enterprising scholars going forward. First, the research literature has little if anything to say about how an organization's pay system choices affect its communication policies (path 1). Scholars have suggested that more objectively determined pay systems would likely be more successful than subjectively determined pay systems in an environment of pay openness (Milkovich, Newman, & Gerhart, 2014; Thompson & Pronsky, 1975). By extension this suggests that organizations with pay systems where pay is determined on the basis of relatively objective criteria would tend to be more likely to choose pay openness policies over pay secrecy policies, but to our knowledge there has been no empirical test of this conjecture. It is also possible that the reverse is true; in organizations where pay openness is mandated (e.g., state and local government agencies), this required openness may shape the pay system to reduce the likelihood that nonobjective criteria would be used to any significant degree for pay determination. So, for example, such an organization might be less likely to adopt a strongly performance-based pay system where performance requires subjective assessment or to implement discretionary bonuses if they had to be disclosed.

A second research question that has received little attention is how organizations' communication policies and practices influence employees' perceptions of the adequacy and accuracy of the information and explanations received (path 2). For example, one might expect that pay openness policies would be seen as more adequate in some ways in that they provide more data, but depending on how the information is communicated (online or by managers), they might be perceived as poor in terms of inviting employee feedback or questions about the data. And what is an employee to think if the data are only partially correct? For example, professors' salaries as shown in public university databases are often only reflective of the nine- or ten-month pay for the academic year and may or may not include additional remuneration for summer pay, overload teaching, or executive education. An employee might check his/her own information as disclosed online, see that it is only partially correct, and actually question the adequacy of the data.

A third avenue for future research is to consider whether an employee's perceptions of the organization's information-sharing practices moderate the degree to which he or she develops accurate knowledge of the pay system and/or the degree to which he or she reacts to the pay system (since these are similar, both of these are labeled as path 3). If pay information systems are seen as adequate, clear, and permitting feedback, is the employee more likely to believe and internalize the information? Do information-sharing practices perceived as frequent, clear, and interactive moderate the reactions to the pay system (e.g., productivity, commitment) in a way that makes the pay system more effective overall? Or can the reverse occur? Can communication practices reduce the effectiveness of the pay system itself, and if so how?

A final avenue for future research is depicted in path 4. Organizations implement pay systems with the proximal aim of affecting employee outcomes, but with the ultimate goal of positively influencing organizational outcomes. To what degree do an organization's communication practices create more consistent, or more varied, reactions among employees that in the aggregate either strengthen or weaken the effect of the pay system on organizational outcomes (e.g., Bowen & Ostroff, 2004)? For example, one might surmise that online pay databases and written policy information, while they have their drawbacks, do ensure a certain level of consistency that managerial discussions with individual employees may not (unless managers are trained to deliver consistent messages about pay to employees).

In closing, we are optimistic about the ability of social science scholars in the disciplines of communication, organizational behavior, and human resource management to advance the research in this area in a way that has applicability to managerial practice. We hope that this overview has provided a launching point for that endeavor.

Note

1 In the United States, the National Labor Relations Board (NLRB) has taken the position, enforced by the Sixth Circuit Court of Appeals, that pay secrecy policies, written or verbal, and even if not routinely enforced, interfere with the rights of employees to discuss their working conditions as protected under federal law (see NLRB v. Main Street Terrace Care Center, 327 NLRB 101, *enfd*. 218 F.3d 531 (6th Cir. 2000).

Bibliography

Adams, J.S. (1965). Inequity in social exchange. In L. Berkowitz (Ed.), *Advances in experimental social psychology, Vol. 2* (pp. 267–299). New York: Academic Press.

Bamberger, P., & Belogolovsky, E. (2010). The impact of pay secrecy on individual task performance. *Personnel Psychology, 63*, 965–996.

Bowen, D.E., & Ostroff, C. (2004). Understanding HRM-firm performance linkages: The role of the "strength" of the HRM system. *Academy of Management Review, 29*, 203–221.

Brown, K.A., & Huber, V.L. (1992). Lowering floors and raising ceilings: A longitudinal assessment of the effects of an earnings-at-risk plan on pay satisfaction. *Personnel Psychology, 45*, 279–311.

Burroughs, J.D. (1982). Pay secrecy and performance: The psychological research. *Compensation & Benefits Review, 14*(3), 44–54.

Card, D., Mas, A., Moretti, E., & Saez, E. (2012). Inequality at work: The effect of peer salaries on job satisfaction. *American Economic Review, 102,* 2981–3003.

Colella, A., Paetzold, R.L., Zardkoohi, A., & Wesson, M.J. (2007). Exposing pay secrecy. *Academy of Management Review, 32,* 55–71.

Dulebohn, J.H., & Martocchio, J.J. (1998). Employee perceptions of the fairness of work group incentive pay plans. *Journal of Management, 24,* 469–488.

Farrell, A.M., Krische, S.D., & Sedatole, K.L. (2011). Employees' subjective valuations of their stock options: Evidence on the distributions of valuations and the use of simple anchors. *Contemporary Accounting Research, 28,* 746–793.

Folger, R., & Konovsky, M.A. (1989). Effects of procedural and distributive justice on reactions to pay raise decisions. *Academy of Management Journal, 32,* 115–130.

Folger, R., Rosenfield, D., Grove, J., & Corkran, L. (1979). Effects of "voice" and peer opinions on responses to inequity. *Journal of Personality and Social Psychology, 37,* 2253–2261.

Futrell, C.M. (1978). Effects of pay disclosure on satisfaction for sales managers: A longitudinal study. *Academy of Management Journal, 21,* 140–144.

Futrell, C.M., & Jenkins, O.C. (1978). Pay secrecy versus pay disclosure for salesmen: A longitudinal study. *Journal of Marketing Research, 15,* 214–219.

Gerhart, B., & Rynes, S. (2003). *Compensation: Theory, evidence, and strategic implications.* Thousand Oaks, CA: Sage.

Huddart, S., & Lang, M. (1996). Employee stock option exercises: An empirical analysis. *Journal of Accounting and Economics, 21,* 5–43.

Judge, T.A. (1993). Validity of the dimensions of the Pay Satisfaction Questionnaire: Evidence of differential prediction. *Personnel Psychology, 46,* 334–355.

Lawler, E.E. (1965). Managers' perceptions of their subordinates' pay and of their superiors' pay. *Personnel Psychology, 18,* 413–422.

Lawler, E.E. (1967). Secrecy about management compensation: Are there hidden costs? *Organizational Behavior and Human Performance, 2,* 182–189.

Lawler, E.E., Benson, G.S., & McDermott, M. (2012). Performance management and reward systems. *WorldatWork Journal, 21*(4), 19–28.

Lawler, E.E., & McDermott, M. (2003). Current performance management practices. *WorldatWork Journal, 12*(2), 49–60. Retrieved from www.worldatwork.org/waw/adimLink?id=16825.

Mahoney, T.A., & Weitzel, W. (1978). Secrecy and managerial compensation. *Industrial Relations, 17,* 245–251.

Milkovich, G.T., & Anderson, P.H. (1972). Management compensation and secrecy policies. *Personnel Psychology, 25,* 293–302.

Milkovich, G.T., Newman, J.M., & Gerhart, B. (2014). *Compensation* (11th ed.). New York: McGraw-Hill Irwin.

Mulvey, P.W., LeBlanc, P.V., Heneman, R.L., & McInerney, M. (2002) *The knowledge of pay study: Emails from the front line.* Scottsdale, AZ: WorldatWork.

Pfeffer, J., & Davis-Blake, A. (1992). Salary dispersion, location in the salary distribution, and turnover among college administrators. *Industrial and Labor Relations Review, 45,* 753–763.

Pritchard, R.D. (1969). Equity theory: A review and critique. *Organizational Behavior and Human Performance, 4,* 176–211.

Scott, K.D., Sperling, R.S., McMillen, T.D., & Bowbin, B. (2008). *Rewards communication and pay secrecy: A survey of policies, practices, and effectiveness.* WorldatWork. Retrieved from www.worldatwork.org/waw/adimLink?id=25110.

Shaw, J.D., & Gupta, N. (2007). Pay system characteristics and quit patterns of good, average, and poor performers. *Personnel Psychology, 60,* 903–928.

Silverman, R.E. (2013, January 30). Psst . . . This is what your co-worker is paid. *Wall Street Journal,* B6.

Sweins, C., & Kalmi, P. (2008). Pay knowledge, pay satisfaction and employee commitment: Evidence from Finnish profit sharing schemes. *Human Resource Management Journal, 18,* 366–385.

Thompson, P., & Pronsky, J. (1975). Secrecy or disclosure in management compensation? *Business Horizons, 18*(3), 67–74.

Williams, J.R., & Levy, P.E. (1992). The effects of perceived system knowledge on the agreement between self-ratings and supervisor ratings. *Personnel Psychology, 45*, 835–847.

WorldatWork. (2010). *The connection between academic research and total rewards professionals: A survey of practitioner knowledge and discussion of research.* Scottsdale, AZ: WorldatWork.

WorldatWork. (2012a, October). *Compensation programs and practices.* Scottsdale, AZ: WorldatWork.

WorldatWork. (2012b, July). *The evolving compensation function.* Scottsdale, AZ: WorldatWork.

16

THE ROLE OF COMMUNICATION IN EMPLOYEE SAFETY AND HEALTH MANAGEMENT

Robert R. Sinclair, Kyle R. Stanyar, Anna C. McFadden, Alice M. Brawley, and Yueng-Hsiang Huang

Each year, several thousand U.S. workers die from work-related illnesses and injuries, and over two million experience nonfatal injuries (United States Bureau of Labor Statistics, n.d.). In addition to the devastating human costs for workers, workplace safety and health create significant costs for employers. The direct workers compensation costs of the ten most disabling injuries totaled $51.1 billion in 2010 (Liberty Mutual Research Institute for Safety, 2012), and indirect costs (e.g., lost productivity, administrative costs) exceed the direct costs (Huang, Leamon, Courtney, Chen, & DeArmond, 2011). Employee health also has significant implications for organizational productivity and profitability (Aldana, 2001; Loeppke et al., 2009). Chronic health conditions such as obesity, depression, and back pain represent an estimated 10.7% of total labor costs (Collins et al., 2005), and unhealthy employees cost the U.S. economy an estimated $1.3 trillion annually (DeVol & Bedroussian, 2007).

These figures indicate the importance of developing proactive strategies to minimize the risk of accidents and injuries by creating safer workplaces *and* to maximize employee health and well-being by promoting positive health behaviors. Communication is central to these efforts. The Centers for Disease Control and Prevention (CDC, 2013) defines health communication as "the study and use of communication strategies to inform and influence individual decisions to enhance health." In this chapter we describe a model linking communication to safety and health outcomes through its effects on organizational climate, employee knowledge, and motivation. We also discuss practical considerations for crafting communication strategies and research directions concerning safety and health communication.

Linking Communication to Safety and Health Outcomes

Figure 16.1 presents our model linking communication with employee safety and health. As the model depicts, we focus on employee behavior as central to safety and health management. Responsibility for safety and health does not reside entirely with employees—particularly those working in inherently dangerous and/or poorly managed work environments. However, individual behavior often plays an important role in health and safety events, and communication can help encourage safe and healthy behavior. We assume that communication affects employee

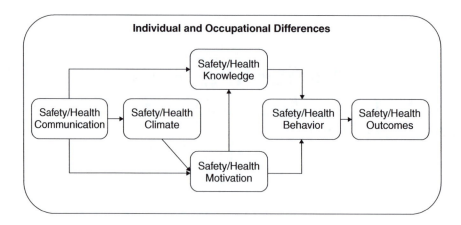

FIGURE 16.1 A conceptual framework linking safety/health communication to safety/health outcomes.

behavior through two primary pathways—knowledge and motivation—and that effective communication strategies must address both. We also assume there is no one-best safety and health communication strategy. Important concerns in one occupational context may be irrelevant in another, and individual differences among employees suggest that no communication strategy is likely to be universally effective. We discuss some of these contingency factors in the following.

Safety and Health Behavior and Outcomes

The first link in the model concerns the behavior-outcome relationship. Behavior refers to specific actions employees take that threaten or enhance their health and safety. Outcome refers to any adverse employee health consequence, including both chronic (e.g., cardiovascular disease, musculoskeletal disorders) and acute conditions (e.g., strains and sprains, loss of limb). Industrial-organizational psychology models of job performance distinguish two broad forms of work-related behavior: *task performance*, which involves behaviors related to core job functions, and *contextual performance*, which involves going above and beyond job requirements to support the organization or to help coworkers (Borman & Motowidlo, 1993). Task performance is more likely to appear in job descriptions and formal reward systems; contextual performance is more discretionary and volitional in nature.

The performance literature suggests distinctions in safety behavior between safety compliance and participation (Griffin & Neal, 2000; Neal & Griffin, 2004, 2006). Safety compliance is analogous to task performance and concerns performance of safety-related job requirements (e.g., using required personal protective equipment, following safety procedures). Examples of safety compliance include construction workers who wear hard hats, nurses who follow appropriate procedures for disposing of biohazards, and long-haul truckers who comply with mandated limits on consecutive hours of driving. Safety participation is analogous to contextual performance and refers to "behavior that does not contribute directly to an individual's personal safety, but that does support safety in the wider organizational context" (Neal & Griffin, 2004, p. 16). Examples of safety participation include joining safety committees, encouraging coworkers to use personal protective equipment, and promoting organizational safety programs. Meta-analytic reviews of a sizable literature show that compliance and participation are distinct and have different patterns of antecedents and outcomes (Christian, Bradley, Wallace, & Burke, 2009; Clarke, 2006).

Health promotion literature draws a similar distinction between voluntary/discretionary and mandatory health behavior. Voluntary behavior refers to participation in non-mandated programs addressing issues such as diet, fitness, or smoking cessation. Mandated health behaviors are required as part of the job and may involve sanctions for a lack of compliance. For example, most companies have drug free–workplace policies; others have implemented on-site smoking bans with mixed success (cf. Borland, Owen, Hill, & Schofield, 1991). Many occupations (e.g., pilots, physicians) have restrictions on mandatory overtime or between-shift rest requirements (Federal Aviation Administration, 2010; Rogers, Wei-Ting, Scott, Aiken, & Dinges, 2004); other occupations (e.g., firefighters, military personnel) have mandatory physical fitness requirements when fitness can be tied to legitimate safety or performance concerns.

The voluntary-mandatory distinction has important implications for communication strategies. For example, some mandatory behaviors are compelled by the legal system (e.g., not using illegal substances). Companies can discourage overtly illegal behavior by emphasizing the negative outcomes of breaking a law (e.g., fines, jail time). In contrast, mandatory but not illegal behavior (e.g., fitness requirements) may be more difficult to enforce, and employees who most need them may be least likely to participate (Marshall, 2004). In addition, organizations often send inconsistent messages about desired behavior—having mandatory policies but being inconsistent in their enforcement. Encouraging desired-but-not-required behavior may require careful tailoring of messages to the target group (Kreuter & Wray, 2003) to ensure that they acquire sufficient knowledge to engage in the desired behavior and are sufficiently motivated to put their knowledge into action.

Knowledge and Motivation

Safety knowledge and motivation are primary pathways through which organizational practices influence employees' safety behavior (Griffin & Neal, 2000; Neal & Griffin 2004, 2006). Safety knowledge encompasses both factual knowledge and safety-related skills. For example, a farm worker might need to know both *what* pesticides are toxic and *how* to properly wear personal protective equipment. Other safety-related skills include recognition and awareness, decision making, and problem solving (Burke & Signal, 2010).

Health and safety messages should be tailored to employees' specific circumstances. Farkas (1999) discussed the importance of procedural discourse—the written and spoken aspects of communication—when crafting messages. For example, a message targeting employees who perform their job in an unsafe manner needs to provide information about how to change behavior in order to follow safety requirements. Hovde (2010) expanded on this by examining how technical communicators tailor messages to help transform declarative knowledge into procedural knowledge. Examples of important considerations include knowledge about the employee, organizational culture, organizational constraints, and the tools and skills used on the job. This literature offers both practical advice for safety/health management and conceptual foundations for future research on safety and health communication.

Safety motivation concerns the willingness to work safely and reflects expected outcomes of performing safety behaviors (Neal & Griffin, 2006). Although we derived our model from safety literature, both motivation and knowledge are similarly relevant to health promotion. We also include a path from safety motivation to knowledge as we expect employees with higher safety/ health motivation to seek out and attend to relevant information.

The motivation-knowledge distinction is important for understanding how communication efforts affect outcomes as well as for identifying the needed content of messages. For example, providing employees with basic safety information is less likely to affect behavior when employees lack motivation to change. Similarly, outcomes may be suboptimal when employees are strongly motivated but lack sufficient knowledge about desired behavior. Communication has an instrumental function as it provides employees with information needed to engage in desired behaviors and information about possible rewards and sanctions. However, safety and health communication programs also have a symbolic function in that they signal to employees what is valued at work (Hofmann & Stetzer, 1998). Clear and consistent communication also contributes to the organizational climate for safety and health.

Organizational Climate

Organizational climate reflects employees' shared perceptions about organizational policies, procedures, and practices (Schneider, Ehrhart, & Macey, 2011). Policy reflects organizational goals, procedures are strategies used to achieve goals, and practices are ways procedures are implemented (Zohar, 2003). Climate typically refers to perceptions about specific sets of policies, practices, and procedures, meaning that organizations have multiple "strategic climates" for attributes such as innovation, service, and quality (Schneider et al., 2011). Zohar (2011) described two key properties of strategic climates—relative priority (which varies from high to low) and strength (the extent to which group members agree). A strong positive climate indicates clear consensus among employees about the relative importance of various strategic priorities.

Safety Climate

In organizations with a strong positive safety climate, most employees believe that top management is committed strongly to employee safety (Zohar, 2008). Several meta-analytic reviews offer sound empirical support for the importance of safety climate as a predictor of safety outcomes (Beus, Payne, Bergman, & Arthur, 2010; Christian et al., 2009; Clarke, 2006, 2010; Nahrgang, Morgeson, & Hoffman, 2011). According to Zohar (2010), safety climate forms through a sense-making process as group members compare and modify their perceptions until they reach some level of agreement on the nature of organizational reality. Organizations can affect the sense-making process through both formal training and informal discussions (Christian et al., 2009). Immediate supervisors also play an important role as employees infer the relative priority of safety from their actions (Zohar & Hofmann, 2012). Safety climate and communication are closely connected (Griffin & Neal, 2000; Neal, Griffin, & Hart, 2000) with some studies supporting a directional relationship from communication to climate (Hofmann & Stetzer, 1998). Our model represents this relationship with a path from safety and health communication to climate.

One of the understudied links in this literature concerns which specific aspects of organizational communication link to employee safety and health. Real and Cooper (2000) studied employees' perceptions of several dimensions of safety communication climate, including communication satisfaction, safety information seeking intensions, and information seeking expectations. They found that these dimensions predicted manufacturing plant employees' safety climate perceptions and self-reported safety behavior. Such findings suggest interesting future research opportunities for communication researchers interested in health and safety issues.

Health Climate

Interestingly, safety climate is also associated with lower burnout (Nahrgang et al., 2011) and better general health (Clarke, 2010), perhaps because of the relationship between safety climate and health climate. Although the safety climate literature is fairly large, few studies have investigated the corresponding concept of health climate. Yet workplace health promotion programs likely influence health behavior in part through effects on organizational climate. Mearns, Hope, Ford, and Tetrick (2010, p. 1447) defined health climate as "shared perceptions of an organization's priorities and practices regarding employee health." As with safety climate, health climate is largely influenced by organizational practices, including company investment into health promotion activities and training in the workplace. Because employees may not expect organizations to heavily invest in health initiatives, such programs strengthen climate in part by demonstrating an organization's value for employee well-being.

Although the relationship between safety climate and health climate has received relatively little attention, research suggests that each predicts different health outcomes (Basen-Engquist, Hudmon, Tripp, & Chamberlain, 1998). Nonetheless, the concepts are positively related—organizations whose employees believe they place a high priority on safety typically also believe the organization values general employee health (Mearns et al., 2010). This may be because both safety and health climate convey a general sense of organizational concern for employees' well-being. Thus, an improved safety climate may be an unintended benefit of efforts to improve health climate; similarly, organizations that do not prioritize safety may experience unintended negative consequences for general health climate.

Health Communication Strategies/Framing

Whereas the safety climate literature highlights the general influence of communication in developing a strong positive safety climate, health communication literature is more useful in understanding how different kinds of messages shape climate or stimulate behavior. A central concern is whether positive or negative messages best achieve desired outcomes. Message framing literature investigates the conditions under which positive and/or negative messages are most effective.

The concept of message framing has its roots in Tversky and Kahneman's (1981) prospect theory, which concerns how potential gains and losses affect decision making. Positive message frames emphasize desirable consequences (e.g., resource gains, prevention of losses) of working safely and/or maintaining ones' health. Negative frames emphasize the harm (potential losses) that may come from dangerous or unhealthy behavior (Block & Keller, 1995). Prospect theory explains that people are highly averse to resource losses and that aversion to loss can affect behavior even in the absence of risk (Kahneman & Tversky, 1979; Kahneman, Knetsch, & Thaler, 1991); messages with goals framed to emphasize potential losses may have stronger effects on behavior than gain frames (Levin, Schneider, & Gaeth, 1998). Similarly, negative stimuli, emotions, and experiences have more powerful effects on people, in part because they have stronger survival value (Baumeister, Bratslavsky, Finkenauer, & Vohs, 2001).

Health communication literature provides several additional guidelines about message framing. Communication is optimized when message frames match the behavior to be promoted

(Rothman & Salovey, 1997). Positive goal frames should be used when the intent is to encourage employees to engage in desired behavior (e.g., dieting, wearing safety equipment); negative frames should be used to encourage employees to refrain from undesirable behavior (e.g., smoking). Positively framed messages require less motivation to process the information and can reinforce the healthy behaviors someone currently practices (Maheswaran & Chaiken, 1991). Positively framed messages also appear to be more persuasive when they come from a credible source such as a doctor or personal trainer (Jones & Sinclair, 2003). Finally, when negative frames are used, it is important to provide information about how to change the targeted behavior (McCaul, Johnson, & Rothman, 2002; Self & Rogers, 1990).

Employees' reactions are likely to differ to even the most carefully crafted safety and health messages. Positively framed messages may be more successful when a person is not motivated to process the message (Block & Keller, 1995). For example, someone who is not suffering from a diet-related health problem may ignore negatively framed diet messages. Similarly, messages aimed at increasing the self-efficacy of a specific behavior should increase the likelihood that the behavior will be practiced (Fletcher & Banasik, 2001). For example, Prestin and Nabi (2012) studied skill and motivation of performing exercise as predictors of self-efficacy to exercise. They found that participants low in motivation exercised more than people who were low in skill, regardless of message quality. However, framing the message as fun, easy, and beneficial tended to increase exercise self-efficacy.

In summary, while there is strong theoretical support for the relative strength of negative frames, they should be used with caution. Extreme or overused threat and fear appeals, while persuasive, can have unintended effects, and practitioners should be wary (Hale & Dillard, 1995). Constant demands for strong immediate responses can promote cynicism and erode employees' willingness to respond. Therefore, negative frames should be used prudently; fear and threat appeals should only be used in emergencies or otherwise threatening situations. When seeking to build long-term patterns of constructive behavior, positive message frames should receive stronger consideration. However, when negative messages are considered necessary, we encourage safety and health researchers to draw from the sizable communication literature dealing with threat communication (e.g., Hale & Dillard, 1995; Witte, 1993).

Research and Practice Recommendations

Our recommendations for research and practice are by no means exhaustive, but all suggest the need for more and better intervention research. However, the following issues are important considerations for organizations seeking to create strong positive safety and health climates and for researchers seeking to understand conditions affecting the efficacy of safety and health communication.

Recognize the Key Role of Supervisors

Perceptions of management commitment to safety strongly predict safety climate (Griffin & Neal, 2000; Neal & Griffin, 2006; Zohar, 2008), and supervisors' behavior is an important actionable influence on workplace safety and health. Employees are highly sensitive to gaps between an organization's espoused policies and its actual practices, a conflict that occurs when supervisors encourage employees to follow unsafe practices or engage in unhealthy behavior. Organizations can increase perceptions of management commitment by ensuring that managers give safety and health concerns appropriate attention. When supervisors discuss safety issues with subordinates, employees better understand the possible outcomes of unsafe behavior (Michael, Guo, Wiedenbeck, & Ray, 2006). Frequent communication also strengthens safety climate (Zohar & Luria, 2003). Indeed, supervisors who frequently discuss health and safety issues with employees may themselves be more aware of significant health and safety threats.

Comfort with upward communication influences employees' willingness to discuss safety issues with their supervisor. Leaders can facilitate upward communication by demonstrating support to and concern for their followers. When leaders cultivate better subordinate relationships, employees are more likely to be comfortable discussing safety and health issues (Hofmann & Morgeson, 1999; Kath, Marks, & Ranney, 2010). Kines et al. (2010) found that coaching foremen to discuss safety issues with workers resulted in increased safety performance. Facilitating upward communication also should lead to other health benefits including reduced stigma associated with seeking help for mental health concerns (Britt & McFadden, 2012).

Consider the Occupational Context

The occupational context may be an important consideration in safety and health communication. For example, sense-making processes may be especially important in dangerous environments (e.g., for deployed military personnel or emergency rescue crews), particularly in the aftermath of traumatic events when team members attempt to make sense of their experiences. For solitary workers, such as long-haul truckers and home health care nurses, the nature of health and safety climate may differ because of their limited opportunities for social interaction (Huang et al., 2013), and, because they are less frequent, communication events may take on greater significance. Finally, night shift workers, such as nurses or factory workers, typically have greater risk of negative health outcomes related to sleep quality (Oishi et al., 2005), highlighting the need to focus health communication specifically on sleep hygiene (National Sleep Foundation, 2013). Safety and health communication strategies must fit the needs of the targeted occupation; communication research can inform this process by investigating how and when occupational contexts affect study findings.

Investigate the Role of Individual Differences

Research on individual differences may provide additional insight into how employees react to various safety and health communication messages. Elliot and Thrash (2002) describe approach and avoidance temperaments as broad biologically based dispositions encompassing peoples' attentiveness to, reactivity to, and behavior toward positive (e.g., rewards, resource gains) and negative (e.g., punishments, resource losses) stimuli. People with an approach temperament are more sensitive to positive stimuli and are risk tolerant; people with an avoidance temperament are more sensitive to negative stimuli and are risk avoidant.

Positive and negative messages about safety and health are likely to affect people differently depending on their temperament. Research on regulatory fit (Higgins, 2000) suggests that the impact of communication is optimal when the risks or gains highlighted by a message match a person's risk-seeking or risk-avoidance orientation. For example, a worker with a strong avoidance temperament might be more sensitive to safety messages emphasizing possible harms associated with failure to follow safety guidelines; someone with a strong approach temperament might be more motivated by the prospect of physical fitness gains stemming from participation in a company-sponsored exercise program. Although some research supports the importance of temperament-message frame fit for health behavior (e.g., Sherman, Mann, & Updegraff, 2006), more research is needed, particularly for safety communication.

Health promotion researchers have long recognized individual differences in peoples' "readiness" to change their health behavior. Prochaska's (1994) transtheoretical model describes five stages people go through when attempting to change behavior. The *pre-contemplation* stage is characterized by a lack of intention to change behavior, and people in this stage may not be aware of risks associated with an unhealthy behavior. In the *contemplation* stage, people are aware that a problem exists and are thinking about changing their behavior but have not committed to change. People in the *preparation* stage intend to change their behavior but have not yet begun to change. In the *action* stage, people have begun to change their behavior but have only practiced it for a short time. Finally, in the *maintenance* stage, people work to prevent relapse and to transform new behaviors into long-lasting habits.

Programs based on Prochaska's (1994) model match treatment to the person's stage of change readiness. For example, a physical activity program focusing on people in stage 1 or 2 should attempt to increase peoples' use of cognitive processes related to health such as increasing awareness of health risks and understanding benefits of healthy behavior. Interventions focusing on people in stages, 3, 4, or 5 should target the desired behavioral changes. Behavioral change methods can include suggesting strategies to begin exercising or maintaining an exercise regimen, rewarding people for achieving goals, and providing materials that encourage people to exercise.

Implement CDC and NIOSH Best Practices

The CDC and the National Institute for Occupational Safety and Health (NIOSH) have developed many useful tools, concepts, and programs to help create safer and healthier workplaces. For example, the CDC (2013) describes several considerations when planning a health communication strategy, including the following:

- Define the problem by reviewing background information (What's out there?).
- Set communication objectives (What do we want to accomplish?).
- Analyze and define target audience (Who do we want to reach?).
- Develop and pre-test message concepts (What do we want to say?).
- Select communication medium (Where do we want to say it?).
- Select, create, and pre-test message and/or products (How do we want to say it?).
- Develop promotion plan/production (How do we get it used?).
- Implement communication strategies and conduct process evaluation (Getting it out there).
- Conduct outcome and impact evaluation (How well did it work?).

NIOSH (2012) describes its Total Worker Health™ program as "a strategy for integrating occupational safety and health protection with health promotion to prevent worker injury and illness and to advance health and well-being." The concept of total worker health highlights the idea that worker health and safety are connected and have synergistic effects on employee well-being. NIOSH describes four facets of total worker health program design and implementation: organizational culture and leadership, program design, program implementation, and program evaluation. Communication practices are important to each.

For example, communication helps organizational leaders display commitment to health and safety and helps involve all levels of management in the program. During program design, coordinated communication across units may help identify potential conflicts between proposed programs and other organizational functions and may help identify redundancies between new and existing initiatives. NIOSH also highlights the need for strategic communication during program implementation that is tailored to the targeted employee groups. Simply, everyone involved in the project should know what the organization is doing and why. The CDC (2013) health communication strategies discussed earlier identify several considerations for effectively tailoring such messages.

Explore Emerging Communication Strategies and Technologies

Internet-based resources can combine the positive attributes of interpersonal and mass communication (Cassell, Jackson, & Cheuvront, 1998). The Health Information National Trends study (Chou, Hunt, Beckjord, Moser, & Hesse, 2009) estimated that 69% of U.S. adults use the Internet, 23% use social media Web sites, 7% reported blogging, and 5% participated in online support groups—figures that have likely increased since then. Moreover, people of differing socioeconomic backgrounds reported using the Internet fairly equally, making it a powerful method for reaching workers. Web-based communication may be particularly effective for reaching geographically isolated workers and for providing a way for people to discuss their health concerns and goals anonymously so they can avoid having coworkers or employers know intimate details about their health.

Internet-based communication greatly facilitates the ability to provide multiple communications about the same topic (through e-mail, blogs, etc.). This raises concerns about whether and how repeating a message increases its efficacy. Stephens and Rains (2011) found that, as compared with repeated use of the same technology, delivering a repeated message through multiple complementary technologies was associated with increased perceptions of informational effectiveness and behavioral intentions.

There are, however, important limitations to newer forms of communication media. Multiple asynchronous communications, such as text messages, may help reinforce the urgency of a crisis but should be viewed as a supplement to, rather than as a substitute for, more direct forms of communication (Stephens, Barrett, & Mahometa, in press). Further, because younger adults use social media more frequently than do older adults (Chou et al., 2009), worker age is an important consideration in communication strategies. Age-diverse workforces may require a wide array of communication strategies. Given rapid technological change, one might expect exciting developments in the not-too-distant future of safety and health communication. One can easily envision greater use of social media for safety and health promotion, as well as embedded technology in warning signs that might, for example, give prerecorded safety warnings in multiple languages. Many smartphone applications already allow users to track their physical health in real-time, such as the distance traveled on a hike, and Web-based programs have greatly expanded educational access for groups facing opportunity constraints, such as rural workers or those in developing countries. These examples suggest the exciting possibilities for future safety and health communication and, ultimately, for creating safer and healthier workplaces.

Bibliography

Aldana, S.G. (2001). Financial impact of health promotion programs: A comprehensive review of the literature. *American Journal of Health Promotion, 15,* 296–320.

Basen-Engquist, K., Hudmon, K.S., Tripp, M., & Chamberlain, R. (1998). Worksite health and safety climate:
Scale development and effects of a health promotion intervention. *Preventative Medicine, 27,* 11–119.

Baumeister, R.F., Bratslavsky, E., Finkenauer, C., & Vohs, K.D. (2001). Bad is stronger than good. *Review of
General Psychology, 5,* 323–370.

Beus, J.M., Payne, S.C., Bergman, M.E., & Arthur, W. (2010). Safety climate and injuries: An examination of
theoretical and empirical relationships. *Journal of Applied Psychology, 95,* 713–727.

Block, L.G., & Keller, P.A. (1995). When to accentuate the negative: The effects of perceived efficacy and
message framing on intentions to perform a health-related behavior. *Journal of Marketing Research, 32,*
192–203.

Borland, R., Owen, N., Hill, D., & Schofield, P. (1991). Predicting attempts and sustained cessation of smoking after the introduction of workplace smoking bans. *Health Psychology, 10,* 336–342.

Borman, W. C., & Motowidlo S.J. (1993). Expanding the criterion domain to include elements of contextual
performance. In N. Schmitt & W. C. Borman (Eds.), *Personnel selection in organizations* (pp. 71–98). San
Francisco: Jossey-Bass.

Britt, T.W., & McFadden, A.C. (2012). Understanding mental health treatment-seeking in high stress occupations. In J. Houdmont, S. Leka, & R.R. Sinclair (Eds.), *Contemporary occupational health psychology: Global
perspectives on research and practice* (pp. 57–73). London: Wiley-Blackwell.

Burke, M.J., & Signal, S. (2010). Workplace safety: A multilevel, interdisciplinary perspective. In J.J. Martocchio, H. Liao, & A. Joshi (Eds.), *Research in personnel and human resource management* (pp. 1–47). Bingley,
UK: Emerald Group.

Cassell, M. M., Jackson, C., & Cheuvront, B. (1998). Health communication on the Internet: An effective
channel for health behavior change? *Journal of Health Communication, 3*(1), 71–79.

Centers for Disease Control and Prevention (CDC). (2013). *Gateway to health communication and social strategies.* Retrieved from www.cdc.gov/healthcommunication/healthbasics/whatishc.html.

Chou, W-Y, S., Hunt, Y.M., Beckjord, E.B., Moser, R.P., & Hesse, B.W. (2009). Social media use in the
United States: Implications for health communication. *Journal of Medical Internet Research, 11,* 1–6.

Christian, M.S., Bradley, J.C., Wallace, J., & Burke, M.J. (2009). Workplace safety: A meta-analysis of the roles
of person and situation factors. *Journal of Applied Psychology, 94,* 1103–1127.

Clarke, S. (2006). The relationship between safety climate and safety performance: A meta-analytic review.
Journal of Occupational Health Psychology, 11, 315–327.

Clarke, S. (2010). An integrative model of safety climate: Linking psychological climate and work attitudes
to individual safety outcomes using meta-analysis. *Journal of Occupational and Organizational Psychology,
83,* 553–578.

Collins, J.J., Baase, C.M., Sharda, C.E., Ozminkowski, R., J., Nicholson, S., Billotti, G.M., & Berger, M.L.
(2005). The assessment of chronic health conditions on work performance, absence, and total economic
impact for employers. *Journal of Occupational and Environmental Medicine, 47,* 547–557.

DeVol, R., & Bedroussian, A. (2007). *An unhealthy America. The economic burden of chronic disease.* Santa Monica
CA: Milken Institute.

Elliot, A.J., & Thrash, T.M. (2002). Approach-avoidance motivation in personality: Approach and avoidance
temperaments and goals. *Journal of Personality and Social Psychology, 82,* 804–818.

Farkas, K.D. (1999). The logical and rhetorical construction of procedural discourse. *Technical Communication,
46,* 42–54.

Federal Aviation Administration. (2010). *Fact sheet-pilot flight time, rest, and fatigue.* Retrieved from www.faa
.gov/news/fact_sheets/news_story.cfm?newsId=6762.

Fletcher, J.S., & Banasik, J.L. (2001). Exercise self-efficacy. *Clinical Excellence for Nurse Practitioners, 5,* 134–143.

Griffin, M.A., & Neal, A. (2000). Perceptions of safety at work: A framework for linking safety climate to
safety performance, knowledge, and motivation. *Journal of Occupational Health Psychology, 5,* 347–358.

Hale, J.L., & Dillard, J. (1995). Fear appeals in health promotion campaigns: Too much, too little, or just right? In E. Maibach & R. Parrott (Eds.), *Designing health messages: Approaches from communication theory and public health practice* (pp. 65–80). Thousand Oaks, CA: Sage.

Higgins, E.T. (2000). Making a good decision: Value from fit. *American Psychologist, 55*(11), 1217–1230.

Hofmann, D.A., & Morgeson, F.P. (1999). Safety-related behavior as a social exchange: The role of perceived organizational support and leader–member exchange. *Journal of Applied Psychology, 84*, 286–296.

Hofmann, D.A., & Stetzer, A. (1998). The role of safety climate and communication in accident interpretation: Implications for learning from negative events. *Academy of Management Journal, 41*, 644–657.

Hovde, R.M. (2010). Creating procedural discourse and knowledge for software users: Beyond translation and transmission. *Journal of Business and Technical Communication, 24*, 164–205.

Huang, Y., Leamon, T.B., Courtney, T.K., Chen, P.Y., & DeArmond, S. (2011). A comparison of workplace safety perceptions among financial decision-makers of medium- vs. large-size companies. *Accident Analysis and Prevention, 43*, 1–10.

Huang, Y.H., Zohar, D., Robertson, M.M., Garabet, A., Lee., J., & Murphy, L.A. (2013). Development and validation of safety climate scales for lone workers using truck drivers as exemplar. *Transportation Research Part F, 17*, 5–19.

Jones, L.W., & Sinclair, R.C. (2003). The effects of source credibility and message framing on exercise intentions, behaviors, and attitudes: An integration of the elaboration likelihood model and prospect theory. *Journal of Applied Psychology, 33*, 179–196.

Kahneman, D., Knetsch, J.L., & Thaler, R.H. (1991). Anomalies: The endowment effect, loss aversion, and status quo bias. *Journal of Economic Perspectives, 5*, 193–206.

Kahneman, D., & Tversky, A. (1979). Prospect theory: An analysis of decision under risk. *Econometrica, 47*, 263–292.

Kath, L.M., Marks, K.M., & Ranney, J. (2010). Safety climate dimensions, leader–member exchange, and organizational support as predictors of upward safety communication in a sample of rail industry workers. *Safety Science, 48*, 643–650.

Kines, P., Andersen, L.S., Spangenberg, S., Mikkelsen, K.L., Dyreborg, J., & Zohar, D. (2010). Improving construction site safety through leader-based verbal safety communication. *Journal of Safety Research, 41*, 399–406.

Kreuter, M.W., & Wray, R.J. (2003). Tailored and targeted health communication: Strategies for enhancing information relevance. *American Journal of Health Behavior, 27*, 227–232.

Levin, I.P., Schneider, S.L., & Gaeth, G.J. (1998). All frames are not created equal: A typology and critical analysis of framing effects. *Organizational Behavior and Human Decision Processes, 76*, 149–188.

Liberty Mutual Research Institute for Safety. (2012, Winter). *2010 workplace safety index, from research to reality.* Retrieved from www.libertymutualgroup.com/omapps/ContentServer?c=cms_document&pagename=LMGResearchInstitute%2Fcms_document%2FShowDoc&cid=1240013854303.

Loeppke, R., Taitel, M., Haufle, V., Parry, T., Kessler, R., & Jinnett, K. (2009). Health and productivity as a business strategy: A multiemployer study. *Journal of Occupational & Environmental Medicine, 51*, 411–428.

Maheswaran, D., & Chaiken, S. (1991). Promoting systematic processing in low motivation settings: Effect on incongruent information on processing and judgment. *Journal of Personality and Social Psychology, 61*, 13–25.

Marshall, A.L. (2004). Challenges and opportunities for promoting physical activity in the workplace. *Journal of Science and Medicine in Sport, 7*, 60–66.

McCaul, K.D., Johnson, R.J., & Rothman, A.J. (2002). The effects of framing and action instructions on whether older adults obtain flu shots. *Health Psychology, 21*, 624–628.

Mearns, K., Hope, L., Ford, M.T., & Tetrick, L.E. (2010). Investment in workforce health: Exploring the implications for workforce safety climate and commitment. *Accident Analysis and Prevention, 42*, 1445–1454.

Michael, J.H., Guo, Z., Wiedenbeck, J.K., & Ray, C.D. (2006). Production supervisor impacts on subordinates' safety outcomes: An investigation of leader-member exchange and safety communication. *Journal of Safety Research, 37*, 469–477.

Nahrgang, J.D., Morgeson, F.P., & Hofmann, D.A. (2011). Safety at work: A meta-analytic investigation of the link between job demands, job resources, burnout, engagement, and safety outcomes. *Journal of Applied Psychology, 96*, 71–94.

National Institute for Occupational Safety and Health (NIOSH). (2012). *Total worker health*. Retrieved from www.cdc.gov/niosh/TWH/totalhealth.html.

National Sleep Foundation. (2013). *Sleep hygiene*. Retrieved from www.sleepfoundation.org/article /ask-the-expert/sleep-hygiene.

Neal, A., & Griffin, M.A. (2004). Safety climate and safety at work. In J. Barling & M.R. Frone (Eds.), *The psychology of workplace safety* (pp. 15–34). Washington, DC: American Psychological Association.

Neal, A., & Griffin, M.A. (2006). A study of the lagged relationships among safety climate, safety motivation, safety behavior, and accidents at the individual and group levels. *Journal of Applied Psychology, 91*, 946–953.

Neal, A.A., Griffin, M.A., & Hart, P.M. (2000). The impact of organizational climate on safety climate and individual behavior. *Safety Science, 34*, 99–109.

Oishi, M., Suwazono, Y., Sakata, K., Okubo, Y., Harada, H., Kobayashi, E., Uetani, M., & Nogawa, K. (2005). A longitudinal study on the relationship between shift work and the progression of hypertension in male Japanese workers. *Journal of Hypertension, 23*(12), 2173–2178.

Prestin, A., & Nabi, L.R. (2012). Examining determinants of efficacy judgments as factors in health promotion message design. *Communication Quarterly, 60*, 520–544.

Prochaska, O.J. (1994). Strong and weak principles for progressing from precontemplation to action on the basis of twelve problem behaviors. *Health Psychology, 13*, 47–51.

Real, K., & Cooper, M.D. (2009, May). *The importance of communication factors to safety climate: An exploratory analysis*. International Communication Association, Chicago, IL. Retrieved from www.allacademic.com /meta/p299149_index.html.

Rogers, A.E., Wei-Ting, H., Scott, L.D., Aiken, L.H., & Dinges, D.F. (2004). The working hours of hospital staff nurses and patient safety. *Health Affairs, 23*, 202–212.

Rothman, A.J., & Salovey, P. (1997). Shaping perceptions to motivate healthy behavior: The role of message framing. *Psychological Bulletin, 121*, 3–19.

Schneider, B., Ehrhart, M.G., & Macey, W.H. (2011). Perspectives on organizational climate and culture. In S. Zedeck (Ed.), *APA handbook of industrial and organizational psychology, Vol. 1: Building and developing the organization* (pp. 373–414). Washington, DC: American Psychological Association.

Self, C.A., & Rogers, R.W. (1990). Coping with threats to health: Effects of persuasive appeals on depressed, normal, and antisocial personalities. *Journal of Behavioral Medicine, 13,* 343–358.

Sherman, D.K., Mann, T., & Updegraff, J.A. (2006). Approach/avoidance motivation, message framing, and health behavior: Understanding the congruency effect. *Motivation and Emotion, 30,* 164–168.

Stephens, K.K., Barrett, A.K., & Mahometa, M.J. (in press). Organizational communication in emergencies: Using multiple channels and sources to combat noise and escalate a sense of urgency. *Human Communication Research.*

Stephens, K.K., & Rains, A.S. (2011). Information and communication technology sequences and message repetition in interpersonal interaction. *Communication Research, 38*, 101–122.

Tversky, A., & Kahneman, D. (1981). The framing of decisions and the psychology of choice. *Science, 211*, 453–458.

United States Bureau of Labor Statistics. (n.d.). *Injuries, Illnesses, and Fatalities Program*. Retrieved from http:// www.bls.gov/iif/.

Witte, K. (1993). Message and conceptual confounds in fear appeals: The role of threat, fear, and efficacy. *Southern Communication Journal, 58*, 147–155.

Zohar, D. (2003). Safety climate: Conceptual and measurement issues. In J. Quick & L.E. Tetrick (Eds.), *Handbook of occupational health psychology* (pp. 123–142). Washington, DC: American Psychological Association.

Zohar, D. (2008). Safety climate and beyond: A multi-level multi-climate framework. *Safety Science, 46*, 376–387.

Zohar, D. (2010). Thirty years of safety climate research: Reflections and future directions. *Accident Analysis and Prevention, 42*, 1517–1522.

Zohar, D. (2011). Safety climate: Conceptual and measurement issues. In J. Quick & L.E. Tetrick (Eds.), *Handbook of occupational health psychology* (2nd ed., pp. 141–164). Washington, DC: American Psychological Association.

Zohar, D., & Hofmann, D.A. (2012). Organizational culture and climate. In S.W.J. Kozlowski (Ed.), *The Oxford handbook of organizational psychology* (pp. 643–666). Oxford: Oxford University Press.

Zohar, D., & Luria, G. (2003). The use of supervisory practices as leverage to improve safety behavior: A cross-level intervention model. *Journal of Safety Research, 34*, 567–577.

17

MANAGING DIVERSITY THROUGH EFFECTIVE COMMUNICATION

Eddy S. Ng and James R. Barker

A key human resource challenge facing employers is managing an increasingly diverse workforce. Diversity encompasses a broad range of human dimensions such as age, disability, sexual orientation, religion, social class, education, national origin, and language (Shore et al., 2009). Projections from the U.S. Census Bureau (2012) suggest that the workforce will become more diverse from a racial and ethnocultural perspective. By the year 2020, the labor participation rate will be highest among Hispanics and Asians, outpacing the rate for Whites. According to the "value-in-diversity" hypothesis (Cox, 1993), workforce diversity when properly managed can be a source of competitive advantage for organizations and employers, including greater creativity and innovation, attraction of the best talents, and greater marketplace success (Cox & Blake, 1991; Robinson & Dechant, 1997). However, workplace diversity when left unmanaged can also detract from organizational performance with issues stemming from group cohesion, communication, and turnover (Grimes & Richard, 2003; Roberge & van Dick, 2010).

Managing diversity is important for organizations and employers because of the following:

- Globalization and immigration will inevitably result in greater ethnocultural diversity in the labor market. For example, low birth rates and an aging labor force in North America will necessitate employing a greater number of foreign workers and immigrants (Statistics Canada, 2011; U.S. Census Bureau, 2012).
- The "business case" for diversity suggests that organizations that can capitalize on the value in diversity will gain a competitive advantage in the marketplace. Research has established that cultural diversity contributes to better financial and market performance for firms (Ng & Tung, 1998; Richard, 2000; Wiegand, 2007).
- Institutional pressures from customers, investors, special interests, and employee groups impel employers to hire and treat fairly employees from diverse backgrounds (i.e., "legitimacy and fairness;" Ely & Thomas, 2001). Executive Order 11246 also requires employers receiving contracts from the U.S. government to implement Affirmative Action.

Although diversity management has been touted for its positive outcomes for organizations and employers, the implementation of diversity practices could backfire when they are not properly managed (e.g., Ely, Padavic, & Thomas, 2012; McKay & Avery, 2005; Verbeek & Groeneveld, 2012). The purpose of this chapter is to review how various human resource practices can promote or hinder diversity in organizations and to highlight the important role communication plays in the effective application of diversity management programs and procedures in organizations.

How Can Organizations Communicate a Commitment to Diversity?

An organization's commitment to diversity can be communicated to members of the public via its top executive's behaviors and human resource practices and consequently has an impact on its labor force. In this regard, we document how top-level managers and the messages contained in recruitment materials can help promote a more diverse workforce.

Leadership Commitment to Diversity

An organization's top executive (e.g., chief executive officer) plays an important leadership role in communicating an organization's commitment to diversity to its members. CEOs convey a strong and symbolic message when they take a public stance on their support for diversity. Ng and Wyrick (2011) suggested that CEOs might be motivated to manage diversity because it is good for business (instrumental motive), because it is the right thing to do in an era of corporate social responsibility (normative motive), and when they want their legacy to be positive (affective motive).

Top executive commitment to diversity is important because the CEO sets the corporate agenda, makes decisions, and allocates the resources necessary for managing diversity, typically a long-term effort whose benefits (e.g., creativity and innovation) are not immediately realized (Robinson & Dechant, 1997). Thus, CEO steadfastness is essential to keep the commitment focused over the long-term in order for the organization to reap the benefits from a diverse workforce. Few studies have investigated CEO commitment to diversity and its implications for organizations. Ng and Burke (2010) found that CEOs in organizations having to comply with affirmative action in Canada reported a greater commitment to diversity. Hambrick and Mason (1984) suggested that organizations are a reflection of their CEOs' values and characteristics. Consistent with this, Ng (2008) proposed that CEO gender, race, age, values, and cognition matter in top executive support for diversity programs. For example, CEOs espousing greater social values also display a greater number of diversity practices in the organizations they lead (Ng & Sears, 2012).

Although diversity managers (or affirmative action officers) frequently implement change (Tatli & Özbilgin, 2009), CEOs initiate change in organizations by assuming highly symbolic roles, such as champions for change. In this regard, the degree of a CEO's personal and private support for diversity is crucial in the implementation of diversity management. Ng (2005) found that human resource managers' perception of CEOs' personal commitment to diversity is more important than CEOs' public support for diversity. In other words, when managers perceive their CEOs to be committed to diversity, they are more likely to implement diversity management programs and practices rigorously. Likewise, a closer reporting relationship between the diversity manager and the CEO signals to organizational members the latter's commitment to diversity. Consistent with this, Pfeffer, Davis-Blake, and Julius (1995) reported that diversity managers' compensation (signaling proximity to the CEO) was related to the number of women and minorities employed in the organization. On this basis, the appointment of a diversity manager working closely with the CEO signals an organization's commitment to the implementation of diversity management.

Communicating a Commitment to Diversity Through Recruitment

Employee recruitment is a key function in staffing an organization. Thomas and Wise (1999) suggested that recruitment aids in the development of candidate pools, helps employers achieve a demographically representative workforce, and ensures that the pool of candidates is qualified to perform the job. Importantly, recruitment can help to ensure that the organization is able to attract a diverse pool of applicants. As applicants may have incomplete information about organizations, they often fill in the gaps in their knowledge by interpreting the recruitment messages found in job ads about their prospective employers. Recruitment messages are particularly salient to minority job applicants because they are less likely to have the same access to informal sources of information as their White counterparts and, thus, have to rely on recruitment messages as cues to an organization's diversity climate (Giscombe & Mattis, 2002).

Studies have shown that racial minority applicants were more attracted to organizations with messages that espouse diversity (Williams & Bauer, 1994) or with job ads that portray other racial minorities (Highhouse, Stierwalt, Bachiochi, Elder, & Fisher, 1999). The representation of minorities in job ads was particularly salient to minority group members because it signals an organization's diversity climate and its willingness to hire a diverse pool of employees. Ng and Burke (2005) reported that messages of diversity (e.g., commitment to affirmative action) contained in employment offers also attracted higher quality job applicants, likely because job applicants believe that the employer is committed to diversity and is willing to promote and advance the careers of ethnic minorities. Additionally, Avery (2003) found racial minority applicants were more attracted to job ads depicting other minorities in supervisory or managerial positions because they suggest the absence of a glass ceiling for minorities (see Breaugh's chapter 3 in this book for additional information regarding recruitment of a diverse workforce).

How Human Resource Practices Can Be Detrimental to Organizational Diversity

Even organizations that are committed to fostering diversity can inadvertently undermine attainment of this goal because the selection practices that they use make it less likely that they will hire minorities, women, or applicants of different nationalities. Although special efforts such as affirmative action to hire and promote members of diverse groups can help to diversify an organization, such efforts may cause significant problems for human resource managers.

Effect of Selection Practices on Diversity

Selection practices play a critical role in affecting the diversity in organizations. Ng and Sears (2010a) found that selection practices predicted the representation of minorities in management after controlling for other diversity initiatives, thereby suggesting that selection is key to ensuring a pipeline of diverse talents for the firm. For example, the hiring of members of minority groups is less likely if human resource managers fail to recognize foreign credentials and work experience (Fang, Samnani, Novicevic, & Bing, 2013; Ng & Sears, 2010b). Hiring decisions also may be influenced by the cultural or religious backgrounds of the applicants (Forstenlechner & Al-Waqfi, 2010). In Canada, for example, new immigrants from non-Anglo countries face barriers in the employment process because of their language accents, religious attires (e.g., turbans for Sikhs or hijabs for Muslims), and a lack of understanding of the "Canadian" way, factors that are unrelated to skills or ability to perform on the job (Conference Board of Canada, 2004). Consequently, many highly skilled and highly educated minorities find themselves underemployed in jobs that do not fully utilize their skills and training (Haq & Ng, 2010).

Even professionally developed selection methods—for example, cognitive ability tests—may inadvertently have an adverse impact against minority group members. Adverse impact occurs when the selection rate for a minority group is less than 80 percent of that for the majority group (Equal Employment Opportunity Commission, 1978). Ng and Sears (2010a) surveyed human resource managers about different selection instruments and found that a majority of the respondents thought cognitive ability tests were "free from bias." In this regard, firms that utilized cognitive ability tests for employee selection also had fewer racial minorities in management, apparently because adverse impact reduced the number of minorities hired and available to be promoted.

Ethnocentric hiring practices run counter to the goal of diversity management, where everyone, regardless of their cultural backgrounds, potentially can contribute to help achieve organizational goals. Hiring managers should be made aware that qualified candidates may be turned away because of ethnocentric hiring practices. Likewise, prospective minority job applicants who perceive a lack of fairness in the selection process are likely to warn other prospective minority job applicants, which could damage the employer's reputation. Employers could also face the threat of action from the Equal Employment Opportunities Commission. Consequently, it is important to inform and train those involved with employee selection about the necessity of using selection methods that do not discriminate unfairly when hiring in a diverse labor market.

Affirmative Action in Employment

One way in which organizations can increase the representation of minorities in the workforce is through the use of affirmative action. However, the issue of affirmative action in hiring and promoting minorities has been controversial and divisive. In general, support for employment equity is strongest when it involves the elimination of unfair discrimination and least when it involves preferential treatment (Kravitz, Bludau, & Klineberg, 2008; Verbeek & Groeneveld, 2012). Likewise, Ng and Wiesner (2007) reported that respondents reacted negatively when they were asked to give preferential treatment to women who were less qualified for a position.

In general, individuals who subscribe to the principle of meritocracy believe that opportunities should be given to the most qualified candidate. They perceive affirmative action to be unfair because preferential treatment is accorded based on factors other than qualification for the job (Kravitz, 2008; Son Hing, Bobocel, & Zanna, 2002). Likewise, the non-beneficiaries of affirmative action (i.e., typically White males) believe such policies eliminate employment opportunities from them, possibly resulting in compensatory backlash and legal action to redress "reverse discrimination" (Harrison, Kravitz, Meyer, Leslie, & Lev-Arey, 2006; Kravitz et al., 2008).

Despite affirmative action efforts to address the underrepresentation of minorities, Stainback and Tomaskovic-Devey (2009) reported that the overrepresentation of White males in managerial positions had remained unchanged since the Civil Rights Act in 1964. White males continue to enjoy greater opportunities but have difficulty acknowledging their dominant status. Thus, their support for affirmative action is weaker (Mujtaba & Sims, 2011; Spanierman, Beard, & Todd, 2012). It has been suggested that the lack of awareness among dominant group members is due to a lack of understanding of their privileged position (Ancis & Szymanski, 2001), but they (White males) could be persuaded to support and commit to fairness and equality (Goodman, 2011). Thus, the need to convey the purpose for affirmative action and their privileged position to dominant organizational members is crucial to winning support (i.e., "White empathy"; see Spanierman et al., 2012) for managing diversity. Furthermore, Ely and colleagues (2012) found that when Whites perceive a more inclusive climate (team learning and interaction), group performance increased. Thus, efforts to capitalize on the benefits of diversity are more likely to be successful when everyone, including the White male majority, is included (Thomas, 1990).

Stigmatization of Affirmative Action Hires

One of the unintended outcomes of affirmative action is stigmatization of affirmative action hires (Aquino, Stewart, & Reed, 2005; Kravitz, 2008). Stigmatization occurs when affirmative action hires are thought to have received a job or a promotion because of their minority status without which they would not have been selected (Evans, 2003). Early research found that affirmative action hires received lower performance ratings (Heilman, Block, & Lucas, 1992). At the same time, the beneficiaries who believed they were hired because of affirmative action also had lower self-confidence and more negative self-perceptions (Heilman, Lucas, & Kaplow, 1990; Heilman, Battle, Keller, & Lee, 1998). On this basis, there is little support for affirmative action even among those who benefit from such policies.

Holzer and Neumark (1999, 2000) investigated the qualifications of affirmative action hires. Although minorities had lower qualifications than non-affirmative action hires, they did not actually have lower performance. When affirmative action is used in concert with other human resource practices (e.g., training), performance deficiencies do not arise, thus producing equally productive employees. Furthermore, when African-Americans were hired into higher level jobs (e.g., managerial positions) using affirmative action, they were not stigmatized in the same way as those who were hired into lower level positions, suggesting that minorities in higher social roles were perceived more favorably than those in lower social roles (Aquino et al., 2005). Specifically, when racial minorities are evaluated in a high social role context (e.g., an African-American lawyer), the stigmatization against the group (e.g., African-Americans in general) may lessen. In this regard, employers should ensure that they have minorities in higher level positions to mitigate the stigmatization of minorities in lower level positions.

Stereotypes Against Minorities

The stigma associated with affirmative action hires may stem from stereotypes about a particular group on the basis of group identity. As an example, African-Americans are known to score, on average, lower than the Whites on cognitive ability tests (Roth & Bobko, 2000; Roth, Bevier, Bobko, Switzer, & Tyler, 2001) and thus have lower predicted organizational performance (Ely et al., 2012). Consequently, some employers may rely on group membership markers (e.g., race) to make predictions about an individual's ability to perform (cf. Al-Waqfi & Jain, 2008). If actual performance differences exist between groups, employers may rely on group membership instead of individual ability to make employment decisions, thus reinforcing the stereotypes of African-Americans as less competent. Hence, it is important to change the attitudes and behaviors of employers who would otherwise make incorrect attributions based on race or cultural backgrounds.

Stereotypes about particular groups may also gain legitimacy through communication within organizations. In an experimental study, White students rated African-American students lower when they "sounded Black" than when they "sounded White" during a speech (cf. Allen 1995). In this regard, managers must be trained to refrain from perpetuating negative stereotypes against minority groups. For example, in a study on communicating about dissimilar others, asking managers to communicate about minority groups in a positive fashion can help change their attitudes in a positive direction and reduce stereotypic beliefs about a particular group (Biernat & Sesko, 2013). Thus, informal organization communication must be monitored to ensure that it does not reinforce the negative stereotypes against individual groups.

The Impact of Stereotype Threats on Minority Performance

Negative stereotypes about a particular group also place additional burdens on its members to dispel "stereotype threats" about themselves. Such a mind-set may actually reinforce the stereotype, especially when individuals are under greater pressure to perform (Roberson & Kulik, 2007). For example, warning individuals about the stereotypes about themselves creates additional anxiety and difficulty in performing the task. Roberson and Kulik (2007) suggested several strategies to reduce stereotype threats, including shifting the focus of the task or changing the conditions upon which stereotype threats are at work. One simple yet effective method in mitigating the stereotype threat is to simply inform the individuals that a particular task requires a certain skill and that anyone possessing that skill can do equally well. For example, to reduce the stereotype that women can't do math, simply telling the test takers that men and women perform equally well on math tests would make the stereotype irrelevant (cf. Roberson & Kulik, 2007).

Promoting an Inclusive Organizational Climate

Context is a critical variable affecting the interpretation of messages. Consequently, the climate of an organization must be considered an important influence on the meanings derived by its members from messages intended to promote diversity.

Managing Expectations to Reduce Minority Turnover

Although many organizations claim that they have an inclusive climate and support diversity, the reality experienced by minorities could be a different one. According to Avery (2003), when prospective minority job applicants see racially diverse cues in recruitment ads, it promotes high person–organization fit expectations with prospective employers. However, when post-hire experiences do not match initial recruitment expectations, minority employees perceive a violation of their psychological contract with their employers. Research has consistently demonstrated a link between diversity climate and psychological withdrawal among minority employees. For example, African-American employees reported lower commitment and had higher absenteeism rates and greater turnover intentions when the organizational diversity climate expectations failed to materialize (Avery, McKay, Wilson, & Tonidandel, 2007; McKay, Avery, Tonidandel, Morris, Hernandez, & Hebl, 2007; Triana, Garcia, & Colella, 2010).

Consequently, employers must ensure that the diversity climate and human resource practices match the image projected in their recruitment messages. Employers can also temper or manage prospective employees' expectations by using realistic job previews during the recruitment process (Avery, 2003) and by communicating their commitment to diversity during site visits (McKay & Avery, 2006). In this regard, having other minority employees convey to prospective applicants the employer's commitment to diversity during site visits may be particularly helpful (Avery et al., 2007).

Internal and External Communications in a Diverse Environment

In an era of increasing "political correctness," organizational communication is frequently conducted in an ethnocentric fashion (Arai, Wanca-Thibault, & Shockley-Zalabak, 2001). Grimes and Richard (2003) pointed out that references such as "your group" and "my group" used by organizational members can create an in-group/out-group distinction and may imply that one group is inferior to the other. As an example, Ross Perot used the term "your people" when addressing African-Americans at a NAACP gathering in 1992 and offended many since it has racist connotations (cf. Tung, 1993). Edmondson, Gupte, Draman, and Oliver (2009) also found that using the term "minorities" to refer to "non-Whites" in corporate communications (e.g., "minority employees," "minority suppliers") should be avoided because it is considered offensive and suggestive of having less power than Whites. The term may also be outdated when non-Whites are becoming the majority group in many places in the U.S. (U.S. Census Bureau, 2012).

The difference in communication patterns between dominant and minority groups is also important with the increasing number of non-White immigrants in the labor force. Historically, immigrants to the U.S. were predominantly from Europe. Recently, immigrants tend to arrive from Latin America, Asia, and the Middle East. According to Hall and Hall (1987), individuals from these countries tend to communicate in a high-context fashion (e.g., indirect, nonconfrontational) in contrast to Anglo-Americans and Europeans who communicate in a low-context manner (e.g., direct, confrontational). As a consequence, employees from high-context cultures may be perceived to lack confidence and assertiveness, traits considered to be necessary to be managers and leaders in Western, low-context cultures, and may thus be passed over for hiring or promotions. The lack of competency in cross-cultural communication can also create misunderstandings, lead to conflicts, and pose barriers to cooperation. In this regard, Tung (1993) suggested ways to develop communication competency from an "unconscious incompetence" to "unconscious competence" to reduce miscommunication among difference groups. The goal for managing diversity is to attain unconscious competence in cross-culture communication, whereby majority and minority group members acknowledge that cultural differences exist between the groups. It is important to genuine attempts to understand that such differences are important (e.g., indirectly asking questions in conversations among high-context communicators should not be interpreted as insecure or insincerity, while assertiveness among low-context communicators should not be interpreted as rude; see Tung, 1993). Given the increasing diversity in the workplace, it is be important to assess leadership effectiveness across different cultures, based on a leader's high- and low-context communication style. Are high- or low-context leaders more effective among a multicultural group of workers? Research on supervisor/superior-subordinate cross-cultural communication has been lacking and merits further investigation. Likewise, it is also important to assess whether "consciously competent" leaders will result in more multicultural organizations and have more diverse top management teams, which could lead to greater firm performance.

Modes of Interaction in Diverse Organizations

Berry and Sabatier (2010) proposed four modes of interaction between members of dominant and minority cultures in Montreal and Paris. The four modes that influence organizational diversity climates (see Figure 17.1) are: assimilation (i.e., adapting to the dominant culture); integration (i.e., choosing and retaining the best of both dominant and minority cultures); marginalization (i.e., rejecting both dominant and minority cultures); and separation (i.e., preserving minority cultures and rejecting dominant cultures). Employers should seek to foster an "integration" climate in which organizational members adopt the best of both dominant and minority cultures. Such an organization (also referred to as the "Multicultural Organization" by Cox, 1993) would ensure the inclusion of minority group input, would promote acceptance without alienating majority group members (e.g., White males), and would promote a positive climate and a productive work environment.

Other modes of interaction such as "separation" or "marginalization" are dysfunctional because they promote ethnocentrism, bias, and prejudice against the nondominant groups (Berry, 1997, 2006). Likewise, "assimilation" requires minority group members to abandon their cultures in favor of the dominant culture, which can lead to conflicts and resentment. Furthermore, the integration of minority cultures with dominant cultures can enhance overall group and organizational performance. As an example, more individualistic cultures (e.g., Anglos) tend to be more competitive, while collectivist cultures (e.g., African-Americans, Asians, and Latinos) tend to be more cooperative, and the inclusion of members from collectivist cultures in workgroups promotes more cooperation (Cox, Lobel, & McLeod, 1991) that can lead to better group and organizational performance. Thus, the integration approach to interaction can improve teamwork and help the organization realize the potential of its multicultural workforce. In this regard, valuing cultural differences between majority and minority group members and combining the positive aspects from both groups can help advance organization goals. As an example, the business case approach whereby minority culture (e.g., language skills and cultural know-how) are preserved and valued can lead to greater marketing success for firms (Cox & Blake, 1991; Tung, 1993). One way to promote the integration of both majority and minority groups is through language training, whereby bilingualism and multilingualism can enhance the understanding and appreciation of each others' culture, which in turn promotes greater communication and workgroup performance (Cox, 1991). In this light, it is important for organizations to foster a climate of acceptance, trust, and mutual admiration of each others' cultures and languages. In multicultural organizations, employees from diverse cultures interact with each other with ease and have a shared understanding in organizational values, missions, and goals. Thus, in times of crisis, organizations can draw upon their diverse pools of talents and resources for problem solving. More research is

	Cultural Preservation	
	Yes	No
Cultural Attractiveness — Yes	Integration	Assimilation
Cultural Attractiveness — No	Separation	Marginalization

FIGURE 17.1 Modes of acculturation.
Source: Adapted from Berry and Sabatier (2010).

needed to demonstrate how language capacity can facilitate greater communication and promote the integration of diverse group members.

Conclusion

Workforce diversity can present both opportunities and challenges to employers. Employers that can harness the diversity in their workforces stand to gain a competitive advantage in the marketplace. In this chapter, we have identified how human resource practices can promote or impede diversity in organizations. In general, organizations that communicate their commitment to diversity can attract a more diverse and talented pool of applicants. However, organizational processes such as selection practices can limit the hiring and promotion of minorities. Prospective minority applicants may self-select themselves out of the recruitment process when they perceive an employer's management practices to be unfair or inequitable. Likewise, poorly implemented affirmative action policies and unchecked internal and external organizational communication can affect the diversity climate, which in turn can affect the commitment and performance of both minority and dominant group members. Minority employees who feel a mismatch between their pre-hiring expectations and organizational realities post-hire will experience a violation of psychological contract and will ultimately withdraw from the organization. Dominant group members will also need to feel included and be brought on board to promote a climate of inclusion for all. Following Berry's work, an organization should strive to foster an integration approach to diversity and should be mindful of both its internal and external communication to ensure that its message on commitment to diversity is consistent throughout the organization, from its CEO to the perceptions held by its organizational members.

Bibliography

Allen, B.J. (1995). "Diversity" and organizational communication. *Journal of Applied Communication Research, 23*(2), 143–155.

Al-Waqfi, M., & Jain, H.C. (2008). Racial inequality in employment in Canada: Empirical analysis and emerging trends. *Canadian Public Administration, 51*(3), 429–453.

Ancis, J.R., & Szymanski, D.M. (2001). Awareness of white privilege among white counseling trainees. *Counseling Psychologist, 29*(4), 548–569.

Aquino, K., Stewart, M.M., & Reed, A. (2005). How social dominance orientation and job status influence perceptions of African-American affirmative action beneficiaries. *Personnel Psychology, 58*(3), 703–744.

Arai, M., Wanca-Thibault, M., & Shockley-Zalabak, P. (2001). Communication theory and training approaches for multiculturally diverse organizations: Have academics and practitioners missed the connection? *Public Personnel Management, 30*(4), 445–455.

Avery, D.R. (2003). Reactions to diversity in recruitment advertising—are differences black and white? *Journal of Applied Psychology, 88*(4), 672–679.

Avery, D.R., McKay, P.F., Wilson, D.C., & Tonidandel, S. (2007). Unequal attendance: The relationships between race, organizational diversity cues, and absenteeism. *Personnel Psychology, 60*(4), 875–902.

Berry, J.W. (1997). Immigration, acculturation, and adaptation. *Applied Psychology: An International Review/Psychologie Appliquee: Revue Internationale, 46*(1), 5–34.

Berry, J.W. (2006). Mutual attitudes among immigrants and ethnocultural groups in Canada. *International Journal of Intercultural Relations, 30*(6), 719–734.

Berry, J.W., & Sabatier, C. (2010). Acculturation, discrimination, and adaptation among second generation immigrant youth in Montreal and Paris. *International Journal of intercultural relations, 34*(3), 191–207.

Biernat, M., & Sesko, A.K. (2013). Communicating about others: Motivations and consequences of race-based impressions. *Journal of Experimental Social Psychology, 49*(1), 138–143.

Conference Board of Canada. (2004). *The voices of visible minorities: Speaking out on breaking down barriers.* Ottawa: Conference Board of Canada.

Cox, T.H. (1991). The multicultural organization. *Academy of Management Executive, 5*(2), 34–47.

Cox, T.H. (1993). *Cultural diversity in organizations: Theory, research & practice.* San Francisco: Berrett-Koehler.

Cox, T.H. Jr., & Blake, S. (1991). Managing cultural diversity: Implications for organizational competitiveness. *Academy of Management Executive, 5*(3), 45–56.

Cox, T.H., Lobel, S.A., & McLeod, P.L. (1991). Effects of ethnic group cultural differences on cooperative and competitive behaviour on a group task. *Academy of Management Journal, 34*(4), 827–847.

Edmondson, V.C., Gupte, G., Draman, R.H., & Oliver, N. (2009). Focusing on communication strategy to enhance diversity climates. *Journal of Communication Management, 13*(1), 6–20.

Ely, R.J., Padavic, I., & Thomas, D.A. (2012). Racial diversity, racial asymmetries, and team learning environment: Effects on performance. *Organization Studies, 33*(3), 341–362.

Ely, R.J., & Thomas, D.A. (2001). Cultural diversity at work: The effects of diversity perspectives on work group processes and outcomes. *Administrative Science Quarterly, 46*(2), 229–273.

Equal Employment Opportunity Commission. (1978). Uniform guidelines on selection procedures. *Federal Register* 43: 38290–38315.

Evans, D.C. (2003). A comparison of the other-directed stigmatization produced by legal and illegal forms of affirmative action. *Journal of Applied Psychology, 88*(1), 121–130.

Fang, T., Samnani, A., Novicevic, M.M., & Bing, M.N. (2013). Liability-of-foreignness effects on job success of immigrant job seekers. *Journal of World Business, 48*(1), 98–109.

Forstenlechner, I., & Al-Waqfi, M. (2010). "A job interview for Mo, but none for Mohammed": Religious discrimination against immigrants in Austria and Germany. *Personnel Review, 39*(6), 767–784.

Giscombe, K., & Mattis, M.C. (2002). Leveling the playing field for women of color in corporate management: Is the business case enough? *Journal of Business Ethics, 37*(1), 103.

Goodman, D.J. (2011). *Promoting diversity and social justice: educating people from privileged groups* (2nd ed.). New York: Routledge.

Grimes, D.G., & Richard, O.C. (2003). Could communication form impact organizations' experience with diversity? *Journal of Business Communication, 40*(1), 7–27.

Hall, E.T., & Hall, M.R. (1987). *Hidden differences: Doing business with Japan.* Garden City, NJ: Anchor Press/Doubleday.

Hambrick, D.C., & Mason, P.A. (1984). Upper echelons: The organization as a reflection of its top managers. *Academy of Management Review, 9*(2), 193–206.

Haq, R., & Ng, E.S.W. (2010). Employment equity and workplace diversity in Canada. In A. Klarsfeld (Ed.), *International handbook on diversity management at work: Country perspectives on diversity and equal treatment.* Cheltenhem: Edward Elgar.

Harrison, D.A., Kravitz, D.A., Meyer, D.M., Leslie, L.M., & Lev-Arey, D. (2006). Understanding attitudes toward affirmative action programs in employment: Summary and meta-analysis of 35 years of research. *Journal of Applied Psychology, 91*(5), 1013–1036.

Heilman, M.E., Battle, W.S., Keller, C.E., & Lee, R.A. (1998). Type of affirmative action policy: A determinant of reactions to sex-based preferential selection? *Journal of Applied Psychology, 83*(2), 190–205.

Heilman, M.E., Block, C.J., & Lucas, J.A. (1992). Presumed incompetent? Stigmatization and affirmative action. *Journal of Applied Psychology, 77*(4), 536–544.

Heilman, M.E., Lucas, J.A., & Kaplow, S.R. (1990). Self-derogating consequences of sex-based preferential selection: The moderating role of initial self-confidence. *Organizational Behavior and Human Decision Processes, 46*(2), 202–216.

Highhouse, S., Stierwalt, S.L., Bachiochi, P., Elder, A.E., & Fisher, G. (1999). Effects of advertised human resource management practices on attraction of African American applicants. *Personnel Psychology, 52*(2), 425–442.

Holzer, H., & Neumark, D. (1999). Are affirmative action hires less qualified? Evidence from employer-employee data on new hires. *Journal of Labor Economics, 17*(3), 534–569.

Holzer, H.J., & Neumark, D. (2000). What does affirmative action do? *Industrial & Labor Relations Review, 53*(2), 240–271.

Kravitz, D.A. (2008). The diversity-validity dilemma: Beyond selection—the role of affirmative action. *Personnel Psychology, 61*(1), 173–193.

Kravitz, D.A., Bludau, T.M., & Klineberg, S.L. (2008). The impact of anticipated consequences, respondent group, and strength of affirmative action plan on affirmative action attitudes. *Group & Organization Management, 33*(4), 361–391.

McKay, P.F., & Avery, D.R. (2005). Warning! Diversity recruitment could backfire. *Journal of Management Inquiry, 14*(4), 330–336.

McKay, P.F., & Avery, D.R. (2006). What has race got to do with it? Unraveling the role of racioethnicity in job seekers' reactions to site visits. *Personnel Psychology, 59*(2), 395–429.

McKay, P.F., Avery, D.R., Tonidandel, S., Morris, M.A., Hernandez, M., & Hebl, M.R. (2007). Racial differences in employee retention: Are diversity climate perceptions the key? *Personnel Psychology, 60*(1), 35–62.

Mujtaba, B.G., & Sims, R.L. (2011). Gender differences in managerial attitudes towards unearned privilege and favoritism in the retail sector. *Employee Responsibilities and Rights Journal, 23*(3), 205–217.

Ng, E.S.W. (2005). Employment equity and organizational diversity performance: The role of CEOs' characteristics and commitment. Unpublished doctoral dissertation, McMaster University, Hamilton, ON.

Ng, E.S.W. (2008). Why organizations choose to manage diversity? Toward a leadership-based theoretical framework. *Human Resource Development Review, 7*(1), 58–78.

Ng, E.S.W., & Burke, R.J. (2005). Person–organization fit and the war for talent: Does diversity management make a difference? *International Journal of Human Resource Management, 16*(7), 1195–1210.

Ng, E.S.W., & Burke, R.J. (2010). A comparison of the legislated employment equity program, federal contractors program, and financial post 500 firms. *Canadian Journal of Administrative Sciences, 27*(3), 224–235.

Ng, E.S.W., & Sears, G.J. (2010a). The effect of adverse impact in selection practices on organizational diversity: A field study. *International Journal of Human Resource Management, 21*(9), 1454–1471.

Ng, E.S.W., & Sears, G.J. (2010b). What women and ethnic minorities want, work values and labor market confidence: A self-determination perspective. *International Journal of Human Resource Management, 21*(5), 676–698.

Ng, E.S.W., & Sears, G.J. (2012). CEO leadership styles and the implementation of organizational diversity practices: Moderating effects of social values and age. *Journal of Business Ethics, 105*(1), 41–52.

Ng, E.S.W., & Tung, R.L. (1998). Ethno-cultural diversity and organizational effectiveness: A field study. *International Journal of Human Resource Management, 9*(6), 980–995.

Ng, E.S.W., & Wiesner, W.H. (2007). Are men always picked over women? The effects of employment equity directives on selection decisions. *Journal of Business Ethics, 76*(2), 177–187.

Ng, E.S.W., & Wyrick, C.R. (2011). Motivational bases for managing diversity: A model of leadership commitment. *Human Resource Management Review, 21*(4), 368–376.

Pfeffer, J., Davis-Blake, A., & Julius, D.J. (1995). AA officer salaries and managerial diversity: Efficiency wages or status? *Industrial Relations, 34*(1), 73–94.

Richard, O.C. (2000). Racial diversity, business strategy, and firm performance: A resource-based view. *Academy of Management Journal, 43*(2), 164–177.

Roberge, M., & van Dick, R. (2010). Recognizing the benefits of diversity: When and how does diversity increase group performance? *Human Resource Management Review, 20*(4), 295–308.

Roberson, L., & Kulik, C.T. (2007). Stereotype threat at work. *Academy of Management Perspectives, 21*(2), 24–40.

Robinson, G., & Dechant, K. (1997). Building a business case for diversity. *Academy of Management Executive, 11*(3), 21–31.

Roth, P.L., Bevier, C.A., Bobko, P., Switzer, F.S. III, & Tyler, P. (2001). Ethnic group differences in cognitive ability in employment and educational settings: A meta-analysis. *Personnel Psychology, 54*(2), 297–330.

Roth, P.L., & Bobko, P. (2000). College grade point average as a personnel selection device: Ethnic group differences and potential adverse impact. *Journal of Applied Psychology, 85*(3), 399–406.

Shore, L.M., Chung-Herrera, B., Dean, M.A., Ehrhart, K.H., Jung, D.I., Randel, A.E., & Singh, G. (2009). Diversity in organizations: Where are we now and where are we going? *Human Resource Management Review, 19*(2), 117–133.

Son Hing, L.S., Bobocel, D.R., & Zanna, M.P. (2002). Meritocracy and opposition to affirmative action: Making concessions in the face of discrimination. *Journal of Personality and Social Psychology, 83*(3), 493–509.

Spanierman, L.B., Beard, J.C., & Todd, N.R. (2012). White men's fears, white women's tears: Examining gender differences in racial affect types. *Sex Roles, 67*(3–4), 174–186.

Stainback, K., & Tomaskovic-Devey, D. (2009). Intersections of power and privilege: Long-term trends in managerial representation. *American Sociological Review, 74*(5), 800–820.

Statistics Canada. (2011). *Projected trends to 2031 for the Canadian labour force*. Retrieved from www.statcan. gc.ca/pub/11-010-x/2011008/part-partie3-eng.htm.

Tatli, A., & Özbilgin, M.F. (2009). Understanding diversity managers' role in organizational change: Towards a conceptual framework. *Canadian Journal of Administrative Sciences, 26*(3), 244–258.

Thomas, K.M., & Wise, P.G. (1999). Organizational attractiveness and individual differences: Are diverse applicants attracted by different factors? *Journal of Business and Psychology, 13*(3), 375.

Thomas, R.R. (1990). From affirmative action to affirming diversity: Diversity is what makes America different; why don't we turn it to our advantage? *Harvard Business Review, 68*(2), 107–117.

Triana, M., Garcia, M.F., & Colella, A. (2010). Managing diversity: How organizational efforts to support diversity moderate the effects of perceived racial discrimination on affective commitment. *Personnel Psychology, 63*(4), 817–843.

Tung, R.L. (1993). Managing cross-national and intra-national diversity. *Human Resource Management, 23*(4), 461–477.

U.S. Census Bureau. (2012). *Employment outlook: 2010–2020. Labor force projections to 2020: A more slowly growing workforce*. Retrieved from www.bls.gov/opub/mlr/2012/01/art3full.pdf.

Verbeek, S., & Groeneveld, S. (2012). Do "hard" diversity policies increase ethnic minority representation? *Personnel Review, 41*(5), 647–664.

Wiegand, R.A. (2007). Organizational diversity, profits, and returns in U.S. firms. *Problems and Perspectives in Management, 5*(3), 69–83.

Williams, M.L., & Bauer, T.N. (1994). The effect of a managing diversity policy on organizational attractiveness. *Group & Organization Management, 19*(3), 295.

18

WORK-LIFE ISSUES

Caryn E. Medved

Throughout the last four decades, work-life issues have attracted considerable media attention, corporate policy effort, and scholarly consideration. Many organizations have work-life policies and practices such as flextime, flex-place, part-time work, maternity and paternity leave, and eldercare or child care referral services. Still, impediments often exist to executive-level collaboration, managerial support, and implementation of work-life policies (Myers, Gaillaird, & Putnam, 2012; Ryan & Kossek, 2008). Different from most industrialized countries, minimal federal-level policy exists in the United States to aid individuals with caregiving responsibilities (Gornick & Myers, 2005). Thus, support with work-life conflicts in the United States primarily rests on employer accommodation and family or community assistance.

Human resource management (HRM) professionals must collaborate with executives, legal departments, management, employees, and, at times, unions to develop optimal solutions, even during difficult economic conditions (Galinsky & Bond, 2010). HRM departments are often responsible for developing work-life programs, gathering and sharing policy information, training or coaching employees, and managing related employee relations issues (Kossek, Bates, & Matthews, 2011). Although all these tasks require specific communication knowledge and skills, only a small but vital corpus of work-life communication research exists, little of which explicitly investigates the role of HRM in communicating effective work-life policies. The goal of this chapter is to bring research on work-life communication, as well as related communication theory and skills, together with the study and practice of HRM. To do so, relevant communication research is organized around three roles an HRM practitioner may play in relation to work-life policy issues: resource, coach, and strategist. In the following each role is explored by (a) detailing practitioner tasks and goals, (b) synthesizing existing communication research, and (c) identifying knowledge gaps critical to HRM research and practice. In closing, I propose a research agenda for scholars interested in further investigating the intersections among HRM, communication, and work-life policy, and I offer suggestions for HRM practice.

To achieve these goals, I weave three literatures together. The interdisciplinary work-life policy research is touched upon to situate the underlying HRM policy context (e.g., Kelly et al., 2008; Matos & Galinsky, 2012; Pitt-Catsouphes, Kossek, & Sweet, 2006). In addition, the small yet bourgeoning body of work-life communication research illustrates the centrality of messages, interaction, and language to successful work-life policy design and implementation (e.g., Hoffman & Cowan, 2008, 2010; Kirby & Krone, 2002; Medved, 2010; Miller, Jablin, Casey, Lamphear-Van Horn, & Ethington, 1996; Ryan & Kossek, 2008; Tracy & Rivera, 2010). Finally, HRM-related work-life communication research is extended and directions for future research forged through considering insights from previously unrelated studies of internal strategic communication planning (Welch & Jackson, 2005), information giving and seeking (Miller & Jablin, 1991; Rowan, 2003; Street, 2003), upward influence (e.g., Olufowote, Miller, & Wilson, 2005), and information richness (Daft & Lengel, 1984; Trevino, Daft, & Lengel, 1990), as well as gender and manager-employee negotiations (Babcock & Laschever, 2003; Meiners & Boster, 2012).

One additional prefatory remark is necessary. Conversations about communication and work-life issues must begin and end with issues of credibility. HRM must provide leadership that is honest, inspiring, and competent with respect to work-life issues (Kouzes & Posner, 2005; O'Keefe, 1990; Ulrich, 1998). To successfully create a supportive organizational work-life culture, HRM credibility must be established across relationships with various organizational stakeholders. Credibility with the C-suite gets HRM a seat at the decision-making table. HRM credibility also is important with midlevel managers, the gatekeepers of policy implementation (Peper, Den Dulk, & van Doorne-Huiskes, 2009). Finally, HRM must be perceived by employees as a credible source of information, advice, and conflict resolution regarding work-life issues. Balancing goodwill for employees' concerns with vital work unit and organizational outcomes is a difficult communicative dance (McCroskey & Teven, 1999). While few would argue with the value of credibility for the success of HRM work-life policies, research on how HRM professionals attain and maintain credibility is sorely needed.

Work-Life Policy: A (Very) Brief Introduction

In the 1980s, work-life initiatives (then labeled "work-family") emerged to attract and retain professional women in the workforce. These programs initially targeted high-performing women who were also mothers who struggled to manage both paid work and "second shift" family responsibilities (Hochschild, 1989). These initiatives over time broadened in scope, popularity, and inclusiveness. Men and women employees experience work-life conflict. Recently, men report increased rates of work-life conflict (Aumann, Galinsky & Matos, 2011; Williams, 2012).

HRM professionals must be knowledgeable about several pieces of legislation that affect both workers and employers in the United States. The Fair Labor Standards Act (1938) established the 40-hour workweek for nonexempt employees, guidelines for overtime pay, and federal minimum wage standards. The Pregnancy Discrimination Act (1978), an amendment to Title VII of the Civil Rights Act (1964), prohibits discrimination by mandating that employers provide pregnant women the same benefits offered other employees. Further, the Patient Protection and Affordable Care Act (2010) requires large employers to provide "appropriate breaks and locations so that working mothers covered by FLSA can pump breast milk" (Boushey, 2011, p. 171). The Family Medical Leave Act (FMLA, of 1993) is the only U.S. legislation designed explicitly to provide employee protection and employer guidance on family caregiving leave (see U.S. Department of Labor, 2013). HRM professionals in organizations employing 50 or more workers must be experts on the terms of the FMLA, including issues of employee eligibility, employer responsibility, documentation procedures, and state-level leave provisions.

Employer-sponsored work-life benefits take various forms. Some policies permit employees to vary work schedules and/or locations around caregiving duties (Galinsky, Sakai, & Wigton, 2011). Specific forms of workplace flexibility include the following: flextime (e.g., traditional flextime, daily flextime, compressed workweeks), reduced time (e.g., part-time work, part-year work), flex-leaves (time off during an individual day, illness time off, paid time off for child care, parental leave), flex-careers and flex-place (e.g., full-time telecommuting, hoteling; Friedman, 2002). Other work-life benefits include employment conditions (e.g., job design, terms of employment) along with organizational and professional cultures and norms (e.g., managerial support, face-time pressures; Kossek, 2005). Recently, benefits have been scrutinized in relation to being "single friendly"; i.e., attention now is being paid to the nonwork needs of employees without children (e.g., Casper, Weltman, & Swesiga, 2007).

Lastly, a strong business case exists for work-life programs and policies (e.g., A Better Balance, 2010; Council of Economic Advisors, 2010). Assisting employees with work-life balance is not only good for employees but also financially benefits the organization in terms of recruitment, retention, health care costs, and productivity. To illustrate, in a survey of 200 human resource managers, two-thirds of respondents identified family supportive policies as the single most important factor in attracting and retaining employees (Williams, 2000). Absenteeism attributed to family caregiving costs U.S. organizations more than $5 billion a year (MetLife, 2006), and 63% of workers using flexible work arrangements said they were absent less from work due to the availability of these policies (Flatley McGuire, Kenney, & Brashler, 2010). Further, work-life balance is the second best predictor, after economic security, of an employee's quality of health, frequency of sleep problems, and level of stress (Aumann & Galinsky, 2009). Finally, employees with access to flexible work schedules tend to have higher job satisfaction and appear to be more willing to work hard (Flatley McGuire et al., 2010).

HRM Work-Life and Communication

Work-life communication research may be organized around three communication roles HRM professionals play in the implementation of work-life policies: resource, coach, and strategist.

Resource

HRM professionals must serve as credible *sources of information* about a range of employment issues (e.g., benefits, compensation, recruitment, etc.). When HRM practitioners assume the work-life *resource* role, they must efficiently and effectively gather, monitor, and disseminate work-life policy information. At a basic level, serving as a resource involves creating awareness among stakeholder groups. HRM professionals as organizational resources must craft organization-wide messages regarding policy details, procedures, and vision. Indeed, credible HRM departments continuously gather and share information about the ever-changing external environment and employee needs (Ulrich, 1998).

Successful policy implementation includes "developing comprehensive and well-organized communication strategies with consistent messaging" (Boston College Center for Work & Family, 2008, p. 6). Effective communication about work-life programs is argued to "signal inclusion and employer caring by demonstrating that policies exist not merely as public relations vehicles" (Ryan & Kossek, 2008, p. 300). That is, the presence of work-life policies de facto has *symbolic value*. The empirical work of Casper and Harris (2008) found that the availability of work-life benefits influenced attachment of female employees to the organization *irrespective of actual policy use*. Conversely, ineffectively communicating about work-life programs limits employee awareness of policy availability and applicability (Christensen, 1999) and creates perceptions of exclusion (Ryan & Kossek, 2008).

Yet as evidenced by the scant organizational-level communication research, we know little about how HRM professionals strategically and effectively gather, monitor, and disseminate work-life information. Consequently, our attention now turns to knowledge gaps and connecting these openings to existing communication research. HRM professionals, for instance, often are charged with preparation of corporate messages for global employee populations or for various internal stakeholder groups (Welch & Jackson, 2007). Research does not exist exploring levels and/or forms of effective communication planning during policy implementation, although it is known that communication affects the acceptance of HRM and managerial innovation (Kossek, 1989). Fruitful investigation might explore the role of storytelling in creating work-life organizational change (Tucker, Yeow, & Viki, 2013) or ways that the media undermines or supports internal messaging about high-profile work-life issues. The recent media frenzy and fallout of Marissa Mayer's global "memo" sent to Yahoo employees about the elimination of all telecommuting only underscores the critical role that internal corporate communication plays in managing work-life initiatives (Kleinman, 2013).

Future research also might investigate questions such as, how should corporate messages be tailored to various employee groups in ways that facilitate uptake and inclusiveness (Welch & Jackson, 2007)? Or, how can communication about work-life programs strategically be used to externally shape corporate image (and, simultaneously, aid in employee recruitment) and internally create employee engagement (Cheney & Christensen, 2001; Saks, 2006)? Studies of communication during policy implementation could explore critical factors in success such as communication needs analysis, message timing, voice, and issue framing (Fairhurst, 2011).

After the announcements and kickoff events are over, HRM's role during the day-to-day management of work-life programs often is that of *informing* stakeholders about basic policy utilization rules and regulations. Informing is the provision of information that generally is not in dispute (Rowan, 2003). Effective explainers offer a variety of examples and counter-examples, encouraging learners to practice, and "communicate familiar but often misunderstood notions by explaining what these notions do not mean as well as what they do mean" (Rowan, 2003, p. 420). To date, investigations have yet to explore the information-giving skills of HRM professionals as well as the information needs of executives (as well as other stakeholders) faced with decisions about supporting work-life policy decisions (Tracy & Rivera, 2010). Existing studies on information giving, primarily conducted in the context of health communication research (e.g. Street, 2003), could be imported into the work-life policy context to provide directions for research to explore assessing the amount of information that executives want, gauging the amount of information that they already possess about work-life issues, and avoiding technical jargon that might alienate executives (Street, 2003). Researchers must also investigate policy implementation materials, including Web site FAQs and HRM handbook materials, in terms of effective information-giving strategies; information giving in the virtual and textual space also has important consequences for policy adoption (Cowan & Hoffman, 2008).

In addition to message content, HRM professionals also make decisions about ways of conveying information via communication technologies. When aiming to be a credible resource about work-life issues, HRM must consider the match between the nature of the information being conveyed and the richness of the communication channel (Daft & Lengel, 1984). Scant research explores Information Richness Theory in the context of new work-life policy adoption. Under what circumstances is lean media perhaps more or less effective during the implementation of a new work and family policy? Conversely, when is a rich media critical to new policy adoption by executives, managers, or employees? Thus, more extensive research on media preferences for communication about work-life policy also could help to inform media richness theory as well as HRM practice.

Coach

HRM professionals, at times, also *coach* managers on the front line of implementing flexibility programs. HRM coaching also assists employees with concerns about when and/or if to raise work-life conflict issues with supervisors (Liu & Buzzanell, 2004; Miller et al., 1996). Supervisory support from a psychological, rather than a communicative perspective often has been a focus of interdisciplinary work-life research (e.g., Thompson, Beauvais, & Lyness, 1999). We know that managerial support is critical to the success of work-family programs and/or policies. Supervisors and coworkers can either facilitate effective policy integration or become stumbling blocks to utilization (Fay & Kline, 2011; Kossek & Nichol, 1992).

A growing body of empirical research has begun to explore the role of communication in constructing managerial support across episodes of work-life conflict and leave negotiations (Buzzanell & Lui, 2007; Kirby, 2000; Kirby & Krone, 2002; Ter Hoeven, Miller, Den Dulk, & Peper, 2012), including the structuration of rules and resources embedded in employee requests for workplace accommodation (Hoffman & Cowan, 2010) and employee decision making about when to "speak up" in the workplace (Edmondson & Detert, 2005).

Kirby's (2000) study of the communication processes shaping work-life conflict and policy utilization at a governmental agency found that managerial support in practice is not simply an issue of management endorsement. Rather, subtle forms of contradictory and ambiguous communication, over and above individual managers' attitudes, shapes policy utilization, including coworker interaction (Fay & Kline, 2011; Kirby & Krone, 2002). Although complex, the central role of managerial communication still cannot be discounted. Peper and colleagues' (2009) case study of a Dutch bank reported, "It was managers who made the difference when it came to flexibility about the company's work-family" benefits (p. 123). Managers' decision making was, at times, perceived by some employees as arbitrary or contradictory.

Further, Ter Hoeven and colleagues (2012) identified four communication tensions inherent in work-life policy implementation, all of which touch on the manager-employee relationship: (a) policy exists but management discourages its use, (b) workplace culture supports policy implementation yet coworkers actively discourage use, (c) policy exists yet career and economic costs for employee negate uptake, and (d) managers want to facilitate use of policies yet workflow and productivity issues prevent their use. Extant research also shows that productivity pressures may discourage managerial approval for employee flexibility (Den Dulk & Ruijter, 2008). Managerial fears of losing control or lack of policy knowledge or resources also may create roadblocks (Boston College Center for Work & Family, 2008).

Workplace accommodation, as aptly noted by Hoffman and Cowan (2010), is not just a function of top-down HRM information dissemination but also immediately results from employee attempts at *upward influence*. Hoffman and Cowan found that employee appeals were made only after careful weighing of risk and were largely framed in terms of organizational, rather than personal, interests. Further, requests that centered on family-related conflicts, versus nonfamily issues, more often were made and supported. Edmondson and Detert (2005) support Hoffman and Cowan's work in their proposal that four conditions influence when an employee will decide to "speak up" or remain silent about work-life conflict: (a) feelings of psychological safety, (b) weighing the costs of anticipated gains, (c) motivations for speaking up, and (d) leadership behaviors.

In addition to identifying and interrogating manager-employee tensions and the nature of employee requests or reasons for speaking up, communication researchers have also *relationally* positioned policy implementation as "role negotiation" (Miller et al., 1996) and "conflict management" processes (Buzzanell & Liu, 2007). Miller and colleagues theorize maternity leave as a three-stage process of role negotiating. Their theoretical model posits antecedents, role negotiation attributes, and outcomes that comprise the role negotiation process. Buzzanell and Liu (2007) empirically explored maternity leave as a communicative process. In their exploration of interviews specifically with women who had been discouraged at the point of beginning their maternity leave, these authors identified three sets of discourses and practices that accounted for both the disparities between these women's expectations and experiences as well as related tensions. Overt, covert, and institutional discourses and practices all served to discourage the manager-employee negotiation process around maternity leave; in fact, many of these discouraged leave-takers expressed an inability or unwillingness to negotiate the details of their maternity leaves with their supervisors.

Future research should dig deeper into the range of successful to unsuccessful leave negotiations and the role of HRM in facilitating leave-taking conversations. In particular, what is the nature of paternity leave negotiations, reasons for lack of negotiations, and/or changing gendered assumptions affecting paternity leave requests? Further, although leader-member exchange (LMX) relationships and other structural and relational variables affect the nature of supervisor-employee negotiations (Meiners & Boster, 2012), no research exists about how LMX specifically affects maternity leave negotiation outcomes and/or satisfaction with outcomes. Finally, how might perceptions of gendered negotiation skills potentially influence outcomes (Babcock & Laschever, 2003)? We need to know more about how gender dynamics are operating, and perhaps changing, in organizational communication about work-life accommodation.

High-intensity teleworkers typically enjoy flexible work arrangements, and this may contribute to their greater satisfaction than office-based workers (Fronner & Roloff, 2010). We know little, however, about how HRM professionals effectively coach employees and managers to have effective conversations about performance in the context of telecommuting or job sharing (see Gordon & Miller, 2012), as well as how to facilitate meaningful and productive coworker interactions given that we know these relationships can be challenging (Fay & Kline, 2011).

Finally, studies could query under what circumstances HRM professionals serve as proactive coaches for managers and employees on work-life issues in comparison to situations in which they act as reactive conflict mediators. Knowing more about how HRM professionals fashion and carry out their work-life communication roles could help diagnose implementation challenges and/or identify strengths (e.g., Pounsford, 2007). Wrench, McCroskey, Berletch, Powley, & Wehr (2008) suggest that organizational coaching is a form of instructional communication and propose to measure effective coaching with the perceived coaching scale. Do higher levels of perceived HRM coaching for either managers or employees relate to more effective work-life negotiations? What communication strategies do HRM professionals use, such as storytelling, in the context of work-life coaching interactions (Pounsford, 2007; Tucker et al., 2013)?

Strategist

The final role that HR professionals can play in the successful development and implementation of work-family policies and practices is to communicate at the strategic level. The *strategist* role allows HRM professionals to shift from a singular focus on specific HRM functions to assess how work-life issues integrate into larger organizational goals and plans. Being a strategist requires being invited to the executive decision-making table at the highest levels of the organization. Yet we know little about the communication aptitudes or skills of HRM professionals who are central to organizational decision making or how credibility is established by HRM at this level regarding work-life policy development.

The strategic level is often framed through the language of the "business case." This role for HRM professionals requires persuasively posing and answering the following question: *What critical business needs or problems can be addressed through work-life programs or initiatives?* To respond to this question, HRM professionals must be well versed in leadership goals and know how to frame work-life issues as solutions to key business problems (Fairhurst, 2011). For instance, if turnover of highly talented women is a leadership concern, HRM can provide data and arguments about possible connections between these incidents of turnover and the availability (or, most likely, lack of availability) of work-life support. Thinking and communicating strategically demands engaging in four intersecting tasks across all organizational levels: assess, design, implement, and evaluate work-life policies (Boston College Center for Work & Family, 2008).

First, to work at the strategic level requires hard data. Assessment means gathering extensive information on various employee needs, communication climate, managerial relationships, performance, work design, technology, and industry best practice. Conducting a thorough work-life needs assessment is essential to policy design and to building support at the highest levels of the organization (Friedman & Galinsky, 1992). Research findings detailed in the previous sections can guide HRM professionals to broaden their scope of data collection to issues such as perceived coworker support (Fay & Kline, 2011), employee willingness to speak up about work-life conflict (Edmondson & Detert, 2005), and perception of current managerial attitudes toward requests (Hoffman & Cowan, 2010).

Second, even armed with high-quality data, strategic-level policy and program design is never easy. In addition to HRM outcomes such as retention and recruitment, design must also take into consideration the functionality of work-life programs vis-à-vis other business units' outcome measures such as those of operations, sales, and finance. Representatives from other business units must have a voice in work-life policy design, when appropriate. Little research exists about ways to effectively frame work-life policy initiatives across organizational units (Fairhurst, 2011). HRM professionals often must formulate internal communication plans for policy rollouts and training as well as proactively address public relations issues. Limited communication research exists to provide HRM practitioners with assistance in the design phase and to connect to the literature on communication and organizational change (Deetz, Tracy, & Simpson, 1999).

Further research on designing communication aspects of new policy development might explore questions such as these: How do employees without children or significant eldercare responsibilities talk about their needs for personal accommodations (see Casper et al., 2007)? How do managers communicate in their workgroups about accommodations in ways that create a climate of perceived fairness? In addition, communication research also urges HRM professionals to question the very language of *flexibility*. Talking about work-life programs through the language of *adaptability* recently is argued to provide a more comprehensive approach to how "organizations and workers mutually adapt to each other's changing needs to benefit both the individuals and the institutions" (Myers, Gaillaird, & Putnam, 2012, p. 213).

After assessing and designing, execution of new strategic initiatives is the third stage the HRM work-life strategist faces. Four work-life policy attributes have been theorized to affect the success and inclusiveness of their implementation: supervisor support, universality, negotiability, and quality of communication (Ryan & Kossek, 2008). Existing communication research supports the criticality and tension-filled nature of supervisor support (Kirby, 2000;Ter Hoeven et al., 2012). Communication research is necessary to explore the attribute of negotiability: What is the nature of manager-employee negotiations and upward influence strategies during non-leave related work-life accommodations? What is the nature of employee information-seeking strategies in addition to direct supervisor requests (Miller & Jablin, 1991)?

Finally, measuring the impact of work-life programs is not easy, yet evaluation is essential to their ongoing realization and success. Evaluation of work-life policies and practices should be executed at the employee, managerial, workgroup, and organizational levels. To fully understand the impact of work-life programs as implied in the aforementioned research, it is essential to include evaluation metrics on the nature of and satisfaction with communication relationships, corporate messaging, and communication about flexibility programs. To date, no communication research focuses on developing metrics and assessment tools for program evaluation (e.g., Wrench et al., 2008). Scholars could make a contribution to practice by developing the tools and research to evaluate the communicative aspects of work-family programs.

An HRM Work-Life Communication Research Agenda

HRM professionals can play three critical communication roles in the design and implementation of work-life policies and programs: resource, coach, and strategist. Although in its infancy, the growing body of communication work-life research has much to offer the study and practice of HRM. Looking across the numerous and peripatetic threads of research initiated in the prior discussion, I close this chapter by prioritizing three future directions for communication scholarship related to HRM and work-life policy.

First, while communication scholars have begun to explore issues of maternity leave, managerial and coworker communication, work-family accommodation requests, and telecommuting, a wide range of work-life accommodation contexts and concepts remain unexplored. The full range of HRM related work-life communication issues sorely needs investigation, including, but not limited to, coworker communication in job-sharing relationships, performance appraisal conversations for telecommuting, coworker and managerial support for eldercare responsibilities, talk about domestic partnerships and gay/lesbian work-life conflicts, career counseling conversations around work-family issues, and workplace interactions between part-time and full-time employees. In short, only a handful of policy contexts comprising the communication HRM research agenda have been explored.

Second, most, if not all, of the communication research is woman and maternity centered. As noted at the outset of this chapter, gendered divisions of labor at home and in the workplace are changing (Medved & Rawlins, 2010). It is critical that the future research agenda not only broaden to explore the role of HRM in facilitating men's work-life balance, but also challenge the unitary categories of femininity and masculinity. As men continue to desire and take on more caregiving and domestic work at home, the workplace stereotypes of men as "ideal workers"—in other words, available to employers 24/7 without family responsibilities—continue to become less viable (Williams, 2000). Negotiations at home shape negotiations in the workplace, and future research must continue to connect both spheres of communication and relationships (Medved, 2004).

Finally, further investigation of communication and the construction of gender, race, and class are critical to HRM practices of work-life and are connected to issues of diversity. Most, if not all, communication work-life research focuses on the professional white-collar workplace. At the same time, low-income workers struggle in different, if not profoundly different, ways with managing caring and earning responsibilities (Council of Economic Advisors, 2010). If HRM professionals truly desire to create supportive work environments for all employees and to contribute to the bottom line of organizations, scholars interested in work-life issues of communication need to broaden their scope of investigation.

Bibliography

A Better Balance. (2010). *The business case for flexibility*. New York: A Better Balance.

Aumann, K., & Galinsky, E. (2009). *The state of health in the American workforce: Does having an effective workplace matter?* New York: Families and Work Institute.

Aumann, K., Galinsky, E., & Matos, K. (2011). *The new male mystique. National study of the changing workforce.* New York: Families and Work Institute.

Babcock, L., & Laschever, S. (2003). *Women don't ask: Negotiation and the gender divide*. Princeton, NJ: Princeton University Press.

Boston College Center for Work & Family. (2008). *Overcoming the implementation gap: How 20 leading companies are making flexibility work*. Boston: Boston College Center for Work & Family.

Boushey, H. (2011). The role of the government in work-family conflict. *Future of Children, 21*, 163–190.

Buzzanell, P.M., & Liu, M. (2007). It's "give and take": Maternity leave as a conflict management process. *Human Relations, 60*, 463–495.

Casper, W. J., & Harris, C. M. (2008). Work-life benefits and organizational attachment: Self-interest utility and signaling theory models. *Journal of Vocational Behavior, 72*(1), 95–109.

Casper, W.J., Weltman, D., & Swesiga, E. (2007). Beyond family friendly: The construct and measurement of singles-friendly work culture. *Journal of Vocational Behavior, 70*, 478–501.

Cheney, G., & Christensen, L. (2001). Organizational identity linkages between internal and external communication. In F. Jablin & L. Putnam (Eds.), *The new handbook of organizational communication: Advances in theory, research and method* (pp. 231–269). Thousand Oaks, CA: Sage.

Christensen, P. (1999). Toward a comprehensive work/life strategy. In S. Parasuraman & J. Greenhaus (Eds.), *Work and family: Challenges and choices for a changing world* (2nd ed., pp. 25–37). Westport, CT: Praeger.

Council of Economic Advisors. (2010). *Work-life balance and the economics of workplace flexibility*. Washington, DC: The White House.

Cowan, R.L., & Hoffman, M.F. (2008). The meaning of work/life: A corporate ideology of work/life balance. *Communication Quarterly, 56*, 227–246.

Daft, R.L., & Lengel, R.H. (1984). Information richness: A new approach to managerial behavior and organizational design. *Research in Organizational Behavior, 6*, 191–233.

Deetz, S.A., Tracy, S.J., & Simpson, J.L. (1999). *Leading organizations through transition: Communication and culture change*. Thousand Oaks, CA: Sage.

Dulk, L. Den, & Ruijter, J. de. (2008). Managing work-life policies: Disruption versus dependency arguments. *International Journal of Human Resource Management, 19*(7), 1222–1236.

Edmondson, A.C., & Detert, J.R. (2005). The role of speaking up in work-life balancing. In E.E. Kossek & S.J. Lambert (Eds.), *Work and life integration: Organizational, cultural and individual perspectives* (pp. 381–406). Mahwah, NJ: Taylor & Francis.

Fairhurst, G.T. (2011). *The power of framing: Creating the language of leadership*. San Francisco, CA: Jossey-Bass.

Fay, M.J., & Kline, S.L. (2011). Co-worker relationships and informal communication in high-intensity telecommuting. *Journal of Applied Communication Research, 39*, 144–163.

Flatley McGuire, J., Kenney, K., & Brashler, P. (2010). *Flexible work arrangements: The fact sheet.* Washington, DC: Georgetown University Law Center. Retrieved from: http://scholarship.law.georgetown.edu/legal/.

Friedman, D.E. (2002). *Workplace flexibility: A guide for companies*. New York: Families and Work Institute.

Friedman, D.E., & Galinsky, E. (1992). Work and family issues: A legitimate business case. In S. Zedeck (Ed.), *Work, families and organizations: Frontiers of industrial and organizational psychology* (pp. 168–207). San Francisco, CA: Jossey-Bass.

Fronner, K.L., & Roloff, M.E. (2010). Why teleworkers are more satisfied with their jobs than are office-based workers: When less contact is beneficial. *Journal of Applied Communication Research, 38,* 336–361.

Galinsky, E., & Bond, J.T. (2010). *The impact of the recession on employers.* New York: Families and Work Institute. Retrieved from http://familiesandwork.org/site/research/reports/Recession2009.pdf.

Galinsky, E., Sakai, K., & Wigton, T. (2011). Workplace flexibility: From research to action. *Future of Children, 21,* 141–161.

Gordon, M.E., & Miller, V.D. (2012). *Conversations about job performance: A communication perspective on the appraisal process.* New York: Business Expert Press.

Gornick, J.C., & Meyers, J.C. (2005). *Families that work: Policies for reconciling parenthood and employment.* New York: Russell Sage.

Hochschild, A.R. (1989). *The second shift.* New York: Avon Books.

Hoffman, M. F., & Cowan, R. L. (2008). The meaning of work/life: A corporate ideology of work/life balance. *Communication Quarterly, 56*(2), 227–246.

Hoffman, M.F., & Cowan, R.L. (2010). Be careful what you ask for: Structuration theory and work/life accommodation. *Communication Studies, 61,* 205–223.

Kelly, E.L., Kossek, E.E., Hammer, L.B., Durham, M., Bray, J., Chermack, K., Murphy, L.A., & Kaskubar, D. (2008). Getting there from here: Research on the effect of work-family initiatives on work-family conflict and business outcomes. *Academy of Management Annals, 2,* 305–349.

Kirby, E.L. (2000). Should I do as you say or as you do?: Mixed messages about work and family. *Electronic Journal of Communication, 10.* Retrieved from www.cios.org.remote.baruch.cuny.edu/EJCPUBLIC/010/3/010313.html.

Kirby, E.L., & Krone, K.J. (2002). "The policy exists but you can't really use it": Communication and the structuration of work-family policies. *Journal of Applied Communication Research, 30,* 50–77.

Kleinman, A. (2013, April 19). Marissa Mayer finally addresses work from home ban. *Huffington Post.* Retrieved from www.huffingtonpost.com/2013/04/19/marissa-mayer-work-from-home_n_3117352.html.

Kossek, E.E. (1989). The acceptance of human resource innovations by multiple stakeholders. *Personnel Psychology, 47*(2), 263–281.

Kossek, E.E. (2005). Workplace policies and practices to support work and families: Gaps in implementation and linkages to individual and organizational effectiveness. In S. Bianchi, L. Casper, & R. King (Eds.), *Work, family health and well-being* (pp. 97–116). Mahwah, NJ: Lawrence Erlbaum Associates.

Kossek, E.E., Bates, B.B., & Matthews, R.A. (2011). How work-family research can finally have an impact in organizations. *Industrial & Organizational Psychology, 4*(3), 352–369.

Kossek, E.E., & Nichol, V. (1992). The effects of on-site childcare on employee attitudes and performance. *Personnel Psychology, 45,* 485–509.

Kouzes, J.M., & Posner, B.Z. (2005). Leading in cynical times. *Journal of Management Inquiry, 14,* 357–364.

Liu, M., & Buzzanell, P. M. (2004). Negotiating maternity leave expectations: Perceived tensions between ethics of justice and care. *Journal of Business Communication, 41*(4), 323–349.

Matos, K., & Galinsky, E. (2012). *National study of employers.* New York: Families and Work Institute.

McCroskey, J.C., & Teven, J.J. (1999). Goodwill: A reexamination of the construct and its measurement. *Communication Monographs, 66,* 90–103.

Medved, C.E. (2004). The everyday accomplishment of work and family: Exploring practical actions in daily routines. *Communication Studies, 55,* 1–45.

Medved, C.E. (2010). Work and family communication. In S. Sweet & J. Casey (Eds.), *Work and family encyclopedia.* Chestnut Hill, MA: Sloan Work and Family Research Network. Retrieved from http://workfamily.sas.upenn.edu/wfrn-repo/object/3kb6k5cb4ft79l8c.

Medved, C.E., & Rawlins, W.K. (2010). At-home fathers and breadwinning mothers: Varieties in constructing work and family lives. *Women & Language, 34,* 9–39.

Meiners, E.B., & Boster, F.J. (2012). Integrative process in manager-employee negotiations: Relational and structural factors. *Journal of Applied Communication Research, 40,* 208–228.

MetLife (2006, July). *The MetLife caregiving costs study: Productivity losses to U.S. Businesses.* Westport, CT: MetLife Mature Market Institute and National Alliance for Caregiving. Retrieved from www.metlife.com/assets/cao/mmi/publications/studies/mmi-caregiver-cost-study-productivity.pdf.

Miller, V.D., & Jablin, F.M. (1991). Information seeking during organizational entry: Influences, tactics, and a model of the process. *Academy of Management Review, 16,* 92–120.

Miller, V.D., Jablin, F.M., Casey, M.K., Lamphear-Van Horn, M., & Ethington, C. (1996). The maternity leave as a role negotiation process. *Journal of Managerial Issues, 8,* 286–309.

Myers, K.K., Gaillaird, B.M., & Putnam, L.L. (2012). Reconsidering the concept of workplace flexibility: Is adaptability a better solution. In C. Salmon (Ed.), *Communication yearbook, 36* (pp. 195–230). Mahwah, NJ: Taylor & Francis.

O'Keefe, D.J. (1990). *Persuasion: Theory and research.* Los Angeles, CA: Sage.

Olufowote, J. O., Miller, V. D., & Wilson, S. R. (2005). The interactive effects of role change goals and relational exchanges on employee upward influence tactics. *Management Communication Quarterly, 18*(3), 385–403.

Peper, B., Den Dulk, L., & van Doorne-Huiskes, A. (2009). Work-family policies in a contradictory culture: A Dutch financial sector corporation. In S. Lewis, J. Brannen, & A. Nilson (Eds.), *Work, families, and organisations in transition: European perspectives* (pp. 113–128). Bristol: Policy Press.

Pitt-Catsouphes, M., Kossek, E.E., & Sweet, S. (Eds.) (2006). *The work and family handbook: Multi-disciplinary perspectives, methods, and approaches.* Mahwah, NJ: Lawrence Erlbaum Associates.

Pounsford, M. (2007). Using storytelling, conversation and coaching to engage: How to initiate meaningful conversations inside your organization. *Strategic Communication Management, 11,* 32–35.

Rowan, K.E. (2003). Informing and explaining skills: Theory and research on informative communication. In J.O. Greene & B. Burleson (Eds.), *Handbook of communication and interaction skills* (pp. 403–438). Mahwah, NJ: Lawrence Erlbaum Associates.

Ryan, A.M., & Kossek, E.E. (2008). Work-life policy implementation: Breaking down or creating barriers to inclusiveness. *Human Resource Management, 47*(2), 295–310.

Saks, A.M. (2006). Antecedents and consequences of employee engagement. *Journal of Managerial Psychology, 21,* 600–619.

Street, R.L. (2003). Interpersonal communication skills in health care contexts. In J.O. Greene & B.R. Burleson (Eds.), *Handbook of communication and social interaction skills* (pp. 909–935). Mahwah, NJ: Lawrence Erlbaum Associates.

Ter Hoeven, C.L., Miller, V., Den Dulk, L., & Peper, B. (2012, May). *"The work must go on": The role of employee and managerial discourse in the implementation and restriction of work-life policy use.* Paper presented at the International Communication Association's 62nd Annual Conference, Phoenix, AZ.

Thompson, C.A., Beauvais, L.L., & Lyness, K.S. (1999). When work-family benefits are not enough: The influence of work-life culture, benefit utilization, organizational attachment, and work-life conflict. *Journal of Vocational Behavior, 54,* 392–415.

Tracy, S.J., & Rivera, K.D. (2010). Endorsing equity and applauding stay-at-home moms: How male voices on work-life reveal aversive sexism and flickers of transformation. *Management Communication Quarterly, 24,* 3–43.

Trevino, L.K., Daft, R.L., & Lengel, R.H. (1990). Understanding managers' media choices: A symbolic interactionist perspective. In J. Fulk & C. Steinfeld (Eds.), *Organizations and communication technology* (pp. 71–94). Newbury Park, CA: Sage.

Tucker, D.A., Yeow, P., & Viki, G.T. (2013). Communicating during organizational change using social accounts: The importance of ideological accounts. *Management Communication Quarterly, 27,* 184–209.

Ulrich, R. (1998). *Delivering results: A new mandate for human resource professionals.* Cambridge, MA: Harvard Business Review Press.

U.S. Department of Labor. (2013). *Wage and hour division: Family medical leave act.* Retrieved from http://www.dol.gov/whd/fmla/.

Welch, M., & Jackson, P.R. (2007). Rethinking internal communication: A stakeholder approach. *Corporate Communications, 12,* 177–198.

Williams, J.C. (2000). *Unbending gender: Why work and family conflict and what to do about it.* New York: Oxford University Press.

Williams, J.C. (2012). *Reshaping the work-family debate: Why men and class matter.* Cambridge, MA: Harvard University Press.

Wrench, J.S., McCroskey, J.C., Berletch, N., Powley, C., & Wehr, A. (2008). Organizational coaching as instructional communication. *Human Communication, 11,* 279–292.

19

MEDIA MANAGEMENT

The Integration of HRM, Technology, and People

Keri K. Stephens, Eric D. Waters, and Caroline Sinclair

Most people agree that human resource management (HRM) plays an integral role in handling employee communication—things like employee benefits, onboarding, and newsletters. But does HRM handle a situation when an employee sets up a controversial blog? Do they assist dispersed team members who need help establishing a Web conference? Is it an HRM issue when the entire company needs to be notified that employees, vendors, and visitors should seek shelter due to impending storms? In the globally distributed, technology-enabled workplace of today, the role HRM plays often crosses over into territory traditionally owned by information technology (IT), public relations (PR), or even legal departments. This blending of roles occurred because employees have a more multiplexed means of information consumption and an employee's behavior is no longer bound by the office walls.

Communication with organizational stakeholders is complex and has risen in importance, due largely to the vast technology landscape of today (Verčič, Verčič, & Sriramesh, 2012). People have more access to information and communication technologies (ICTs), which affords them many options for retrieving and sharing information. Research suggests that workers use a wide variety of over 20 different ICTs, with 88% of people using e-mail at work, 85% using an intranet (D'Urso & Pierce, 2009), and a rising number (15%) using newer tools such as Twitter (Smith & Brenner, 2012). Although several other chapters in this book have discussed ICTs in general, this chapter focuses on two major changes in communication practices—organizational translucency and eHRM, or self-service HRM—that have resulted from the pervasiveness of ICTs. Before discussing these changes, we will provide an overview of the diverse fields and theoretical perspectives that have guided the research in this broad area of organizational ICT use.

Theoretical Perspectives on HRM-Related ICT Use

In the past decade, theoretical perspectives on organizational ICT use have progressed from the mind-set of simply comparing one ICT to another—for example, is e-mail better than face-to-face communication for delivering emotional messages?—to exploring how people use ICTs combinatorially and as integral tools in day-to-day work and life. This progression has created a focus on explaining how people *actually* use ICTs in day-to-day work/life. While there is still valuable research that relies on traditional media theories that focus on differences between media, like media richness theory (Daft & Lengel, 1986) and social presence theory (Short, Williams, & Christie, 1976), many researchers now examine dimensions of media that are shared across a variety of ICTs—for example, synchronicity—to develop more nuanced understanding (e.g., Dennis, Fuller, & Valacich, 2008; Stephens, Barrett, & Mahometa, 2013). Several organizational theorists now propose that we identify mixes of technologies (Rice, Hiltz, & Spencer, 2004), or what has been called combinatorial ICT use (Stephens, 2007), to help expand our knowledge of new organizational practices. These perspectives focus on the contemporary reality that people do not use ICTs in isolation and that more of a longitudinal and combinatorial perspective on ICT use can better guide our research.

While ICTs are types of material artifacts that have concrete features (e.g., a call waiting signal), ICTs are used by people, and that use cannot be separated from a social context (Leonardi, 2009). This relationship between the material and social considerations is referred to as a sociomaterial perspective (Orlikowski, 2007). This perspective is congruent with adaptive stucturation theory (DeSanctis & Poole, 1994), which states that technology appropriation occurs as groups produce and reproduce their own structures and validate them through use. Technology itself does not produce organizational outcomes. Therefore, it is the *use* of technology that becomes central to understanding the organization's communication practices (DeSanctis & Poole, 1994; Orlikowski, 2007). For example, consider any popular e-mail software. The software itself likely has hundreds of features, yet most individuals use only a small percentage of the capabilities. Often workgroups choose the specific features that allow them to socially adapt to each other and accomplish their work.

While these are some overarching trends in technology theorizing, much of the empirical research relevant for HRM practices relies less on ICT theories and more on theories that guide related constructs or outcomes of interest. For example, studies of intranet use for HRM purposes often are based on theories such as diffusion of innovations (Rogers, 1995) or employ the technology acceptance model (Venkatesh & Davis, 2000) because these studies focus on diffusion of practices and access to ICTs. In contrast, studies that consider workplace norms and how technologies are used to help people accomplish goals tend to be based on theories such as the social influence model (Fulk, Schmitz, & Steinfield, 1990) or social exchange theory (Emerson, 1976). Finally, in research that considers online learning, scholars invoke theories such as self-regulation (Mithaug, 1993). A theoretical review of the organizational ICT use literature reveals many options for guiding this research and opportunities for the future. To organize the current research being conducted in areas related to HRM, let us examine each of the two changes being brought about by contemporary ICT use: organizational translucency and eHRM.

Organizations Become Translucent

For quite some time, scholars have argued against the use of a container metaphor for organizations because it is so difficult to distinguish between what is cleanly "inside" and "outside" an organization (McPhee & Poole, 2001). Yet practitioners and scholars still use terms like "internal communications" to describe what gets communicated intraorganizationally, and some scholars argue that we need even more focus on these types of communicative activities (e.g., Ruck & Welch, 2012). Similarly, internal/external distinctions are found in organizations to differentiate group roles, for example, where HRM handles "internal" communication and PR speaks to the world outside the organization (Eyre & Littleton, 2012; Sha, 2009). However, now that organizations have multiple Web and social media sites, and the employees of these organizations have personal and professional online presences, the public has much more access to organizational activities than before. This access to previously concealed organizational information creates a paradigm shift from a "contained" organization to a translucent one; organizations are not necessarily transparent, but their activities are more public than they have been historically.

Organizations have responded to this explosion of communication opportunities by creating additional departments and positions such as corporate communications, marketing communications, the communications team, training and development, organization development, and communication operations. Organizational translucency has complicated most types of organizational communication and heightened the necessity for managing communication and ICTs. Let us examine three major changes that have resulted from the increase in organizational translucency: recruiting, cybervetting, and meeting practices.

Recruiting

The process of introducing and onboarding new employees into an organization has changed considerably in the past decade. Today, recruiters and potential employees rely on technological tools to inform or learn about job and work expectations. Before employees join an organization, they begin to form impressions about the potential employer. Known as anticipatory socialization, individuals gain information and form expectations about potential job choices from many resources ranging from childhood family conversations about career choices (Simpson, 1962) to the first days of work (Feldman, 1981; Stephens & Dailey, 2012). As employees anticipate employment, they make assumptions about the organizational culture and assess whether organizational norms match their own beliefs about how an organization should operate (Jablin, 2001). Further, while in active pursuit of a position, job seekers typically find information from either a prospective organization's information resources (e.g., job advertisements, corporate reports, Web sites) or through interpersonal interactions (e.g., interviews, friends, other social ties; Granovetter, 1995). This information helps form their job expectations. Recent research suggests that prospective employees can learn a significant amount about the organization and its culture from its Web site (Braddy, Meade, & Kroustalis, 2006; Stephens, Cho, & Ballard, 2012), including whether work will be fast paced, if employees will be expected to be accessible outside of work hours, and the anticipated workload (Stephens et al., 2012). In addition, when people are exposed to an organization before they begin working there, those experiences can shape how quickly they feel membership in their new organization if they accept a position (Stephens & Dailey, 2012). Therefore, the online presence of an organization can become a pivotal factor in the type of employees who are attracted to apply for an open position.

Potential employees might begin their job search using an official organizational Web site, but increasingly recruiting efforts reach beyond company-owned sites to social (e.g., Facebook or Twitter) and recruiting sites (e.g., Monster or Career Builder). In one 2001 study, 90% of all Fortune 500 businesses used at least some online recruiting tactics (Capelli, 2001). In 2011, Monster Worldwide, parent company of Monster.com and the largest online recruiter, listed more than 80,000 job posts a day (Backhaus, 2004).

The recruiting function is now an online sales process. Just as a human recruiter's appearance can affect impressions in a face-to-face interview, the online presence of a company also affects a job seeker's impression of the organization. Job seekers critique companies based on their Web site attractiveness and usability (Thompson, Braddy, & Wuensch, 2008). Recruiters need access to

Web design experts and should have an intricate understanding of Web-based networking tools to attract the right types of employees. Recruiters also need to be aware that sometimes they should pay the extra fees to become premier members on professional social networking sites—for example, LinkedIn has such a service—to target their recruiting. These are all changes in HRM processes that highlight the growing need for HRM professionals to be knowledgeable about ICTs.

Cybervetting in Hiring and Promotion

The majority of employers vet job candidates prior to offering them employment or even before offering interviews (Dipboye, 1982). This vetting process includes an evaluation of the candidate's credentials, the formal interview, and the post-interview decision to hire, reject, or continue evaluation (Dipboye, 1982). In her work on cybervetting, Berkelaar (2013) studied how employers acquire and evaluate information from search engines, social network sites (e.g., Facebook profiles), blogs, and other digital materials to make hiring and promotion decisions. This is common when hiring personnel are concerned that the employee has engaged in deception, excessive impression management, and limited their access to credible references from former employers. Her findings suggest that employers use access to these tools to inform personnel decisions and that online information can (problematically) affect their decisions. The issues include matters like bias, decision effectiveness, retention, and organizational reputation.

In addition to the active cybervetting process used to hire and promote employees, there are also times when controversial content (ethically or morally questionable) about an employee appears online and HRM can be called upon to intervene. The ease of using ICTs to post personal and work-related content to blogs, social media sites, and Web sites can place HRM professionals in a quandary. In their research about blogging, Valentine, Fleischman, Sprague, and Godkin (2010) advise HRM professionals to cautiously match the severity of discipline to the blog's content. Terminating an employee for harmless, innocent blog posts can be viewed as more unethical than firing an employee for negative work-related blogging. Such an unethical perception may fester into employee dissent and backlash (Valentine et al., 2010). The equivocality of HRM's role in managing employee social media interaction was exemplified in the case of Rhonda Lee, a meteorologist who was fired from her job at KTBS in Shreveport, Louisiana, for responding (politely) to viewer comments via Facebook (Smith, 2012).

The legality of managing employee use of social media and cybervetting practices will likely be debated for some time. In late 2012, residents of Michigan, Maryland, New Jersey, Delaware, California, and Illinois voted to forbid employers from demanding social networking site access from job applicants (Levy, 2012). It is plausible that other states may follow suit, making HRM's use of cybervetting to recruit and promote employees a subject of intense legal and ethical debate. This is something for HRM professionals to discuss inside their organizations and monitor as the courts become involved.

Meeting Technology Use and Meeting Policies

Major changes in organizational meeting practices are a result of the ubiquity of mobile devices and connectivity around the globe. Much of the early research on meetings focused on actions occurring in a meeting—like decision making—instead of examining meetings themselves as a topic worthy of research. In the scholarly literature, Helen Schwartzman (1989) began the focus on meetings as a topic, which has continued today resulting in a special issue of *Small Group*

Research in 2011 (e.g., Scott, Shanock, & Rogelberg, 2011) and best paper proceedings at management conferences (Dittrich, Guerard, & Seidl, 2011).

Meetings are so common in many organizations that they are considered the place in organizational life where work gets done (Chudoba, Watson-Manheim, Crowston, & Lee, 2011). Nevertheless, most people publicly complain about attending meetings (Rogelberg, Scott, & Kello, 2007). Research into meetings finds that people who attend many meetings do not necessarily feel less productive, but a high meeting load does negatively affect people's well-being (Luong & Rogelberg, 2005). Furthermore, when people are satisfied with meetings, they are also more satisfied with their job (Rogelberg, Allen, Shanock, Scott, & Shuffler, 2010). Issues of employee well-being are clearly related to human relations, and, thus, HRM can get involved in these recurring organizational practices.

HRM might also find itself involved in training supervisors about meeting practices because research suggests that supervisors have a strong impact on employees' meeting experiences (Baran, Shanock, Rogelberg, & Scott, 2012). Baran and colleagues (2012) found that when managers use good meeting practices, they can benefit from more positive relationships with their employees. They suggest that organizations train and coach supervisors on good meeting practices like scheduling meetings at times congruent with employee needs, starting and ending on time, and soliciting input for meeting agendas.

Dispersed Meetings

Meetings today often involve non-colocated participants (Chudoba et al., 2011). In their study of Intel's meetings, Chudoba et al. (2011) found that HRM was actively involved in trying to help workgroups manage the explosion of meeting types that involve technology. Specifically, HRM promoted the use of meeting agendas and minutes to increase individual productivity in meetings, but the workgroups implemented these practices in diverse ways by using different technologies and tools.

When meeting attendees are dispersed, they often use a variety of technology tools to help them meet. Several studies have found that geographically dispersed meetings are more frequently used when attendees work for the same organization (Arnfalk & Kogg, 2003; Denstadli, Julsrud, & Hjorthol, 2012) and that dispersed meetings are most effective for short, repetitive, follow-up, and information task meetings (Arnfalk & Kogg, 2003). Relational links among team members seem to be important determinants for the effectiveness of information exchange in Web-based meetings (Warkentin, Sayeed, & Hightower, 1997). In a study of more than 60 international organizations, Maynard, Mathieu, Rapp, and Gilson (2012) found that transactive memory systems—creating ways to document practices—and preparation activities were crucial for virtual team effectiveness in meetings and beyond.

Multitasking in Dispersed Meetings

Chudoba et al. (2011) argue that ICTs are fundamentally changing the way we work, and the ease of using them for multitasking is a key issue in contemporary organizational meetings. In addition, the prolific use of ICTs has elevated the importance of and access to meetings such that meetings are now integral to work performance in team-centered organizations (Chudoba et al., 2011). These scholars also emphasize that the use of ICTs in (and out) of the workplace has heightened tensions between group and personal objectives because the technology enables the blending of personal and work lives. Studying an organization where most of their workforce meets regularly through teleconferences and Web conferences, Wasson (2004) found that meeting participants' skills at multitasking affected the perception others had of them. There were several factors that shaped the amount of multitasking they observed: barriers between interactional spaces, personal skill, meeting activity, topic relevance, and the urgency of competing claims between local space and meeting space.

Multicommunicating

While multitasking has emerged as a prominent practice in organizations, a similar practice, known as multicommunicating (Reinsch, Turner, & Tinsley, 2008)—using a mobile device to carry on multiple conversations—is growing in many organizational meetings. The practice of multicommunicating is being more widely explored, and theoretical frames are emerging. For example, Stephens (2012) created a scale to measure the actual behaviors involved in multicommunicating. She created a 23-item instrument that represents five factors that describe what people do when they multicommunicate in meetings. Those practices include informing, influencing, supporting others, participating in parallel meetings, and being available. She suggests that being available during a meeting is an important practice because it highlights the fact that human communication involves multiple people. This research provides HRM practitioners with an instrument that can be used to identify the behaviors their employees are using when they multicommunicate. This scale could be helpful since there are currently conflicting views about this practice, likely because it is new and rules for its utilization have not been established (Cameron & Webster, 2010). This scale and the early research conducted on multicommunicating practices provide a solid and fertile area for future communication research.

Videoconference Meetings

In addition to meeting via audio bridge or instant messaging, people in some organizations are using videoconferencing to meet. In their study of 1,411 Norwegian business travelers, Denstadli and colleagues (2012) found that the larger the company, the more likely the employees had access to videoconferencing. While most people in their study used videoconferencing in a traditional meeting-room format (81%), slightly over a third reported that their companies were using PC-based videoconferencing platforms, and almost 20% of them were capable of using videoconferencing through portable devices. Top-level and middle-level managers used videoconferencing more than non-managers. When asked if their face-to-face meetings could be replaced with videoconference meetings, most of the business travelers said no. Their reasons concerned the need for more social contact with meeting partners and the belief that videoconferencing was unsuitable for many of their business situations. Denstadli and colleagues (2012) did find that videoconference meetings saved time, reduced the strain of business travel, and were quite useful for ad hoc gatherings of workgroups geographically dispersed.

Meeting Policies

In many organizations HRM professionals may be called on to make recommendations on whether formal policies are needed for ICT use in meetings. For example, there have been several popular press and scholarly reports of companies having "laptop-down" policies (e.g., Chudoba et al., 2011; Marquez, 2008) to help people stay on task. But what happens when people need to access fundamental information in the middle of a meeting to make progress? Indeed, some scholars advise careful consideration of the costs and benefits of technology in meetings; cutting off all extraneous contact during meetings can also mean cutting off access to potentially helpful information (Stephens & Davis, 2009b). In their research specifically on meeting multitasking policies, Stephens and Davis (2009a) found that people interpret formal meeting rules fairly clearly, especially when mobile devices are prohibited. But when there are no formal rules, people (a) assume that others' behavior is an indicator of a rule, (b) use their job roles and types to justify behavior, and (c) are suspicious of others using mobile devices. One of the biggest struggles that their research uncovered was people's needs to respond to a supervisor even when they were busy in a meeting where multitasking was viewed unfavorably. This finding is clearly linked to other communication research on topics such as concertive control and the power dynamics found in much of the supervisor/subordinate literature. Now that mobile devices have infiltrated most organizations, there are many new opportunities for communication researchers to explore these types of issues.

eHRM Shifts HRM's Role

The second major change that technology has prompted in many organizations is the reliance on an organization-wide intranet and, in the case of HRM, an electronic human resources management system or eHRM. HRM plays an expanded role in organizations today—one that often involves an intricate knowledge of how to use the latest media and technology tools to store and disseminate information. HRM can be asked to partner with information technology (IT) to codevelop online training platforms and to consult their legal team about technology use policies (Bulgurcu, Cavusoglu, & Benbasat, 2010; Siponen & Vance, 2010).

As organizations expand their reach around the globe, HRM has moved away from exclusively providing one-on-one assistance and has adopted a self-service or eHRM type of one-to-many support (Bell, Lee, & Yeung, 2006; Voermans & van Velhoven, 2007). The move toward having a central repository for benefit information has been made possible by the proliferation of corporate intranets and the availability of outsourced services that provide needed IT support. Now that HRM functions are more automated, HRM professionals have been relieved of some of their administrative tasks and freed up to participate in more strategic organizational activities (Bell et al., 2006). This means a paradigm shift from a role that was largely operational to one that is more consultative and strategic. HRM professionals are now expected to work closely with senior management to solve problems and make informed business decisions. As a result of eHRM, successful HRM professionals must be proficient not only in their traditional organizational role, but also in their organization's business environment (Bell et al., 2006).

While eHRM systems are touted for their ability to create efficient information dissemination, employees must have sufficient skills and access to the Internet to use these systems effectively. When employees lack these skills and access to the Internet, implementation of eHRM systems is less successful (Panayotopoulou, Vakola, & Galanaki, 2007). Often, it is assumed that employees are computer savvy and have access to Internet connections when they need them. This, in fact, is not always the case. One study that compared different types of organizational workers, some with constant connections to the Internet at work and others whose work was more manual labor, found that over 30% of the latter did not have regular Internet access (Stephens et al., 2008). Although some research has identified a lack of education and/or economic gaps as antecedents of this discrepancy, other research suggests roots in psychosocial barriers such as relevance, fear, and self-concept (Stanley, 2003). Stanley (2003) gives several psychosocial reasons for disconnected workers. Some, he says, are disinterested or uninformed with respect to the utility or relevance of a computer or Internet connection. Others avoid the technology because they fear it is too complex or difficult to use. Finally, others simply do not view themselves as computer users and resist adopting the technology as a result of their self-concept (Stanley, 2003). Until this organizational digital divide narrows, eHRM systems will not realize their full potential (Panayotopoulou et al., 2007). As an HRM professional, in practical terms, this research translates to (a) understanding the landscape of the organization in terms of technology access and employee skills and (b) providing alternative support and training for individuals who are struggling to adopt the new technology solutions.

Online Training

While HRM often oversees the training of employees, there has been an explosion in the use of online or Web-based training, which has supplemented or replaced face-to-face or instructor-led training. Therefore, HRM professionals must shift from a traditional focus on interpersonal relationships with trainees to a focus on the usability and effectiveness of online training. Research suggests that HRM professionals who successfully prompt employee self-regulation in technologically mediated training—helping employees take responsibility for their own training progress—affect employees' learning and performance over time (Sitzmann, Bell, Kraiger, & Kanar, 2009). Higher levels of cognitive ability and self-efficacy on the part of the employees intensified these effects (Sitzmann et al., 2009). This prompting may come in the form of HRM professionals helping employees understand how the technology functions and/or how it can be utilized to achieve learning goals (London & Hall, 2011).

Research also indicates that employees who exhibit higher levels of self-regulatory behaviors such as self-evaluation and self-monitoring will be more likely and better suited to embrace more advanced Web-based technologies for work-related training (London & Hall, 2011). When these employees and HRM professionals alike take full advantage of more advanced tools available in what has been called Web 2.0 (e.g., capabilities to track progress, build curricula, and produce detailed reports), learning outcomes could include enhanced organizational problem solving and multiple skill set development (London & Hall, 2011).

Large-Scale Message Dissemination

One convenient function often automated in an eHRM system is large-scale communication (Ruck & Welch, 2012; Welch, 2012). Frequently, globally relevant organizational messages are disseminated via e-mail managed through the eHRM. Even when e-mail distribution lists are not inside an eHRM system, HRM typically acquires that information when people join their organization, and they often manage message distribution to employees. Currently, there is limited research on how these messages are received and interpreted by employees though ICTs like e-mail and social media. For example, in their communication survey of a large organization, Stephens et al. (2008) found that workers who used the computer regularly in their jobs were more likely to request fewer e-mails, while employees who only used computers occasionally—due primarily to the nature of their manual labor work—wanted more e-mail on most topics. Research is needed to determine the job functions, message content, and specific ICTs that contribute to negative work perceptions and could lead employees to miss important information.

Since research has revealed that people cite e-mail as their top source of work stress (Barley, Meyerson, & Grodal, 2011), HRM professionals should weigh the convenience of messaging mass audiences with the potential message overload of the reader.

In addition to work-provided ICTs like e-mail, there is growing evidence that employees bring their personal mobile devices to work and expect their employer communication to be compatible with their personal devices. This trend, often referred to as BYOD, or "bring your own device" to work (Personal devices at work, 2012), presents difficulty to IT departments who determine how to keep company data safe when it is being accessed through so many mobile devices (Personal devices at work, 2012). Yet this trend is also highly relevant for HRM departments and their need to send messages that will reach their intended recipients. In an investigation of the importance of multiple emergency messages sent sequentially by an organization, Stephens et al. (2013) found that the first organizational message received by most people was delivered through a text message (often via a personal mobile device). In the organization they studied, employees were not required to provide their organization a mobile number for emergency notifications. Stephens et al. (2013) claim that, even in emergency messaging systems, organizations face the dilemma of needing to ask "permission" to send messages to employee's mobile devices, and there is no research on how this occurs.

Conclusion

This review of ICTs and HRM technology should illustrate that HRM's role in the organization has been transformed due to the increased use of communication technology in the workplace. From automated dissemination of messages to virtual training systems, HRM departments face new challenges and, at the same time, have many new opportunities, all of which require consideration and planning. Although there is a growing body of research in the area of technology use in the workplace (e.g., multitasking, multicommunicating, virtual meetings, group messaging systems, and intranets), there are plenty of opportunities for researchers to further explore HRM's new role in the globally dispersed organization.

Bibliography

Arnfalk, P., & Kogg, B. (2003). Service transformation: Managing a shift from business travel to virtual meetings. *Journal of Cleaner Production, 11,* 859–872.

Backhaus, K. (2004). An exploration of corporate recruitment descriptions on Monster.com. *Journal of Business Communication, 41,* 115–136.

Baran, B.E., Shanock, L.R., Rogelberg, S.G., & Scott, C.W. (2012). Leading group meetings: Supervisors' actions, employee behaviors, and upward perceptions. *Small Group Research, 43,* 330–355.

Barley, S.R., Meyerson, D.E., & Grodal, S. (2011). E-mail as a source and symbol of stress. *Organization Science, 22,* 887–906.

Bell, B.S., Lee, S.W., & Yeung, S.K. (2006). The impact of eHRM on professional competence in HRM: Implications for the development of HR professionals. *Human Resource Management, 45,* 295–308.

Berkelaar, B.L. (2013). Joining and leaving organizations in a global information society. In E. Cohen (Ed.), *Communication Yearbook, 37* (pp. 33–64). Thousand Oaks, CA: Sage.

Braddy, P.W., Meade, A.W., & Kroustalis, C.M. (2006). Organizational recruitment website effects on viewers' perceptions of organizational culture. *Journal of Business and Psychology, 4,* 525–543.

Bulgurcu, B., Cavusoglu, H., & Benbasat, I. (2010). Information security policy compliance: An empirical study of rationality-based beliefs and information security awareness. *Management Information Systems Quarterly, 34,* 523–548.

Cameron, A.F., & Webster, J. (2010). Relational outcomes in multicommunicating: Integrating incivility and social exchange perspectives. *Organizational Science, 22,* 754–771.

Capelli, P. (2001). Making the most of on-line recruiting. *Harvard Business Review, 7,* 139–146.

Chudoba, K.M., Watson-Manheim, M.B., Crowston, K., & Lee, C.S. (2011). Participation in ICT-enabled meetings. *Journal of Organizational and End User Computing, 23,* 15–36.

Daft, R.L., & Lengel, R.H. (1986). Organizational information requirements, media richness, and structural design. *Management Science, 32,* 554–571.

Dennis, A.R., Fuller, R.M., & Valacich, J.S. (2008). Media, tasks, and communication processes: A theory of media synchronicity. *MIS Quarterly, 32,* 575–600.

Denstadli, J.M., Julsrud, T.E., & Hjorthol, R.J. (2012). Videoconferencing as a mode of communication: A comparative study of the use of videoconferencing and face-to-face meetings. *Journal of Business and Technical Communication, 26,* 65–91.

DeSanctis, G., & Poole, M.S. (1994). Capturing the complexity in advanced technology use: Adaptive structuration theory. *Organization Science, 5,* 121–147.

Dipboye, R.L. (1982). Self-fulfilling prophecies in the selection-recruitment interview. *Academy of Management Review, 7,* 579–586.

Dittrich, K., Guerard, S., & Seidl, D. (2011, August). The role of meetings in the strategy process: Towards an integrative framework. *Academy of Management Best Paper Proceedings.* Retrieved from http://dx.doi.org/10.2139/ssrn.1989794.

D'Urso, S.C., & Pierce, K.M. (2009). Connected to the organization: A survey of communication technologies in the modern organizational landscape. *Communication Research Reports, 26,* 75–81.

Emerson, R.M. (1976). Social exchange theory. *Annual Review of Sociology, 2,* 335–362.

Eyre, D.P., & Littleton, J.R. (2012). Shaping the zeitgeist: Influencing social processes as the center of gravity for strategic communications in the twenty-first century. *Public Relations Review, 38,* 179–187.

Feldman, D.C. (1981). The multiple socialization of organization members. *Academy of Management Review, 6,* 309–318.

Fulk, J., Schmitz, J., & Steinfield, C.W. (1990). A social influence model of technology use. In J. Fulk & C. Steinfield (Eds.), *Organizations and communication technology* (pp. 117–140). Newbury Park, CA: Sage.

Granovetter, M. (1995). *Getting a job: A study of contacts and careers* (2nd ed.). Chicago: University of Chicago Press.

Jablin, F.M. (2001). Organizational entry, assimilation, and disengagement/exit. In F.M. Jablin & L.L. Putman (Eds.), *The new handbook of organizational communication: Advances in theory, research, and methods* (pp. 732–818). Thousand Oaks, CA: Sage.

Leonardi, P.M. (2009). Crossing the implementation line: The mutual constitution of technology and organizing across development and use activities. *Communication Theory, 19,* 277–309.

Levy, G. (2012). *Facebook password laws go into effect in 5 states.* Retrieved from www.upi.com/blog/2012/12/31/Facebook-password-laws-go-into-effect-in-5-states/9231356986835/.

London, M., & Hall, M.J. (2011). Unlocking the value of Web 2.0 technologies for training and development: The shift from instructor-controlled, adaptive learning to learner-driven, generative learning. *Human Resource Management, 50,* 757–775.

Luong, A., & Rogelberg, S.G. (2005). Meetings and more meetings: The relationship between meeting load and the daily well-being of employees. *Group Dynamics: Theory, Research, and Practice, 9,* 58–67.

Marquez, L. (2008, March 31). *Why Silicon Valley employees are going to meetings laptopless.* Retrieved from http://abcnews.go.com/Technology/story?id=4560823Going topless to office meetings.

Maynard, M., Mathieu, J.E., Rapp, T.L., & Gilson, L.L. (2012). Something(s) old and something(s) new: Modeling drivers of global virtual team effectiveness. *Journal of Organizational Behavior, 33,* 1099–1379.

McPhee, R.D., & Poole, M.S. (2001). Organizational structures and configurations. In F.M. Jablin & L.L. Putnam (Eds.), *The new handbook of organizational communication: Advances in theory, research, and methods* (pp. 504–544). Thousand Oaks, CA: Sage.

Mithaug, D.E. (1993). *Self-regulation theory: How optimal adjustment maximizes gain.* Westport, CT: Praeger/Greenwood.

Orlikowski, W.J. (2007). Sociomaterial practices: Exploring technology at work. *Organizational Studies, 28,* 1435–1448.

Panayotopoulou, L., Vakola, M., & Galanaki, E. (2007). E-HR adoption and the role of HRM: Evidence from Greece. *Personnel Review, 36,* 277–294.

Personal devices at work. (2012). *PC Today, 10,* 44–46.

Reinsch, N.L., Turner, J.W., & Tinsley, C.H. (2008). Multicommunicating: A practice whose time has come? *Academy of Management Review, 33,* 391–403.

Rice, R.E., Hiltz, S.R., & Spencer, D. (2004). Media mixes and learning networks. In S.R. Hiltz & R. Goldman (Eds.), *Learning together online: Research on asynchronous learning* (pp. 215–237). Mahwah, NJ: Erlbaum.

Rogelberg, S.G., Allen, J.A., Shanock, L., Scott, C., & Shuffler, M. (2010). Employee satisfaction with meetings: A contemporary facet of job satisfaction. *Human Resource Management, 49,* 149–172.

Rogelberg, S.G., Scott, C., & Kello, J. (2007, Winter). The science and fiction of meetings. *MIT Sloan Management Review,* 18–21.

Rogers, E.M. (1995). *Diffusion of innovations* (4th ed.). New York: Free Press.

Ruck, K., & Welch, M. (2012). Valuing internal communication: Management and employee perspectives. *Public Relations Review, 38,* 294–302.

Schwartzman, H.B. (1989). *The meeting: Gatherings in organizations and communities.* New York: Plenum.

Scott, C.W., Shanock, L.R., & Rogelberg, S.G. (2012). Meetings at work: Advancing the theory and practice of meetings. *Small Group Research, 43,* 127–129.

Sha, B.L. (2009). Exploring the connection between organizational identity and public relations behaviors: How symmetry trumps conservation in engendering organizational identification. *Journal of Public Relations Research, 21,* 295–317.

Short, J., Williams, E., & Christie, B. (1976). *The social psychology of telecommunications.* London: John Wiley & Sons.

Simpson, R.L. (1962). Parental influence, anticipatory socialization, and social mobility. *American Sociological Review, 27,* 517–522.

Siponen, M., & Vance, A. (2010). Neutralization: new insights into the problem of employee information systems security policy violations. *MIS Quarterly, 34,* 487.

Sitzmann, T., Bell, B.S., Kraiger, K., & Kanar, A.M. (2009). A multilevel analysis of the effect of prompting self-regulation in technology-delivered instruction. *Personnel Psychology, 62,* 697–734.

Smith, A., & Brenner, J. (2012). *Twitter use 2012.* Pew Research Center's American Life Project, Washington, DC. Retrieved from http://pewinternet.org/Reports/2012/Twitter-Use-2012.aspx.

Smith, J. (2012). *Meteorologist fired after defending her "ethnic" hair.* Retrieved from http://tv.msnbc.com/2012/12/12/meteorologist-fired-after-defending-her-ethnic-hair/.

Stanley, L.D. (2003). Beyond access: Psychosocial barriers to computer literacy. *Information Society, 19,* 407–416.

Stephens, K.K. (2007). The successive use of information and communication technologies at work. *Communication Theory, 17,* 486–507.

Stephens, K.K. (2012). Multiple conversations during organizational meetings: Development of the multicommunicating scale. *Management Communication Quarterly, 26,* 195–223.

Stephens, K.K., Barrett, A., & Mahometa, M.L. (2013). Organizational communication in emergencies: Using multiple channels and sources to combat noise and capture attention. *Human Communication Research,* articles in advance. doi: 10.1111/hcre.12002.

Stephens, K.K., Cho, J., & Ballard, D.I. (2012). Simultaneity, sequentiality, and speed: Organizational messages about multiple-task completion. *Human Communication Research, 38,* 23–47.

Stephens, K.K., & Dailey, S. (2012). Situated organizational identification in newcomers: Impacts of preentry organizational exposure. *Management Communication Quarterly, 26,* 402–422.

Stephens, K.K., Dailey, S.L., Peterson, B., Cho, J., Inman, D., Muldiar, P. et al. (2008). *Communication practices in university operations.* Austin: University of Texas. Retrieved from www.utexas.edu/operations/files/UniversityOperationsReport_1109_details.pdf.

Stephens, K.K., & Davis, J.D. (2009a). *Electronic multitasking in meetings: A challenge for organizational policy.* Paper presented at the International Conference on Mobile Communication and Social Policy, New Brunswick, NJ.

Stephens, K.K., & Davis, J.D. (2009b). The social influences on electronic multitasking in organizational meetings. *Management Communication Quarterly, 23,* 63–83.

Thompson, L.F., Braddy, P.W., & Wuensch, K.L. (2008). E-recruitment and the benefits of organizational Web appeal. *Computers in Human Behavior, 24,* 2384–2398.

Valentine, S., Fleischman, G.M., Sprague, R., & Godkin, L. (2010). Exploring the ethicality of firing employees who blog. *Human Resource Management, 49,* 87–108.

Venkatesh, V., & Davis, F.D. (2000). A theoretical extension of the technology acceptance model: Four longitudinal field studies. *Management Science, 46,* 186–204.

Verčič, A., Verčič, D., & Sriramesh, K. (2012). Internal communication: Definition, parameters, and the future. *Public Relations Review, 38,* 223–230.

Voermans, M., & van Veldhoven, M.J.P.M. (2007). Attitude towards E-HRM: An empirical study at Philips. *Personnel Review, 36,* 887–902.

Warkentin, M.E., Sayeed, L., & Hightower, R. (1997). Virtual teams versus face-to-face teams: An exploratory study of a Web-based conference system. *Decision Sciences, 28,* 975–996.

Wasson, C. (2004). Multitasking during virtual meetings. *Human Resource Planning, 27,* 47–60.

Welch, M. (2012). Appropriateness and acceptability: Employee perspectives of internal communication. *Public Relations Review, 38,* 246–254.

20

GLOBAL OPERATIONS

William D. Schneper and Mary Ann Von Glinow

Plus ca change, plus c'est la meme chose redux?

Globalization has been transforming our world for over half a century. Although no individual or organization is immune from the increasing flows of information, capital, and other resources across national borders, scholars have long held a special interest in the relationship between globalization and multinational firms. In the same speech that the term "multinational corporation" (MNC) was coined, for instance, Lilienthal (1960) pointed out how firms of the future would need to dedicate greater attention to identifying and training employees for foreign assignments, dealing with the complexities of international communication, and developing a cadre of "cosmopolitan" managers. Just a few years later, Perlmutter (1969) presented his famous framework on how MNCs evolve over time.

Early international human resource management (IHRM) research took inspiration from these and other early international business writings but focused narrowly on the most salient and pressing challenges distinguishing MNCs from domestic firms. Thus, the IHRM literature of the 1980s and early 1990s dedicated its attention largely to such topics as identifying managers for international assignments, expatriate adjustment, and the international transfer of practices (Hall & Wailes, 2010). Although these topics remain vitally important today, researchers have increasingly begun devoting their energies to a range of other issues as varied as globally dispersed teams and cross-border mergers and acquisitions.

In their evaluation of the HRM field, Kerr and Von Glinow (1997) identified several newly emerging business trends still relevant today, including outsourcing and the growing corporate social responsibility movement. Ultimately they concluded "plus ca change, plus c'est la meme chose"—the more things change, the more they stay the same. While globalization and other environmental forces continue to transform the business world, HRM managers and scholars should continue to draw upon many of the same well-established theories and practices that have previously offered guidance. In other words, the future of HRM will look like the past in many important and surprising ways.

One issue that has remained paramount to international management since its foundations has been the importance placed on addressing the communication challenges inherent in global business. In this chapter, we provide a contemporary evaluation of the IHRM field and the role that communication plays in managing human resources across global operations. We proceed as follows. First, we take a closer look at the globalization phenomenon. Specifically, we discuss the role that computer-mediated communications (CMCs) and language have played in bringing about globalization. We also consider the overall impact of globalization on the HRM field. Next, we present two classic international business models (Perlmutter's [1969] cultural attitudes and Bartlett and Ghoshal's [1989] integration/responsiveness framework), arguing that they still serve as fundamental elements of the IHRM field. Finally, we explore some of the key challenges facing IHRM professionals today. We also consider what role past ideas and practices will hold in the future of IHRM.

Globalization: Causes and Consequences

We would be remiss if we did not draw special attention to the role communications technologies have played in bringing about globalization. In *The Consequences of Modernity*, sociologist Anthony Giddens (1990, p. 77) treats globalization as a long-term process resulting in large part from an extended series of communications innovations dating back to the introduction of mechanical printing in 15th-century Europe. In *The World Is Flat*, journalist Thomas Friedman (2005) assigns a similar causal role to the convergence of computing and communications. He argues that we have entered a new stage of globalization where economic competitors across the world now face off against each other on much more equal terms. During recent years, Internet search engines such as Google, Baidu in China, and Naver in South Korea have helped democratize access to information. Social networking services provide individuals and organizations with the opportunity to voice their ideas and opinions internationally and instantaneously across the globe, but perhaps without sufficient concern about the legitimacy and credibility of the source (Lidsky & Connor, 2007). Cellular communications and portable computing devices have placed even greater constraints on the length of time that many of us are able to isolate ourselves from our shrunken world. Such changes can be especially hard felt among the employees of MNCs. The sun truly never sets on firms with global organizations.

Some of the statistics on communications and information flows are among the most striking indicators of globalization. According to the World Bank (2013), the number of Internet users worldwide has grown from about 2.6 million in 1990 to over 2.6 billion in 2011. Telephone lines have also increased globally from about 158 million in 1970 to almost 1.2 billion in 2010. Cell phones are the primary way that many people in developing economies will gain access to the Internet. As of 2011, the number of cellular subscriptions per 100 people was about 73 percent in both India and China. In Brazil, Russia, and South Africa, the number of cellular subscriptions already exceeds the total population. Some communication scholars posit that globalization would not have been possible without the emergence of a universal language, namely English, as the lingua franca (Louhiala-Salminen & Kankaanranta, 2011). Charles (2007, p. 261) estimates that nonnative speakers (NNS) of English now outnumber native speakers (NS) nine to one.

Despite such evidence, skeptics suggest the world's population tends to be more parochial and less globally connected than commonly presumed (see Hirst & Thompson, 1996). Ghemawat (2011) reports that individuals receive 95 percent of their news information from domestic sources. International telephone calls account for just 2 percent of all telephone traffic, and 90 percent of the world's population will never leave the country where they were born. Although some individuals tally thousands of friends and connections from places both near and far on social media Web sites, Facebook, for instance, reports that most users devote the bulk of their communication to only three to ten other users (Dunbar, 2012; Ghemawat, 2011). Charles (2007, p. 266) ponders the degree to which NNSs are marginalized and viewed as "sources of trouble" in some MNCs. The limited contact that most individuals have with foreign people, information sources, and ideas presents a daunting challenge to MNCs striving for a globally oriented workforce (Javidan & Teagarden, 2011).

Some research has sought to identify the impact of globalization and CMCs on HRM (Friedman, 2007; Kapoor, 2011). Advances in communications as well as transportation technologies have played important roles in bringing about increased outsourcing and the global dispersion of value chain activities (Friedman, 2005). Due to such technologies, the McKinsey Global Institute reports that about 11 percent of all service jobs worldwide could be conducted remotely (Farrell, Laboissière, & Rosenfeld, 2006). At the same time, firms operating in the United States and many other developed countries are experiencing skills shortages partially due to slowing population growth (Kapoor, 2011; Vance & Paik, 2011). The World Economic Forum (2010) projects that the United States would need to add 46 million high-skilled employees to its talent pool by 2030 to sustain the economic growth rate it experienced from 1988 to 2008. While the stock of high-skilled workers is growing five times faster in low-wage countries, McKinsey Global Institute (2005) estimates that just 13 percent of recent college graduates from these nations would currently be considered viable candidates at most foreign MNCs due to inadequate foreign language skills, lack of cultural fit, or inexperience at group work.

More than ever, HRM departments must be flexible and innovative in controlling costs, boosting productivity, and finding ways of hiring and developing workers with diverse backgrounds (Kapoor, 2011; see chapter 17 by Ng and Barker for a discussion of diversity issues). Not surprisingly, IHRM increasingly has turned toward CMCs to meet these challenges (Florkowski & Olivas-Lujan, 2006). For instance, Dermot O'Brien (2013), ADP's chief human resources officer, suggests that recruiting through social media Web sites is especially important for MNCs because they often seek individuals with highly specialized and difficult-to-find skills. He urges MNCs to move beyond popular social media and career Web sites and establish proprietary blogs and forums to attract communities of practice. Unfortunately, the literature provides limited information on social media and other CMCs and their relationship to IHRM outcomes. Clearly, more empirical work is needed. Several already prominent international business and communications frameworks and concepts can offer guidance in this endeavor.

Classic Theoretical Frameworks

One of the first attempts to explain the nature of communication flows within MNCs continues to be among the most influential. Perlmutter (1969) proposed that the top management mind-sets in MNCs progress through three stages: ethnocentric, polycentric, and geocentric.[1] In MNCs where an ethnocentric mind-set dominates, communication tends to flow downstream from the corporate headquarters to subsidiaries in the form of advice, counsel, and instructions. People, ideas, and practices from the home country are considered superior, and home country nationals hold all important management positions.

The polycentric mind-set inspires a shift in authority from the headquarters to relatively independent national subsidiaries. Compared to earlier and later stages, there is less communication flow between headquarters and subsidiaries. Communication across subsidiaries is insignificant. Subsidiaries are largely in charge of their own staffing, and the most powerful positions are held by host country citizens. Finally, under a geocentric mind-set, MNCs seek the best people and ideas at a truly global level. Lines of communication and influence throughout the organization are complex, dynamic, and multidirectional (Schneper & Von Glinow, 2013). Headquarters and subsidiaries maintain a collaborative relationship, and groups of subsidiaries work together closely. Training is also conducted on a global level.

Perlmutter's model has proven to be immensely helpful across the international business field, and many observers still consider it the basis for understanding communication flows and HRM policies within MNCs (Von Glinow & Schneper, 2013). Perlmutter believed that the cultural attitudes within a firm progressed from ethnocentrism to polycentricism and then toward the ideal state of geocentricism, perhaps without ever fully attaining it. Recent research suggests that firms do not always evolve the way Perlmutter predicted but that these mind-sets are often the relatively long-term outcome of such factors as industry characteristics, administrative heritage, and country of origin (Schneper & Von Glinow, 2013). Many U.S. firms, for instance, have traditionally maintained an ethnocentric approach due to the importance of their home market to overall performance. Prior to the emergence of the common market, European MNCs tended toward polycentricism because they had to compete across several relatively smaller national markets, each with significantly different cultures, standards, and practices. A recent phenomenon involves the tendency for some firms in developing countries to be "born global" and follow a geocentric mind-set to move beyond the limited opportunities presently available at home.

This is not to say that communication patterns within MNCs cannot change dramatically because they do, sometimes quite rapidly. Corporate restructurings are often aimed at altering organizational chains of communication and authority (Daft, 2012). In one of the most closely studied examples, N.V. Philips (Netherlands) was transformed from a relatively headquarters-centric organization ultimately to a more network-based form after communication channels between headquarters and subsidiaries were disrupted during World War II (Bartlett, 2011). Some survey-based research has also explored how HRM and other organizational practices shape communication activity within MNCs. Most of these studies, however, were limited to just a single time period. Ghoshal, Korine, and Szulanski (1994) found that deliberate lateral socialization efforts by management (such as task forces and joint work in teams) increased the frequency of both parent-subsidiary and intersubsidiary communication. Surprisingly, they found no discernible relationship between subsidiary autonomy and the frequency of communication with either headquarters or other subsidiaries. Research is needed to determine how MNC communication flows affect top management attitudes and strategies.

One of the most important theories inspired by Perlmutter is Bartlett and Ghoshal's (1989) integration/responsiveness framework, which distinguishes between multinational, global, international, and transnational companies. Each category represents an adaptive response to the relative strength of two competing environmental pressures. Multinational companies are roughly analogous to Perlmutter's polycentric firms and tend to be most successful when there are strong pressures for responsiveness to national differences but little need for global integration. By contrast, transnational corporations are more like Perlmutter's geocentric firms. They must manage operations in a way that balances needs for local responsiveness and global integration. The greatest contribution of Bartlett and Ghoshal's model to IHRM is its emphasis on the tradeoffs between implementing universal policies and practices versus tailoring the firm's approach to the local environment. Although MNCs might prefer a universal approach to its HRM systems to reduce complexity and promote efficiency, managers discover that policies and practice cannot always be transferred effectively or appropriately across countries. Thus, MNCs must often customize their approach across countries and regions. Bartlett and Ghoshal also took inspiration from Perlmutter in realizing that becoming a transnational corporation means less about formal structure and authority than it does about mind-set and informal communication ties. According to Bartlett and Ghoshal (1989, p. 34), management must pursue a wide array of IHRM policies and "integrative mechanisms" such as annual conferences, international rotation of managers, language and cultural training, and cross-subsidiary forums to exchange ideas and express differences. Through such activities, these scholars argued that MNCs could create a network of close interpersonal relationships that facilitate interunit communication and a broader understanding of the global environment.

Contemporary Trends and Future Directions

Just as early research stressed, the identification and development of managers for foreign assignments remains one of the most important IHRM tasks. Today, many IHRM professionals view global mind-set as one of the most important attributes in selecting leadership prospects and candidates for expatriate positions (Schneper & Von Glinow, 2013). Perlmutter's work on geocentric mind-set and Bartlett and Ghoshal's notion of transnationalism were both among the most important theoretical inspirations for the contemporary conception of global mind-set. Javidan and Teagarden (2011) describe global mind-set as people's ability to influence other individuals, groups, organizations, and systems that are unlike themselves or their own. They suggest that global mind-set depends on possessing three forms of capital: intellectual, psychological, and social. Among these three, social capital is probably the most directly associated with communication. Javidan (2010) suggests that social capital requires the ability to experience and express empathy with people from different cultures. Defined as the ability to perceive others' situation, thoughts, and feelings, empathy enables individuals to assess the information needs of their audience (Hogan & Henley, 1970). As Lustig and Koester (2013) suggest, people who are perceived as empathetic tend to be judged more favorably by their communication partners. Expressions of empathy can be verbal (such as relating a similar experience or feeling from one's past) or nonverbal (e.g., a knowing glance).

The notion of global mind-set can be compared to the concept of intercultural communication competence (ICC) in communication research. Although no consensus on a definition exists, ICC may be described as the ability to interact with people from a different culture in a way that is both effective and appropriate (Hajek & Giles, 2003; Lustig & Koester, 2013). Despite their differences, both global mind-set and ICC are commonly believed to require psychological adaptation (e.g., the ability to cope with frustration and the stress brought on by new situations) and cultural awareness (an understanding of the values, customs, or norms of foreign persons; Chen, 2007; Levy, Beechler, Taylor, & Boyaçigiller, 2007). Although global mind-set places greater emphasis on influencing others, some research conceptualizes ICC similarly as the ability to control outcomes and achieve personal objectives (Hajek and Giles, 2003; Parks, 1994). Unlike ICC, global mind-set has traditionally focused little attention on spoken or written foreign language proficiency. ICC is also sometimes defined in terms of adequacy, or the minimal level of ability necessary for effectiveness (Wiemann & Bradac, 1989). An English NNS may not need to be nearly as proficient as an English NS to be considered competent in conducting global business, particularly when dealing with other English NNSs (see Babcock & Du-Babcock, 2001). A study conducted in five Finnish MNCs that adopted English as the official corporate language found business professionals viewed English grammar ability and a broad, general vocabulary less important than possessing the specialized knowledge and vocabulary of their business field: "The basic message seemed to be that 'adequately' good grammar and vocabulary were sufficient" (Louhiala-Salminen & Kankaanranta, 2011, p. 253).

The extant literature on ICC is much broader and arguably more developed than the one on global mind-set. Careful consideration of the ICC literature may prove especially helpful when researching global mind-set. For instance, empirical studies of ICC training program effectiveness might help produce cues for developing global mind-set competencies in both business and educational learning environments. Future research also might explore the degree that foreign language ability affects perceptions of global mind-set (both self-reports and those of third parties). Finally, IHRM professionals could utilize ICC research when deciding the content of foreign language training programs or determining the minimum language requirements for a particular job (Louhiala-Salminen & Kankaanranta, 2011).

Language policy is another fertile research topic that crosses both IHRM and communications disciplines. In order to optimize global integration and local responsiveness, Luo and Shenkar (2006), following Bartlett and Ghoshal (1989), propose that MNCs ought to use a common corporate language for intraorganizational communication and the local language when dealing with external parties in host countries. This approach can lead to poor interunit communication, however, if home language proficiency in the subsidiaries is weak (Piekkari, 2006; van den Born & Peltokorpi, 2010).

Although van den Born and Peltokorpi (2010) agree with Luo and Shenkar (2006) about matching language policies with corporate strategy, they instead follow Perlmutter's (1969) model for evaluating MNC strategic orientation. Within ethnocentric settings, for instance, MNCs should emphasize home country language skills in both headquarters and foreign subsidiaries. Home country language ability should also be a priority in recruitment for subsidiaries and expatriate selection. Within polycentric subsidiaries, local languages should receive emphasis, but the adoption of a common lingua franca can facilitate communication at the interunit level. Geocentric MNCs should promote the lingua franca in both inter- and intraunit communication but should be able to switch to the host country language in a situations where the lingua franca creates communication difficulties (van den Born & Peltokorpi, 2010).

One frequent theme in MNC language policy was how language ability was a source of power (Charles, 2007). Individuals lacking corporate language skill may be denied access to critical information sources or become beholden to those with superior language abilities. Failure to know the corporate language can be a terminal barrier to advancement for many otherwise promising employees unless the MNC provides language training. Employees at all levels of the organization may be perceived as less intelligent or talented if they possess relatively weak foreign language abilities (Piekkari, 2006). Although these factors would seem to benefit NSs, social identity theory (Tajfel & Turner, 1979) suggests that these individuals may be negatively affected if NNSs band together and treat NSs as outsiders (Charles, 2007).

Language abilities can shape organizational dynamics in unanticipated ways. Barner-Rasmussen and Björkman (2007) report on an interview with one CEO who admitted to visiting a French subsidiary less frequently because he couldn't speak the language. Similarly, Piekkari (2006) notes how the national subsidiaries of one MNC formed informal coalitions and communicated more frequently with one another based on common language.

The choice of an official language can have an enduring impact on an MNC's identity and the type of employees it attracts (Piekkari, 2006). Some MNCs might avoid naming an official language due to concerns over intraorganizational politics. Scandinavian Airlines, the product of a cross-border merger and a flag carrier in Denmark, Norway, and Sweden, chose not to have an official language in order to reduce conflict among constituencies from these three countries (Piekkari, 2006).

English is the most common choice as an official corporate language (Charles, 2007; Piekkari, 2006). This is due largely to the historical prominence of U.S. MNCs, the importance of Anglophone product and capital markets to MNCs, and, perhaps to some degree, the popularity of English-language entertainment (Peng, 2008). Due to the growth of China and several other emerging economies, the choice of English as lingua franca might erode during next few decades. Lewis (2009) reports that the language with the most NS is Mandarin Chinese with 845 million. Spanish is second (329 million), while English is a close third (328 million). The large number of NNS and high-level English proficiency in some of the world's fastest growing markets (e.g., India) will act as countervailing forces to sustain English's dominant role.

Another communication principle that may prove especially relevant to IHRM scholarship is media naturalness theory (Kock, 2004). According to this theory, human beings are biologically designed to communicate through face-to-face contact. By substituting communication methods that are increasingly less similar to face-to-face interaction (i.e., those that don't require colocation and synchronicity and limit the ability to convey or perceive body language, facial expressions, or speech), participants will experience increased cognitive difficulty, communication ambiguity, and reduced physiological arousal.[2]

Media naturalness theory provides one reason why some efforts to incorporate CMCs in IHRM practices may prove disappointing. MNCs might encourage expatriates to use social media to ease adjustment and maintain personal and professional ties back home, for example, but these interactions might turn out to be emotionally unfulfilling for many users (see Kock, 2005). In some cases, CMCs are already contributing to reduced expatriate use, which, at first blush, would appear to be a plus given that the costs of expatriates are two to three times the cost of their domestic counterparts in these countries. The Association of Executive Search Consultants reports that the percentage of expatriates in senior executive positions in China, India, Brazil, Middle East, and Russian subsidiaries decreased to 12 percent, compared to 56 percent ten years earlier (Holstein, 2008). However, MNCs instead are relying upon "virtual expatriate assignments," which combine short travel trips with high use of telephone, e-mail, teleconferencing, corporate intranet, and other CMCs (Vance & Paik, 2011). We predict that the success of such initiatives will hinge on the continuation of periodic face-to-face contact in order to foster mutual understanding, trust, and emotional commitment (see MacDuffie, 2007). As Armstrong and Cole (2002) report, "most distributed groups do not attain the ideal of being a real team: a work group with a stable and defined membership that has established a shared working process in the pursuit of a common goal that they can only achieve together" (p. 187).

Following Perlmutter (1969), international business scholars recognized the advantageousness of the MNC's ability to scan the global environment for new ideas and practices and adopt those most likely to enhance firm performance. Yet most MNCs still seem to favor ideas and practices from their home countries, or at least those that originated in the largest and most developed economies. One HRM approach that has attained best practice status in many MNCs has been the increased use of direct feedback in performance management and appraisal systems. This trend is unlikely to change in the United States and some other (mostly Western) countries, where the term "feedback" has taken on a near mystical connotation associated with almost miraculous transformative power (Cameron, 2000). According to a survey by the staffing firm Hudson, younger generations of workers crave feedback much more than earlier generations. In fact, 25 percent of employees born between 1965 and 1979 felt it was important to receive feedback directly from their boss at least once a week, compared to just 11 percent among workers born between 1928 and 1945 (Gallo, 2007). The increased popularity of feedback among some employees and HRM experts has also led to the increased use of multisource feedback. HRM professionals must be careful, however, about transplanting these practices to different cultural settings (Bartlett & Ghoshal, 1989). Chinese culture, for instance, is characterized by a profound respect for authority and strong collectivist orientation. Since the Chinese work system traditionally favors strong hierarchical relationships, employees may resist being evaluated by anyone other than their immediate supervisor (Bailey & Fletcher, 2008). The types of two-way conversations between supervisor and subordinate that characterize many Western performance appraisal models may not be appropriate in high cultural context countries where open conflict in communication is avoided (Milliman, Taylor, & Czaplewski, 2002).

While comparative research on the use of performance appraisal systems remains limited, Chinese supervisors were reluctant to engage in two-way communication during the performance process, and employees participated minimally in self-evaluations (Huo & Von Glinow, 1995). Similarly, Tang, Lai, and Kirkbride (1995) found evidence suggesting that the purpose of performance appraisals differs in Hong Kong organizations (where the emphasis is reviewing past performance) and those in the United States and UK (where significant attention is also placed on counseling and identifying developmental opportunities). Milliman et al. (2002) theorize that performance appraisals are less likely to be used as a developmental tool in countries with a strong external locus since individual performance tends to be viewed largely as the product of one's environment. These researchers suggest that supervisors should respond to this tendency by seeking a consensus with workers regarding which aspects of their job performance are individually controllable.

Similar cultural concerns should be raised about following the common advice that emotional conflict in workgroups should be managed first and foremost by simply "talking things out" (Von Glinow, Shapiro, & Brett, 2004; cf. Cameron, 2000). Candid dialogue may not work well in multicultural teams with members from cultures that generally express feelings of conflict in more indirect ways. Expressing the things that bother you about another person or a situation may be perceived as being selfish or overly aggressive in some non-Western cultures (Von Glinow, Shapiro, & Brett, 2004). Foreign language skills are also a concern here. Describing one's feelings during times of anger, stress, and frustration can be one of the most difficult things for an individual to express even in his or her native tongue. This problem becomes even more apparent given the realization that comparable terms used to express emotional states might not exist across languages. MNCs must find alternatives to talk to manage emotional conflict and promote organizational harmony. One creative alternative could be to promote aesthetic activities among team members (Von Glinow, Shapiro, & Brett, 2004). There is a history in firms from both Eastern and Western countries to encourage employees to sing company songs or participate in other corporate rituals (Nissley, 2002). In Murnighan and Conlon's (1991) study of British string quartets, the researcher found that the most successful groups avoided discussing their differences but instead channeled their frustrations into their music. We look forward to witnessing the first virtual MNC music concert where team members perform together from different locations around the world.

Conclusion

Make new friends but keep the old, one is silver the other gold.[3]

Scholars sometimes refer to established theories, frameworks, and practices as "old friends" (e.g., Ambrose & Kulik, 1999, p. 231). This designation not only reflects a certain intimacy, but also recognition of the idea's ongoing importance. The frameworks set forth by Perlmutter (1969) and Bartlett and Ghoshal (1989) have earned the right to be called old friends within the IHRM field as they continue to yield insights and a common understanding among scholars and managers alike. Communication scholars also have begun applying these frameworks to conceptualize global operations and better understand the present-day challenges facing IHRM professionals (see van den Born & Peltokorpi, 2010). These frameworks are excellent starting points for other communication scholars interested in exploring IHRM questions as varied as information flows in MNCs, the global mind-set construct, and the viability of a particular language or technology policy across different countries.

People also have a tendency to discard what is old in favor of what is shiny and new. Technology-enhanced communications have likewise earned a place within IHRM and in an MNC's global operations. The usefulness of CMCs will undoubtedly grow as technologies continue to improve and as scholars and HRM professionals gain a greater awareness of these technologies' advantages and limits. Just as virtual friendships are unlikely to replace traditional relationships, however, CMCs will remain only a partial substitute for older, more immediate forms of communication.

Notes

1 In later treatments, Perlmutter added a fourth category, viz., regiocentric, that foreshadowed present-day interest in the regional strategies of MNCs (Wind, Douglas, & Perlmutter, 1973).
2 See also Daft & Lengel's (1984) theory on information richness and Sproull and Kiesler's (1986) lack of social context hypothesis.
3 Traditional Girl Scouts camping song. Writer unknown.

Bibliography

Ambrose, M.L., & Kulik, C.T. (1999). Old friends, new faces: Motivation research in the 1990s. *Journal of Management, 39*(3), 231–292.

Armstrong, D.J., & Cole, P. (2002). Managing distances and differences in geographically distributed work groups. In S.E. Jackson & M.N. Ruderman (Eds.), *Diversity in work teams: Research paradigms for a changing workplace* (pp. 167–187). Washington, DC: American Psychological Association.

Babcock, R.D., & Du-Babcock, B. (2001). Language-based communication zones in international business communication. *Journal of Business Communication, 38*(4), 372–412.

Bailey, C., & Fletcher, C. (2008). International performance management and appraisal: Research perspectives. In M.M. Harris (Ed.), *Handbook of research in international human resource management* (pp. 125–144). New York: Taylor & Francis.

Barner-Rasmussen, W., & Björkman, I. (2007). Language fluency, socialization and inter-unit relationships in Chinese and Finnish subsidiaries. *Management and Organization Review, 3*(1), 105–128.

Bartlett, C.A. (2011). *Philips versus Matsushita: The competitive battle continues.* Boston: Harvard Business School Press.

Bartlett, C.A., & Ghoshal, S. (1989). *Managing across borders: The transnational solution.* Boston: Harvard Business School Press.

Cameron, D. (2000). *Good to talk? Living and working in a communication culture.* Thousand Oaks, CA: Sage.

Charles, M. (2007). Language matters in global communication. *Journal of Business Communication, 44*(3), 260–282.

Chen, G.-M. (2007). A review of the concept of intercultural effectiveness. In M. Hinner (Ed.), *The influence of culture in the world of business* (pp. 95–116). Hamburg: Peter Lang.

Daft, R.L. (2012). *Organization theory and design*. Mason, OH: South-Western.

Daft, R.L., & Lengel, R.H. (1984). Information richness: A new approach to managerial behavior and organizational design. *Research in Organizational Behavior, 6*, 191–233.

Dunbar, R.I.M. (2012). Can the internet buy you more friends? [Video file]. Retrieved from http://tedx talks.ted.com/video/TEDxObserver-Robin-Dunbar-Can-t.

Farrell, D., Laboissière, M.A., & Rosenfeld, J. (2006, November). Sizing the emerging global labor market: Rational behavior from both companies and countries can help it work more efficiently. *Academy of Management Perspectives*, 23–34.

Florkowski, G.W., & Olivas-Lujan, H.R. (2006). The diffusion of human resource information technology innovations in US and non-US firms. *Personnel Review, 35*, 684–710.

Friedman, B.A. (2007). Globalization implications for human resource management roles. *Employee Responsibilities and Rights Journal, 19*(3), 157–171.

Friedman, T.L. (2005). *The world is flat: A brief history of the twenty-first century*. New York: Picador.

Gallo, C. (2007, January 31). Why leadership means listening. *Business Week*. Retrieved from www.business week.com/stories/2007-01-31/why-leadership-means-listeningbusinessweek-business-news-stock -market-and-financial-advice.

Ghemawat, P. (2011). *World 3.0: Global prosperity and how to achieve it*. Boston: Harvard Business School Press.

Ghoshal, S., Korine, A., & Szulanski, G. (1994). Interunit communication in multinational corporations. *Management Science, 40*(1), 96–110.

Giddens, A. (1990). *The consequences of modernity*. Stanford, CA: Stanford University Press.

Hajek, C., & Giles, H. (2003). New directions in intercultural communication competence: The process model. In J.O. Greene & B.R. Burleson (Eds.), *Handbook of communication and social interaction skills* (pp. 935–957). Mahwah, NJ: Lawrence Erlbaum.

Hall, R., & Wailes, N. (2010). International and comparative human resource management. In A. Wilkinson, N. Bacon, T. Redman, & S. Snell (Eds.), *The Sage handbook of human resource management* (pp. 115–132). Thousand Oaks, CA: Sage.

Hirst, P., & Thompson, G. (1996). *Globalization in question*. Cambridge, UK: Polity.

Hogan, R., & Henley, N. (1970). *A test of the empathy-effective communication hypothesis*. Baltimore, MD: Center for Social Organization of Schools, Johns Hopkins University. Retrieved from http://files.eric.ed.gov /fulltext/ED043642.pdf.

Holstein, W.J. (2008, July 29). The decline of the expat executive. *strategy+business*. Retrieved from www .strategy-business.com/article/li00086?pg=all.

Huo, Y.P., & Von Glinow, M.A. (1995). On transplanting human resource practices to China: A culture driven approach. *International Journal of Manpower, 16*, 3–15.

Javidan, M. (2010). *Bringing the global mindset to leadership*. Retrieved from http://blogs.hbr.org/imagining -the-future-of-leadership/2010/05/bringing-the-global-mindset-to.html.

Javidan, M., & Teagarden, M.B. (2011). Conceptualizing and measuring global mindset. *Advances in Global Leadership, 6*, 13–39.

Kapoor, B. (2011). Impact of globalization on human resource management. *Journal of International Management Studies, 6*(1), 46–53.

Kerr, S., & Von Glinow, M.A. (1997). The future of HR: Plus ca change, plus c'est la meme chose. *Human Resource Management, 36*(1), 115–119.

Kock, N. (2004). The psychobiological model: Towards a new theory on computer-mediated communication based on Darwinian evolution. *Organization Science, 15*(3), 327–348.

Kock, N. (2005). Media richmess or media naturalness? The evolution of our biological communication apparatus and its influence on our behavior toward e-communication tools. *IEEE Transactions on Professional Communication, 48*(2), 117–130.

Levy, O., Beechler, S., Taylor, S., & Boyaçigiller, N.A. (2007). What we talk about when we talk about "global mindset": Managerial cognition in multinational corporations. *Journal of International Business Studies, 38*(2), 231–258.

Lewis, M.P. (2009). *Ethnologue: Languages of the world* (16th ed.). Dallas: SIL International.

Lidsky, L.B., & Connor, T.F. (2007). Authorship, audiences, and anonymous speech. *Notre Dame Law Review, 82*, 1537–1604.

Lilienthal, D.E. (1960). The multinational corporation. In M. Anshen & G.L. Bach (Eds.), *Management and corporations, 1985* (pp. 119–158). New York: McGraw Hill.

Louhiala-Salminen, L., & Kankaanranta, A. (2011). Professional communication in a global business context: The notion of global communicative competence. *IEEE Transactions on Professional Communication, 54*(3), 244–262.

Luo, Y., & Shenkar, O. (2006). The multinational corporation as a multilingual community: Language and organization in a global context. *Journal of International Business Studies, 37*, 321–339.

Lustig, M.W., & Koester, J. (2013). *Intercultural competence: Interpersonal communications across cultures*. Upper Saddle River, NJ: Pearson.

MacDuffie, J.P. (2007). HRM and distributed work: Managing people across distances. *Academy of Management Annals, 1*(1), 549–615.

McKinsey Global Institute. (2005). *The emerging global labor market*. Retrieved from www.mckinsey.com /insights/mgi/research/labor_markets/the_emerging_global_labor_market.

Milliman, J., Taylor, S., & Czaplewski, J. (2002). Cross-cultural performance feedback in multinational enterprises: Opportunity for organizational learning. *Human Resource Planning, 25*(3), 29–43.

Murnighan, J.K., & Conlon, D.E. (1991). The dynamics of intense work groups: A study of British string quartets. *Administrative Science Quarterly, 36*, 165–186.

Nissley, N. (2002). Tuning-in to organizational song as aesthetic discourse. *Culture and Organization, 8*(1), 51–68.

O'Brien, D. (2013). *Solutions for multinational corporations: Recruiting through social media*. Retrieved from www.adp.com/solutions/employer-services/solutions-for-multinationals/insights/mnc-insight-detail .aspx?id={6E7DE237-FDEC-4141-A693-48BDA902EE30}.

Parks, M.R. (1994). Communicative competence and interpersonal control. In M.L. Knapp & G.R. Miller (Eds.), *Handbook of interpersonal communication* (pp. 589–618). Thousand Oaks, CA: Sage.

Peng, M.W. (2008). *Global business*. Mason, OH: South-Western.

Perlmutter, H.V. (1969). The tortuous evolution of the multinational corporation. *Columbia Journal of World Business, 4*(1), 9–18.

Piekkari, R. (2006). Language effects in multinational corporations: A review from an international human resource management perspective. In G. Stahl & I. Björkman (Eds.), *Handbook of research in international human resource management* (pp. 536–550). Northampton, MA: Edward Elgar.

Schneper, W.D., & Von Glinow, M.A. (2013). Cultural attitudes in MNCs. In E.H. Kessler (Ed.), *Encyclopedia of management thought* (pp. 173–175). Thousand Oaks, CA: Sage.

Sproull, L., & Kiesler, S. (1986). Reducing social-context cues—electronic mail in organizational communication. *Management Science, 32*(11), 1492–1512.

Tajfel, H., & Turner, J.C. (1979). An integrative theory of intergroup conflict. In W.G. Austin & S. Worchels (Eds.), *The social psychology of intergroup relations* (pp. 33–47). Monterey, CA: Brooks/Cole.

Tang, S.F.Y., Lai, E.W.K., & Kirkbride, P.S. (1995). *Human resource management practices in Hong Kong: Survey report*. Hong Kong: Hong Kong Institute of Human Resource Management.

van den Born, F., & Peltokorpi, V. (2010). Language policies and communications in multinational companies: Alignment with strategic orientation and human resource management practices. *Journal of Business Communication, 47*(2), 97–118.

Vance, C.M., & Paik, Y. (2011). *Managing a global workforce: Challenges and opportunities in international human resource management*. New York: M.E. Sharpe.

Von Glinow, M.A., & Schneper, W.D. (2013). Global leadership. In R. Griffin (Ed.), *Oxford bibliographies in management*. Oxford: Oxford University Press. Retrieved from www.oxfordbibliographies.com/browse ?module_0=obo-9780199846740.

Von Glinow, M.A., Shapiro, D.L., & Brett, J.M. (2004). Can we talk, and should we? Managing emotional conflict in multicultural teams. *Academy Management Review, 29*(4), 578–592.

Wiemann, J.M., & Bradac, J.J. (1989). Metatheoretical issues in the study of communicative competence: Structural and functional approaches. In B. Dervin & M.J.Voight (Eds.), *Progress in communication sciences* (pp. 261–284). Norwood, NJ: Ablex.

Wind, Y., Douglas, S.P., & Perlmutter, H.V. (1973). Guidelines for developing international marketing strategies. *Journal of Marketing, 37*(2), 14–23.

World Bank. (2013). *World development indicators database,* Retrieved from http://databank.worldbank.org /data/views/reports/tableview.aspx.

World Economic Forum. (2010). *Stimulating economies through fostering talent mobility.* Retrieved from www3 .weforum.org/docs/WEF_PS_TalentMobility_report_2010.pdf.

21

IMPLICATIONS OF COMMUNICATION RESEARCH FOR IMPROVING CONSERVING POLICIES, PROCEDURES, AND FUNCTIONS

Gary P. Latham

Human Resource Management (HRM) initiatives that are intended to ensure the availability of employees to fill their organizational roles include attitude surveys, compensation systems, demographic diversity, safety practices, work-life balance, global operations, and media/information systems. Thus seven chapters in this book have been devoted to these topics. My commentary on these chapters is written through the lens of a former staff psychologist employed full-time in the private sector, a consultant, and an academic.

Attitude Surveys

Thurstone (1929) defined an attitude as affect or overall degree of favorability regarding an object. The anonymous employee-attitude survey as a method for data collection in organizational settings has remained popular since the 1930s. Both Eagly (1992) and Ajzen (2001) have shown that there is now a strong basis for the argument that attitudes are important causes and strong predictors of manifest behavior. Markham and Brendl (2000) argued that people evaluate objects in relation to their goals. Today, many organizations, including the Center for Creative Leadership, use attitude surveys to gauge employee satisfaction with the job, the leadership team, and the organization as a whole.

In chapter 14, Leonardi, Treem, Barley, and Miller provided a descriptive role of HRM professionals in assessing employee attitudes as an explorer, advocate, and/or facilitator. What is missing in this chapter is prescription. They pointed out what we don't know about each of these roles. Doing so is useful for fostering future research. HRM professionals, however, would likely have benefitted from the authors' collective experience on what HRM might start, stop, or consider doing differently within the context of each of these three roles.

Leonardi et al. do HRM scholars a service by describing the knowledge gaps in different methods for attitude assessment. They concluded their chapter with a brief case description of how these different methods were actually used to the benefit of an organization. The chapter would likely have increased its value for HRM professionals and consultants had it included prescriptions on ways to better use these methods singularly and as an aggregate.

Compensation Systems

In chapter 15, Fulmer and Chen did an excellent job of summarizing both the historical and the current scholarly findings on attitudinal and behavioral reactions to one's pay. They came to the startling conclusion that despite the voluminous studies on this topic, the vast majority have failed to take pay communication issues into account. Instead, the focus has been on pay system designs rather than communication issues on implementation. Hence, age-old controversies such as pay secrecy versus openness continue unabated. However, the authors do a good job of identifying possible individual difference variables that likely affect the answer to this particular controversy, as well as the method that might be used to disseminate pay data information to employees.

This chapter should prove valuable to HRM practitioners and consultants. For example, the authors point out the ongoing necessity for taking steps to ensure that employees understand the organization's compensation philosophy, explaining how to value stock options, and explaining the relationship between an employee's performance appraisal and a salary increase/bonus. Additional prescriptions/hypotheses, based on the authors' everyday experiences as well as their review of the literature, would have been helpful for readers of this chapter.

Employee Safety and Health Management

Sinclair, Stanyar, McFadden, Brawley, and Huang's chapter on the role of communication in employee safety and health management (chapter 16) struck the appropriate balance between theory and empirical research versus action steps that can be immediately taken by HRM professionals and consultants. This may reflect the fact that one of the authors, Huang, works in industry.

Maier (1955) was among the first to propose that performance = ability × motivation. Accordingly, Sinclair et al. present a communication model that focuses on two primary communication pathways—namely, knowledge (ability) and motivation to bring about safety/health related behaviors. They correctly distinguish between task and contextual performance. Recommendations for practice are based directly on theory (e.g., prospect theory) and research on both macro (e.g., organizational culture/context) and micro variables (framing communication positively versus negatively).

Social cognitive theory (Bandura, 2000) was not mentioned by the authors, yet it might prove helpful as a framework for managing health and safety. In brief, the theory posits triadic reciprocal determinism among three variables: person (e.g., factual knowledge and safety-related skills; risk seeking/avoidance), environment (e.g., organizational safety climate, health climate), and behavioral (e.g., task and contextual performance). That is, these three factors influence and are influenced by one another. Consistent with the discussion in this chapter, social cognitive theory also discusses the importance of setting specific goals, communicating the relationship between what people are doing and the outcomes they can expect, and communicating ways to increase self-efficacy (domain-specific confidence) that the person can do what is required to attain the goals (e.g., health and safety).

Managing Diversity

Both the Conference Board (Hart, 1997) and the Society for Human Resource Management (Lockwood, 2005) have reported that workforce diversity is a business imperative for organizational effectiveness and sustained competitiveness. An emphasis on diversity enables an organization to attract and retain the best global talent and to increase market share worldwide.

In chapter 17, Ng and Barker effectively translated the academic literature on this subject for practitioners and consultants. Their chapter is chock full of helpful dos and don'ts. For example, do have the CEO continually discuss senior management's commitment to demographic diversity with the workforce; do use recruitment messages as a method for espousing value for diversity and for depicting minorities in supervisory positions; and do recognize foreign credentials and work experience. Don't use the term "your people."

There is misplaced criticism of using cognitive ability tests for selection purposes when the empirical evidence shows that these tests are indeed valid for predicting job performance. Moreover, cognitive ability tests do not under-predict the performance of minority group members (Sackett, Borneman, & Connelly, 2008). If Ng and Barker are aware of alternative selection methods with equal, if not higher, criterion-related validity, they failed to say so.

A surprising omission from this chapter is a discussion of the communication of societal cultural values on the acceptance of diversity by a nation's workforce. This omission is surprising in that the authors of this chapter are residents of Canada, yet they relied primarily on data collected from the United States to address diversity. The importance of multiculturalism to Canada as a country is communicated in its Charter of Rights. What effect has this espoused value had on Canadian residents? The Canadian government emphasizes the importance of a "mosaic" in contrast to the United States, where the value of a "melting pot" is emphasized. Is an emphasis on a mosaic superior or inferior to an emphasis on a melting point for gaining citizens' acceptance of diversity in the workforce? Singapore as a country officially celebrates the religious holidays of Buddhists, Christians, Hindus, Muslims, and Taoists (Latham & Napier, 1989). What effect has this government policy had on valuing diversity in the workplace?

Still another issue not discussed in this chapter is the U.S. Department of Labor's new affirmative action and nondiscrimination obligations for federal contractors in regard to veterans and individuals with disabilities. These rules include additional reporting and training obligations. Because these rules are arguably onerous and difficult to apply, how HRM communicates these requirements to senior management will likely require a great deal of thought.

Work-Life Issues

Work-life programs and policies, as noted by Medved in chapter 18, are not only good for employees, they also benefit an organization in terms of recruitment, retention, health care costs, and productivity. Medved begins the chapter with a rather profound and despairing observation. There is a paucity of studies on how HRM professionals can attain and maintain credibility on this or any other subject. What makes this issue so troublesome is that in most organizations it is typically the HRM department that is tasked with preparing corporate messages to employees on this subject. This chapter contains a wealth of information for graduate students who are searching for a worthwhile topic for a doctoral dissertation. Answers to the following issues identified by Medved are likely to be quickly published and highly cited:

- When aiming to be a critical resource about work-issues, under what circumstances should HRM use "lean media"? When is a "rich media" critical to new policy adoption?
- In what ways do HRM professionals fashion and carry out their work-life communication roles? What communication strategies do HRM professionals use in the context of work-life coaching interactions?

- How should work-life issues as solutions to important business problems (e.g., operations, sales, revenue) be framed? How should these initiatives be framed to employees who do not have responsibilities for children or elder relatives?
- The extant research on work-life balance has focused largely on white-collar jobs. Are the issues different for other occupations?

Doctoral students and faculty interested in pursuing answers to questions such as these are likely to face little difficulty in obtaining research grants (e.g., SHRM Foundation).

As for the observation that HRM professionals lack credibility, HRM researchers and practitioners might find the principles of organizational justice helpful (Folger & Cropanzano, 1998). The essence of this theory is that for leaders to be effective they must not only be fair, but they must be perceived as fair. The theory then explains ways of doing so in terms of distributive justice (i.e., what is distributed to whom), procedural justice (i.e., procedures on how to determine what is to be distributed to whom), and interactional justice. The latter is particularly relevant for HRM as the theory states that for leaders to be respected and trusted, employees must understand the logic of what a leader says and does, and the leader must be seen as sincere. The theory specifies ways of accomplishing this goal.

Media Management

Chapter 19 is fascinating in that one comes away with the sense that the wave of the future for information and communication technology (ICT) has already occurred for us ignorant majority. Stephens, Waters, and Sinclair do a wonderful job of bringing us ol' timers up-to-date on how organizational translucency has affected recruiting, cybervetting, and meeting practices. For example, the online presence of an organization is now a pivotal factor in the type of employees who decide to apply for an open position. HRM professionals cybervet by evaluating information from search engines, blogs, and other digital materials. To ensure the effectiveness of virtual teams, HRM professionals use transactive memory systems to document practices and preparation activities. Multi-communicating is currently on the horizon.

The Society for Human Resource Management (SHRM) has 270,000 members in more than 150 countries. As of the beginning of 2013, SHRM has successfully released and used these technologies to better engage, interact with, and serve the society's membership (e.g., provided a mobile version of the Web site on the CMS infrastructure; enhanced the SHRM Web site's search capabilities; added products that further expand SHRM's e-commerce unified shopping cart; and integrated the e-commerce platform with accounting software). In 2014, SHRM will further develop its Web site for mobile devices and improve the media experience. The latter is a critical objective for enhancing communication with the society's members.

Despite these exciting technological breakthroughs, the authors also report that the business community states that something so straightforward as videoconferencing is not a substitute for face-to-face meetings. This finding is consistent with media naturalness theory described in the next chapter. That theory states that human beings are biologically designed to communicate face-to-face in order to perceive body language, facial expressions, and speech.

This finding reminded me of the book *Megatrends* (Naisbett, 1982), in which the prediction was made that the world is likely to return to the preference for "high touch." This is especially likely as HRM moves further and further away from one-on-one employee assistance to a self-service e-HRM type of support. As HRM functions become increasingly automated so as to allegedly free HRM professionals for "strategic thinking," I predict entire HRM departments are likely to be outsourced in favor of hiring professional consulting firms on a need-only basis. The outsourcing of HRM departments is especially likely given that they lack credibility in what they communicate, as noted in chapter 18.

Global Operations

In chapter 17, Ng and Barker argued the importance of becoming multilingual as a strategy for bringing about acceptance of diversity in the workforce. In chapter 20, Schneper and Von Glinow painted a dismal picture for the likelihood of this occurrence. They cited statistics showing that 90% of the world's population is unlikely to leave the country where they were born. Arguably worse is their finding that only 13% of recent college graduates from low-wage countries are viable candidates for multinational corporations (MNCs) due in part to inadequate foreign language skills. Consistent with observations made in the previous chapter, MNCs are beginning to seek individuals with highly specialized skills through social media Web sites. Especially needed is intercultural communication competence, namely an individual's ability to interact with people from a different culture in effective and appropriate ways. Adding further evidence to Ng and Barker's emphasis in chapter 17 on multilingualism is the finding reported in the present chapter that language fluency shapes organizational dynamics in unanticipated ways. CEOs may visit divisions in countries where they do not speak the language far less frequently than divisions located in countries where they are fluent in the spoken language. Nevertheless, North American organizations, including SHRM, are attempting to enter the market place in Asia, Africa, and Latin America. As they do so, they will likely meet Chinese organizations with similar objectives where almost all employ individuals who are fluent in more than one language.

Conclusions

These seven chapters make clear that an HRM department serves the entire organization. An HRM department's operational success hinges largely on how well it communicates and in doing so gains the support of organizational stakeholders (e.g., senior management). To be viewed as the trusted thought leader on people management issues such as attracting and retaining high-quality employees, building roadmaps for career advancement, and formulating an HRM strategy that enables an organization to evolve in the future requires mastering the art and science of communication. The seven chapters discussed here contain gems of wisdom that will facilitate the attainment of this objective.

Bibliography

Ajzen, I. (2001). Nature and operation of attitudes. *Annual Review of Psychology, 10*, 27–58.
Bandura, A. (2000). Social cognitive theory: An agentic perspective. *Annual Review of Psychology, 52*, 1–26.
Eagly, A.H. (1992). Uneven progress: Social psychology and the study of attitudes. *Journal of Personality and Social Psychology, 63*(5), 693–710.
Folger, R., & Cropanzano, R. (1998). *Organizational justice and human resource management.* Thousand Oaks, CA: Sage.
Hart, M.A. (1997). *Managing diversity for sustained competitiveness.* New York: Conference Board.

Latham, G.P., & Napier, N. (1989). Chinese human resource practices in Hong Kong and Singapore: An exploratory study. In K. Rowland & J. Ferris (Eds.), *International human resources management* (pp. 173–199). Greenwich, CT: JAI Press.

Lockwood, N.R. (2005). Workforce diversity: Leveraging the power of difference for competitive advantage. *SHRM Research Quarterly, 2,* 1–13.

Maier, N.R.F. (1955). *Psychology in industry* (2nd ed.). Boston: Houghton Mifflin.

Markham, A.B., & Brendl, C.M. (2000). The influence of goals on value and choice. *Psychology of Learning and Motivation, 39,* 97–128.

Naisbett, J. (1982). *Megatrends: Ten directions for transforming our lives.* New York: Warner Books.

Sackett, P.R., Borneman, M.S., & Connelly, B. (2008). High-stakes testing in higher education and employment: Appraising the evidence for validity and fairness. *American Psychologist, 63,* 215–227.

Thurstone, L.L. (1929). Theory of attitude measurement. *Psychological Review, 36,* 222–241.

PART V
EPILOGUE

22

MAPPING THE "TRADING ZONES" OF COMMUNICATION AND HUMAN RESOURCE MANAGEMENT

Vernon D. Miller and Michael E. Gordon

Peter Galison (1997), the Harvard professor of the history of science, created the "trading zone" metaphor in order to elucidate the collaborations across academic departments that enabled the development of multidisciplinary or interdisciplinary fields of study. The basis for the trading zone metaphor appears to be anthropological investigations of commercial exchanges of goods and services between members of different cultures who often spoke different languages and who entered bartering with divergent ideas for the use of the traded commodities. Baird and Cohen (1999) applied Galison's ideas to show how the joint input of physicists and medical researchers was necessary to modify then-popular, but incorrect, settings of magnetic resonance imaging machines in order to reconsider widespread misdiagnoses and realize the machine's full potential. The inspiration for this book was to identify both the goods and services that might have mutual appeal to researchers in the fields of HRM and communication. To this end, we hope that we will have introduced representatives of the two fields to the conceptual traditions and epistemological strengths of the other's studies, thus creating a trading zone.

This chapter has two purposes. First, we reiterate the call for research within the HRM-communication nexus in order to generate theoretically rich research that is relevant to HRM practices. As Lawler (2007), Rynes (2007), and others have argued with regard to disconnects between management research and application by HRM professionals, a primary goal of academic research is to improve the lives of others. "If I had to choose one change that would make a difference, ... I would not argue that [business schools] should get out of the basic research business, but I would argue that they should produce more research and writing that focuses on practice" (Lawler, 2007, p. 1036). In this chapter, we review major research issues from the book and link these issues to the benefit of organizations and their employees. This integration seems fitting as the suggested research directions have been developed by HRM, management, psychology, and communication scholars, and as such they are not the sole property of one academic discipline.

Second, applying the trading zone metaphor, we see this book to be an initial and mutually beneficial conversation of HRM and communication scholars about the intersection of theory and research from their respective fields. Echoing the sentiments and statements expressed by the contributors of each chapter, we argue that opportunities for theoretically and practically valuable discoveries await at this intersection. Consequently, this chapter identifies a number of communication issues that appear throughout the book and suggest starting points for research into staffing, developing, and conserving HRM functions. We hope that faculty, graduate students, and practitioners will make haste to investigate the research questions and, in the process, develop methods to surmount the difficulties and conundrums that each chapter's author(s) identify.

Recurring Issues

The preceding chapters make it apparent that communication is central to every HRM function. Therefore, whether pertaining to the production of messages about organizational policies, the development of training programs, the solicitation of input from employees on HRM policies or programs, the provision of feedback to executives or managers, or the determination of the viability of established programs, it is assumed that HRM professionals will be models of communication excellence for the organization and will be effective in facilitating others' communication behaviors. Consequently, confidence in the communication competence of HRM professionals makes it appear unnecessary to question the effectiveness of their information dissemination and feedback systems. The fact of the matter, however, is that HRM professionals, like all people, vary in their communication competencies, thereby causing organizations, in turn, to differ in their information sharing capabilities (Jablin, Cude, House, Lee, & Roth, 1994; Jablin & Sias, 2001). Thus, a number of personnel and performance difficulties might be traced to the communication skills of HRM personnel, to the organization's employees, and to systemic communication issues in the organization's operations.

Molar Constructs

With regard to recurring communication issues, the authors identify a range of core communication competencies that are central to HRM functions. As depicted in Figure 22.1, molar constructs, so named for their foundational and pervasive character, transcend all message exchanges and interactions. Two constructs stem from professionals' behaviors as well as written and spoken acts: credibility and openness. Credibility refers to perceptions of trustworthiness, competence, and goodwill and, in essence, strongly influence a sender's believability and trustworthiness (Gordon & Miller, 2012; Redding, 1972). Openness is a two-pronged construct, relating to perceptions of approachability or information receiving and perceptions of forthright sharing or information giving (Jablin, 1979).

Credibility and openness may easily serve HRM professionals well or alternatively undercut their efforts. Importantly, both constructs refer to communication phenomena that affect the willingness of organizational members to participate in the information sharing that is the basis for the social construction of HRM practices that affect the manner in which they are understood and affect organizational behavior. For instance, Gordon (chapter 7) suggests that exiting employees, who perceive the HRM representative as competent and trustworthy as well as receptive to whatever they might say, should be more inclined to share a candid appraisal of their experiences than departing personnel who are suspicious of the representative or who perceive the representative as uninterested or too busy to learn about their perspective. Further, Tourish (chapter 11) describes effective organizational leaders as individuals who tolerate dissent, thereby fostering greater employee agency that produces engagement in discussions and that leads to the development of mutually agreeable stances to deal with important organizational issues, including many in the realm of HRM. Credibility and openness may also contribute to employees'

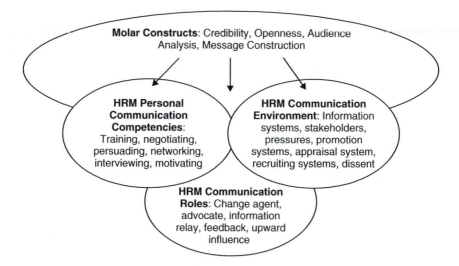

FIGURE 22.1 HRM-communication research themes.

willingness to engage HRM representatives in discussions related to work-life balance (Medved, chapter 18). For example, employees' approach to negotiations involving paternity leave are likely to be influenced by perceptions of HRM's receptivity to such discussions. Leonardi et al. (chapter 14) remind us that employees asked to participate in surveys, focus groups, or interviews, or be observed while performing their jobs, must believe that those collecting the information as well as top management are sincere in their quest to understand employees' points of view. Finally, Stephens et al. (chapter 19) note that corporate and employee use of the Web and e-mail presents a new level of translucency to individuals' attitudes and intentions, where criticisms about the credibility and openness of the organization can be posted on internal information systems or displayed on external Web sites for others to read.

The remaining pair of molar constructs in Figure 22.1 concern strategic acts by individuals that affect the delivery of information: audience analysis and message construction. Audience analysis, one aspect of rhetorical sensitivity, involves properly assessing the information receivers' receptivity to positions or rationales, their personal ability to comprehend complex messages, and the degree to which situational factors interfere with their access to information (Hart & Burks, 1972). At the risk of oversimplification, the analysis of others' orientations also is critical to developing and conveying messages effectively. Knowing how to frame messages, construct arguments, or impart stories that convey targeted meanings to employees or management is vital to message dissemination, decision making, organizing, and socialization (Weick & Browning, 1986).

It seems particularly important to consider how HRM evaluates its audiences in order to construct messages suited to them. For example, Breaugh (chapter 3) points out that HRM must consider the perspective of job applicants in fashioning recruiting messages. Further, audience analysis is exemplified by the longstanding tradition in the training field of conducting a needs analysis of each employee in order to determine which instructional programs will offer appropriate preparation for performing her/his job duties. Given that training is a rhetorical process, Fyke and Buzzanell (chapter 9) insist that training must be audience centered and that trainers must adapt and adjust instruction to trainees' current communicative capacities.

Audience analysis also influences the success with which managers are able to affect employees' responses to announcements about organizational change. According to Lewis (chapter 12), it is vital to address the special concerns of each stakeholder group regarding organizational change, and one of several commonly perceived predictors of failure of change announcements is the failure to adapt messages to different audiences. Finally, Stephens et al. (chapter 19) consider the readiness of employees to receive messages via e-mail and corporate Web pages. Researchers interested in investigating potential problems associated with the user interface are advised not to assume that employees are trained and ready to participate in digital synchronous or asynchronous interactions.

One of the familiar refrains repeated throughout the book pertains to the differences in HRM professionals' message-construction abilities and the consequent variability in the effectiveness of the HRM programs that they administer. A typical HRM department often is tasked with disseminating more than its fair share of mundane messages, including notifications regarding insurance, parking, holidays, and so forth. At the same time, HRM must demonstrate sensitivity and dexterity in message construction whenever misconstruing one of its missives could have considerable negative consequences upon employees' attitudes and organizational behavior. Thus, given the pandemic status of misperceptions about pay, Fulmer and Chen (chapter 15) stress the importance of constructing messages that will create accurate perceptions of compensation policies and practices. As noted in Latham's (chapter 21) remarks, message construction is especially critical when treating difficult compensation topics such as pay secrecy and when formulating responses to questions posed by employees who expect very different information about their pay. Finally, Sinclair and his associates (chapter 16) underscore the importance of matching positive- and negative-message frames to safety and health issues, to various work settings, and to employee readiness and motivation to respond to such messages.

The familiar proverb "Actions speak louder than words" suggests that what people do may convey more credible messages than what they say. There are many instances reported in this book that highlight the significance of messages constructed and conveyed by the actions taken by organizational authorities. For example, Sinclair et al. (chapter 16) observe that the behavior of HRM professionals and managers provides important symbols and examples of appropriate health and safety behavior that employees are expected to follow. Further, the observable pattern of personal characteristics of individuals hired (Dipboye, chapter 4) and promoted (Kramer and Hoelscher, chapter 6) contains important messages regarding the type of employee valued by the organization.

The contributors frequently make the case for a more sophisticated view of communication in HRM that is characterized by co-constructed messages. Though basic communication competencies and facilitating upward and downward message exchanges are critical to well-functioning organizations, the dynamic that both message recipients and senders participate in the communication act and establish shared meanings (Cooren, 2000; Fairhurst & Putnam, 2006; Poole, 2011; Weick & Browning, 1986) often is endorsed here. For instance, Tourish (chapter 11) notes that the assent or dissent of followers are just as important as the leaders' communications, and Fyke and Buzzanell (chapter 9) observe that in training, leadership is relational and reverse mentoring does occur. Bauer, Erdogan, and Simon (chapter 5) point out that socialization in many ways thrives on the reciprocal influence of newcomers on their supervisors and coworkers, Gordon and Miller (chapter 10) recommend that the appraiser and appraisee co-construct the appraisal interview, and Lewis (chapter 12) argues that HRM professionals should go beyond superficial responses and solicit input from employees about proposed or enacted organizational changes. Of course, Sias (chapter 13) opines on the communicative constitution of organizations (CCO; Cooren, 2000), reinforcing the idea that organizations and organizing emerge through communication, importantly by means of both formal and informal messaging.

In sum, matters of credibility, openness, audience analysis, and message construction are fundamental to HRM functions and to this book. In a number of instances, the contributors challenge conventional thinking that the credibility of individual HRM professionals or the HRM department, for example, are consistently at high levels or are inconsequential. Instead, they question whether or not HRM professionals and their departments are perceived as credible and open, and they go so far as to question how professionals can repair perceptions if employees view them negatively in matters of trustworthiness, sincerity, accuracy, concern for employees, willingness to listen, and fairness. The contributors also argue for greater awareness of the cocreation of meaning and the possibility that unintended meanings are derived from HRM professionals' (and executive leadership's) choices in what to say, mediums of expression, and engagement in dialogue with employees. Messages sent by the "organization" are revealed in the actions that HRM takes, and the contributors call for more thorough investigation of tensions, dilemmas, and contradictions that HRM professionals face. Naturally, research questions emerge regarding the extent to which HRM, as an extension of executive leadership, demonstrates an understanding of the power of conversation, stories, use of specific terminology, networking, and the creation of informal information networks.

HRM Personal Communication Competencies

Because they gravitated into HRM careers, and given their customary responsibilities that require interacting with employees at every level of the organization, HRM professionals are expected to be excellent communicators. Yet a body of materials for the development of HRM professionals' communication competencies is difficult to locate. Materials related to instruction in public speaking and writing appear regularly in HRM curricula. Yet materials on constructing and giving feedback, interviewing, or relational development, just to name three, are difficult to locate. The need for such materials seems apparent. The normal duties of HRM professionals in training, negotiating, persuading, networking, interviewing, and motivating, to name a few, require highly developed communication skills. For example, Schneper and Von Glinow (chapter 20) point out that HRM departments interacting with employees on international assignments or with employees of different nationalities in their native country must be sensitive to nuances associated with their cultures (e.g., power distance) and language. Breaugh (chapter 3) observes that HRM professionals responsible for recruiting prospective employees face challenges of developing materials describing the organization and position(s) in accurate *and* attractive ways. Fyke and Buzzanell (chapter 9) identify the need for trainers to adjust their training materials to trainees' knowledge and skill levels, deliver an engaging program that improves the targeted knowledge domains and skills, and follow up with an evaluation of the long-term effectiveness of their training materials and delivery. Each of these actions requires trainers to seek information, be sensitive to feedback, adjust their messages, and coordinate with others rather than to assume that information given is information digested and acted upon—in other words, that their materials generate the desired outcomes.

Moreover, Schmitt (chapter 8) calls for research on the consistency of messages across recruiting, selecting, socializing, and promoting domains. Such research should examine the effect of inconsistencies in messages that employees perceive the organization to be conveying. More to the point of this section on HRM personal communication competencies, it does not require much speculation to anticipate that HRM professionals, who effectively contribute to strategy, keep priorities on track among units, and solicit and relay feedback to keep messages consonant, must exercise considerable tact, timing, and savvy in their interactions with all organizational members. Following this logic, HRM professionals might be assumed to be models of information sharing, information acquisition, conflict management, upward and downward influence, and workgroup development and management using a variety of media, including face-to-face, e-mail, and Web sites. However, the extent to which professionals have strong communication skills appropriate for their respective areas of responsibility (e.g., training, compensation, employee safety and health management) is unclear.

We are not saying that all individuals must be trained in interpersonal or conflict management skills, for example, as many professional already possess highly developed abilities in these skill domains. However, we are calling for an acknowledgement that there are pre-competency, competency, and post-competency stages of communication abilities (Jablin & Sias, 2001). HRM professionals would benefit from targeted coaching or mentoring consistent with their competency stage. Development of communication competencies might considerably improve HRM functions and organizational operations.

A neglected area of study concerns the practice of informal communication across staffing, developing, and conserving programs. By informal communication, we mean unscheduled interactions in which conversational, two-way exchanges (i.e., both parties are able to ask for and share information) provide the basis for relational development, understanding of others' points of view, and knowledge acquisition. Informal conversations are vital in a number of respects. Whereas the development and dissemination of official information on HRM policies or the preparation of training materials require skills in audience assessment and message production, informal communication requires a higher level of communication competencies in order to approach an employee, manager, or executive at an opportune time, to avoid putting the other party on the defensive, and to manage conversations so that mutual understanding can develop (Jablin et al., 1994; Jablin & Sias, 2001). Whether conversations are "small talk," friendly FYIs, or off-the-record chats, informal conversations are in many ways the glue of organizing that enables cooperative relationships to flourish and that facilitate vital information exchanges (Poole, 2011; Weick & Browning, 1986). The ability to engage in what Lewis (chapter 12) refers to as "collaborative communication" is essential to problem identification, analysis, and solution generation.

The contributors identified organizational situations such as established meeting contexts and informal conversations that enable HRM to fulfill its roles. Paradoxically, little is known about the function of informal communication in organizations in general (Weick & Browning, 1986) and in HRM in particular. Certainly, individuals converse more easily with some groups of people than others, perhaps due to similar backgrounds and training, personalities, and assignments. Yet HRM professionals must interact with individuals from diverse backgrounds, many of whom arrive with various preconceptions of the interaction, who may differ in terms of information relevant to the conversation. In a single day, an HRM professional may interact with executive-level officers and day laborers, and he or she would be expected to carry out these episodes with aplomb and effectiveness. Assuming that HRM professionals have the ability to engage in informal conversation with individuals at every level of the organization, it is unclear at present to what extent professionals see the need to spend a portion of their day engaging individuals throughout the organization and have the time in their schedule to do so. Further, the degree to which executives value their HRM professionals taking time to engage others in informal conversations is also unknown.

HRM Communication Roles

In addition to the need to embody a range of communication competencies, HRM professionals must enact one or more vital communication roles in fulfillment of their duties. It should be noted that there is considerable danger in limiting the description of "communication" behavior to a conduit metaphor (Axley, 1984) because communication serves more purposes than the delivery of information vertically and horizontally in the organization (Cooren, 2000; Poole, 2011; Weick & Browning, 1986). For example, negotiating, shared decision making, and information gathering, to name a few, are key organizational communication behaviors that reside outside information transfer activities. That being said, organizations consistently have information relay challenges (Poole, 2011), and a number of contributors place successes and failures in information sharing on HRM's shoulders. For example, prior to, during, and following organizational change efforts, Lewis (chapter 12) advocates that HRM professionals solicit input from those influenced by the change and relay their input to executives and those directing the change. Both Lewis and Leonardi et al. (chapter 14) note a propensity to withhold information from other divisions or units (e.g., "communication silos"). The extent to which HRM professionals serve (and serve well) as official or unofficial liaisons between these units during planned organizational change has important ramifications for employees and organizations and should be a high priority in future investigations. Similarly, Schneper and Von Glinow (chapter 20) discuss the important role of HRM in the flow of information from executive levels to employees in dispersed nations and cultures. They advocate the development of partnerships to aid in the fidelity of message exchanges.

In addition, HRM professionals are uniquely situated to engage in and promote collaboration between parties. In fact, their ability to enlist and in some cases prepare managers and employees to be full participants is critical to matters related to diversity (Ng and Barker, chapter 17), to employees' adapting change efforts to their work contexts (Lewis, chapter 12), and to ensuring employee safety and promoting health in the workplace (Sinclair et al., chapter 16), to name a few. As Sinclair et al. note, there is considerable difference between employee compliance with safety regulations and participation in the adoption of new standards. In the former, employees follow rules in order to avoid disciplinary action while in the latter, employees are apt to develop an understanding of the rationale for safety and become agents of change.

HRM professionals' actions that promote collaboration with managers are also critical to the development of effective feedback systems. Schneper and Von Glinow (chapter 20) as well as Gordon and Miller (chapter 10) argue that effective feedback systems rely on managers engaging their employees in performance reviews and that HRM involvement is often necessary for organizations to develop multisource and timely feedback. In effect, whether it is safety enforcement or developing thoughtful and constructive appraisals, the extent to which HRM professionals form collaborative relationships with managers may well determine the overall effectiveness of those programs.

One other role emerging from these chapters that merits further investigation is that of organizational change agent. HRM professionals have unique opportunities through their access to executive management to advocate for policy, program, and value change. For instance, Ng and Barker (chapter 17) portray HRM as an advocate that is responsible for protecting stigmatized employees and marginalized groups in the organization. Medved (chapter 18) notes that HRM professionals not only are involved in the development of programs promoting work-life balance, but often they must show executives how work-life policies can benefit the organization. Furthermore, HRM change agent efforts also can be downward directed. Sinclair et al. (chapter 16) stress the importance of involving key supporters and opinion leaders in promoting safety and health. Schneper and Von Glinow (chapter 20) discuss the differences between organizational policy at headquarters and its implementation locally. In these cases, the extent to which HRM professionals are able to understand and address local managers' attitudes toward and challenges to policy implementation may well determine policy success.

HRM Communication Environment

It is unlikely that one would dispute the fact that HRM operations are not created or implemented in a vacuum. Organizations' climate and culture, structure, technology, market characteristics and competition, and relative life cycle development can easily generate fast-changing, stressful work environments (Aldrich, 1979). However, HRM personnel and their programs can have both allies and obstacles in the corporate communication environment, which is shaped by its ITC systems, strategic and operational decision-making processes, promotion systems, appraisal systems, and toleration of dissent. Technologically speaking, some aspects of how employees and HRM professionals interact synchronously and asynchronously are changing radically in all aspects of staffing, developing, and conserving functions. And certainly, as Hutchinson (chapter 2) observes, HRM's strategic prominence, primary functions in their organizations, and situational challenges, in turn, influence how professionals seek to enact their roles.

Yet in keeping with the earlier discussion of molar concepts, the credibility and perceived openness of HRM professionals determine, almost more than any other factor, the extent to which employees cooperate with HRM's initiatives. It is possible that a communication environment that is more open will allow professionals more room to consult freely with multiple members, publicly convene stakeholders engaged in contentious issues, and schedule forums for the discussion of delicate policies that are expected to be challenged and in which give-and-take is the norm. In contrast, in communication environments that are more closed, HRM professionals themselves may be unable to broach issues with executives or offer replies bordering on "take it or leave it" to employees who identify flaws in policies.

The communication environment also influences how HRM work may have to be conducted in the midst of awkward binds and complicated demands. For instance, Fulmer and Chen (chapter 15) describe potential struggles when professionals are responsible for implementing policies set forth from executive management that may be at odds with policies stemming from standard HRM practice. Likewise, they note that HRM professionals are in the unique position to see compensation issues from potentially incompatible management and employee perspectives. Lewis (chapter 12) notes that HRM professionals are often under pressure from executive management to implement the "people side" of change but struggle to determine whether or how to relay employees' negative feedback upward or how to resolve dilemmas without losing their own prestige. More generally, Leonardi et al. (chapter 14) discuss the possibility that HRM may be obliged to relay feedback from employees that will not be to executives' liking. Ng and Barker (chapter 17) note that at times HRM professionals are placed in the position of compelling leaders to act or behave appropriately. These challenges are rarely discussed by researchers, but they present yet other potential opportunities for study that might greatly benefit HRM professionals. For example, it would be useful to understand how HRM professionals cultivate credibility and openness with both executive management and employees in the face of conflicting demands. Another related topic worthy of investigation is how HRM professionals restore credibility and openness from the employees' perspective after events may have discredited them.

Developing Trading Zones

Creating trading zones between academic disciplines requires scholars to embrace any relevant intersecting perspectives, theory, and research in the two fields. Certainly, a starting point for any trading zone activity is broadening one's theoretical framework and considering alternative ways of conceptualizing and examining a phenomenon (Baird & Cohen, 1999). A second step would seem to be engaging in conversations with individuals trained in a different tradition but who are interested in related issues. Collaborations across organizationally interested disciplines have resulted in fruitful outcomes (e.g., Poole & Van de Ven, 2004; Weick & Browning, 1986). Such conversations may lead to research ventures.

Throughout the book, there are numerous recommendations for research into HRM functions that can be pursued through multiple methodologies. Moreover, each chapter calls for research investigations into issues that can be perplexing but that, if explored from a different disciplinary perspective, would offer theoretical and practical benefits. Latham (chapter 21), for example, commented on the usefulness of Leonardi et al.'s discussion of the knowledge gaps in different methods for attitude assessment. For instance, Tourish (chapter 11) calls for research on helping leaders to resist subordinate ingratiation and flattery and to promote dissent, both of which would benefit from the analysis of language in conversations. Similarly, Gordon (chapter 7) and Gordon and Miller (chapter 10) discuss longstanding problems with exit and appraisal interviews that may be addressed by gaining a greater understanding of the interaction dynamics occurring during these conversations. Fyke and Buzzanell (chapter 9) direct attention to trainers' use of narratives and framing to help trainees apply materials to their workplace. In turn, Bauer et al. (chapter 5) seek multi-wave longitudinal studies that capture communication patterns between incumbents and newcomers in order to better assess how positive and negative relationships develop among employees. Kramer and Hoelscher (chapter 6) call for research investigating the similarities and differences in social support and information sharing between domestic and international job transfers. Finally, included in Medved's (chapter 18) recommended research agenda are future studies of successful and unsuccessful maternity leave–related negotiations in order to understand what aspects of these conversations were successful or unsuccessful, reasons for these outcomes, the role of skill in negotiations, and changes in gendered assumptions affecting negotiations.

There are two points worth noting here. First, the research topics singled out in this chapter as well as the multitudes in the book not identified here can be explored through more than one methodology and in the long run should be (Miller, Poole, & Seibold, 2011). For example, the appraisal interview should be studied with conversation analysis, a staple methodology of a number of communication scholars, as a way of supplementing what has been learned by HRM researchers that rely on questionnaires and laboratory experiments (Gordon & Miller, chapter 10). Second and most importantly, the exemplars here illustrate calls for more authentic research. Gordon (chapter 7) calls for conversation analysis as a means for studying the exit interview, an HRM program that only has been investigated by means of surveys and simulated conversations about organizational disengagement.

Investigations that address issues that frustrate or enliven employees, HRM professionals, and managers are critical to undertake, and exploration of the various manifestations of communication phenomena can assist in this undertaking. Speculation regarding why HRM professionals are not up-to-date with recent research trends or applying key findings have been extensively set forth (e.g., Lawler, 2007; Rynes, 2007; Rynes, Giluk, & Brown, 2007). It is our belief that the failure of researchers to explore issues of pressing concern to HRM professionals and employees as they experience HRM functions is largely to blame. Thus, we encourage researchers to develop their own trading zones, alliances, working groups, and think tanks with interested others to explore issues carefully and fully.

As part of this initial conversation, there must be recognition of the interdependencies among the specific practices in HRM. For example, a company may not need to devote as much time and effort to the training of new workers if it is able to recruit and select new employees who already possess most of the critical skills and knowledge necessary to perform their particular organizational roles (Kristof, 1996). Hence, not only is the adequate preparation of materials suited to the new hires' abilities and interests (i.e., foundational audience analysis and message construction acts) an important consideration in the delivery of specific training programs, but it is vital for the HRM department to integrate the training of recruiters with organizational and department goals and, in turn, to ensure feedback from recruiters to the HRM department and the new employees' supervisors. Given the task set forth before the contributors to consider a single HRM practice, the matter of interdependencies did not receive adequate attention in the earlier chapters. So, while we discuss specific communication issues primarily relevant to one HRM task, we believe it is incumbent upon us to remind our readers that it is natural that the same issue may have considerable importance in another aspect of HRM's tasks or in the organization's operations.

Final Thoughts

Individuals who are HRM professionals perform critical services for organizations and for their employees. HRM jobs are not without conflicting goals and competing stakeholder demands, and professionals working in this field with whom we have chatted over the years often note a lack of support from key elements within their organization. Returning to the Lawler (2007) quote at the beginning of this chapter, our hope is that this book will stimulate communication research that focuses on practices that will assist HRM professionals, employees, and ultimately their organizations.

Bibliography

Aldrich, H.E. (1979). *Organizations and environments*. Englewood Cliffs, NJ: Prentice Hall.

Axley, S.R. (1984). Managerial and organizational communication in terms of the conduit metaphor. *Academy of Management Review, 9*(3), 428–437.

Baird, D., & Cohen, M.S. (1999). Why trade? *Perspectives on Science, 7*(2), 231–254.

Cooren, F. (2000). *The organizing property of communication*. Amsterdam: John Benjamins.

Fairhurst, G.T., & Putnam, L. (2006). Organizations as discursive constructions. *Communication Theory, 14*(1), 5–26.

Galison, P. (1997). *Image and logic: A material culture of microphysics*. Chicago: University of Chicago Press.

Gordon, M. E., & Miller, V. D. (2012). Conversations about job performance: A communication perspective on the appraisal process. New York: Business Expert Press.

Hart, R.D., & Burks, D. (1972). Rhetorical sensitivity and social interaction. *Communication Monographs, 39*(2), 75–91.

Jablin, F.M. (1979). Superior-subordinate communication: The state of the art. *Psychological Bulletin, 86*(6), 1201–1222.

Jablin, F.M., Cude, R.L., House, A., Lee, J., & Roth, N.L. (1994). Communication competence in organizations: Conceptualizations and comparison across multiple levels of analysis. In L. Thayer & G. Barnett (Eds.) *Emerging perspectives in organizational communication, Vol. 4* (pp. 114–140). Norwood, NJ: Ablex.

Jablin, F.M., & Sias, P.M. (2001). Communication competence. In F.M. Jablin & L.L. Putnam (Eds.), *The new handbook of organizational communication: Advances in theory, research, and methods* (2nd ed.) (pp. 819–864). Newbury Park, CA: Sage.

Kristof, A.L. (1996). Person–organization fit: An integrative review of its conceptualizations, measurement, and implications. *Personnel Psychology, 49*(1), 1–49.

Lawler, E.E. III. (2007). Why HR practices are not evidence-based. *Academy of Management Journal, 50*(5), 1033–1036.

Miller, V.D., Poole, M.S., Seibold, D.R., with Meyers, K., Park, H.S., Monge, P.R., Fulk, J. Frank, L., Margolin, D., Schultz, C., Cuihua, S., Weber, M., Lee, S., & Shumate, S. (2011). Advancing research in organizational communication through quantitative methodology. *Management Communication Quarterly, 25*(1), 1–43.

Poole, M.S. (2011). Communication. In S. Zedeck (Ed.), *APA handbook of industrial and organizational psychology, Vol. 3* (pp. 249–270). Washington, DC: American Psychological Assocation.

Poole, M.S., & Van de Ven, A. (Eds.). (2004). *Handbook of organizational change and innovation.* New York: Oxford University Press.

Redding, W.C. (1972). *Communication within the organization: An interpretive review of theory and research.* New York: Industrial Communication Council.

Rynes, S.L. (2007). Let's create a tipping point: What academics and practitioners can do, alone and together. *Academy of Management Journal, 50*(5), 1046–1054.

Rynes, S.L., Giluk, T.L., & Brown, K.G. (2007). The very separate worlds of academic and practitioner periodicals in human resource management: Implications for evidence-based management. *Academy of Management Journal, 50*(5), 987–1008.

Weick, K.E., & Browning, L.D. (1986). Argument and narration in organizational communication. *Journal of Management, 12*(2), 243–259.

CONTRIBUTORS

James R. Barker (Ph.D., University of Colorado) is a professor and the Herbert S. Lamb Chair in Business Education at Dalhousie University, Canada. His research interests focus on the role of organizational behavior in the development of safe and sustainable knowledge, innovation, and change initiatives and the consequences of these initiatives on organizational governance systems, markets, and practices. He is the immediate past editor-in-chief of *Management Communication Quarterly*.

William C. Barley (M.A., Northwestern University) is a Ph.D. candidate in the Department of Communication Studies at Northwestern University. He studies the communicative processes that enable successful collaboration among people from different disciplinary backgrounds. He has examined employees' attitudes toward collaboration in organizational contexts including automobile design, applied weather research, pediatric emergency rooms, and professional service firms.

Talya N. Bauer (Ph.D., Purdue University) is the Cameron Professor of Management at Portland State University. Her research spans the employee life cycle from recruitment, onboarding, and leadership and appears in the top journals of management and psychology. Dr. Bauer is the former editor of the *Journal of Management* and is an associate editor at the *Journal of Applied Psychology*. She is a co-author of such textbooks as *Organizational Behavior* and *Principles of Management* and is the co-editor of *The Oxford Handbook of Leader-Member Exchange*. She is a fellow of the Society for Industrial and Organizational Psychology, the American Psychological Association, and the American Psychological Society. Her work has been cited in the *Harvard Business Review*, *New York Times*, and *USA Today*.

Alice M. Brawley (B.A., Louisiana Tech University) is a doctoral student of industrial-organizational psychology at Clemson University. Her research interests include organizational climate, situational influence and interactionism, and message framing.

James Breaugh (Ph.D., Ohio State University) is a professor of management in the College of Business Administration at the University of Missouri–St. Louis. He has conducted research on the topics of employee recruitment, selection, work-family balance, and turnover. His articles have appeared in the *Annual Review of Psychology, Journal of Applied Psychology, Journal of Management, Organizational Research Methods, Personnel Psychology*, and *Academy of Management Review*. His research contributions have resulted in his being voted to fellowship status in three professional organizations.

Patrice M. Buzzanell (Ph.D., Purdue University) is a professor of communication in the Brian Lamb School of Communication (and professor of engineering education by courtesy) at Purdue University. Her research centers on the everyday negotiations and structures that produce and are produced by the intersections of career, gender, and communication, particularly in social change and STEM (science, technology, engineering, and math). With Jeremy Fyke, she has published "The Ethics of Conscious Capitalism: Wicked Problems in Leading Change and Changing Leaders" in *Human Relations.*

Yan Chen (MHRIR, University of Illinois at Urbana-Champaign) is a doctoral student at Rutgers School of Management and Labor Relations. Her research interests include human resources management, compensation, and benefits.

Robert L. Dipboye (Ph.D., Purdue University) is a professor of psychology at the University of Central Florida. He has conducted research on a variety of topics in organizational psychology with particular emphasis on employment discrimination, staffing, and training. More recently he has investigated implementation issues in human resource management. He has published in journals such as the *Journal of Applied Psychology* and the *Academy of Management Review*. He co-edited a book, *Discrimination at Work*, and a special issue (*Stigma in Organization*) in the *Academy of Management Review*. He was associate editor of the *Journal of Applied Psychology*. He is a fellow of the American Psychological Association, the American Psychological Society, and the Society for Industrial and Organizational Psychology (SIOP).

Berrin Erdogan (Ph.D., University of Illinois at Chicago) is a professor of management at Portland State University. Her research focuses on interpersonal relationships at work with a focus on manager-employee relationships. Dr. Erdogan is a former associate editor for *European Journal of Work and Organizational Psychology* and is an associate editor for *Personnel Psychology*. She is an author of dozens of journal articles as well as two textbooks, *Organizational Behavior* and *Principles of Management*. She is the co-editor of *The Oxford Handbook of Leader-Member Exchange*. She is a fellow of the Society for Industrial and Organizational Psychology. Her work on overqualification has been cited in the *Harvard Business Review* and *New York Times*.

Ingrid Smithey Fulmer (Ph.D., Vanderbilt University) is an associate professor in the Human Resource Management Department in the School of Management and Labor Relations at Rutgers University. Dr. Fulmer serves as an associate editor for the *Academy of Management Review* and the *International Journal of Human Resource Management*. In her research, she studies relationships among human resource practices, worker attitudes, and organizational performance, with particular interest in compensation and employee benefits.

Jeremy P. Fyke (Ph.D., Purdue University) is an assistant professor in the J. William and Mary Diederich College of Communication at Marquette University. His research focuses on topics in organizational/managerial communication, including well-being and individual and organizational transformation, training, and leadership development and ethics. Recently, his article with Patrice Buzzanell, "The Ethics of Conscious Capitalism: Wicked Problems in Leading Change and Changing Leaders," was published in *Human Relations*.

Michael E. Gordon (Ph.D., University of California, Berkeley) is a professor emeritus in the Department of Management and Global Business at the Rutgers Business School. After years of research on the relationship between unions and their members, his research over the past few years has focused on organizational communication. His paper on the exit interview was the recipient of *Management Communication Quarterly*'s Article of the Year Award for 2011, and with Vernon Miller he co-authored a book entitled *Conversations About Job Performance: A Communication Perspective*.

Carrisa S. Hoelscher (M.A., West Texas A&M University) is a Ph.D. student in the Department of Communication at the University of Oklahoma. Her research interests broadly involve the intersection of organizational and intercultural communication. Specifically, she is interested in the organizational socialization experiences of expatriate employees in multinational corporations.

Yueng-Hsiang Huang (Ph.D., Portland State University) is a senior research scientist at Liberty Mutual Research Institute for Safety in Hopkinton, Massachusetts. Dr. Huang also serves as an associate editor for the *Journal of Accident Analysis and Prevention*. Her research interests involve organizational safety climate and culture, occupational injury, and accident prevention.

Sue Hutchinson (B.A., Hons University of Exeter) is associate professor in HRM at the University of the West of England, where she is also associate head of the HRM teaching and research group. Her main research interests focus on the link between people management and performance, the role of line managers in HRM, and involvement and consultation. Previous work experiences include research and teaching at Bath University, policy advisor for the Chartered Institute of Personnel and Development, and industrial relations advisor in the paper industry. In 2013, she authored the book *Performance Management: Theory and Practice*.

Michael W. Kramer (Ph.D., University of Texas at Austin) is a professor and chair in the Department of Communication at the University of Oklahoma. His research has focused on transitions individual experience as part of the assimilation/socialization process from pre-entry to exit and led to his two books, *Managing Uncertainty in Organizational Communication* and *Organizational Socialization: Joining and Leaving Organizations*. His most recent research is focused on volunteers. It has resulted in an edited book with Laurie Lewis and Loril Gossett, *Volunteering and Communication: Studies in Multiple Contexts*.

Gary P. Latham (Ph.D., University of Akron) is the Secretary of State Professor of Organizational Effectiveness in the Rotman School of Management at the University of Toronto. In addition he serves on the board of directors of the Society for Human Resource Management. His research interests include selection, performance management, self-regulation, and, most importantly, the goal-performance relationship in the workplace. His most recent book, published in 2013 with his co-author, Edwin Locke, is *New Developments in Goal Setting and Task Performance*.

Paul M. Leonardi (Ph.D, Stanford University) is the Pentair-Nugent Associate Professor at Northwestern University in the departments of Communication Studies and Industrial Engineering &

Management Sciences. His research focuses on how organizations can use advanced information technologies to more effectively create and share knowledge. As part of this work, he regularly conducts assessments of organizational members' willingness to try new innovations and assesses their attitudes toward planned organizational change.

Laurie Lewis (Ph.D., University of California, Santa Barbara) is professor and chair in the Department of Communication at Rutgers University. Dr. Lewis also serves as an associate editor for *Management Communication Quarterly*. Her research focuses on communication during organizational change processes. She is the author of *Organizational Change: Creating Change Through Strategic Communication*. She also has research interests in nonprofit collaboration and the management and experience of volunteering.

Anna C. McFadden (M.S., Clemson University) is a doctoral student in industrial-organizational psychology at Clemson University, concentrating in occupational health psychology. Her areas of research include the work-nonwork interface, organizational safety, military psychology, and group-level influences on occupational health.

Caryn E. Medved (Ph.D., University of Kansas) is an associate professor in the Department of Communication Studies of Baruch College, City University of New York. Dr. Medved served as editor for *Journal of Family Communication*. Her research focuses on communication at the nexus of our work and family lives. Her work has been published in outlets such as *Women's Studies Quarterly*, *Management Communication Quarterly*, *Journal of Family Communication*, *Journal of Marriage and Family*, and *Communication Yearbook*. Her current study of the renegotiation of gender in the lives of unconventional earning couples is funded by the Alfred P. Sloan Foundation and PSC-CUNY.

Vernon D. Miller (Ph.D., University of Texas at Austin) is an associate professor in the Department of Communication and Department of Management at Michigan State University. He also serves as an associate editor for *Management Communication Quarterly*. His research focuses on the communicative aspects of organizational entry and role negotiation. With Michael Gordon, he co-authored *Conversations About Job Performance: A Communication Perspective*.

Eddy S. Ng (Ph.D., McMaster University) is an associate professor at Dalhousie University, Canada. His research focuses on diversity and inclusion, including public policy on equal treatment, managing diversity for organizational competitiveness, changing work values, and career issues for women, minorities, older workers, and the millennial generation. He is an associate editor for *Personnel Review*, and he recently edited a book (with Sean Lyons and Linda Schweitzer) on *Managing the New Workforce: International Perspectives on the Millennial Generation*.

Neal Schmitt (Ph.D., Purdue University) is a professor emeritus in the Department of Psychology at Michigan State University. He is former editor of *Journal of Applied Psychology* and past president of the Society for Industrial and Organizational Psychology and Division 5 (Measurement, Evaluation, and Statistics) of the American Psychological Association. With Robert Ployhart and Ben Schneider, he co-authored *Staffing Organizations*. Most recently, he edited *The Oxford Handbook of Personnel Assessment and Selection* and co-edited with Scott Highhouse *The Handbook of Psychology: Vol. 12, Industrial and Organizational Psychology*. He also has published approximately

250 chapters and peer-reviewed papers, most of which involve some aspect of personnel selection or measurement.

William D. Schneper (Ph.D., University of Pennsylvania) is an assistant professor in the Business, Organizations & Society Department at Franklin & Marshall College. His work examines the consequences of globalization and how workers as well as other stakeholders contribute to differences in business practices and perspectives across countries. His research has been published in a variety of noted research outlets including *Administrative Science Quarterly*.

Patricia M. Sias (Ph.D., University of Texas at Austin) is the director of the McGuire Entrepreneurship Program and senior lecturer of leadership and organizational communication at the University of Arizona's Eller College of Management. She also serves as an associate editor for *Management Communication Quarterly*. Her research centers on workplace relationships, uncertainty, and the sociocultural processes of innovation in entrepreneurial teams. She has published in many academic journals and authored the book *Organizing Relationships: Traditional and Emerging Perspectives on Workplace Relationships*.

Lauren Simon (Ph.D., University of Florida) is an assistant professor of management at Portland State University. Her research focuses on interpersonal relationships among employees and, in particular, how these relationships emerge, develop, and change over time. Her research has appeared in top psychology and management journals, including the *Journal of Applied Psychology* and the *Journal of Management*. Her work has also been cited in popular outlets such as the *Wall Street Journal*, *Science Daily*, and WebMD.

Caroline Sinclair (M.A., University of Texas at Austin) is an assistant instructor in the Department of Communication Studies at the University of Texas while seeking her Ph.D. in communication studies. She has over twenty years of management experience in the field of digital communication technologies and online communication. Her research focuses on communication technology and the virtual workplace.

Robert R. Sinclair (Ph.D., Wayne State University) is a professor of industrial-organizational psychology at Clemson University. He is a founding member and past president of the Society for Occupational Health Psychology. His research focuses on safety, health, and well-being issues in military personnel, nurses, low-income/retail workers, and college students. His recent published work includes edited volumes titled *Building Psychological Resilience in Military Personnel: Theory and Practice* (with Tom Britt) and *Research Methods in Occupational Health Psychology: Measurement, Design, and Data Analysis* (with Mo Wang and Lois E. Tetrick).

Kyle R. Stanyar (M.S., Clemson University) is a doctoral student of industrial-organizational psychology at Clemson University, with a specialization in occupational health psychology. His research focuses on health and safety promotion in the workplace, health behaviors, occupational stress, and organizational behavior.

Keri K. Stephens (Ph.D., University of Texas at Austin) is associate professor in the Department of Communication Studies at the University of Texas at Austin. Her research focuses on organizational communication and technology. She examines redundancy and multiple technology use during meetings, and in health and emergency contexts. Prior to academia, Dr. Stephens spent ten years in sales, program management, and training in the high-technology industry.

Dennis Tourish (Ph.D., University of Aberdeen) is the professor of leadership and organization studies at Royal Holloway, University of London, and a fellow of the Leadership Trust Foundation. He is a co-editor of the journal *Leadership* and previously served as an associate editor for *Management Communication Quarterly.* His most recent book is *The Dark Side of Transformational Leadership: A Critical Perspective*, published by Routledge in 2013.

Jeffrey W. Treem (Ph.D., Northwestern University) is an assistant professor of communication studies at the University of Texas at Austin. His research explores how workers come to be seen as knowledgeable by peers and how communication influences perceptions of who knows what within organizations. His work draws upon a variety of methodological approaches—interviews, observations, network analysis, and surveys—to connect workers' attitudes and communicative actions with organizational outcomes.

Mary Ann Von Glinow (Ph.D., Ohio State University) is the Knight Ridder Eminent Scholar Chair in International Management and CIBER director at Florida International University. She is immediate past president (2010–2012) of the Academy of International Business (AIB) and is a fellow of both the Academy of Management and AIB. Her work is largely on offshoring/outsourcing to/from China and the multiple embedded contexts she refers to as "polycontextuality."

Eric D. Waters (M.B.A., University of Texas at Arlington) is a doctoral student in organizational communication at the University of Texas at Austin. His research centers on the interdependent relationship between information and communication technologies (ICTs) and organizational structures such as policies or social norms.

INDEX